Fantastic Four

LOST ADVENTURES

FANTASTIC FOUR: LOST ADVENTURES BY STAN LEE. Contains material originally published in magazine form as THE LAST FANTASTIC FOUR STORY, FANTASTIC FOUR: LOST, and FANTASTIC FOUR #296 and #543. First printing 2008. ISBN# 978-0-7851-3097-0. Published by MARVEL PUBLISHING, INC., a subsidiary of MARVEL ENTERTAINMENT, INC. OFFICE OF PUBLICATION: 417 5th Avenue, New York, NY 10016. Copyright © 1996, 2007 and 2008 Marvel Characters, Inc. All rights reserved. $24.99 per copy in the U.S. and $26.50 in Canada (GST #R127032852); Canadian Agreement #40668537. All characters featured in this issue and the distinctive names and likenesses thereof, and all related indicia are trademarks of Marvel Characters, Inc. No similarity between any of the names, characters, persons, and/or institutions in this magazine with those of any living or dead person or institution is intended, and any such similarity which may exist is purely coincidental. Printed in the U.S.A. ALAN FINE, CEO Marvel Toys & Publishing Divisions and CMO Marvel Entertainment, Inc.; DAVID GABRIEL, SVP of Publishing Sales & Circulation; DAVID BOGART, SVP of Business Affairs & Talent Management; MICHAEL PASCIULLO, VP of Merchandising & Communications; JIM O'KEEFE, VP of Operations & Logistics; DAN CARR, Executive Director of Publishing Technology; JUSTIN F. GABRIE, Director of Editorial Operations; SUSAN CRESPI, Editorial Operations Manager; OMAR OTIEKU, Production Manager; STAN LEE, Chairman Emeritus. For information regarding advertising in Marvel Comics or on Marvel.com, please contact Mitch Dane, Advertising Director, at mdane@marvel.com. For Marvel subscription inquiries, please call 800-217-9158.

10 9 8 7 6 5 4 3 2 1

CLICK

Fantastic Four
LOST ADVENTURES

Writer: Stan Lee

"The Menace of the Mega-Men"
Pencilers: Jack Kirby with Ron Frenz
Embellisher: Joe Sinnott
Colorist: Chris Sotomayor
Letterer: Artmonkey's Dave Lanphear

"The Monstrous Mystery of the Nega-Man"
Pencilers: Jack Kirby, John Buscema & John Romita Sr.
Inker: Joe Sinnott
Letterer: Sam Rosen

"World's End"
Penciler: John Romita Jr.
Inker: Scott Hanna
Colorist: Morry Hollowell
Letterer: Virtual Calligraphy's Joe Caramagna

"Homecoming!"
Plotter: Jim Shooter
Pencilers: Barry Windsor-Smith, Kerry Gammill, Ron Frenz,
Al Milgrom, John Buscema, Marc Silvestri & Jerry Ordway
Inkers: Barry Windsor-Smith, Vince Colletta, Bob Wiacek,
Klaus Janson, Steve Leialoha, Joe Rubinstein & Joe Sinnott
Letterer: John Workman

"If This Be... Anniversary!"
Penciler: Nick Dragotta
Inker: Mike Allred
Colorist: Laura Allred
Letterer: Rus Wooton

Assistant Editors: Molly Lazer & Aubrey Sitterson
Editors: Tom Brevoort & Mike Carlin

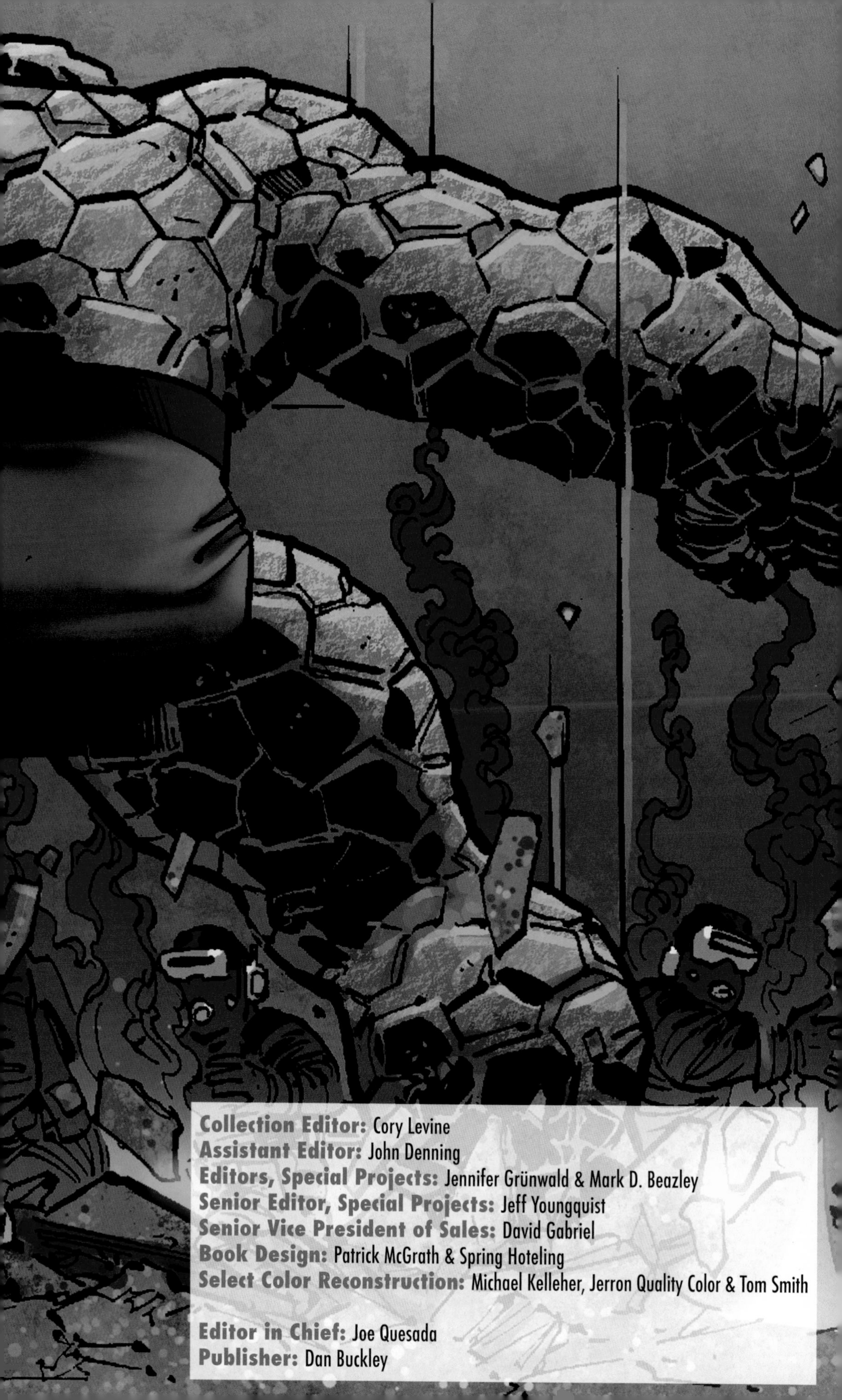

Collection Editor: Cory Levine
Assistant Editor: John Denning
Editors, Special Projects: Jennifer Grünwald & Mark D. Beazley
Senior Editor, Special Projects: Jeff Youngquist
Senior Vice President of Sales: David Gabriel
Book Design: Patrick McGrath & Spring Hoteling
Select Color Reconstruction: Michael Kelleher, Jerron Quality Color & Tom Smith

Editor in Chief: Joe Quesada
Publisher: Dan Buckley

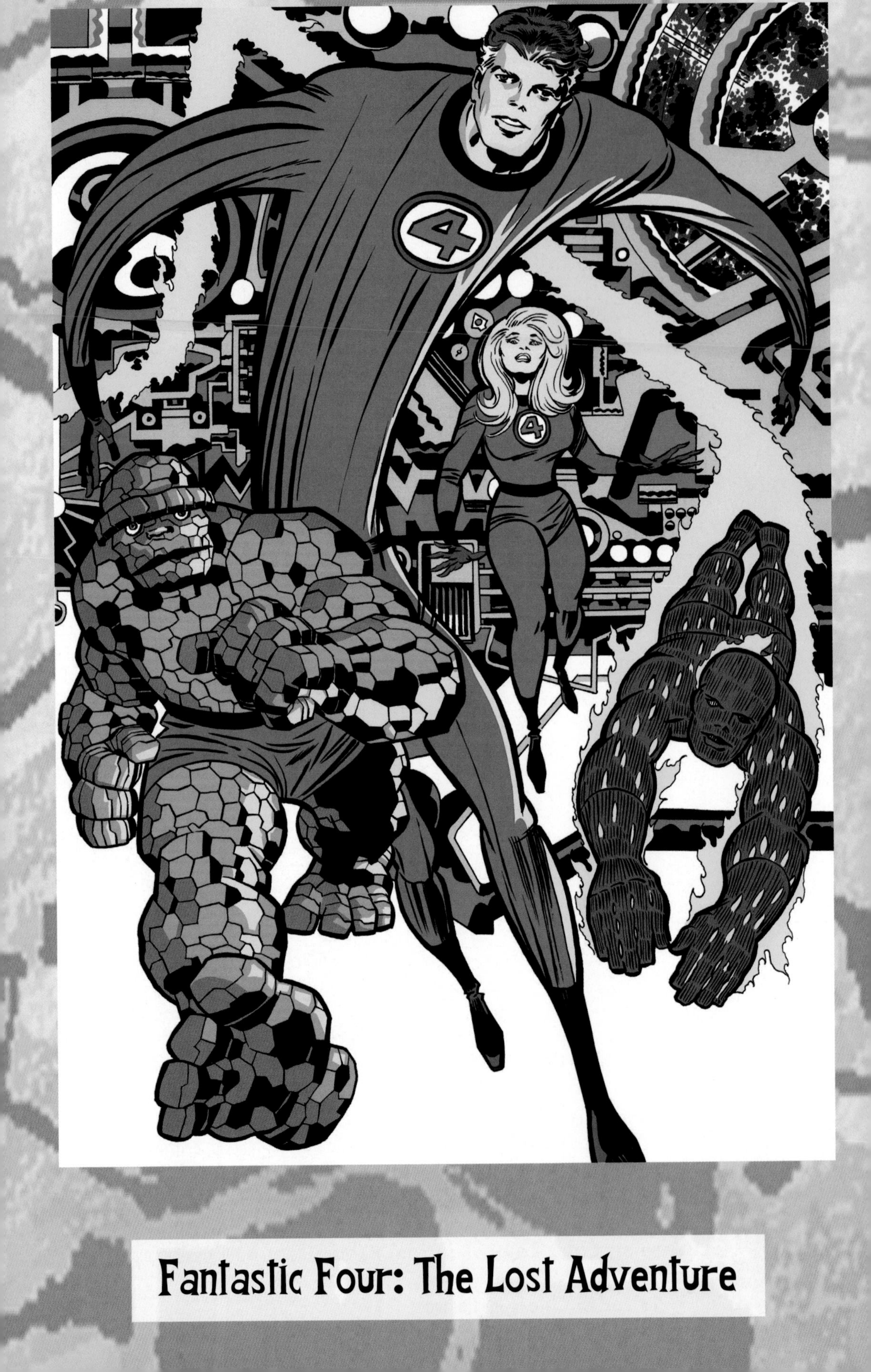

Fantastic Four: The Lost Adventure

Stan Lee & Jack Kirby

Fantastic Four ®
THE LOST ADVENTURE

Between 1961 and 1970, Stan Lee and Jack Kirby produced 102 consecutive issues of FANTASTIC FOUR, as well as six Annuals. However, there was a 103rd issue that they'd begun working on, but never completed.

While portions of that story saw print some months later as an extended flashback sequence in FANTASTIC FOUR #108, the original incarnation of that tale has never been finished--until now!

Working from Jack Kirby's penciled pages and their extensive border notes, Stan Lee and Joe Sinnott have reunited to complete what they'd begun 38 years earlier, aided in part by Ron Frenz and Chris Sotomayor.

This is
FANTASTIC FOUR: THE LOST ADVENTURE

"THE MENACE OF THE MEGA-MEN!"

A Stan Lee and Jack Kirby Production

Additional Pencils by **Ron Frenz**
Embellisher – **Joe Sinnott**
Colorist – **Chris Sotomayor**
Letterer – **Artmonkey's Dave Lanphear**

"FANTASTIC FOUR #108: KIRBY'S WAY"

Writer – **John Morrow**
Designer – **Rommel Alama**

FANTASTIC FOUR #108: "THE MONSTROUS MYSTERY OF THE NEGA-MAN!"

Writer – **Stan Lee**
Pencilers – **Jack Kirby, John Buscema & John Romita Sr.**
Inker – **Joe Sinnott**
Letterer – **Sam Rosen**
Color Reconstruction – **Michael Kelleher**

Assistant Editor – **Molly Lazer**
Editor – **Tom Brevoort**
Editor in Chief – **Joe Quesada**
Publisher – **Dan Buckley**

Special Thanks to Jeff Youngquist, Mark Beazley, Lisa Kirby and the Kirby Estate

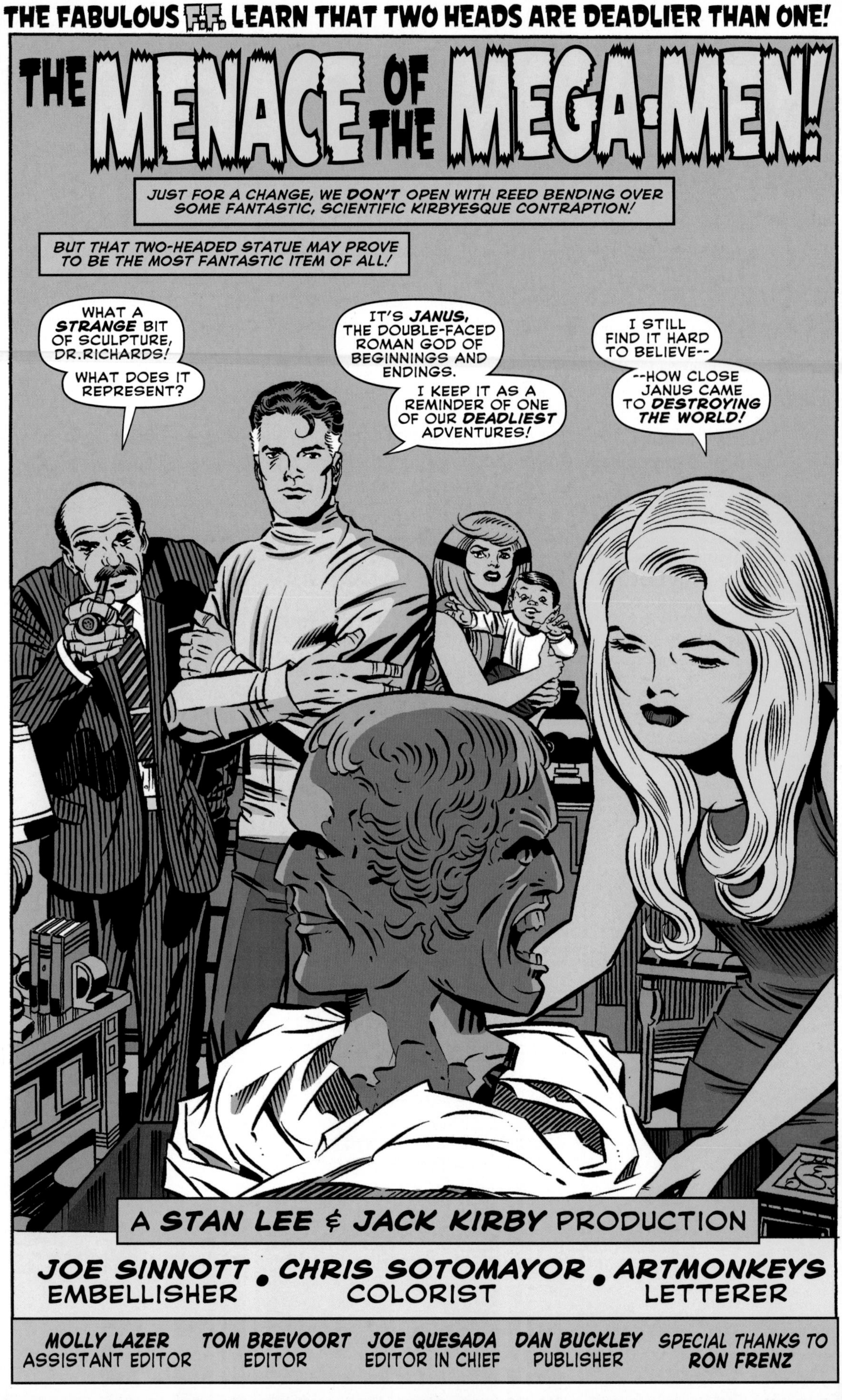

THE FABULOUS F.F. LEARN THAT TWO HEADS ARE DEADLIER THAN ONE!
THE MENACE OF THE MEGA-MEN!
JUST FOR A CHANGE, WE DON'T OPEN WITH REED BENDING OVER SOME FANTASTIC, SCIENTIFIC KIRBYESQUE CONTRAPTION!
BUT THAT TWO-HEADED STATUE MAY PROVE TO BE THE MOST FANTASTIC ITEM OF ALL!
WHAT A STRANGE BIT OF SCULPTURE, DR.RICHARDS!
WHAT DOES IT REPRESENT?
IT'S JANUS, THE DOUBLE-FACED ROMAN GOD OF BEGINNINGS AND ENDINGS.
I KEEP IT AS A REMINDER OF ONE OF OUR DEADLIEST ADVENTURES!
I STILL FIND IT HARD TO BELIEVE--
--HOW CLOSE JANUS CAME TO DESTROYING THE WORLD!
A STAN LEE & JACK KIRBY PRODUCTION
JOE SINNOTT EMBELLISHER • CHRIS SOTOMAYOR COLORIST • ARTMONKEYS LETTERER
MOLLY LAZER ASSISTANT EDITOR
TOM BREVOORT EDITOR
JOE QUESADA EDITOR IN CHIEF
DAN BUCKLEY PUBLISHER
SPECIAL THANKS TO RON FRENZ

DESTROYING THE WORLD, ***INDEED!***
I'M A ***SCIENTIST,*** MY DEAR SUSAN.
I DON'T DEAL IN COMICBOOK PHRASEOLOGY.
THERE WAS NO OTHER WAY TO PUT IT, MY FRIEND.
IT'S STILL HARD TO BELIEVE IT EVER HAPPENED!
I CAPTURED MOST OF THE INCREDIBLE EVENT ON MY NANO-DIGITAL NUCLEOSCAN.
A ***NUCLEOSCAN,*** REED?
SOUNDS LIKE SOMETHING NO LAB SHOULD BE WITHOUT.
MUST WE WITNESS THE WHOLE HORRIBLE EVENT AGAIN?
DR. CLAYMORE FEELS YOU WERE INDULGING IN HYPERBOLE, SUE.
AFTER HE SEES WHAT I'M ABOUT TO SHOW HIM--
--PERHAPS HE'LL HAVE MORE RESPECT FOR "COMICBOOK PHRASEOLOGY"!
REED, WE'VE BEEN FRIENDS FOR YEARS.
I'M WELL AWARE OF YOUR AMAZING EXPLOITS.
BUT I'VE NEVER HEARD OF ANY SO-CALLED ***JANUS*** CAPER!
THAT'S RIGHT, CLAY. I'VE NEVER SPOKEN OF IT.
BUT I WANT TO PROVE TO YOU THAT MY LOVELY WIFE DIDN'T EXAGGERATE--
--WHEN SHE SAID JANUS ALMOST DESTROYED THE WORLD!
*"YOU WERE AT AN ARCHEOLOGICAL DIG IN TIBET, CLAY, WHEN A STRANGE, GYROSCOPIC **AIRCRAFT** ATTACKED THE CENTER OF NEW YORK!"*
WOW! WILLYA LOOK AT ***THAT?***
WHAT'S IT ADVERTISING?

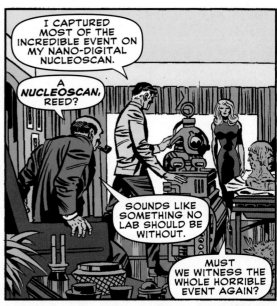

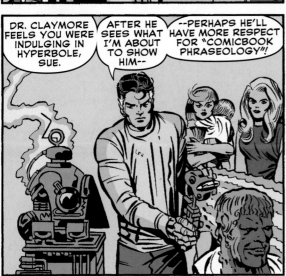

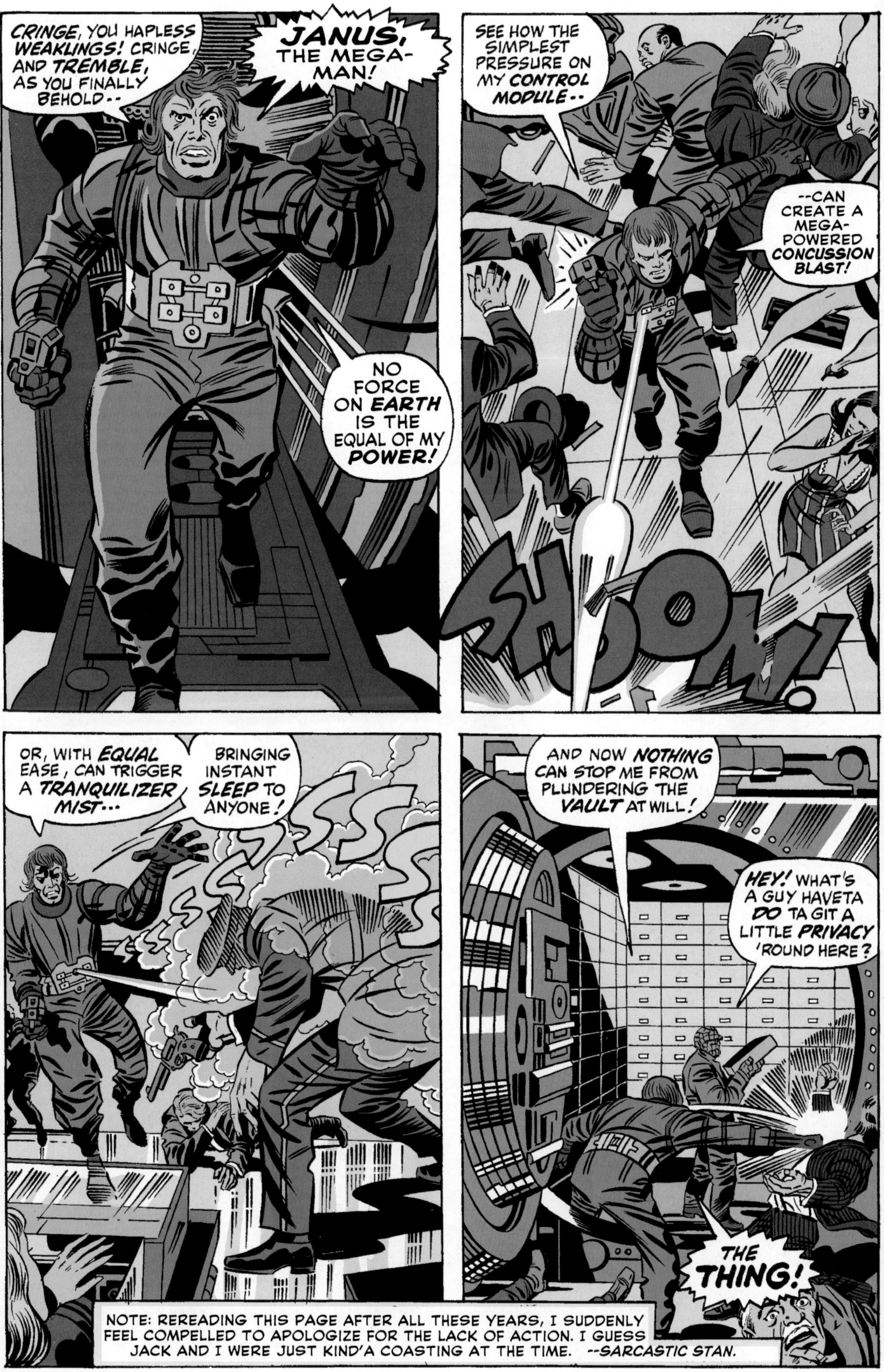
CRINGE, YOU HAPLESS WEAKLINGS! CRINGE, AND TREMBLE, AS YOU FINALLY BEHOLD--
JANUS, THE MEGA-MAN!
NO FORCE ON EARTH IS THE EQUAL OF MY POWER!
SEE HOW THE SIMPLEST PRESSURE ON MY CONTROL MODULE--
--CAN CREATE A MEGA-POWERED CONCUSSION BLAST!
SHOOM!
OR, WITH EQUAL EASE, CAN TRIGGER A TRANQUILIZER MIST...
BRINGING INSTANT SLEEP TO ANYONE!
AND NOW NOTHING CAN STOP ME FROM PLUNDERING THE VAULT AT WILL!
HEY! WHAT'S A GUY HAVETA DO TA GIT A LITTLE PRIVACY 'ROUND HERE?
THE THING!
NOTE: REREADING THIS PAGE AFTER ALL THESE YEARS, I SUDDENLY FEEL COMPELLED TO APOLOGIZE FOR THE LACK OF ACTION. I GUESS JACK AND I WERE JUST KIND'A COASTING AT THE TIME. --SARCASTIC STAN.

WHAT ARE YOU DOING INSIDE THIS VAULT?
PUTTIN' A LITTLE NEST EGG ASIDE FER A RAINY DAY.
NOW GIT LOST, SONNY. YER STARTIN' TA BREATHE ON ME.
YOU GROTESQUE, OVER-RATED CLOD! YOU'RE TALKING TO JANUS, THE MEGA-MAN!
LOOK, CORNBALL--YA'LL BE JANUS WIT' THE FAT LIP IF YA DON'T GIT OFFA MY BACK!
VERY WELL--YOU ASKED FOR IT.
ALL I NEED DO IS SET THE MODULE--
--AND THE THING WILL TROUBLE ME NO MORE!
OKAY, BUTTERCUP--IF THIS IS WHAT YER TRYIN' TA DO---
YA SHOULDA SAID SO.
NOW GO PLAY WIT' YER TOYS SOMEWHERE ELSE, HUH?
I DUNNO WHY ALL THE CRACKPOTS LATCH ONTA ME!
NEVER AGAIN WILL YOU CALL JANUS A CRACKPOT--
NOT AFTER I'VE INCREASED THE MASS OF MY ATOMIC STRUCTURE--
BY PRESSING MY CONTROL MODULE TO HIGHEST INTENSITY.

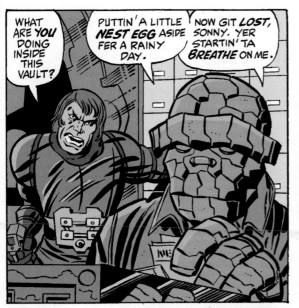

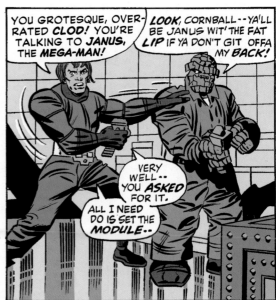

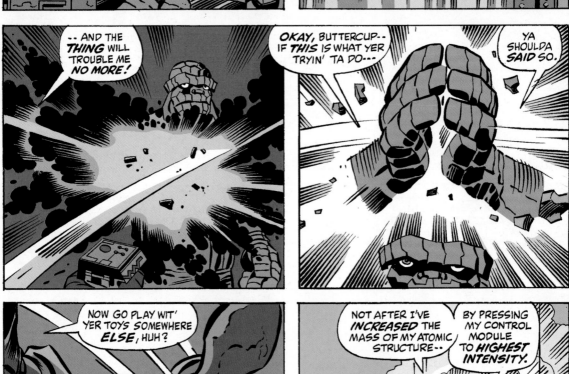

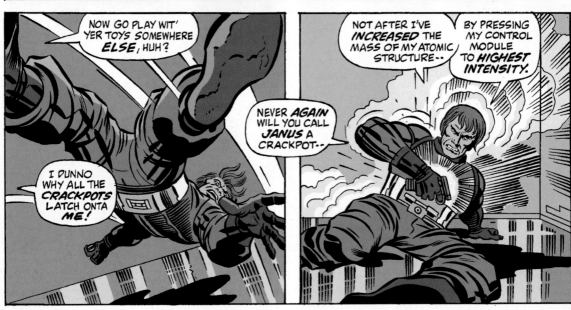

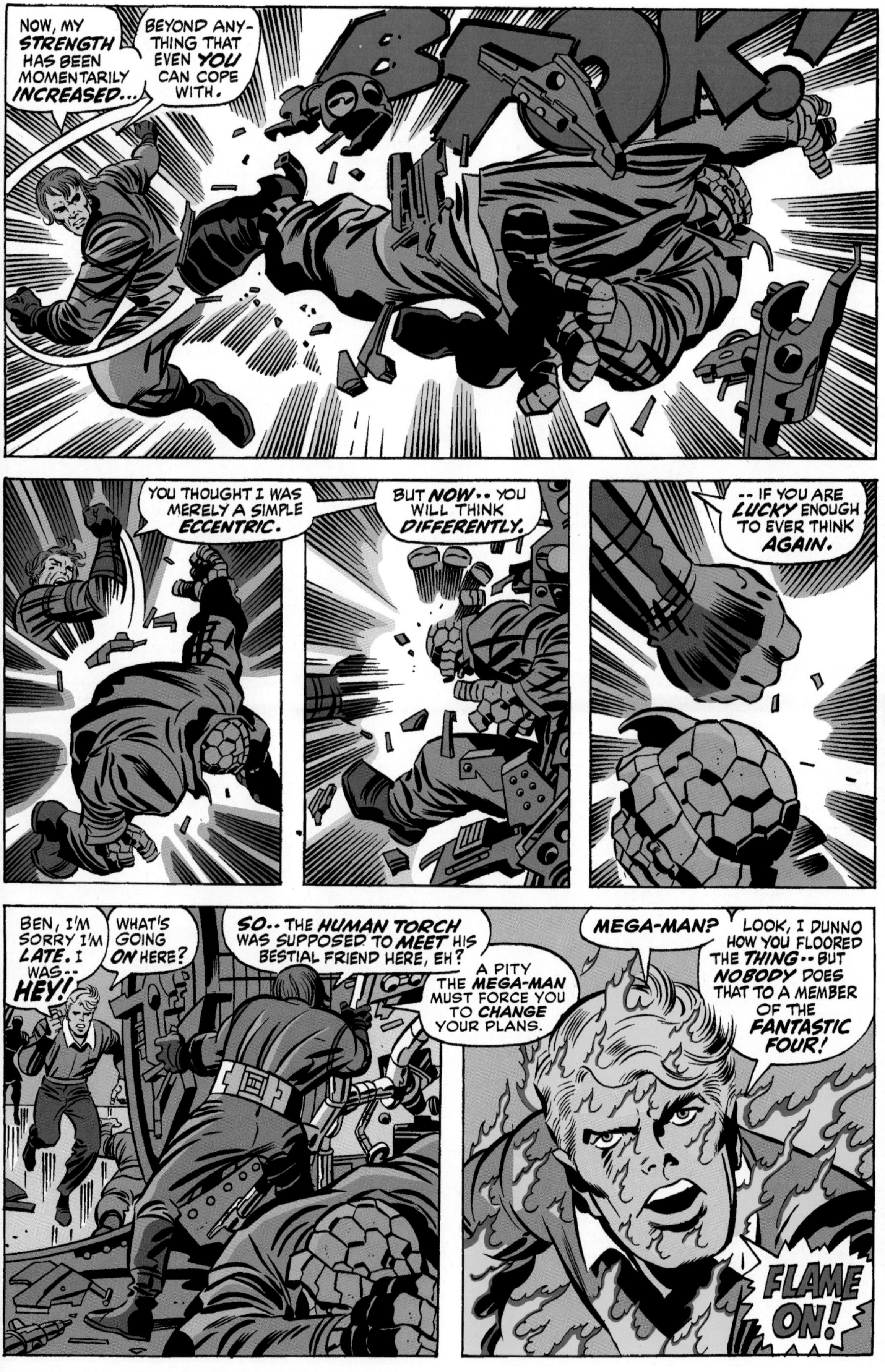

NOW, MY STRENGTH HAS BEEN MOMENTARILY INCREASED...
BEYOND ANYTHING THAT EVEN YOU CAN COPE WITH.
BTOK!
YOU THOUGHT I WAS MERELY A SIMPLE ECCENTRIC.
BUT NOW -- YOU WILL THINK DIFFERENTLY.
-- IF YOU ARE LUCKY ENOUGH TO EVER THINK AGAIN.
BEN, I'M SORRY I'M LATE. I WAS-- HEY!
WHAT'S GOING ON HERE?
SO-- THE HUMAN TORCH WAS SUPPOSED TO MEET HIS BESTIAL FRIEND HERE, EH?
A PITY THE MEGA-MAN MUST FORCE YOU TO CHANGE YOUR PLANS.
MEGA-MAN?
LOOK, I DUNNO HOW YOU FLOORED THE THING -- BUT NOBODY DOES THAT TO A MEMBER OF THE FANTASTIC FOUR!
FLAME ON!

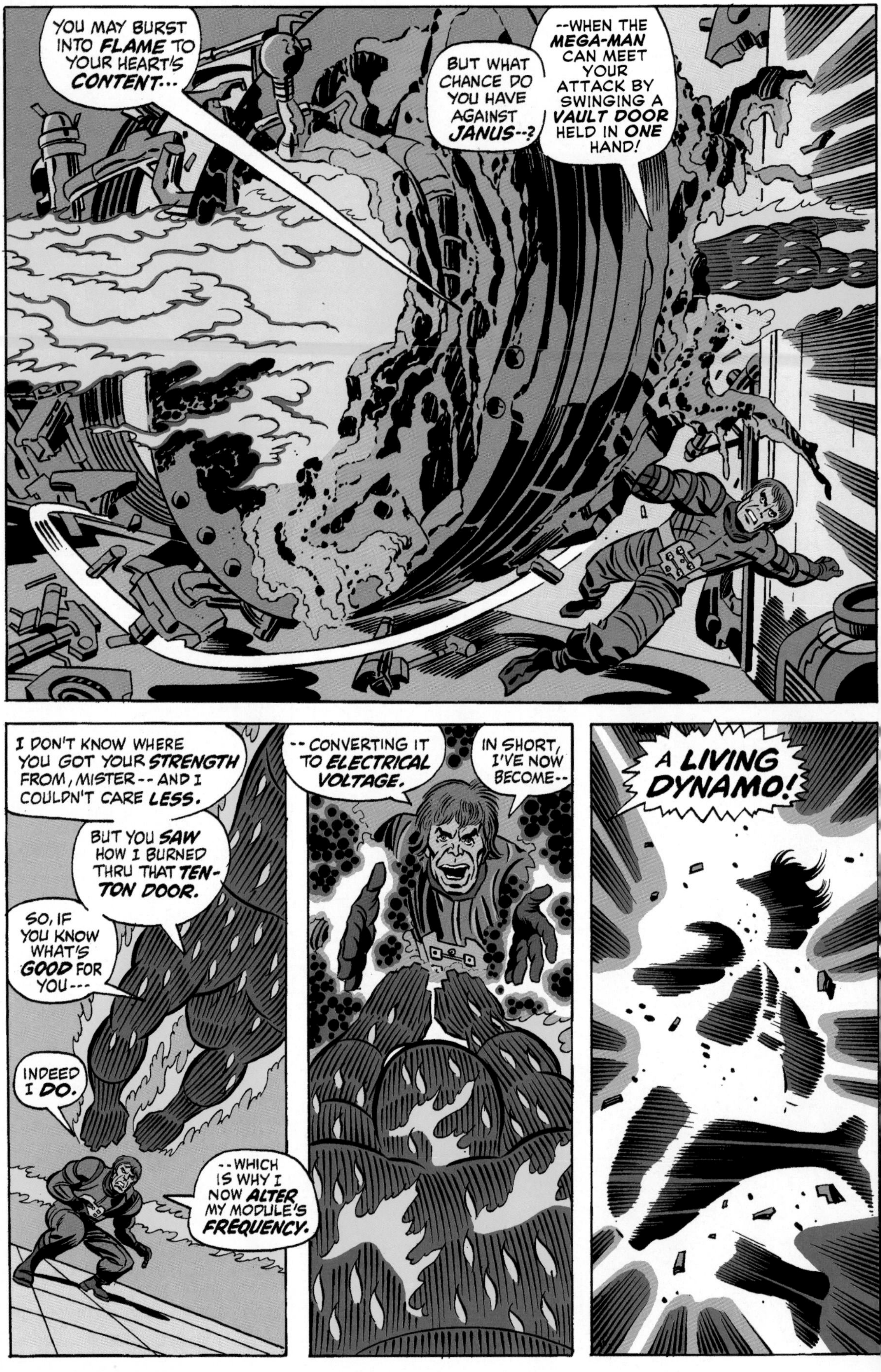

YOU MAY BURST INTO FLAME TO YOUR HEART'S CONTENT...
BUT WHAT CHANCE DO YOU HAVE AGAINST JANUS--?
--WHEN THE MEGA-MAN CAN MEET YOUR ATTACK BY SWINGING A VAULT DOOR HELD IN ONE HAND!
I DON'T KNOW WHERE YOU GOT YOUR STRENGTH FROM, MISTER-- AND I COULDN'T CARE LESS.
BUT YOU SAW HOW I BURNED THRU THAT TEN-TON DOOR.
SO, IF YOU KNOW WHAT'S GOOD FOR YOU---
INDEED I DO.
--WHICH IS WHY I NOW ALTER MY MODULE'S FREQUENCY.
--CONVERTING IT TO ELECTRICAL VOLTAGE.
IN SHORT, I'VE NOW BECOME--
A LIVING DYNAMO!

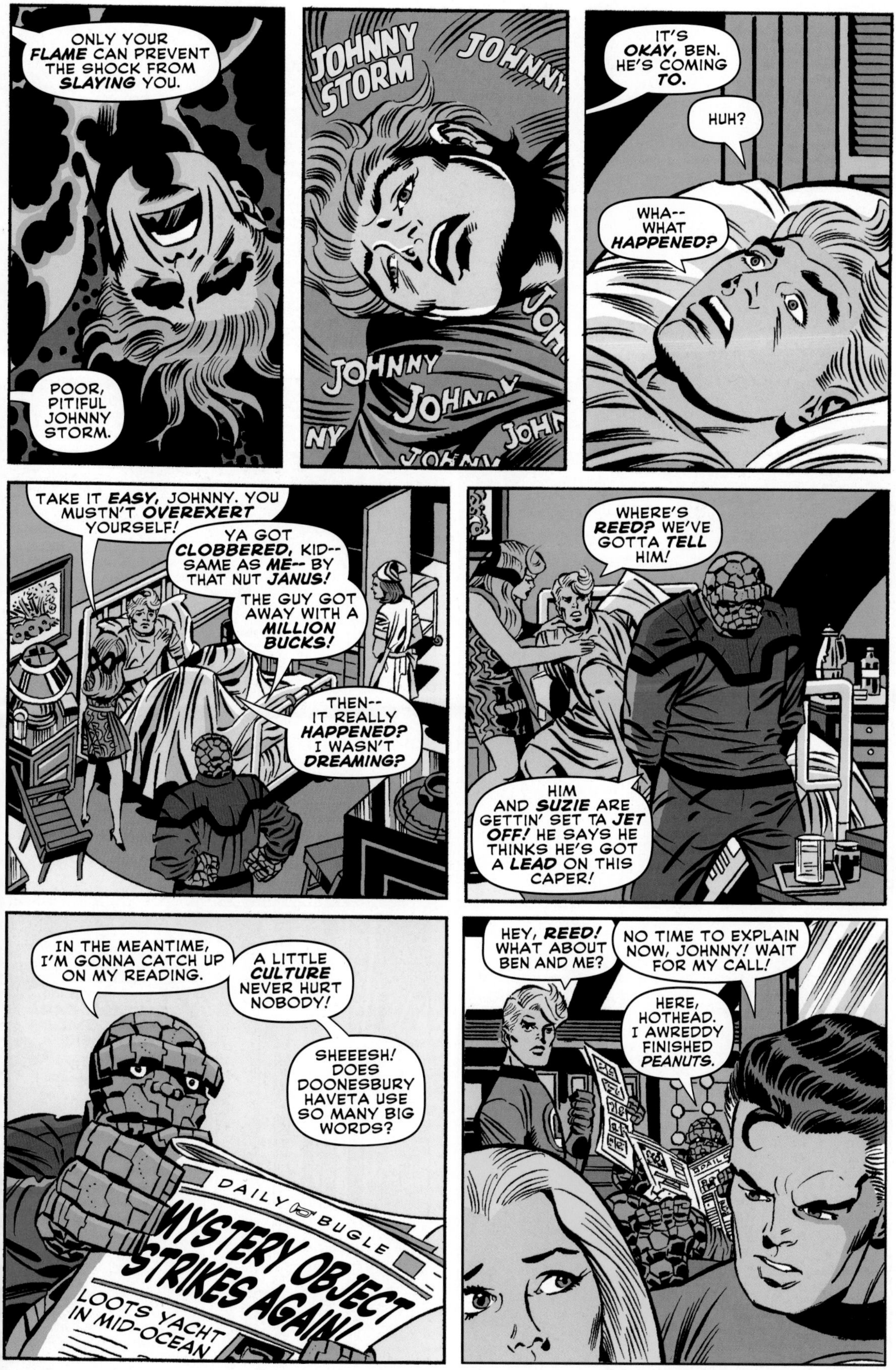
ONLY YOUR FLAME CAN PREVENT THE SHOCK FROM SLAYING YOU.
POOR, PITIFUL JOHNNY STORM.
JOHNNY STORM
JOHNNY
JOHNNY
JOHNNY
IT'S OKAY, BEN. HE'S COMING TO.
HUH?
WHA-- WHAT HAPPENED?
TAKE IT EASY, JOHNNY. YOU MUSTN'T OVEREXERT YOURSELF!
YA GOT CLOBBERED, KID-- SAME AS ME-- BY THAT NUT JANUS!
THE GUY GOT AWAY WITH A MILLION BUCKS!
THEN-- IT REALLY HAPPENED? I WASN'T DREAMING?
WHERE'S REED? WE'VE GOTTA TELL HIM!
HIM AND SUZIE ARE GETTIN' SET TA JET OFF! HE SAYS HE THINKS HE'S GOT A LEAD ON THIS CAPER!
IN THE MEANTIME, I'M GONNA CATCH UP ON MY READING.
A LITTLE CULTURE NEVER HURT NOBODY!
SHEEESH! DOES DOONESBURY HAVETA USE SO MANY BIG WORDS?
DAILY BUGLE
MYSTERY OBJECT STRIKES AGAIN!
LOOTS YACHT IN MID-OCEAN
HEY, REED! WHAT ABOUT BEN AND ME?
NO TIME TO EXPLAIN NOW, JOHNNY! WAIT FOR MY CALL!
HERE, HOTHEAD. I AWREDDY FINISHED PEANUTS.

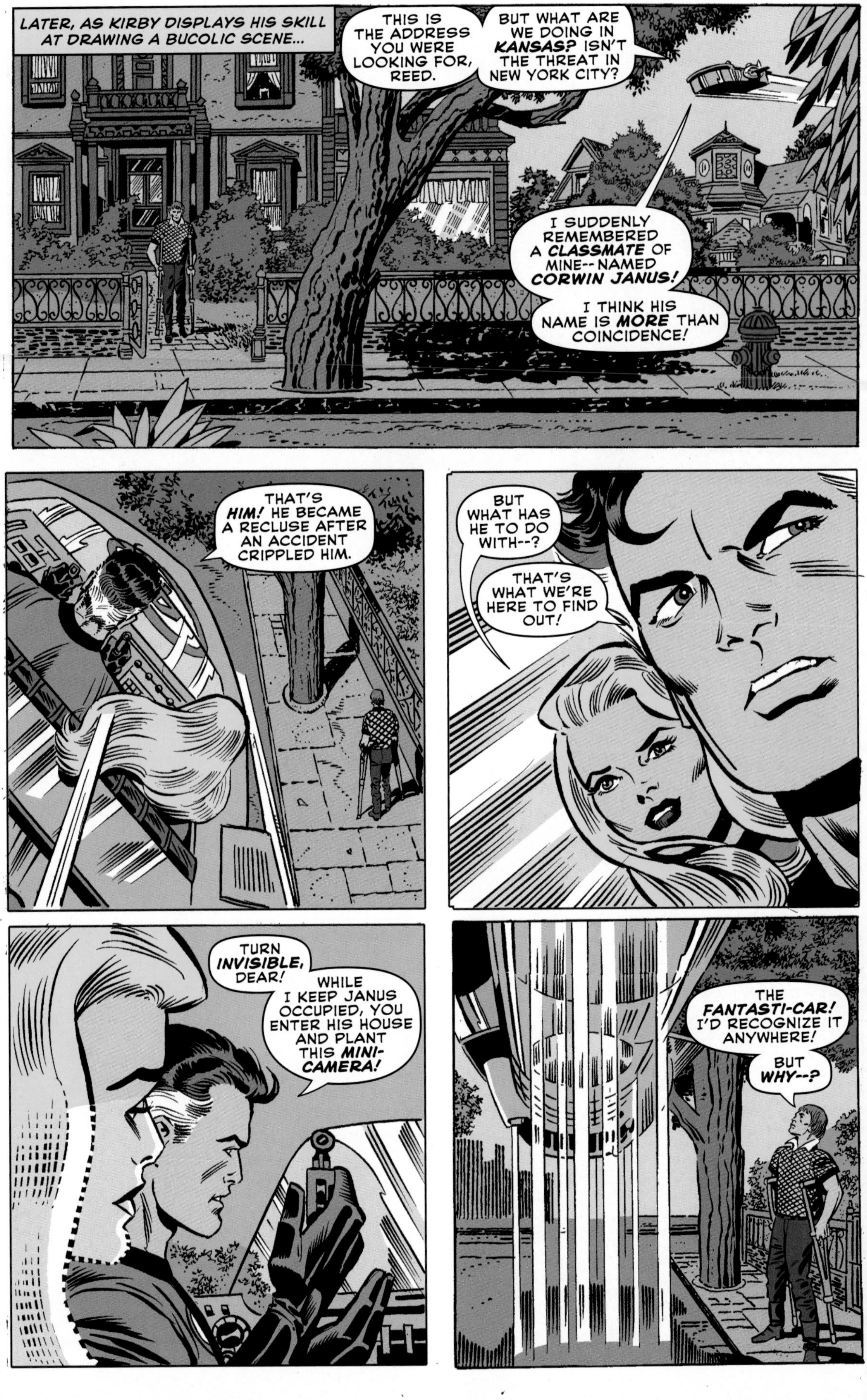

LATER, AS KIRBY DISPLAYS HIS SKILL AT DRAWING A BUCOLIC SCENE...
THIS IS THE ADDRESS YOU WERE LOOKING FOR, REED.
BUT WHAT ARE WE DOING IN KANSAS? ISN'T THE THREAT IN NEW YORK CITY?
I SUDDENLY REMEMBERED A CLASSMATE OF MINE--NAMED CORWIN JANUS!
I THINK HIS NAME IS MORE THAN COINCIDENCE!
THAT'S HIM! HE BECAME A RECLUSE AFTER AN ACCIDENT CRIPPLED HIM.
BUT WHAT HAS HE TO DO WITH--?
THAT'S WHAT WE'RE HERE TO FIND OUT!
TURN INVISIBLE, DEAR!
WHILE I KEEP JANUS OCCUPIED, YOU ENTER HIS HOUSE AND PLANT THIS MINI-CAMERA!
THE FANTASTI-CAR! I'D RECOGNIZE IT ANYWHERE!
BUT WHY--?

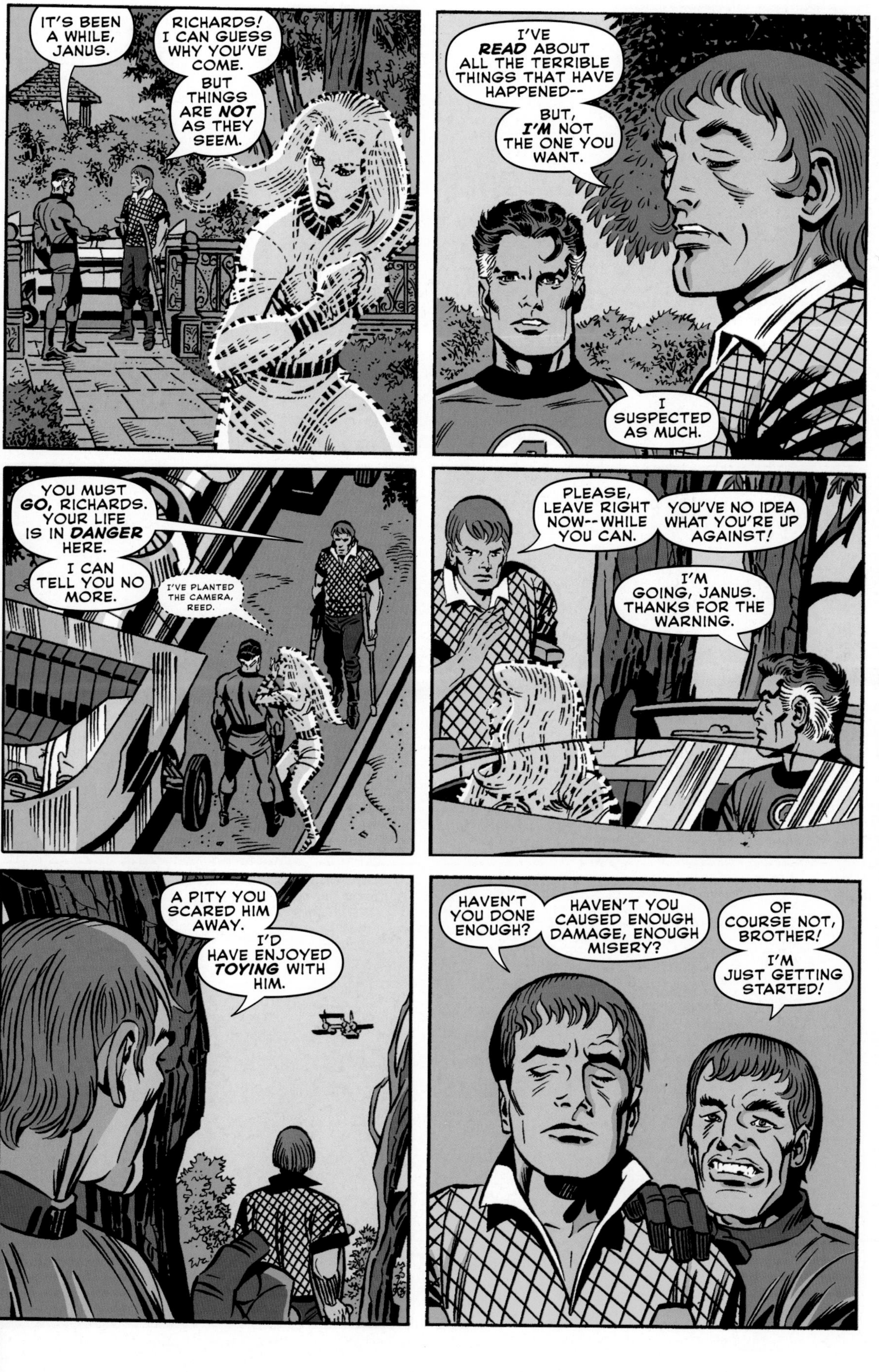
IT'S BEEN A WHILE, JANUS.
RICHARDS! I CAN GUESS WHY YOU'VE COME.
BUT THINGS ARE NOT AS THEY SEEM.
I'VE READ ABOUT ALL THE TERRIBLE THINGS THAT HAVE HAPPENED--
BUT, I'M NOT THE ONE YOU WANT.
I SUSPECTED AS MUCH.
YOU MUST GO, RICHARDS. YOUR LIFE IS IN DANGER HERE.
I CAN TELL YOU NO MORE.
I'VE PLANTED THE CAMERA, REED.
PLEASE, LEAVE RIGHT NOW--WHILE YOU CAN.
YOU'VE NO IDEA WHAT YOU'RE UP AGAINST!
I'M GOING, JANUS. THANKS FOR THE WARNING.
A PITY YOU SCARED HIM AWAY.
I'D HAVE ENJOYED TOYING WITH HIM.
HAVEN'T YOU DONE ENOUGH?
HAVEN'T YOU CAUSED ENOUGH DAMAGE, ENOUGH MISERY?
OF COURSE NOT, BROTHER!
I'M JUST GETTING STARTED!

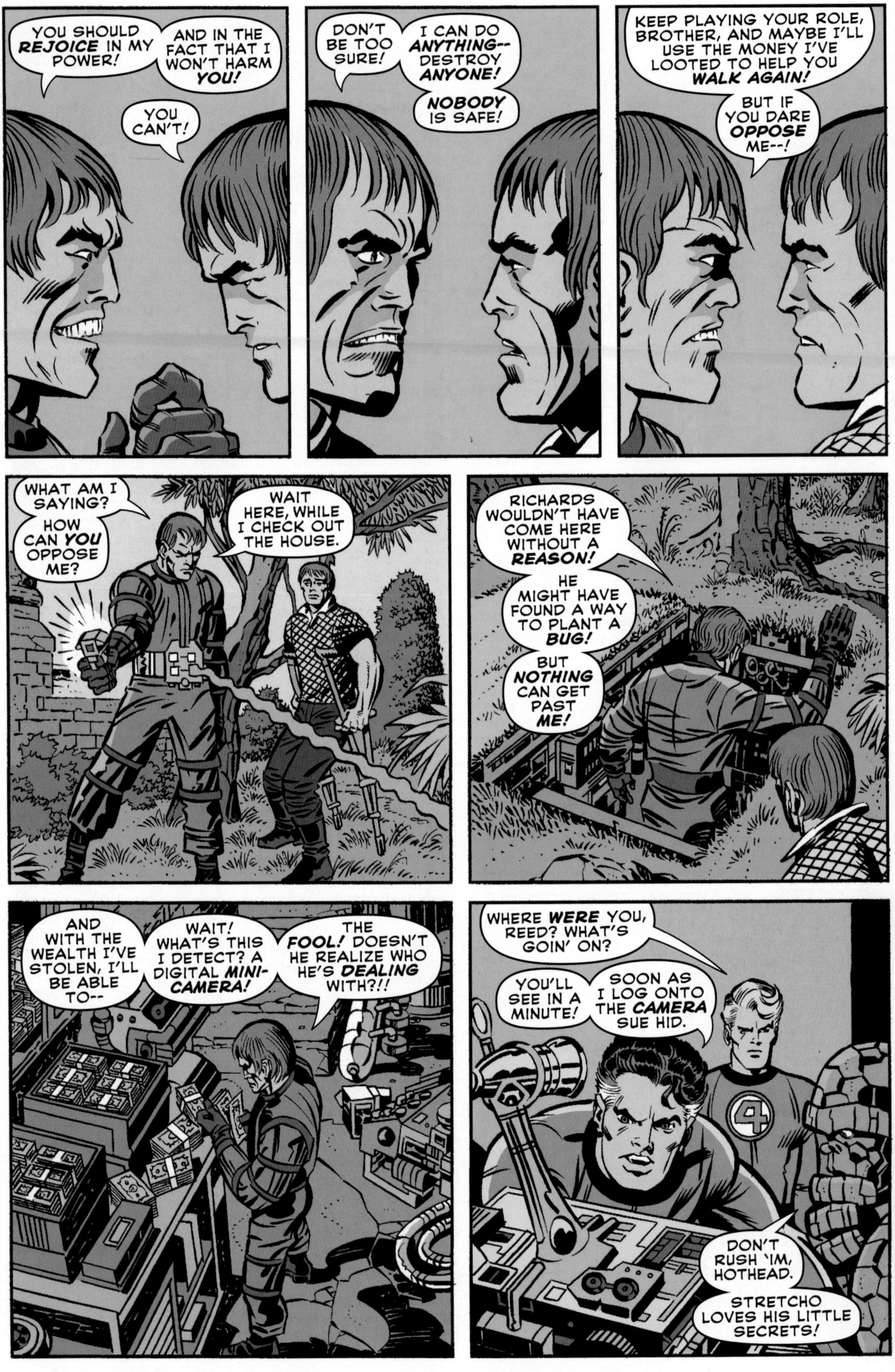
YOU SHOULD REJOICE IN MY POWER!
AND IN THE FACT THAT I WON'T HARM YOU!
YOU CAN'T!
DON'T BE TOO SURE!
I CAN DO ANYTHING-- DESTROY ANYONE!
NOBODY IS SAFE!
KEEP PLAYING YOUR ROLE, BROTHER, AND MAYBE I'LL USE THE MONEY I'VE LOOTED TO HELP YOU WALK AGAIN!
BUT IF YOU DARE OPPOSE ME--!
WHAT AM I SAYING? HOW CAN YOU OPPOSE ME?
WAIT HERE, WHILE I CHECK OUT THE HOUSE.
RICHARDS WOULDN'T HAVE COME HERE WITHOUT A REASON!
HE MIGHT HAVE FOUND A WAY TO PLANT A BUG!
BUT NOTHING CAN GET PAST ME!
AND WITH THE WEALTH I'VE STOLEN, I'LL BE ABLE TO--
WAIT! WHAT'S THIS I DETECT? A DIGITAL MINI-CAMERA!
THE FOOL! DOESN'T HE REALIZE WHO HE'S DEALING WITH?!!
WHERE WERE YOU, REED? WHAT'S GOIN' ON?
YOU'LL SEE IN A MINUTE!
SOON AS I LOG ONTO THE CAMERA SUE HID.
DON'T RUSH 'IM, HOTHEAD.
STRETCHO LOVES HIS LITTLE SECRETS!

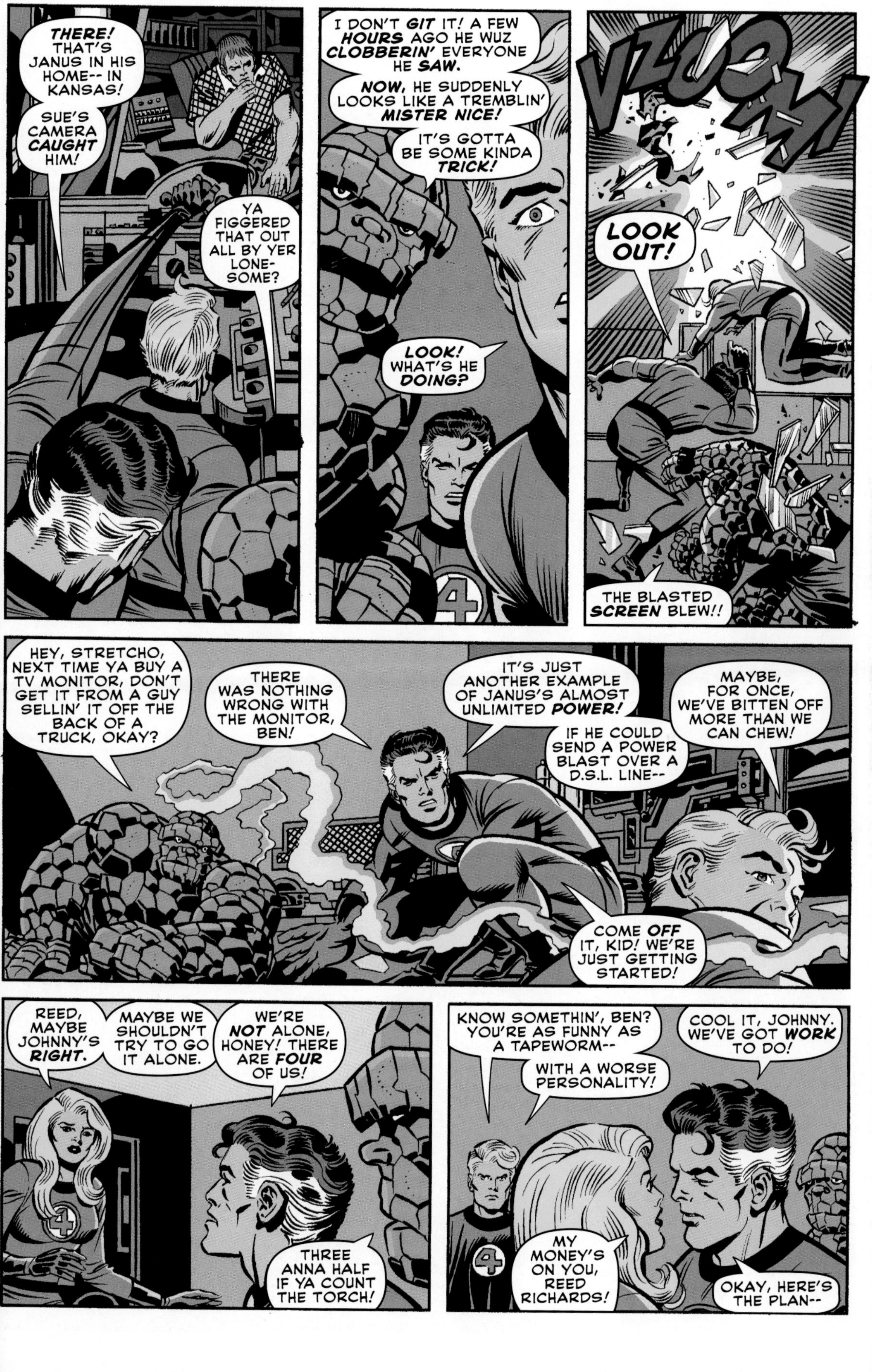

THERE! THAT'S JANUS IN HIS HOME-- IN KANSAS!
SUE'S CAMERA CAUGHT HIM!
YA FIGGERED THAT OUT ALL BY YER LONESOME?
I DON'T GIT IT! A FEW HOURS AGO HE WUZ CLOBBERIN' EVERYONE HE SAW.
NOW, HE SUDDENLY LOOKS LIKE A TREMBLIN' MISTER NICE!
IT'S GOTTA BE SOME KINDA TRICK!
LOOK! WHAT'S HE DOING?
VZOOOM!
LOOK OUT!
THE BLASTED SCREEN BLEW!!
HEY, STRETCHO, NEXT TIME YA BUY A TV MONITOR, DON'T GET IT FROM A GUY SELLIN' IT OFF THE BACK OF A TRUCK, OKAY?
THERE WAS NOTHING WRONG WITH THE MONITOR, BEN!
IT'S JUST ANOTHER EXAMPLE OF JANUS'S ALMOST UNLIMITED POWER!
IF HE COULD SEND A POWER BLAST OVER A D.S.L. LINE--
MAYBE, FOR ONCE, WE'VE BITTEN OFF MORE THAN WE CAN CHEW!
COME OFF IT, KID! WE'RE JUST GETTING STARTED!
REED, MAYBE JOHNNY'S RIGHT.
MAYBE WE SHOULDN'T TRY TO GO IT ALONE.
WE'RE NOT ALONE, HONEY! THERE ARE FOUR OF US!
THREE ANNA HALF IF YA COUNT THE TORCH!
KNOW SOMETHIN', BEN? YOU'RE AS FUNNY AS A TAPEWORM--
WITH A WORSE PERSONALITY!
COOL IT, JOHNNY. WE'VE GOT WORK TO DO!
MY MONEY'S ON YOU, REED RICHARDS!
OKAY, HERE'S THE PLAN--

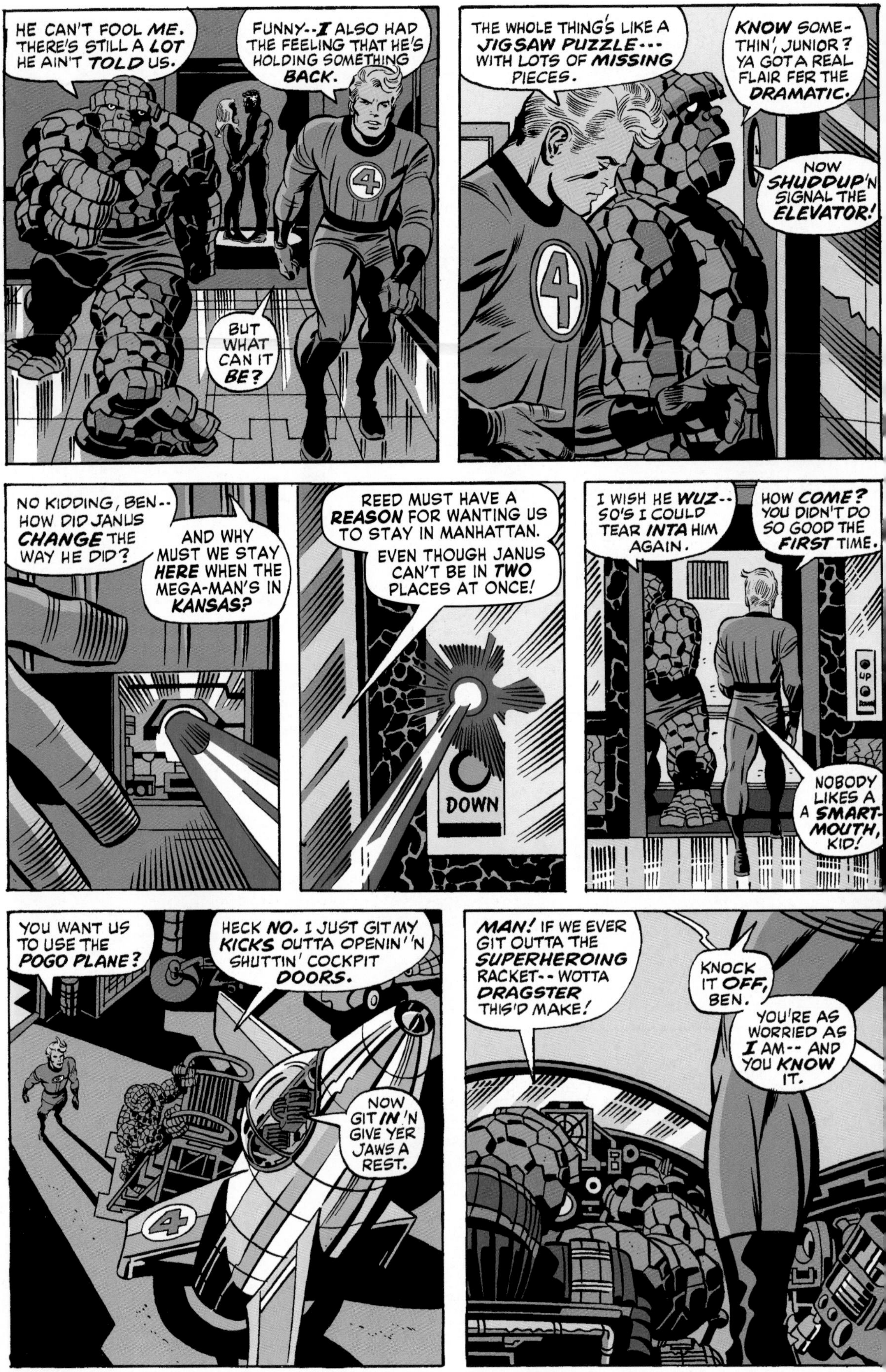
HE CAN'T FOOL ME. THERE'S STILL A LOT HE AIN'T TOLD US.
FUNNY--I ALSO HAD THE FEELING THAT HE'S HOLDING SOMETHING BACK.
BUT WHAT CAN IT BE?
THE WHOLE THING'S LIKE A JIGSAW PUZZLE--- WITH LOTS OF MISSING PIECES.
KNOW SOMETHIN', JUNIOR? YA GOT A REAL FLAIR FER THE DRAMATIC.
NOW SHUDDUP'N SIGNAL THE ELEVATOR!
NO KIDDING, BEN-- HOW DID JANUS CHANGE THE WAY HE DID?
AND WHY MUST WE STAY HERE WHEN THE MEGA-MAN'S IN KANSAS?
REED MUST HAVE A REASON FOR WANTING US TO STAY IN MANHATTAN.
EVEN THOUGH JANUS CAN'T BE IN TWO PLACES AT ONCE!
DOWN
I WISH HE WUZ-- SO'S I COULD TEAR INTA HIM AGAIN.
HOW COME? YOU DIDN'T DO SO GOOD THE FIRST TIME.
UP
DOWN
NOBODY LIKES A A SMART-MOUTH, KID!
YOU WANT US TO USE THE POGO PLANE?
HECK NO. I JUST GIT MY KICKS OUTTA OPENIN' 'N SHUTTIN' COCKPIT DOORS.
NOW GIT IN 'N GIVE YER JAWS A REST.
MAN! IF WE EVER GIT OUTTA THE SUPERHEROING RACKET-- WOTTA DRAGSTER THIS'D MAKE!
KNOCK IT OFF, BEN.
YOU'RE AS WORRIED AS I AM-- AND YOU KNOW IT.

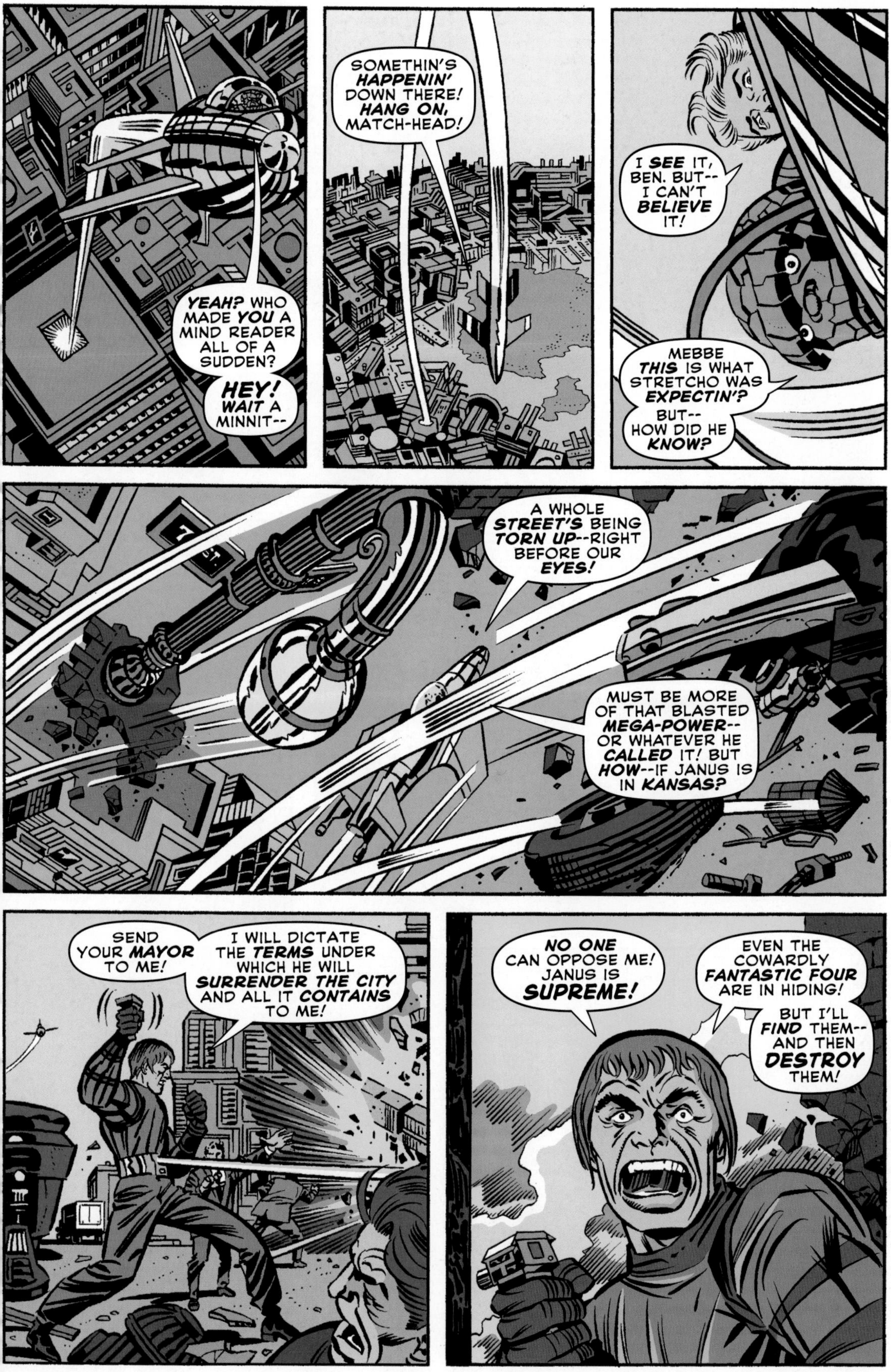
SOMETHIN'S HAPPENIN' DOWN THERE! HANG ON, MATCH-HEAD!
YEAH? WHO MADE YOU A MIND READER ALL OF A SUDDEN?
HEY! WAIT A MINNIT--
I SEE IT, BEN. BUT-- I CAN'T BELIEVE IT!
MEBBE THIS IS WHAT STRETCHO WAS EXPECTIN'?
BUT-- HOW DID HE KNOW?
A WHOLE STREET'S BEING TORN UP--RIGHT BEFORE OUR EYES!
MUST BE MORE OF THAT BLASTED MEGA-POWER-- OR WHATEVER HE CALLED IT! BUT HOW--IF JANUS IS IN KANSAS?
SEND YOUR MAYOR TO ME!
I WILL DICTATE THE TERMS UNDER WHICH HE WILL SURRENDER THE CITY AND ALL IT CONTAINS TO ME!
NO ONE CAN OPPOSE ME! JANUS IS SUPREME!
EVEN THE COWARDLY FANTASTIC FOUR ARE IN HIDING!
BUT I'LL FIND THEM-- AND THEN DESTROY THEM!

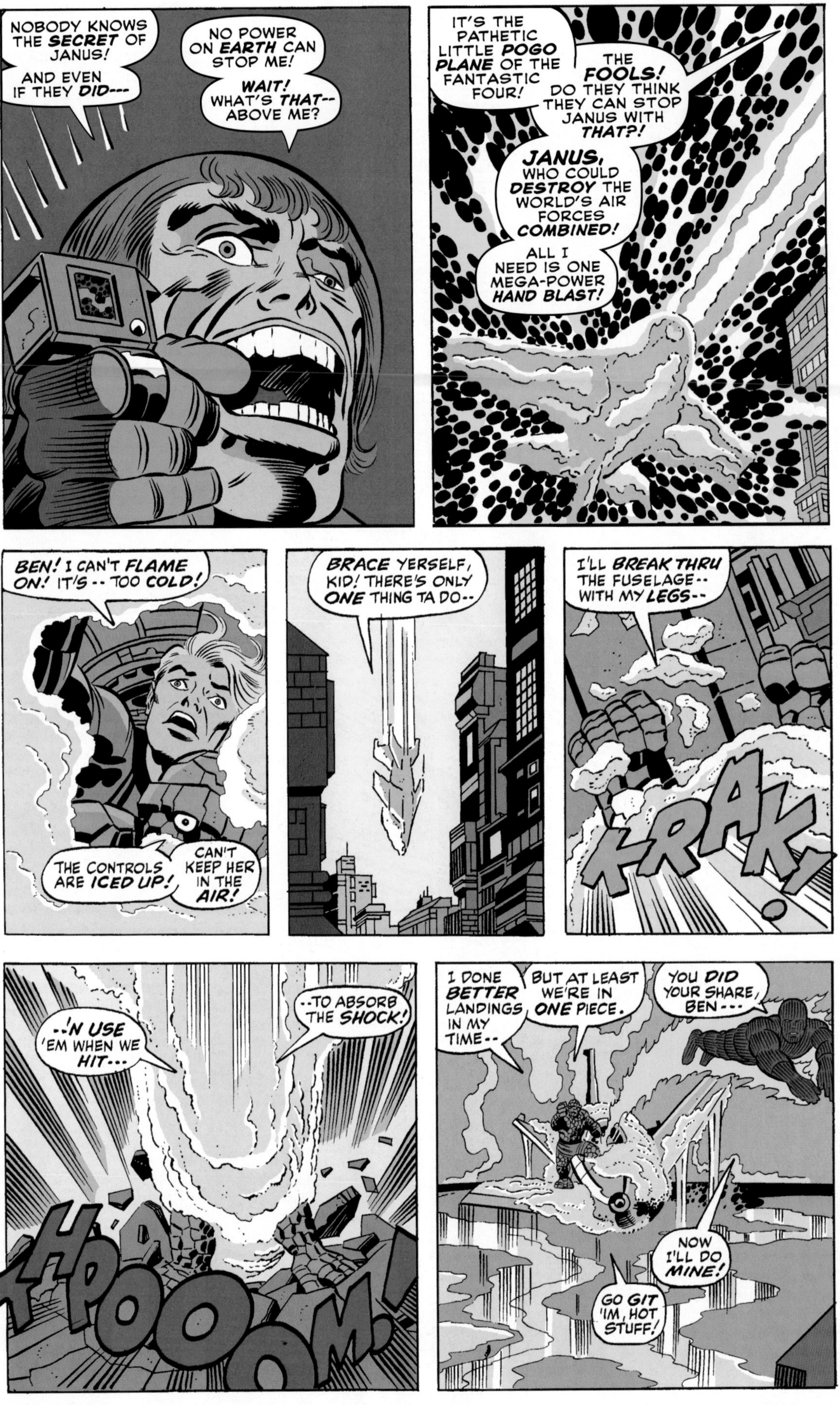
NOBODY KNOWS THE SECRET OF JANUS!
AND EVEN IF THEY DID---
NO POWER ON EARTH CAN STOP ME!
WAIT! WHAT'S THAT-- ABOVE ME?
IT'S THE PATHETIC LITTLE POGO PLANE OF THE FANTASTIC FOUR!
THE FOOLS! DO THEY THINK THEY CAN STOP JANUS WITH THAT?!
JANUS, WHO COULD DESTROY THE WORLD'S AIR FORCES COMBINED!
ALL I NEED IS ONE MEGA-POWER HAND BLAST!
BEN! I CAN'T FLAME ON! IT'S -- TOO COLD!
THE CONTROLS ARE ICED UP!
CAN'T KEEP HER IN THE AIR!
BRACE YERSELF, KID! THERE'S ONLY ONE THING TA DO--
I'LL BREAK THRU THE FUSELAGE-- WITH MY LEGS--
KRAK!
--'N USE 'EM WHEN WE HIT...
--TO ABSORB THE SHOCK!
THPOOOM!
I DONE BETTER LANDINGS IN MY TIME--
BUT AT LEAST WE'RE IN ONE PIECE.
YOU DID YOUR SHARE, BEN---
NOW I'LL DO MINE!
GO GIT 'IM, HOT STUFF!

NUTS! I CAN'T FIND HIM *ANYWHERE!*

BUT WHERE COULD HE HAVE *GONE?* --AND *WHY?*

HE DIDN'T DO ALL OF *THIS* JUST FOR *LAUGHS.*

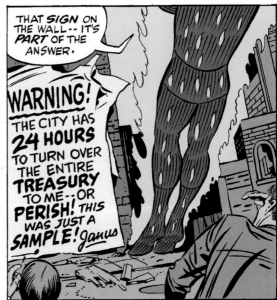

THAT *SIGN* ON THE WALL -- IT'S *PART* OF THE ANSWER.

WARNING! THE CITY HAS **24 HOURS** TO TURN OVER THE ENTIRE **TREASURY** TO ME -- OR **PERISH!** THIS WAS JUST A **SAMPLE!** *Janus*

THE *TORCH!* YOU AND YOUR SHOW-OFF *PARTNERS* WERE A GREAT HELP!

WHERE WERE YA WHEN WE *NEEDED* YOU?

WHO'S PUTTIN' MY *BUDDY* DOWN?

ANYONE GOT ANY *GRIPES?* YA CAN TAKE 'EM UP WITH THE BLUE-EYED *THING!*

HAH! LOOK AT THE CREEPS *RUN!*

NEVER MIND *THEM,* BEN, I'M WONDERING IF *JANUS* TOOK OFF FOR *KANSAS*-- AND FOR *REED?*

NOT LONG AFTER, IN THE HEART OF KANSAS...

THE SO-CALLED *GREAT* FANTASTIC FOUR!

BAH! THEY'RE *YESTERDAY'S* NEWS! OVER-THE-HILL *HAS-BEENS!*

NOW TO *SETTLE* THINGS WITH MY WEAKLING BROTHER--

ONCE AND FOR ALL!

KLIK!

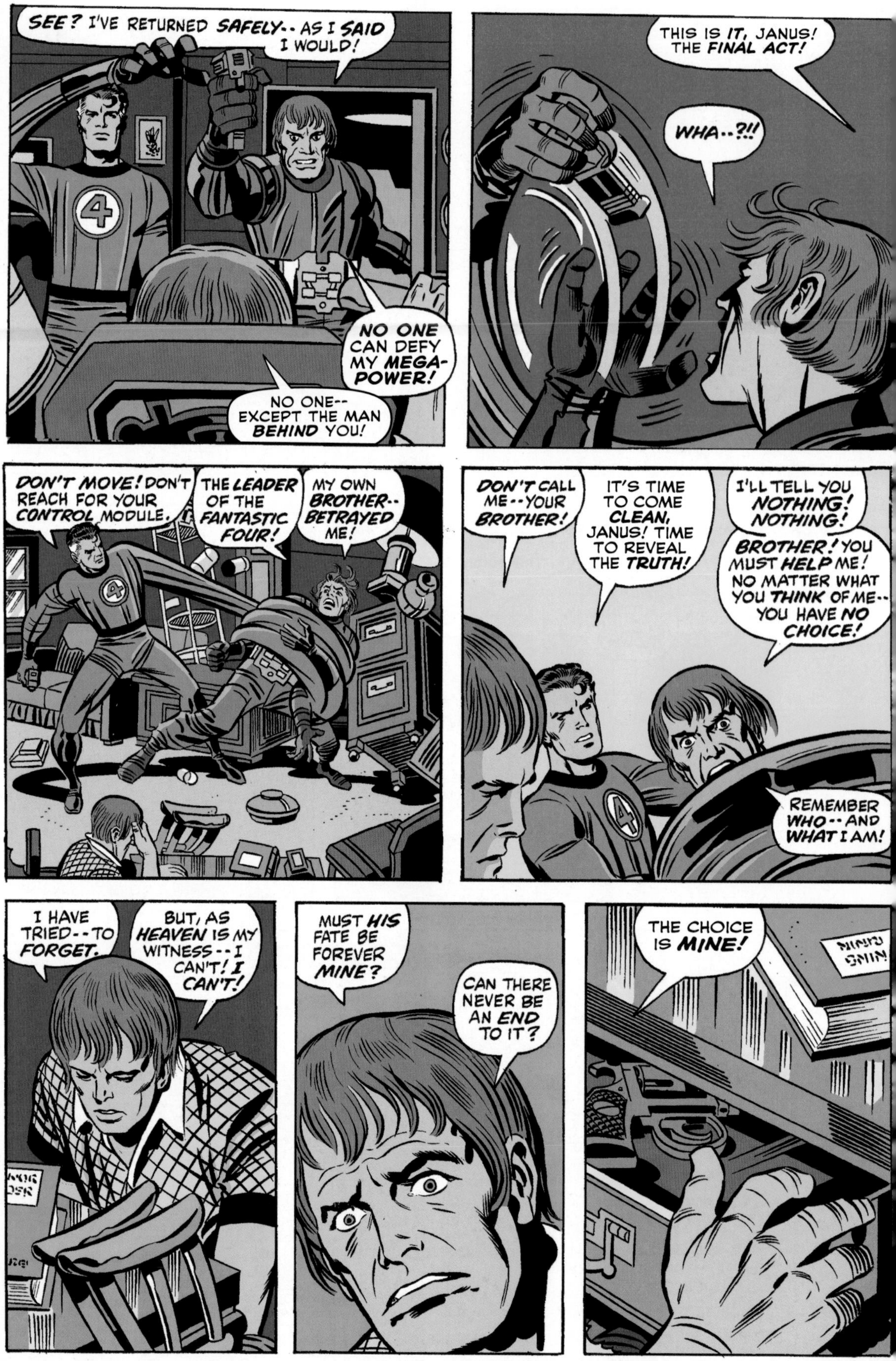
SEE? I'VE RETURNED SAFELY-- AS I SAID I WOULD!
NO ONE CAN DEFY MY MEGA-POWER!
NO ONE-- EXCEPT THE MAN BEHIND YOU!
THIS IS IT, JANUS! THE FINAL ACT!
WHA--?!!
DON'T MOVE! DON'T REACH FOR YOUR CONTROL MODULE.
THE LEADER OF THE FANTASTIC FOUR!
MY OWN BROTHER-- BETRAYED ME!
DON'T CALL ME--YOUR BROTHER!
IT'S TIME TO COME CLEAN, JANUS! TIME TO REVEAL THE TRUTH!
I'LL TELL YOU NOTHING! NOTHING!
BROTHER! YOU MUST HELP ME! NO MATTER WHAT YOU THINK OF ME-- YOU HAVE NO CHOICE!
REMEMBER WHO-- AND WHAT I AM!
I HAVE TRIED-- TO FORGET.
BUT, AS HEAVEN IS MY WITNESS-- I CAN'T! I CAN'T!
MUST HIS FATE BE FOREVER MINE?
CAN THERE NEVER BE AN END TO IT?
THE CHOICE IS MINE!

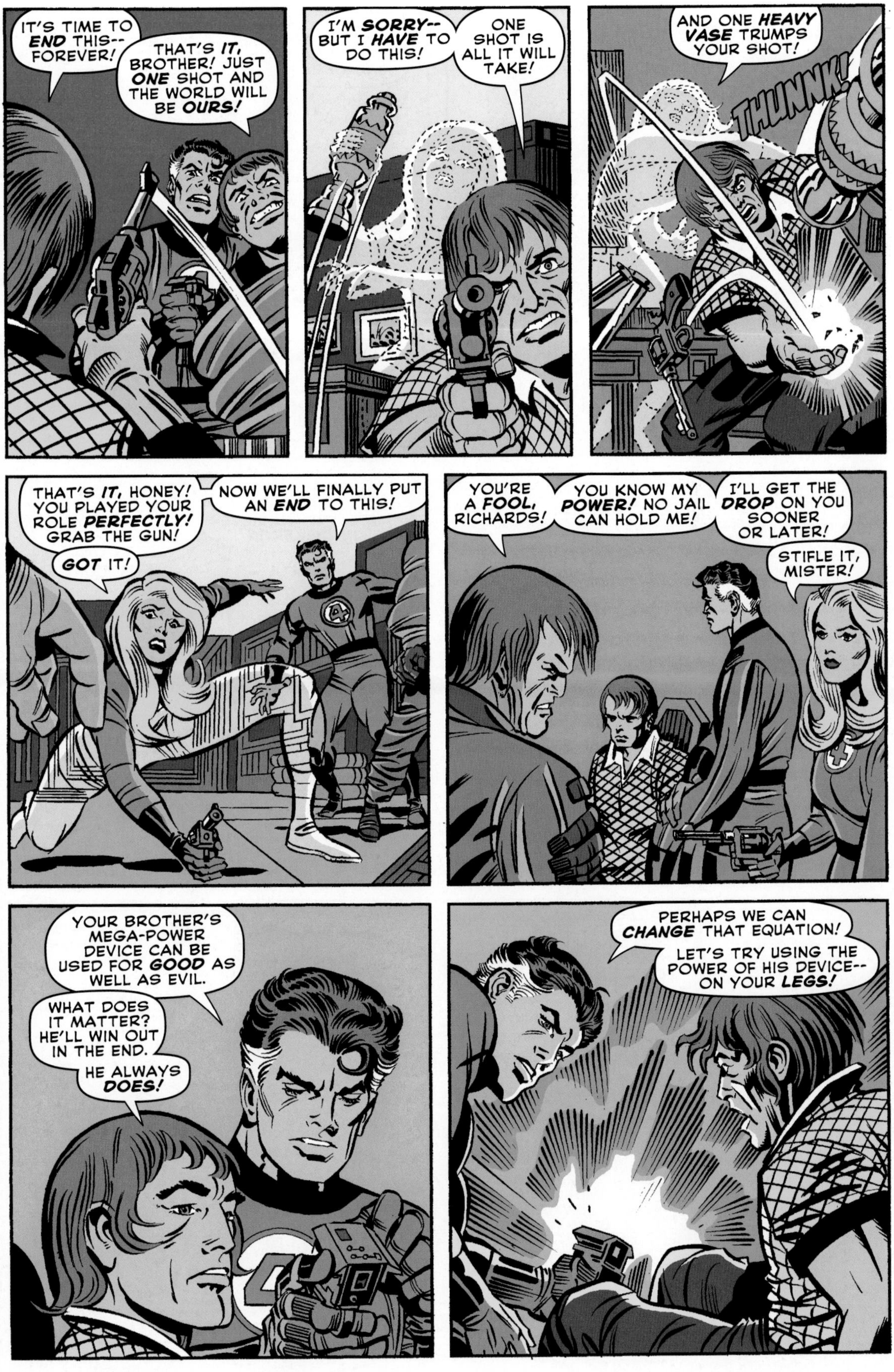
IT'S TIME TO END THIS-- FOREVER!
THAT'S IT, BROTHER! JUST ONE SHOT AND THE WORLD WILL BE OURS!
I'M SORRY-- BUT I HAVE TO DO THIS!
ONE SHOT IS ALL IT WILL TAKE!
AND ONE HEAVY VASE TRUMPS YOUR SHOT!
THUNNK!
THAT'S IT, HONEY! YOU PLAYED YOUR ROLE PERFECTLY! GRAB THE GUN!
NOW WE'LL FINALLY PUT AN END TO THIS!
GOT IT!
YOU'RE A FOOL, RICHARDS!
YOU KNOW MY POWER! NO JAIL CAN HOLD ME!
I'LL GET THE DROP ON YOU SOONER OR LATER!
STIFLE IT, MISTER!
YOUR BROTHER'S MEGA-POWER DEVICE CAN BE USED FOR GOOD AS WELL AS EVIL.
WHAT DOES IT MATTER? HE'LL WIN OUT IN THE END.
HE ALWAYS DOES!
PERHAPS WE CAN CHANGE THAT EQUATION!
LET'S TRY USING THE POWER OF HIS DEVICE-- ON YOUR LEGS!

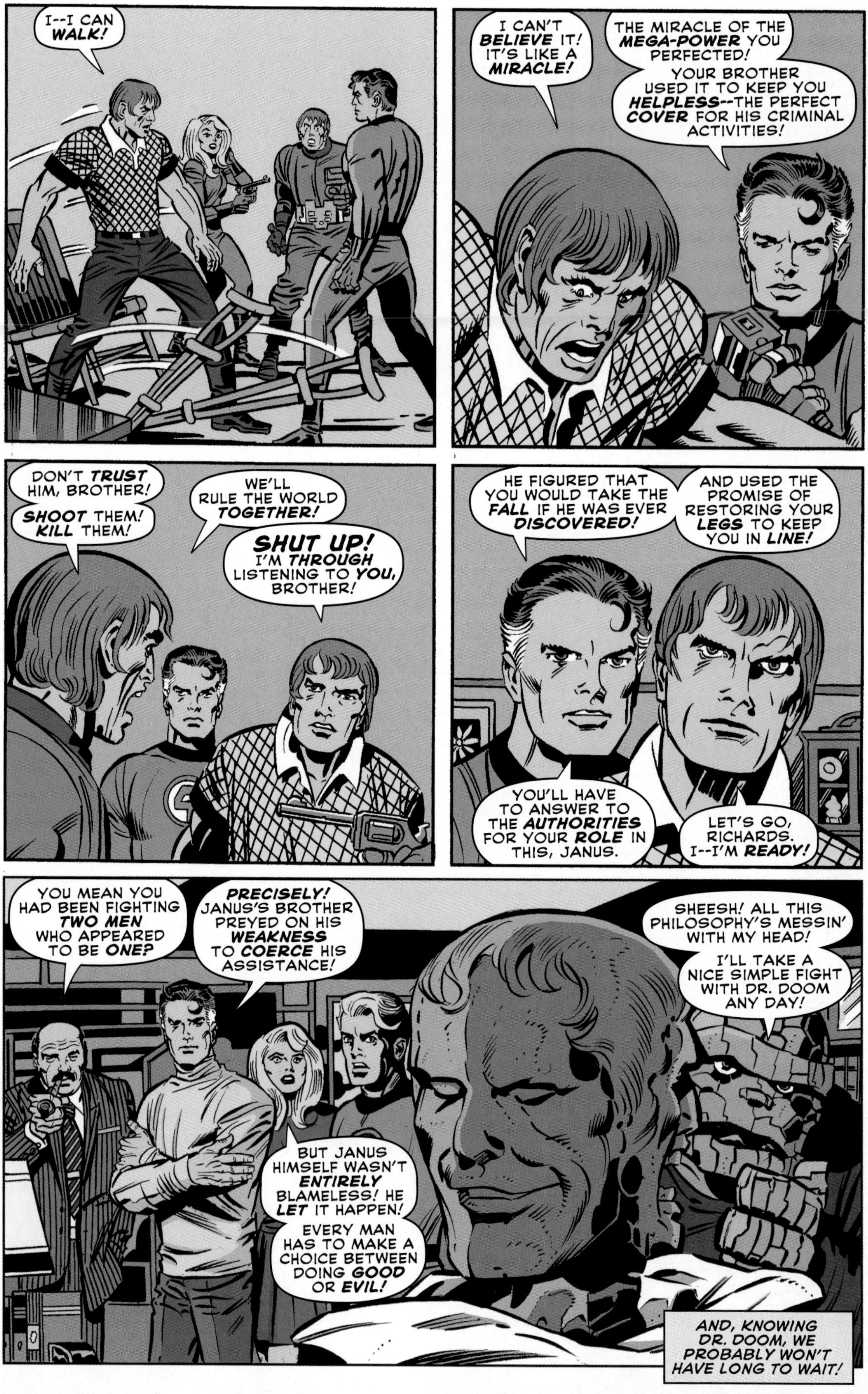

I--I CAN WALK!
I CAN'T BELIEVE IT! IT'S LIKE A MIRACLE!
THE MIRACLE OF THE MEGA-POWER YOU PERFECTED!
YOUR BROTHER USED IT TO KEEP YOU HELPLESS--THE PERFECT COVER FOR HIS CRIMINAL ACTIVITIES!
DON'T TRUST HIM, BROTHER!
SHOOT THEM! KILL THEM!
WE'LL RULE THE WORLD TOGETHER!
SHUT UP! I'M THROUGH LISTENING TO YOU, BROTHER!
HE FIGURED THAT YOU WOULD TAKE THE FALL IF HE WAS EVER DISCOVERED!
AND USED THE PROMISE OF RESTORING YOUR LEGS TO KEEP YOU IN LINE!
YOU'LL HAVE TO ANSWER TO THE AUTHORITIES FOR YOUR ROLE IN THIS, JANUS.
LET'S GO, RICHARDS. I--I'M READY!
YOU MEAN YOU HAD BEEN FIGHTING TWO MEN WHO APPEARED TO BE ONE?
PRECISELY! JANUS'S BROTHER PREYED ON HIS WEAKNESS TO COERCE HIS ASSISTANCE!
BUT JANUS HIMSELF WASN'T ENTIRELY BLAMELESS! HE LET IT HAPPEN!
EVERY MAN HAS TO MAKE A CHOICE BETWEEN DOING GOOD OR EVIL!
SHEESH! ALL THIS PHILOSOPHY'S MESSIN' WITH MY HEAD!
I'LL TAKE A NICE SIMPLE FIGHT WITH DR. DOOM ANY DAY!
AND, KNOWING DR. DOOM, WE PROBABLY WON'T HAVE LONG TO WAIT!

NTASTIC FOUR #10
IRBY'S WA

BY JOHN MORROW

Fantastic Four #108 has quite a history behind it. t was originally meant to be #102, but Stan Lee apparently felt that Jack Kirby's story, as submitted, wasn' dialogueable. So Stan ran the story intended for *FF #103* (which Kirby turned in along with his resignation from Marvel in 1969) in #102, and put the rejected art on the shelf for a few months. The Bullpen eventually chopped Kirby's originals up, rearranged panels, had John Buscema add some filler art, changed the ending, sent the whole thing to Joe Sinnott to ink, and published it (not so coincidentally) the same month Kirby's *New Gods #* came out at DC Comics. The end result was a real mess that, quite frankly, didn't make much sense.

But just how bad was Kirby's original story? Judge for yourself. Presented here is my attempt to pu he story back into its original form, using the Kirby art that didn't make the cut. Comic art dealer Mitch tkowitz came across many of the discarded pencils in the Marvel files a few years ago, and had them eturned to Jack. A few panels are still missing, and you'll see those indicated by question marks. Since Kirby's original story and the published version had major differences, I deleted the published dialogue and page numbers to avoid confusion. In quotes (" ") accompanying the pencil panels are Jack's origina margin notes for Stan Lee to dialogue by (these are numbered to coincide with the panel numbers). With ust the few margin notes here to accompany Kirby's powerful art, it's easy enough to get an idea of the story he set out to tell originally.

Some of the later pages were renumbered more than once during the alterations, making reassem oly a difficult task (apparently, the hatchet job went through several revisions). One thing that helped mmensely in reassembling this story was the fact that Kirby worked on a grid. By simply following his standard FF grid from this period, you can usually tell if panels were falling in the right place on a given page.

There were some major differences in the two versions. Just what is going on in the introduction on page 2 is unclear, and maybe this confusion at the opening of the story is the reason Stan decided i was unusable. Unlike the published version of this story, Kirby's version dealt with a force called Mega Power, not Nega-Power, and had nothing to do with the Negative Zone. And the villain Janus didn't die n the end (a plot twist that I always thought seemed very un-Kirbylike).

This story didn't break any new ground, but there are some really nice bits that got left on the Bullpen loor; those simple, down-to-earth touches like Reed and Sue's casual clothes on page 2 and the Thing's sweater on page 8, and Sue taking baby Franklin from Crystal on page **2.** These seemingly minor details make he FF seem like real people, and were a big part of the sense of family fans felt reading the comics of the Lee Kirby era. The very lack of this type of storytelling detail is one of the reasons the FF has never reached the heights it attained while Kirby was on it.

But rather than dwell on the negative, let's celebrate the end of the classic Lee/Kirby run on Fantastic Four by enjoying this look at one of Jack's final efforts on the FF, as he originally intended it to be seen

---

John Morrow is editor and publisher of The Jack Kirby Collector, *a quarterly magazine about Kirby's ife and career that is currently in its 14th year of publication. His company, TwoMorrows Publishing aunched in 1994 and is the industry's leading publisher of books and magazines about comics artist*

PAGE 1

1. "Famous archeologist has dug up statue of twin god Janus--wants to verify its date with Reed Richards' equipment--" **2.** STAN LEE BORDER NOTE: "Art dealer--why did Alicia do that strange statue?" **3.** STAN LEE BORDER NOTE: "Reed--it represents one of our greatest cases." **4.** "One face of statue is calm--wholesome. Other face is evil--savage." **5.** "Why should statue have been unearthed at this particular time? Strange."

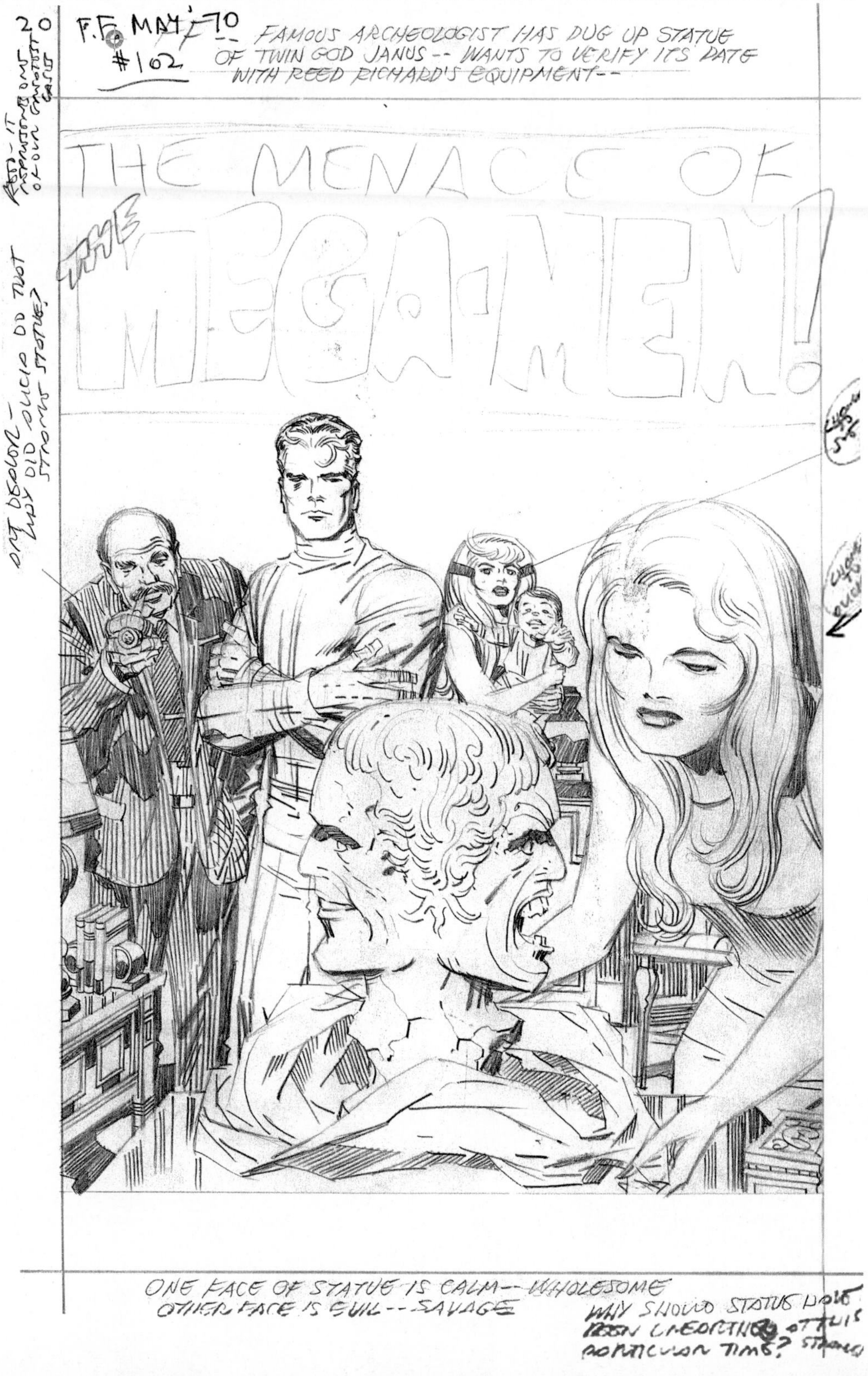

20
F.F. MAY '70
#102
FAMOUS ARCHEOLOGIST HAS DUG UP STATUE OF TWIN GOD JANUS -- WANTS TO VERIFY ITS DATE WITH REED RICHARD'S EQUIPMENT--
THE MENACE OF THE MEGA-MEN!
ONE FACE OF STATUE IS CALM -- WHOLESOME
OTHER FACE IS EVIL -- SAVAGE

PAGE 2

1. "Even ancients pondered problem that still plagues man today." **2.** "This radiation test will prove date conclusively." **3.** "The rays react." **4.** "This intensity meter places statue at 4000 B.C." **5.** "That fierce face--thank goodness we've progressed today." **6.** (From *FF #108*, Page **1.** The panel was cropped when published.)

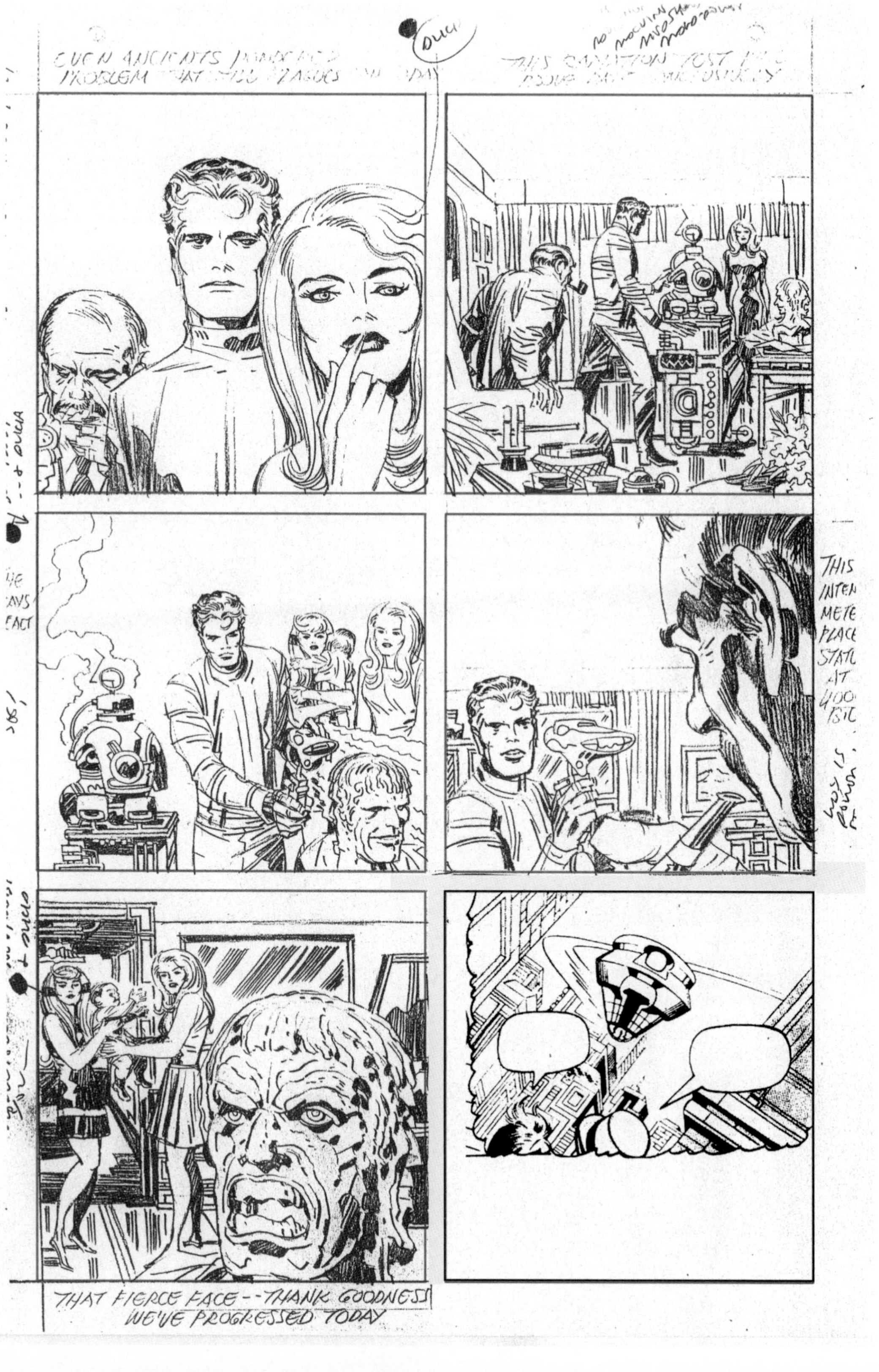
THAT FIERCE FACE--THANK GOODNESS
WE'VE PROGRESSED TODAY

(As published in *FF #108*, pages 2-5.)

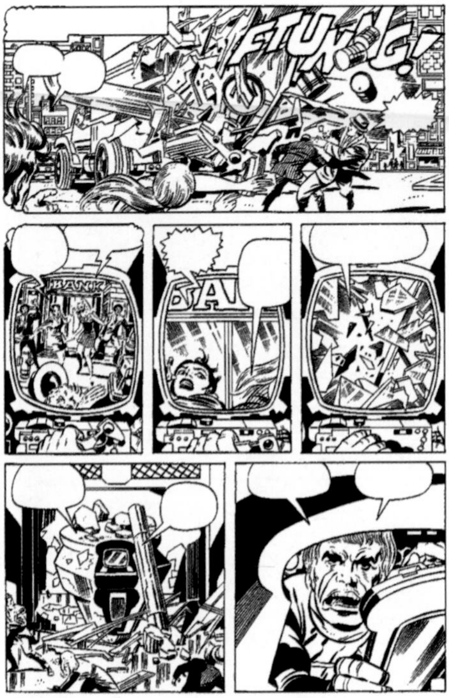
BANK

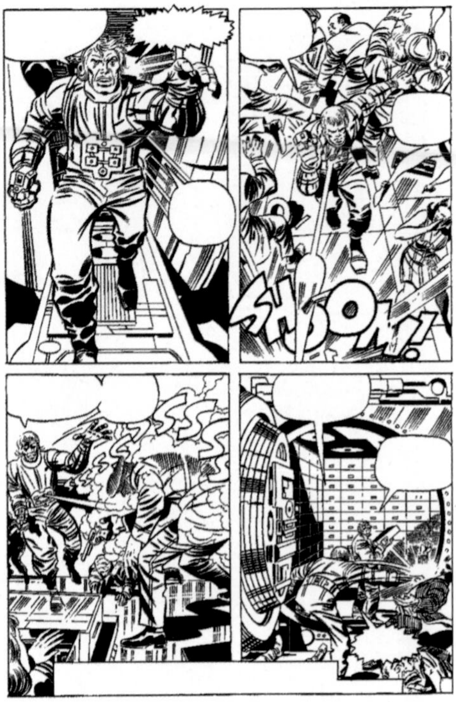
SHOOM!

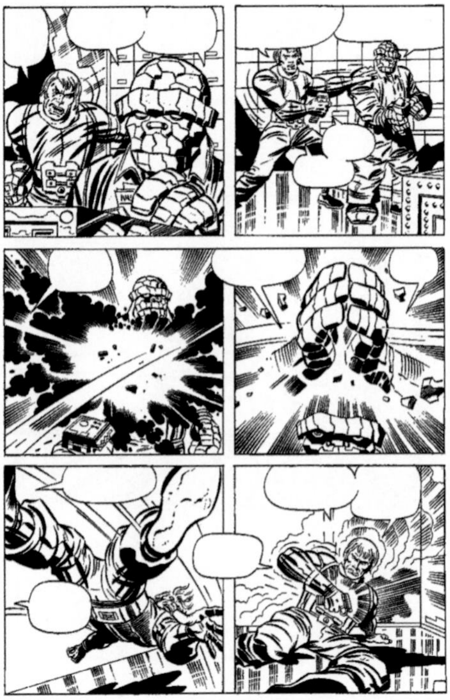

PAGE
6

1. “This gives intruder temporary strength of Thing--he bops Ben hard.” **2.** “Then like beast he hammers away without mercy.” **5.** “Torch comes to meet Ben--instead finds shambles.” **6.** “I don’t know how you did all this--but it’s over!”

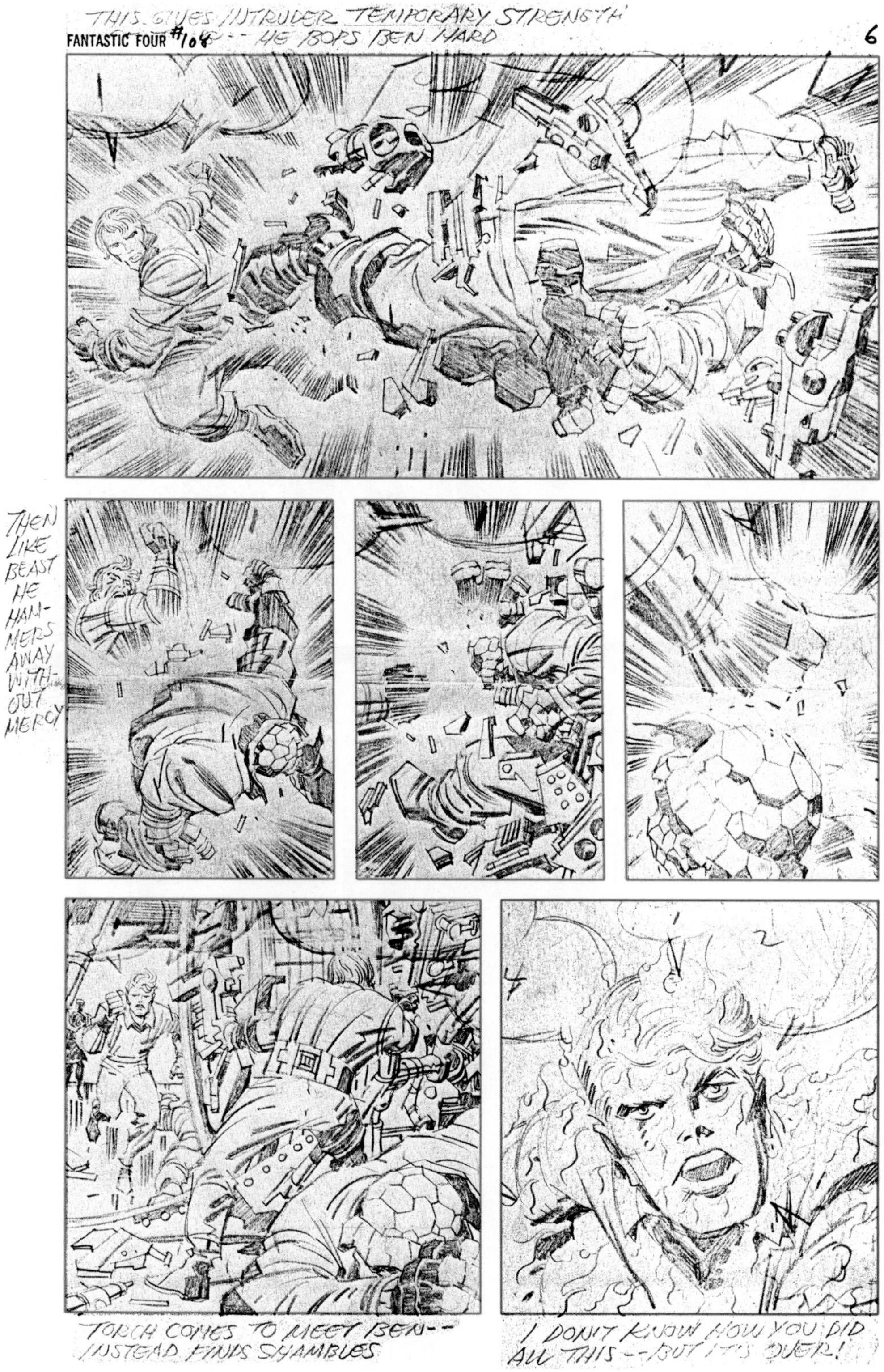
THIS GIVES INTRUDER TEMPORARY STRENGTH
FANTASTIC FOUR #108 -- HE BOPS BEN HARD
6
THEN LIKE BEAST HE HAM-MERS AWAY WITH-OUT MERCY
TORCH COMES TO MEET BEN-- INSTEAD FINDS SHAMBLES
I DON'T KNOW HOW YOU DID ALL THIS--BUT IT'S OVER!

PAGE
7

(As published in *FF #108*, Page 6.)

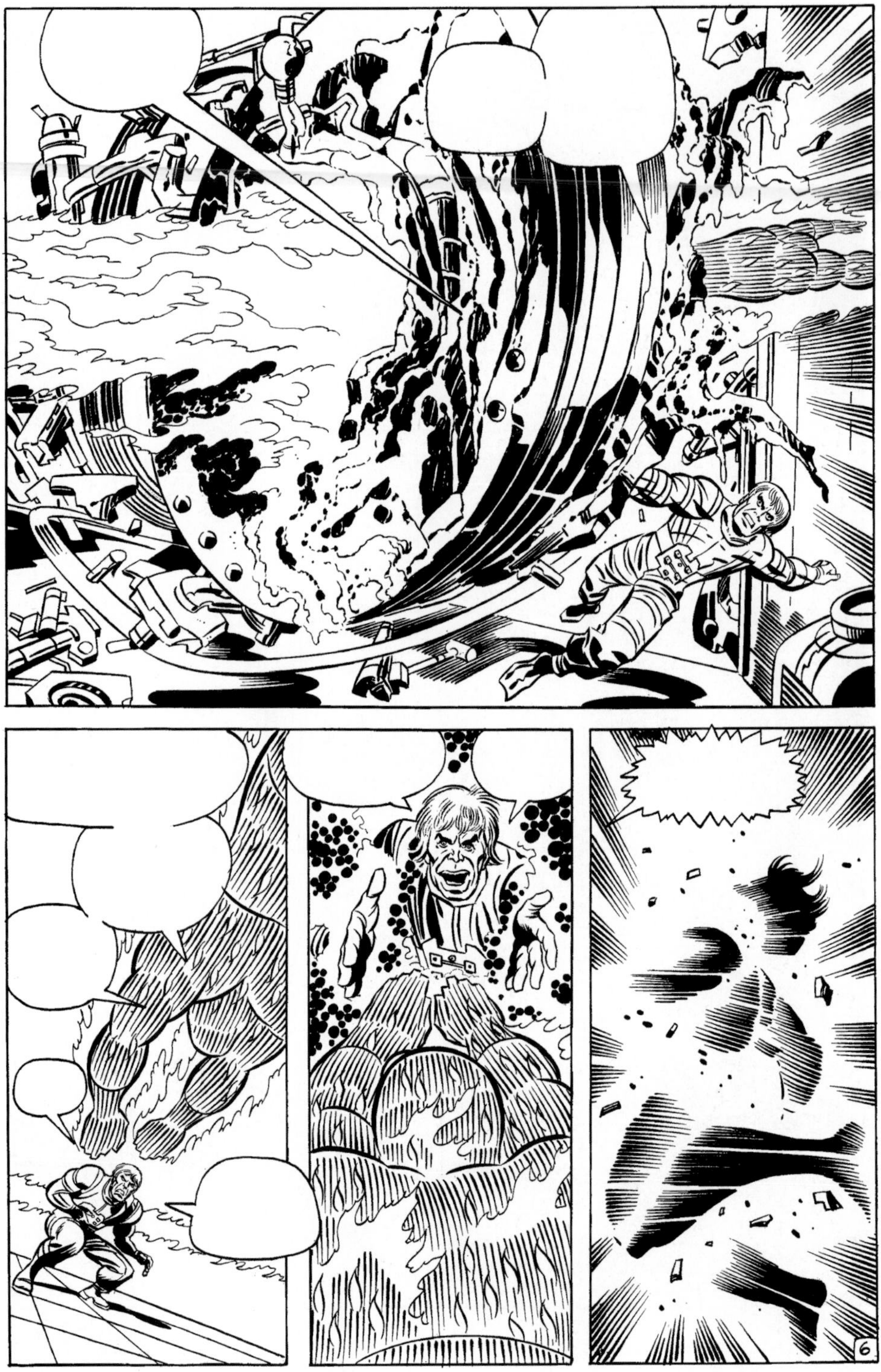

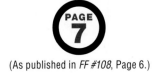

PAGE 8

1. "Torch whirls in ________ nightmare." (From *FF #108*, Page 7, Panels 1-3.) **2.** "__________ like bad dream." **3.** "Torch wakes up in _________" **4.** "Ben says we blew it--the guy got away with a million bucks." **5.** (missing panel.)
6. "Yeah--he's now number one--on the ten most wanted felons!"
7. "We can't stay here! Let's get him--" "Reed says cool it--he's following a lead."

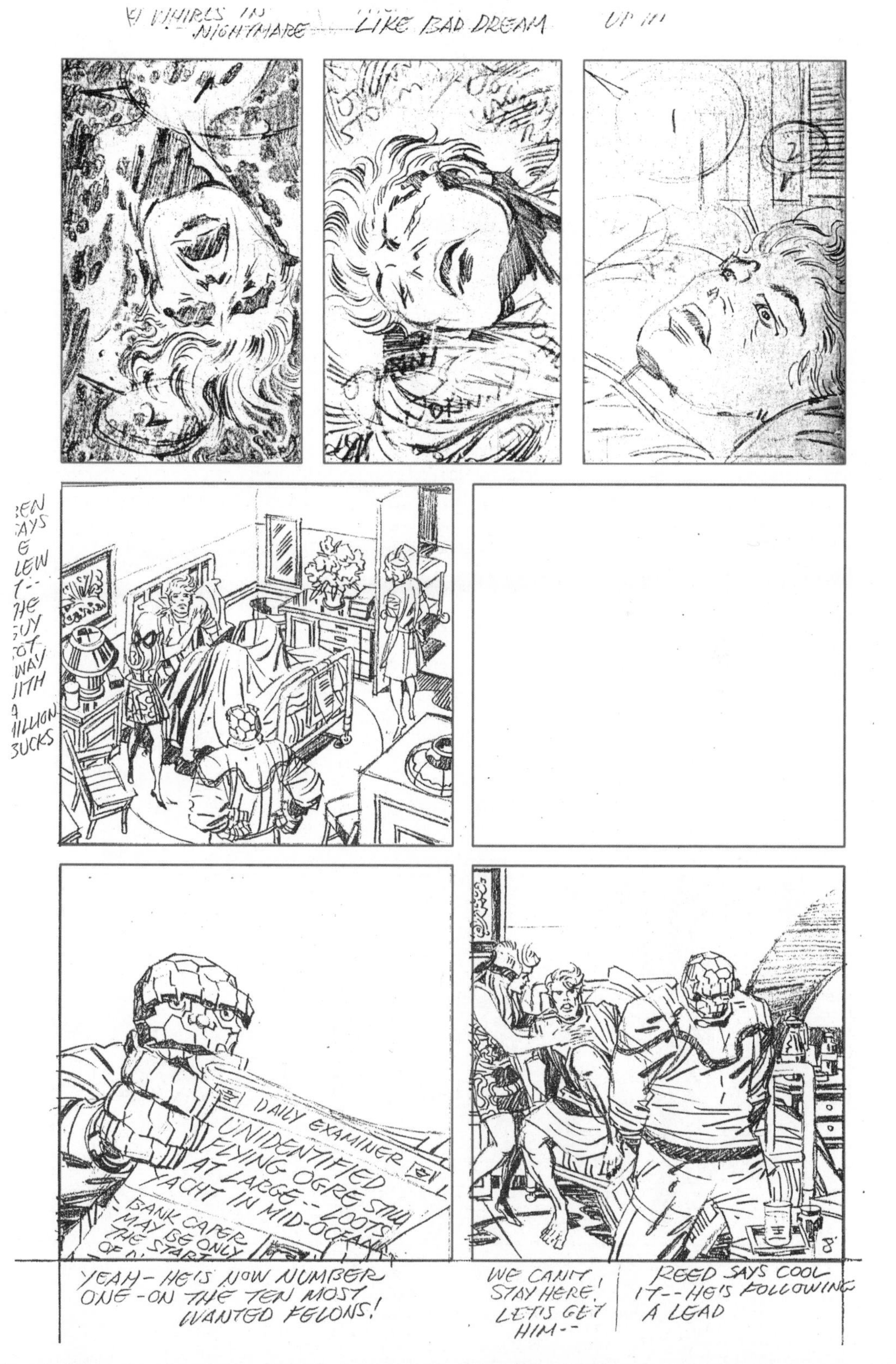

WHIRLS IN NIGHTMARE
LIKE BAD DREAM
UP IN
DAILY EXAMINER
UNIDENTIFIED FLYING OGRE STILL AT LARGE -- LOOTS YACHT IN MID-OCEAN
BANK CAPER MAY BE ONLY THE START
YEAH- HE'S NOW NUMBER ONE-ON THE TEN MOST WANTED FELONS!
WE CAN'T STAY HERE! LET'S GET HIM--
REED SAYS COOL IT--HE'S FOLLOWING A LEAD

PAGE 9

1. (From *FF #108*, page 15, panel 4.) 2-5. (Missing Panels, probably showing Sue planting a Mini-Camera In Janus' house.

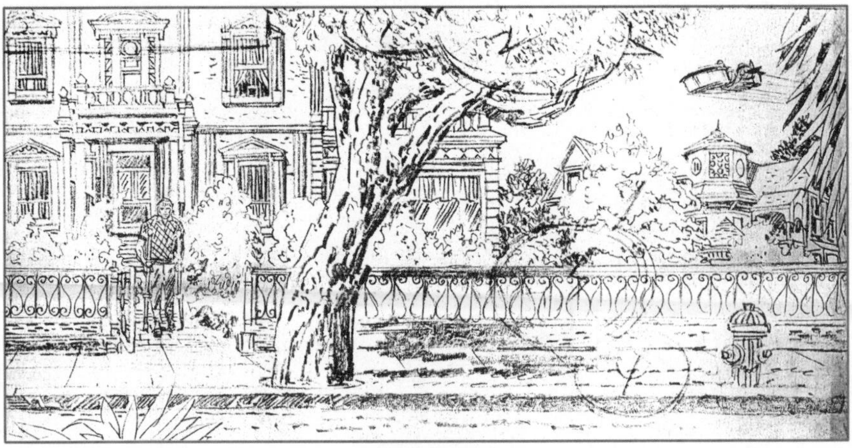

PAGE 10

1-2. (Missing Panels, probably showing Sue planting a Mini-Camera In Janus' house.) **3.** "Reed is amazed at mildness of Prof, who is complete opposite of Ben's description." **5.** "Meanwhile, the Prof's evil brother has been watching--he says Richards must be flabbergasted." **6.** "Prof says--why did you have to come after all these years?" "Because you're a perfect cover, brother--"

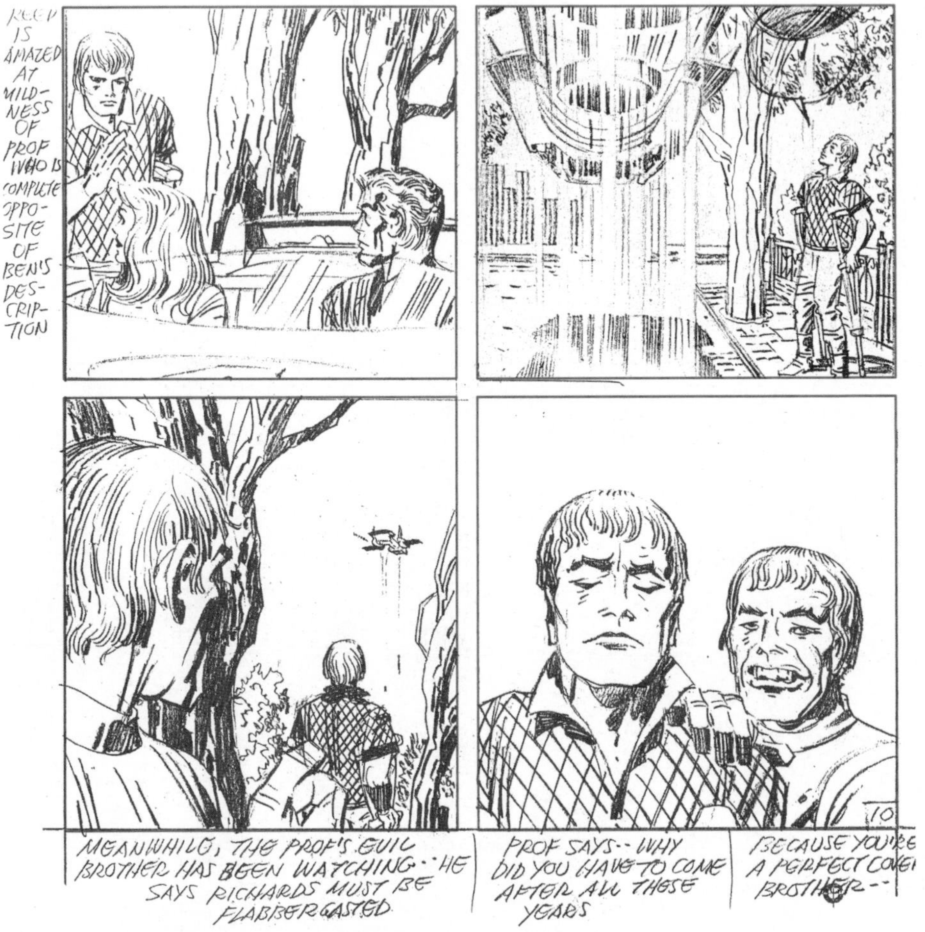
IS AMAZED AT MILD-NESS OF PROF WHO IS COMPLETE OPPO-SITE OF BEN'S DES-CRIP-TION
10
MEANWHILE, THE PROF'S EVIL BROTHER HAS BEEN WATCHING--HE SAYS RICHARDS MUST BE FLABBERGASTED
PROF SAYS--WHY DID YOU HAVE TO COME AFTER ALL THESE YEARS
BECAUSE YOU'RE A PERFECT COVER BROTHER--

PAGE 11

1. "I've been away perfecting Mega-Power. Now--I'll gain money-power." **2.** "You won't talk. The town won't talk--or it's curtains!" **3.** "Stick with me. With Mega-Power--I may even help you walk again." **4.** "Right now I'm gong to be busy in lab. Richards didn't go away without bugging the house." **5.** "I've got instruments to trace his bugs and destroy them. Now leave me." **6.** "Yes--my plans don't stop here--I'll empty that whole city of its money." **7.** (From *FF #108*, Page 7, Panel 6.)

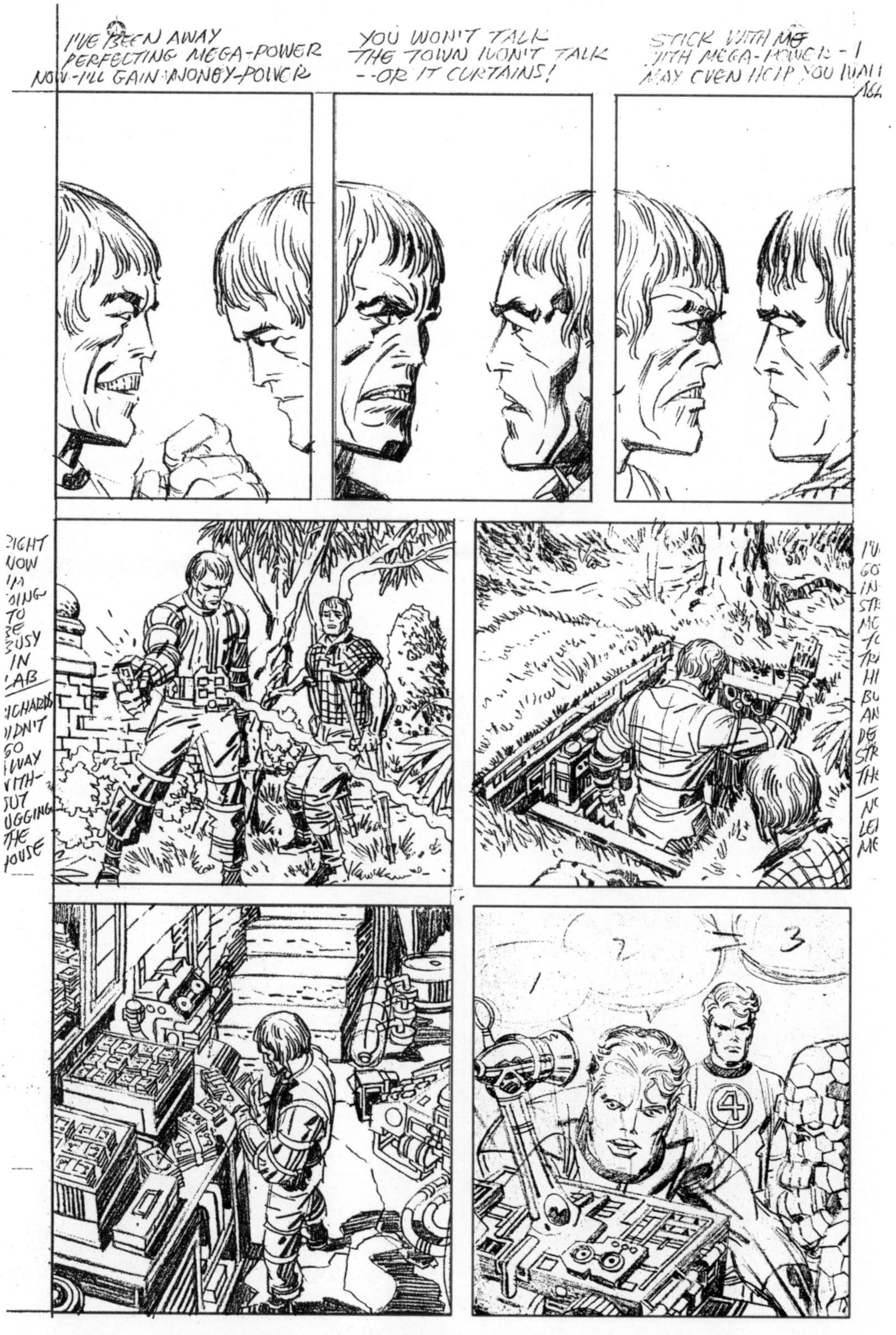
I'VE BEEN AWAY
PERFECTING MEGA-POWER
YOU WON'T TALK
THE TOWN WON'T TALK
--OR IT CURTAINS!

PAGES 12-13

This page would have been split into two half pages, with ads running under them--A practice that got a 20-page story out of only 19 pages of art. **1-2.** (From *FF #108*, Page 8, Panel 2 and 3.) **3.** (From *FF #108*, Page 8, Panel 6.) **4.** ____________________ with mini-camera (From *FF #108*, Page 9, Panel 1.) **5.** "What Happened?" "Ben says--Reed's mini-camera blew up in our faces--that's what!" **6.** "That was no malfunction--that was Mega-Power. Listen Sue--I have a nutty idea--"

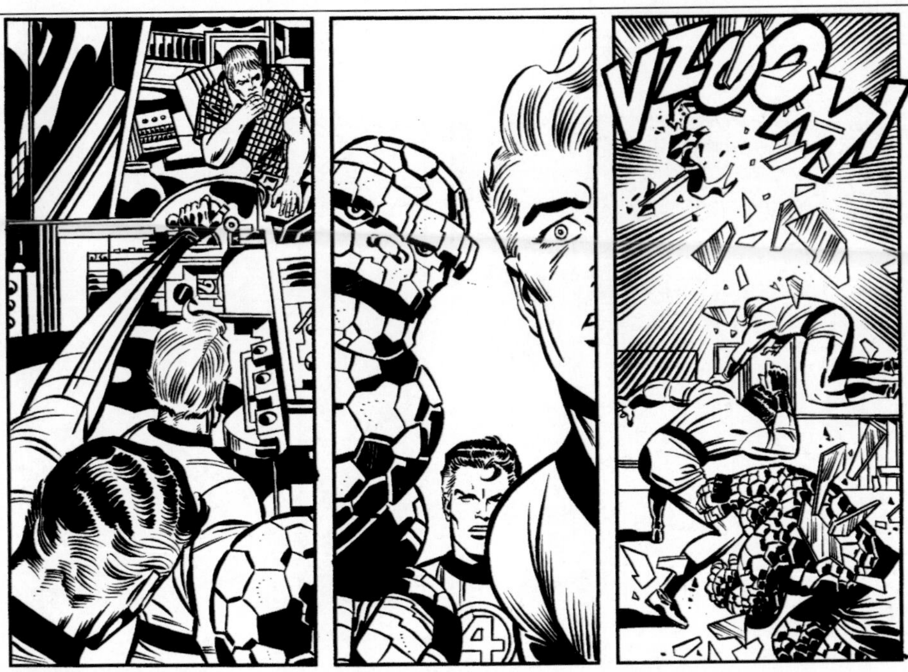
VZOOM!

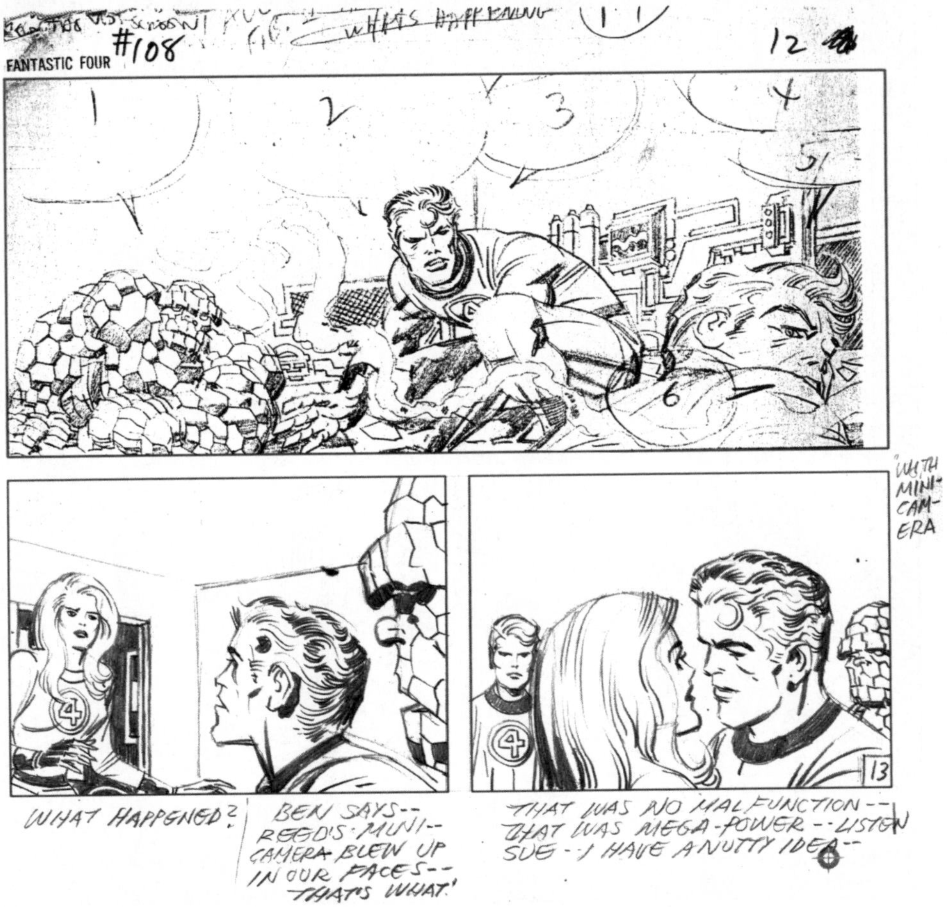
FANTASTIC FOUR #108
12
1
2
3
4
5
6
13
"WITH MINI-CAMERA
WHAT HAPPENED?
BEN SAYS--REED'S MINI-CAMERA BLEW UP IN OUR FACES--THAT'S WHAT!
THAT WAS NO MALFUNCTION--THAT WAS MEGA-POWER--LISTEN SUE--I HAVE A NUTTY IDEA--

PAGE
14

1. "Let him give her crazy ideas--I'll take action--the real culprit must be in city ___________ right now!" **2.** "We'll take Pogo Plane on upper floor. We'll scout around until we nail this bird." **3.** "Ray shoots out from Johnny's belt. It strikes "up" button." **6.** "Ben says--you can't have girls tagging along all the time--Alicia's visiting ________________" **7.** "Boy--these controls feel great--did you know I was a World War 2 ace?"

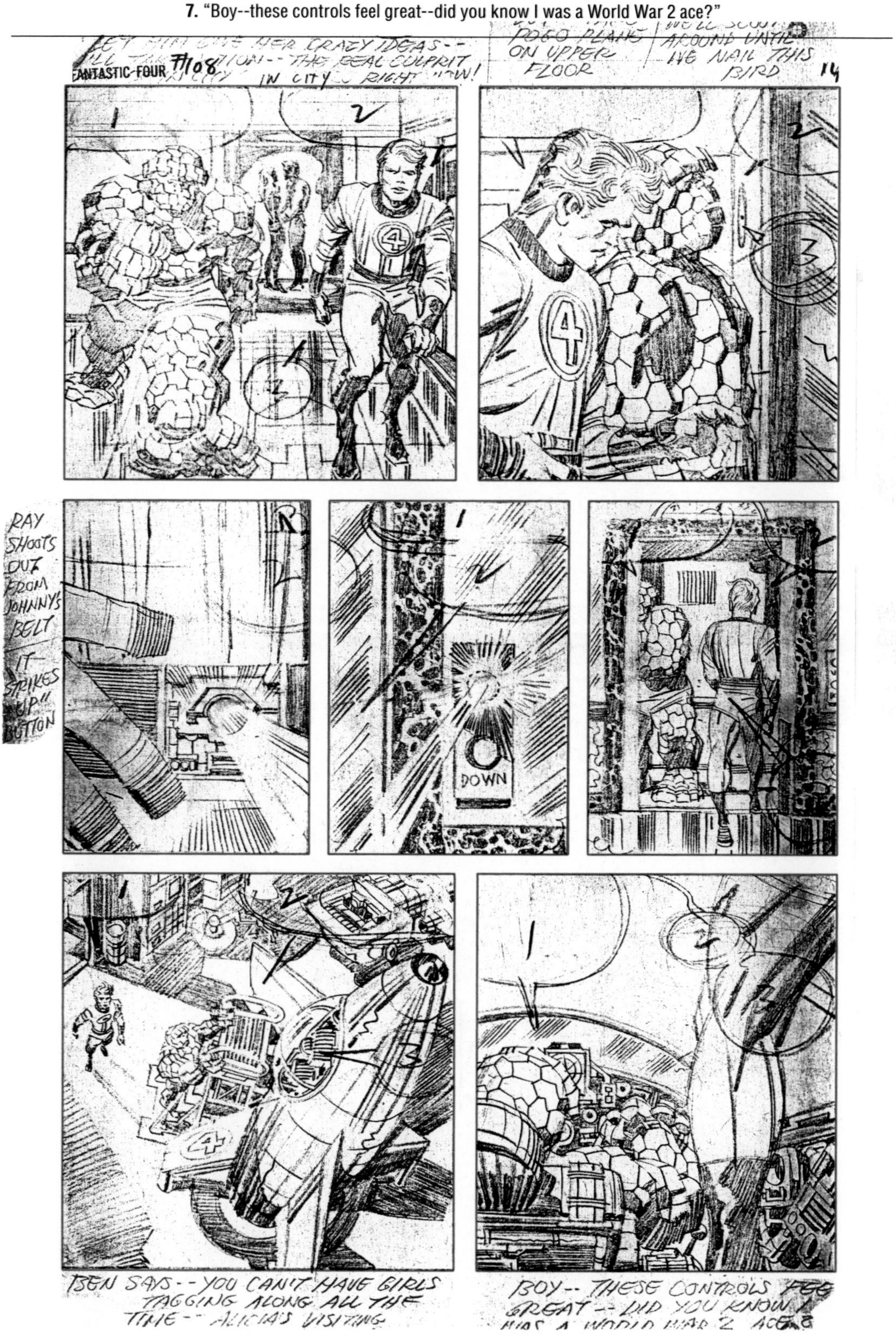

FANTASTIC FOUR 7/108
ON UPPER FLOOR
WE NAIL THIS BIRD
14
RAY SHOOTS OUT FROM JOHNNY'S BELT
IT STRIKES "UP" BUTTON
DOWN
BEN SAYS -- YOU CAN'T HAVE GIRLS TAGGING ALONG ALL THE TIME -- ALICIA'S VISITING
BOY -- THESE CONTROLS FEE
GREAT -- DID YOU KNOW

PAGE 15

1. "How's this for a takeoff--she handles great!" **2.** "_______ friend's crummy craft! I'll take him like the Red Baron."
3. "You see what I see?" **4.** "Flying debris from street below. Ripped out by Mega-Power! Let's go!"
6. "He sees plane! I can't leave without a parting shot--"

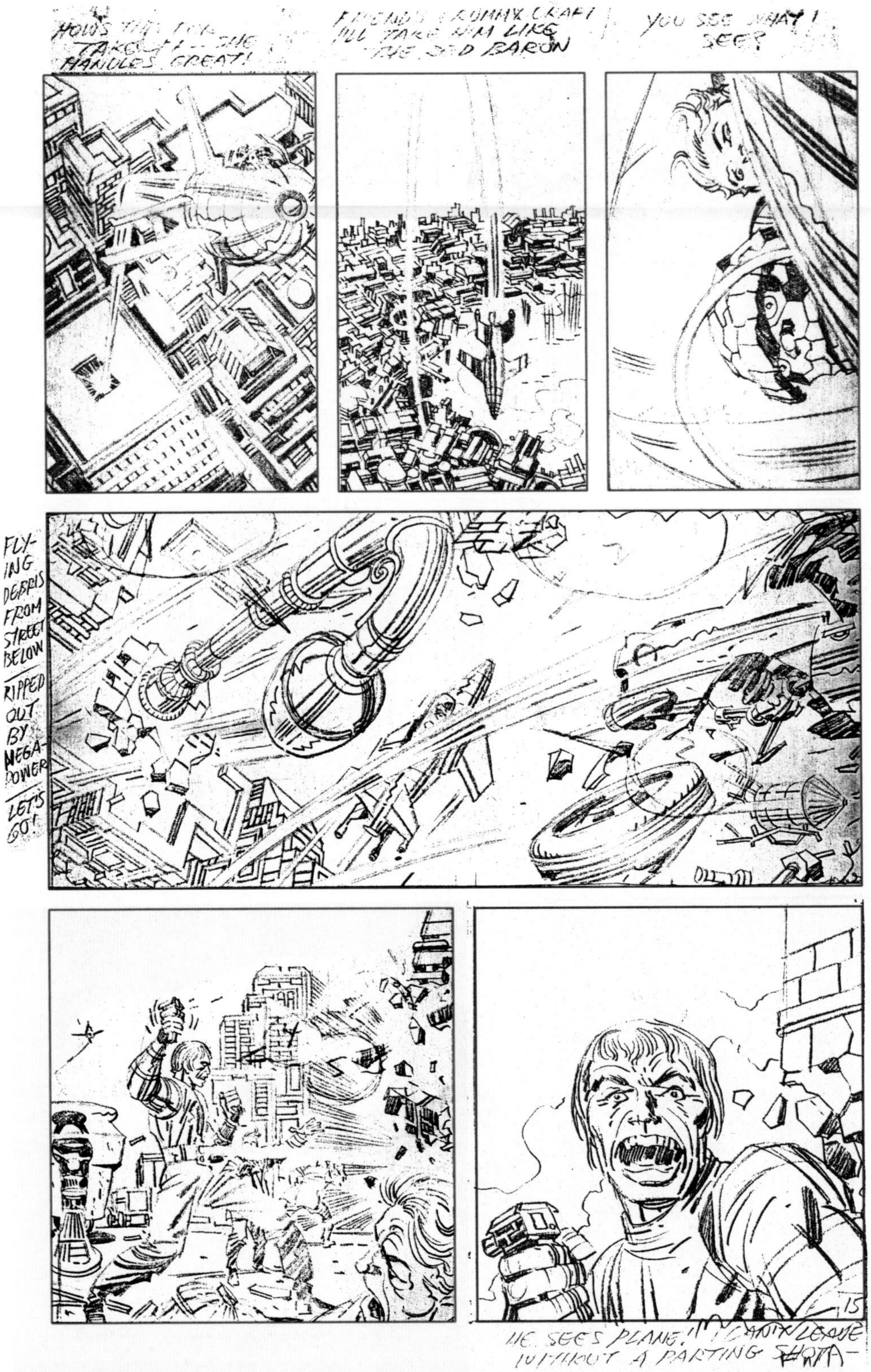
FLY-ING DEBRIS FROM STREET BELOW RIPPED OUT BY MEGA-POWER LET'S GO!
15

PAGE 16

1-2. (From *FF #108*, Page 13, Panel 1-2. Originals were cropped.) **3.** "Ben! The cockpit's frozen tight! Ben says Flame On, kid. Get out! I can't control it." **3-7.** (From *FF #108*, Page 14, Panel 1-5.)

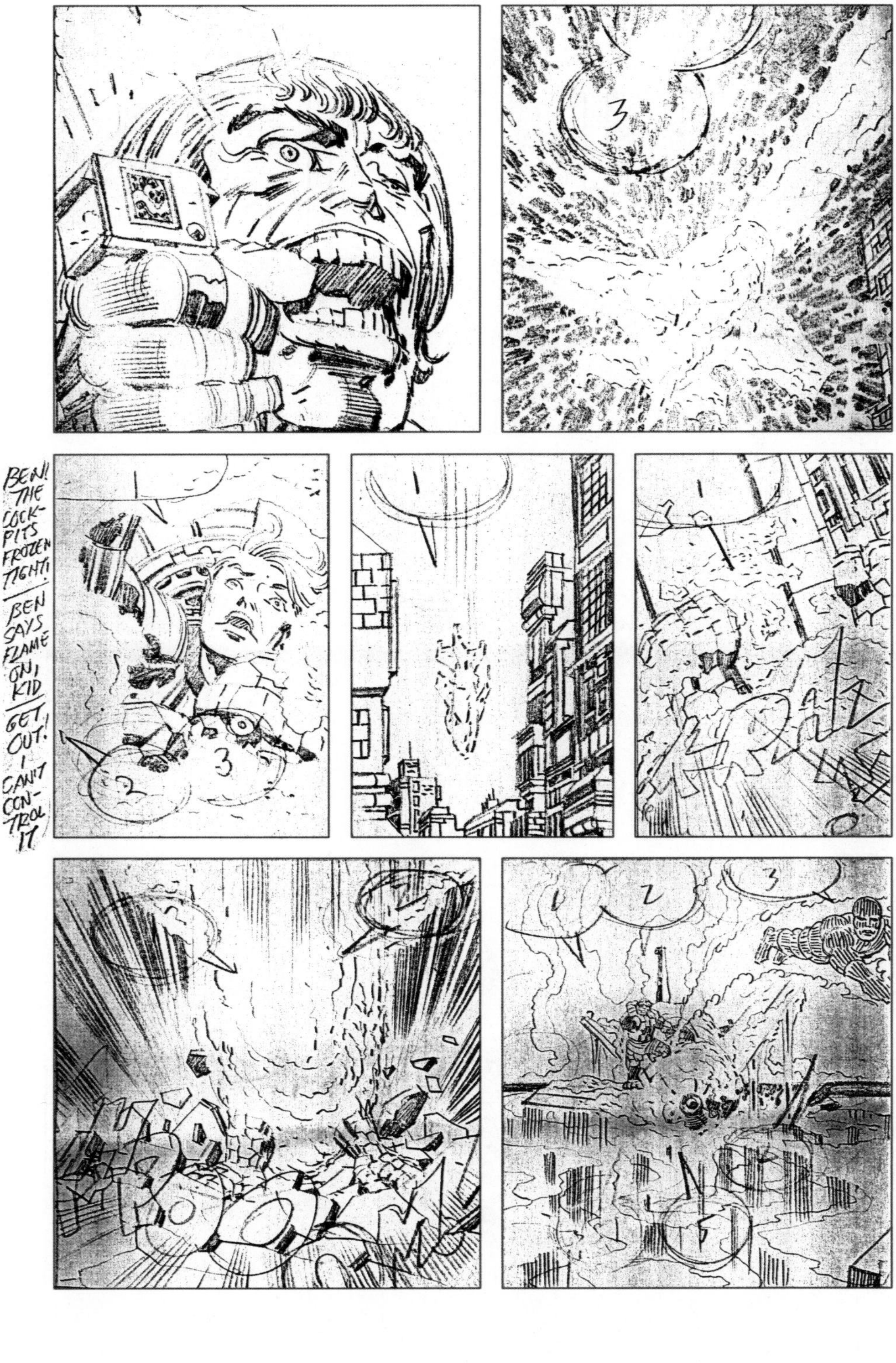
BEN! THE COCK-PITS FROZEN TIGHT!
BEN SAYS FLAME ON, KID
GET OUT! I CAN'T CON-TROL IT

PAGE 17

1-2. (From *FF #108*, Page 14, Panel 6-7.) **3.** "Bruised people say--are we in his power? Can you stop him?" **3-5.** (From *FF #108*, Page 15, Panel 1-3.) **6-7.** (From *FF #108*, Page 16, Panel 3-4.)

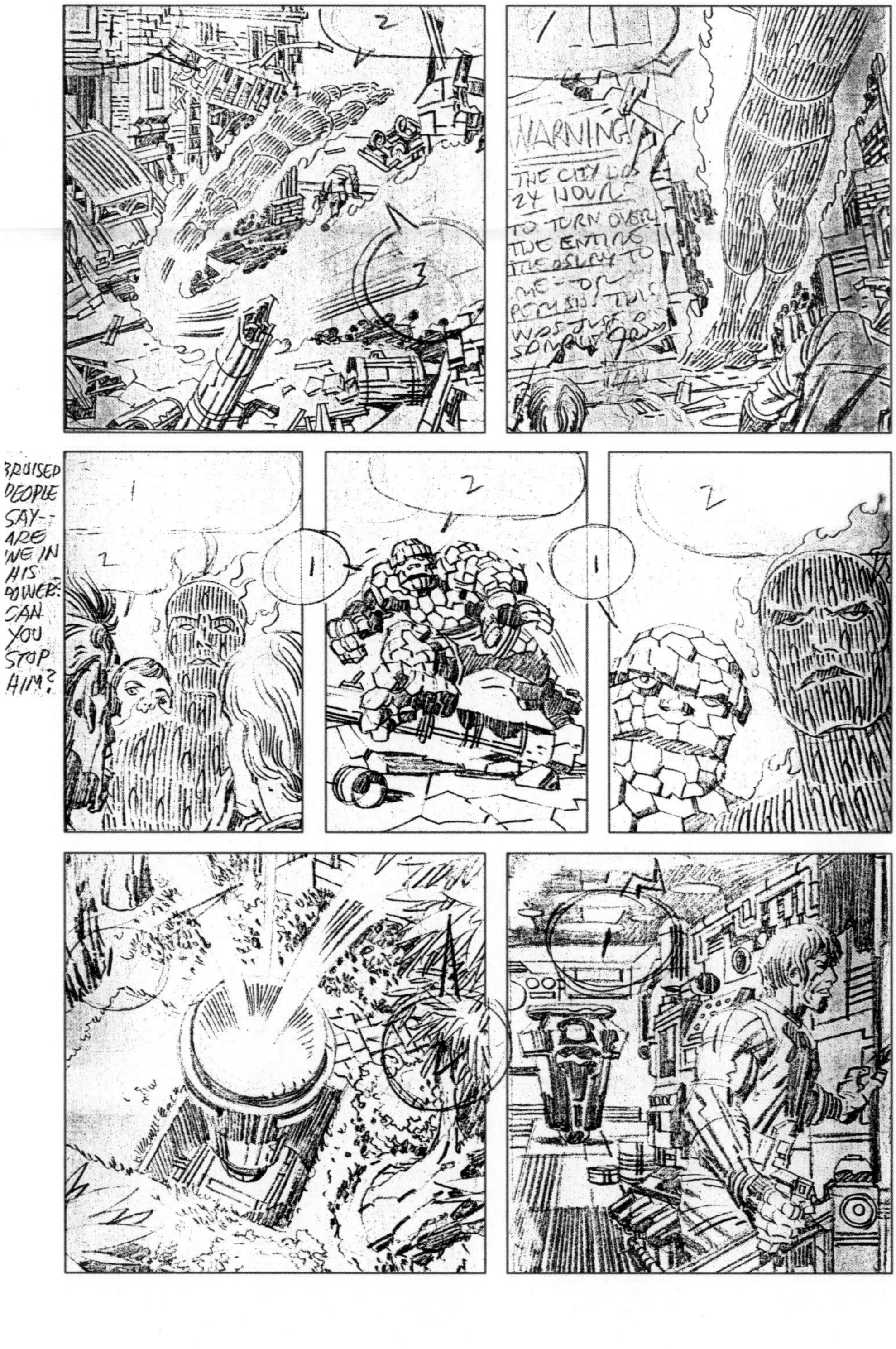

WARNING!
BRUISED PEOPLE SAY-- ARE WE IN HIS POWER? CAN YOU STOP HIM?

PAGE 18

1-2. (From *FF #108*, Page 16, Panel 5-6.) **3-7.** (From *FF #108*, Page 17, Panel 1-5.)

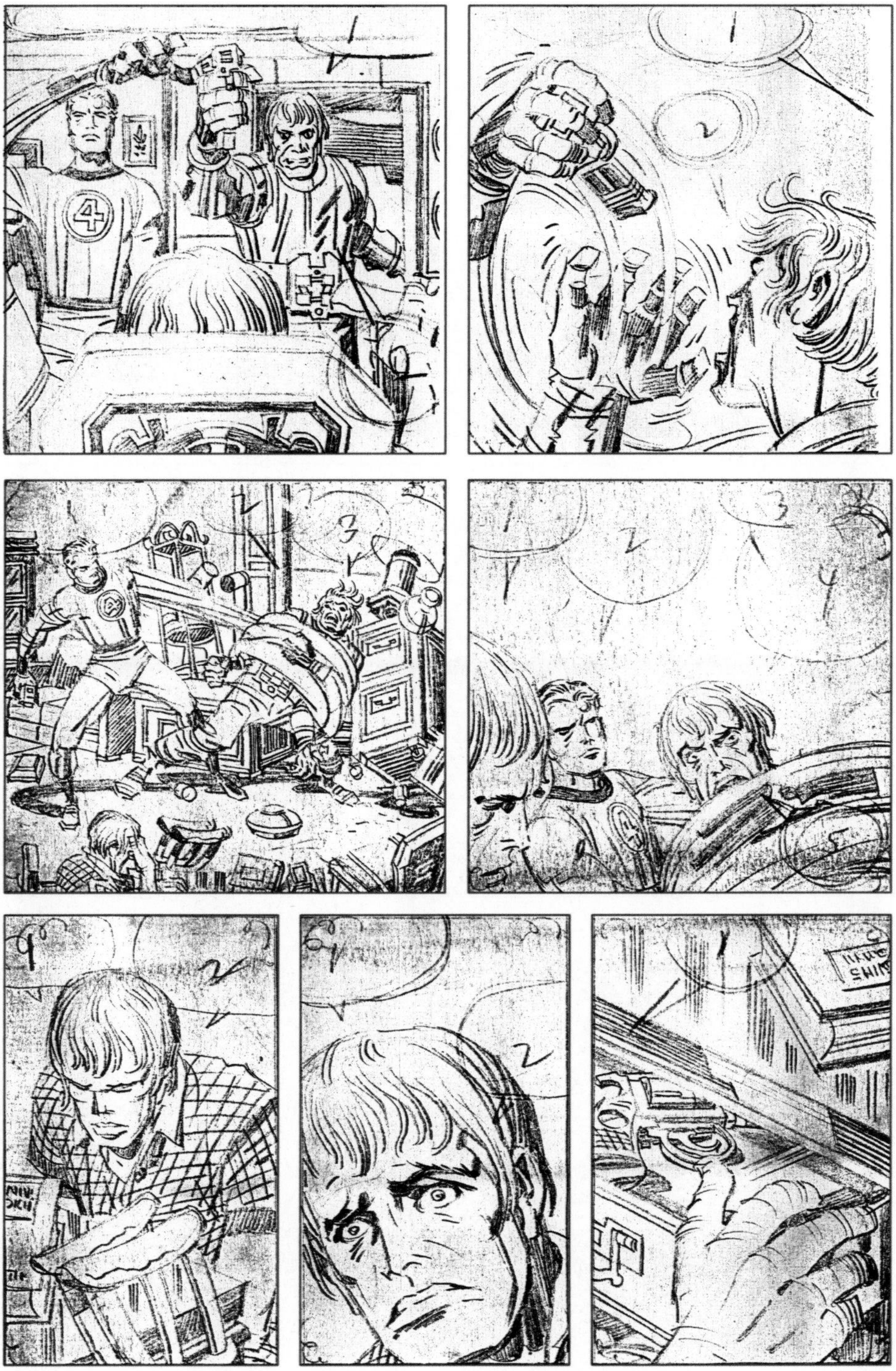

PAGE 19

1. (From *FF #108*, Page 17, Panel 6.) **2-3.** (No Margin Notes Visible.) **4.** "She grabs gun before twin can reach for it." "Reed says--use gun to cover bad twin, Sue!" **5.** "Reed says to good twin--you're a fool you know. The criminal's path is no solution." **6.** (Margin notes are erased.) **7.** "Reed touches good twin's feet with trigger." (The page number "19" has been erased, but is visible.)

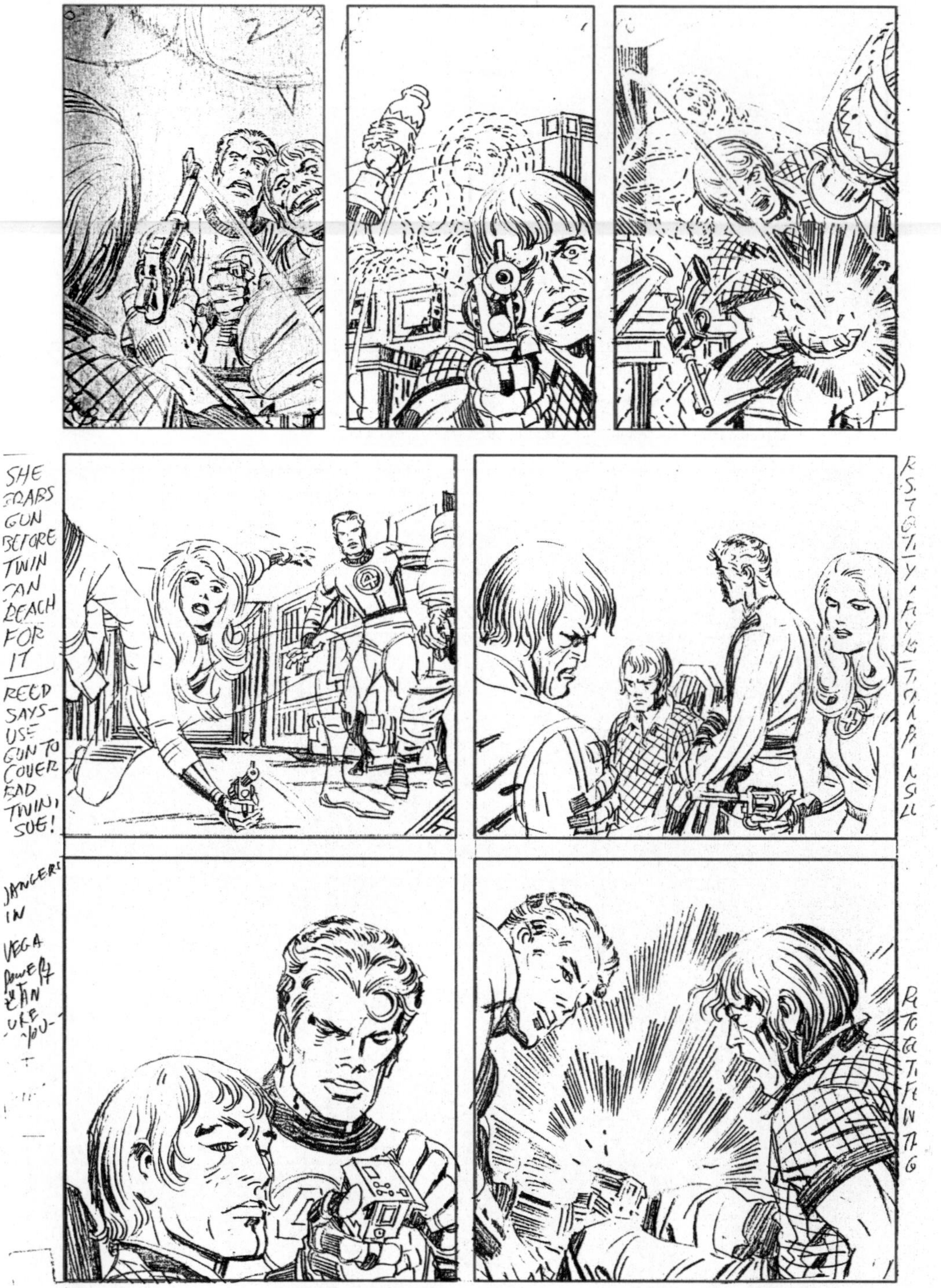
SHE
GUN
BEFORE
TWIN
REACH
FOR
IT
REED
SAYS-
USE
GUN TO
COVER
TWIN,
SUE!
IN
VEGA

PAGE 20

1. (Margin Notes have been erased.) **2.** "Who can tell what Mega-Power can do?" **3.** "Don't trust him! Get him while you can! I'll handle the girl!" (Note the scalloped corners, indicating this was considered for a flashback scene in *FF #108*.) **4.** (Margin Notes have been erased.) **5-7.** (Missing Panels.)

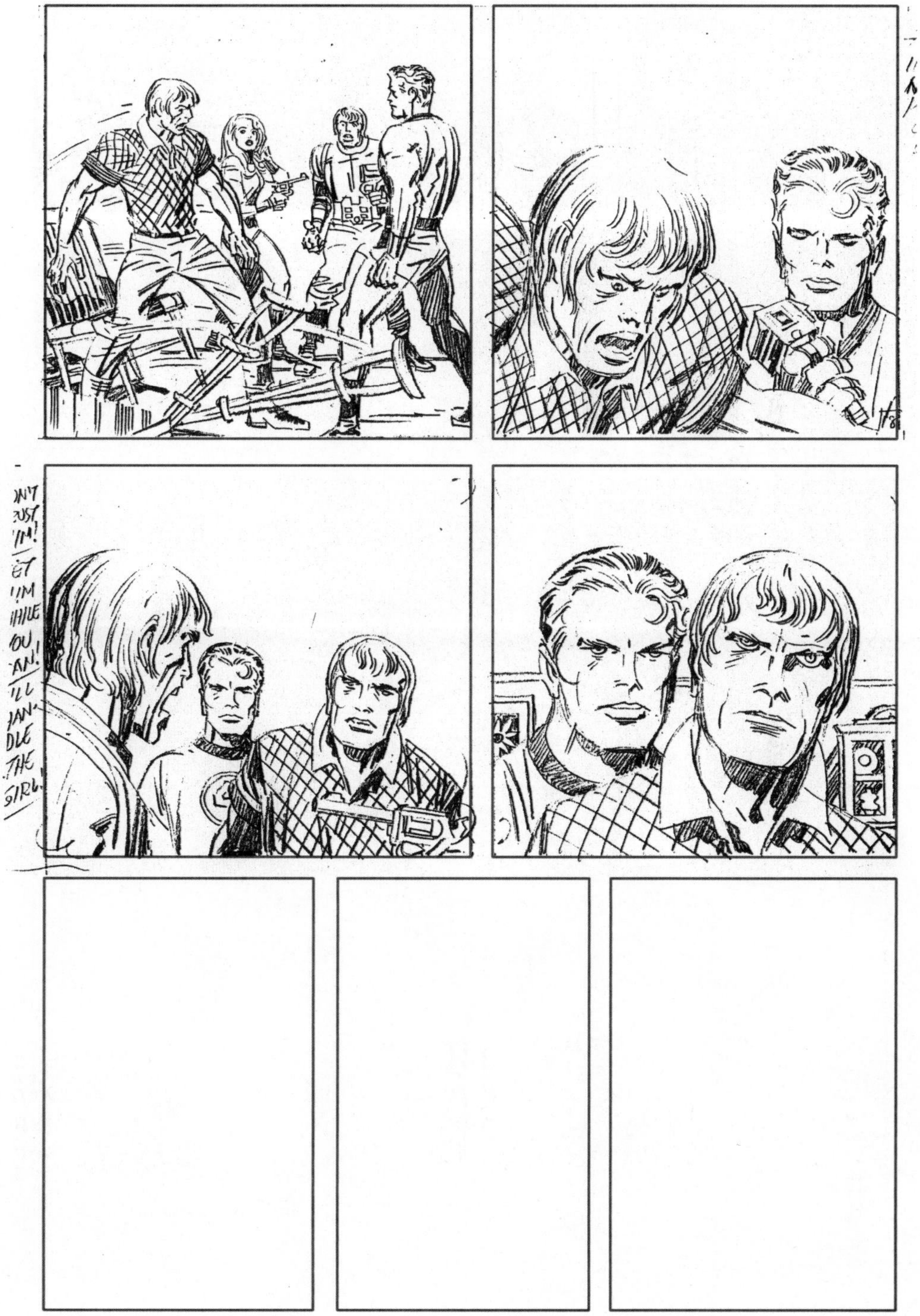

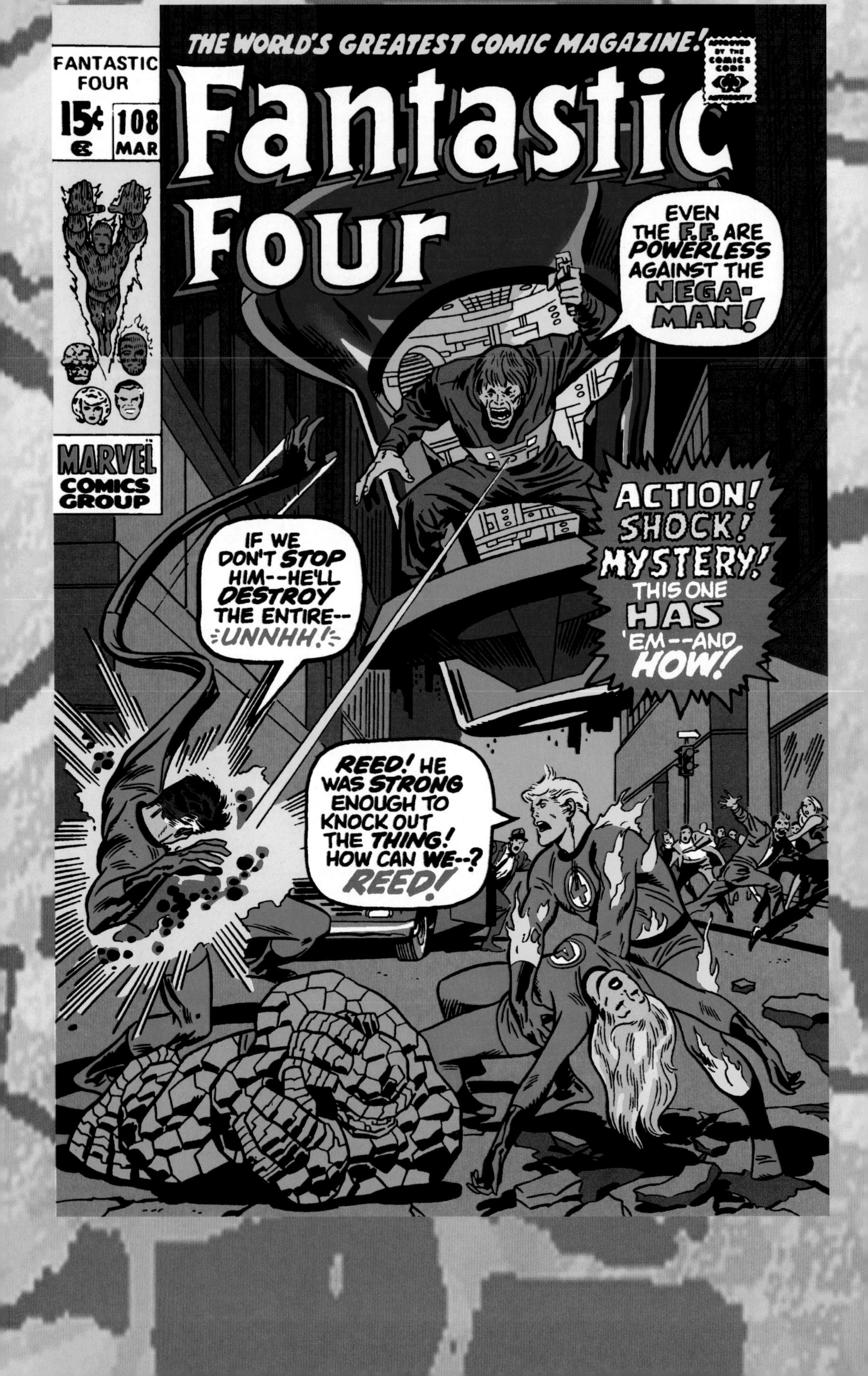
THE WORLD'S GREATEST COMIC MAGAZINE!
FANTASTIC FOUR
15¢
108 MAR
MARVEL COMICS GROUP
Fantastic Four
EVEN THE F.F. ARE POWERLESS AGAINST THE NEGA-MAN!
ACTION! SHOCK! MYSTERY! THIS ONE HAS 'EM--AND HOW!
IF WE DON'T STOP HIM--HE'LL DESTROY THE ENTIRE-- UNNHH!
REED! HE WAS STRONG ENOUGH TO KNOCK OUT THE THING! HOW CAN WE--? REED!

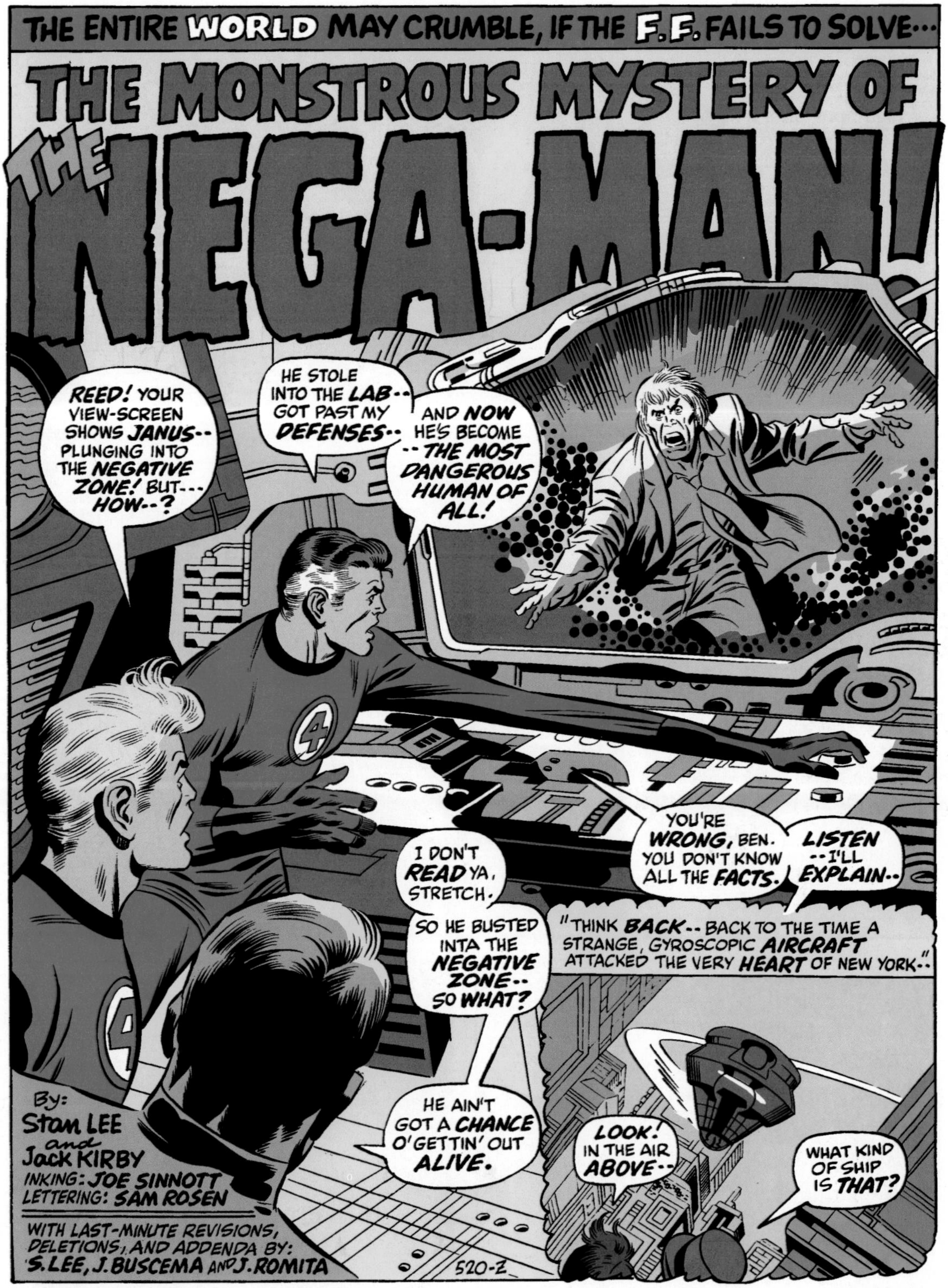
THE ENTIRE WORLD MAY CRUMBLE, IF THE F.F. FAILS TO SOLVE...
THE MONSTROUS MYSTERY OF THE NEGA-MAN!
REED! YOUR VIEW-SCREEN SHOWS JANUS-- PLUNGING INTO THE NEGATIVE ZONE! BUT--- HOW--?
HE STOLE INTO THE LAB-- GOT PAST MY DEFENSES--
AND NOW HE'S BECOME --THE MOST DANGEROUS HUMAN OF ALL!
I DON'T READ YA, STRETCH.
SO HE BUSTED INTA THE NEGATIVE ZONE-- SO WHAT?
HE AIN'T GOT A CHANCE O'GETTIN' OUT ALIVE.
YOU'RE WRONG, BEN. YOU DON'T KNOW ALL THE FACTS.
LISTEN --I'LL EXPLAIN--
"THINK BACK-- BACK TO THE TIME A STRANGE, GYROSCOPIC AIRCRAFT ATTACKED THE VERY HEART OF NEW YORK--"
LOOK! IN THE AIR ABOVE--
WHAT KIND OF SHIP IS THAT?
By: Stan LEE and Jack KIRBY
INKING: JOE SINNOTT
LETTERING: SAM ROSEN
WITH LAST-MINUTE REVISIONS, DELETIONS, AND ADDENDA BY: S. LEE, J. BUSCEMA AND J. ROMITA
520-2

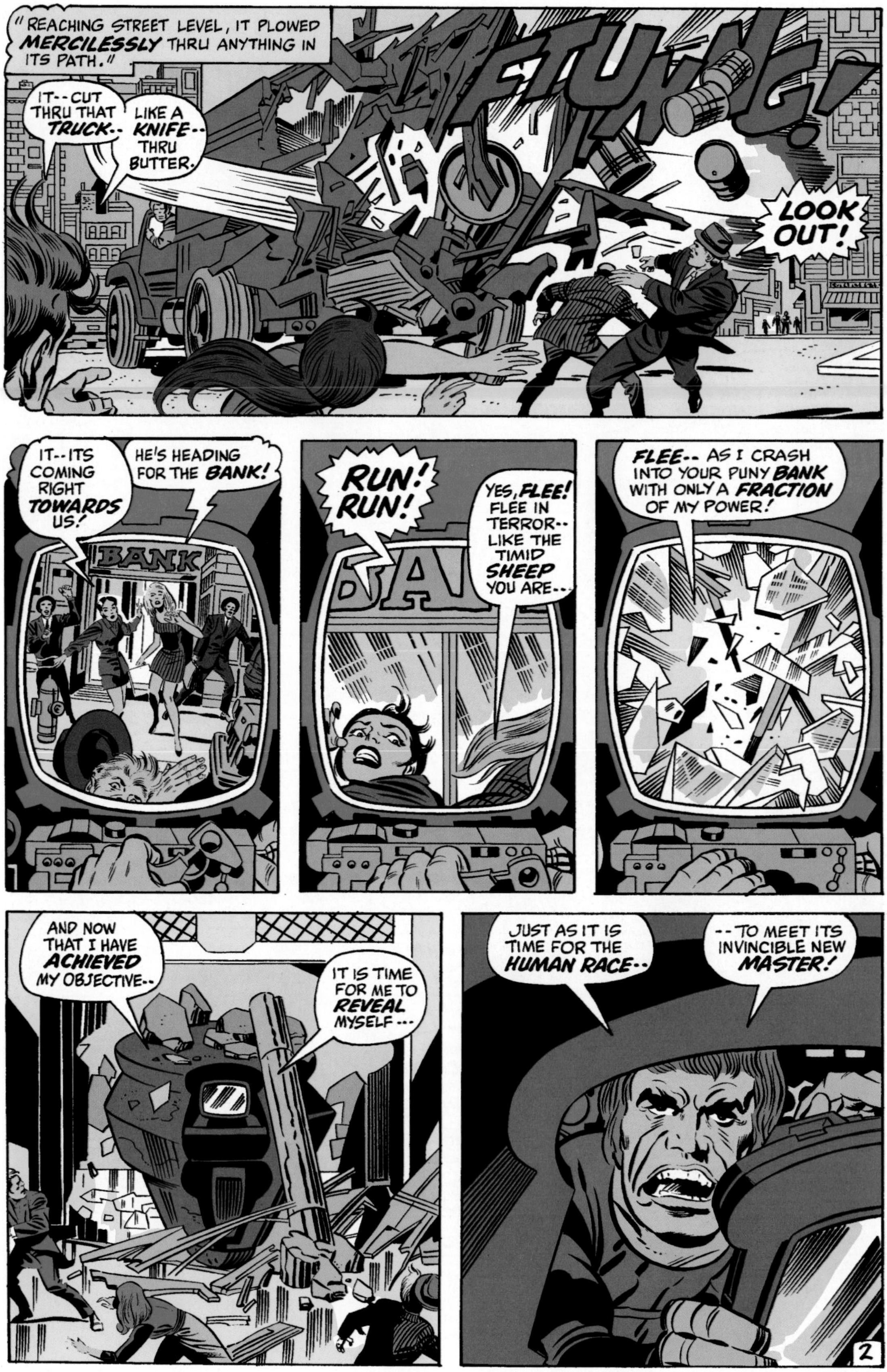
"REACHING STREET LEVEL, IT PLOWED MERCILESSLY THRU ANYTHING IN ITS PATH."
FTUNNG!
IT--CUT THRU THAT TRUCK--
LIKE A KNIFE--THRU BUTTER.
LOOK OUT!
IT--ITS COMING RIGHT TOWARDS US!
HE'S HEADING FOR THE BANK!
BANK
RUN! RUN!
YES, FLEE! FLEE IN TERROR--LIKE THE TIMID SHEEP YOU ARE--
FLEE-- AS I CRASH INTO YOUR PUNY BANK WITH ONLY A FRACTION OF MY POWER!
AND NOW THAT I HAVE ACHIEVED MY OBJECTIVE--
IT IS TIME FOR ME TO REVEAL MYSELF---
JUST AS IT IS TIME FOR THE HUMAN RACE--
--TO MEET ITS INVINCIBLE NEW MASTER!
2

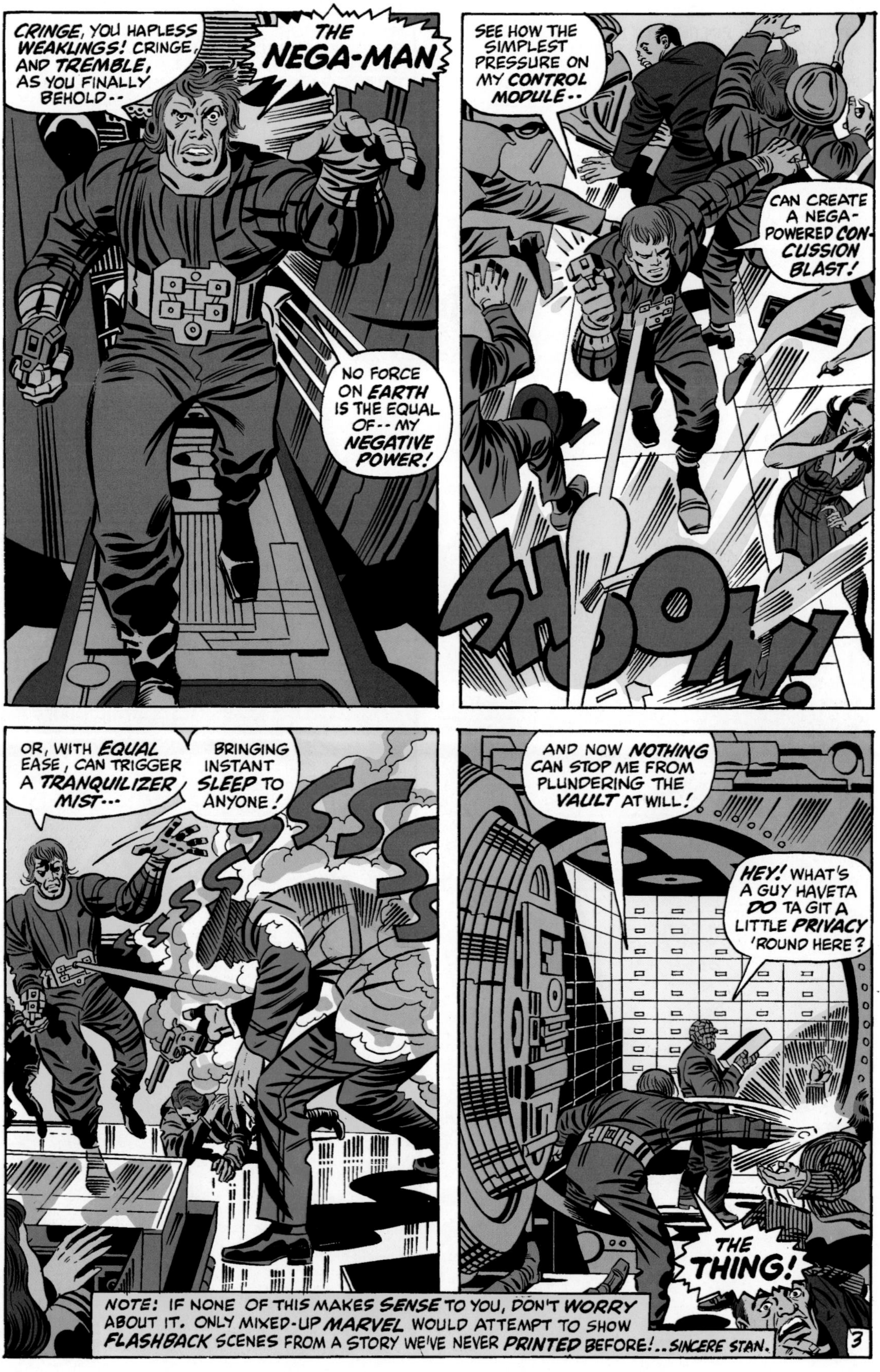

CRINGE, YOU HAPLESS WEAKLINGS! CRINGE, AND TREMBLE, AS YOU FINALLY BEHOLD--
THE NEGA-MAN
NO FORCE ON EARTH IS THE EQUAL OF-- MY NEGATIVE POWER!
SEE HOW THE SIMPLEST PRESSURE ON MY CONTROL MODULE--
CAN CREATE A NEGA-POWERED CONCUSSION BLAST!
SHOOM!
OR, WITH EQUAL EASE, CAN TRIGGER A TRANQUILIZER MIST--
BRINGING INSTANT SLEEP TO ANYONE!
SSSSS
AND NOW NOTHING CAN STOP ME FROM PLUNDERING THE VAULT AT WILL!
HEY! WHAT'S A GUY HAVETA DO TA GIT A LITTLE PRIVACY 'ROUND HERE?
THE THING!
NOTE: IF NONE OF THIS MAKES SENSE TO YOU, DON'T WORRY ABOUT IT. ONLY MIXED-UP MARVEL WOULD ATTEMPT TO SHOW FLASHBACK SCENES FROM A STORY WE'VE NEVER PRINTED BEFORE!.. SINCERE STAN.
3

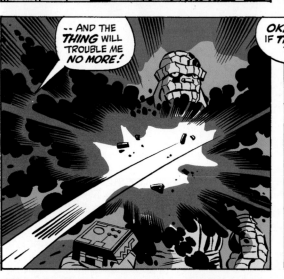

4

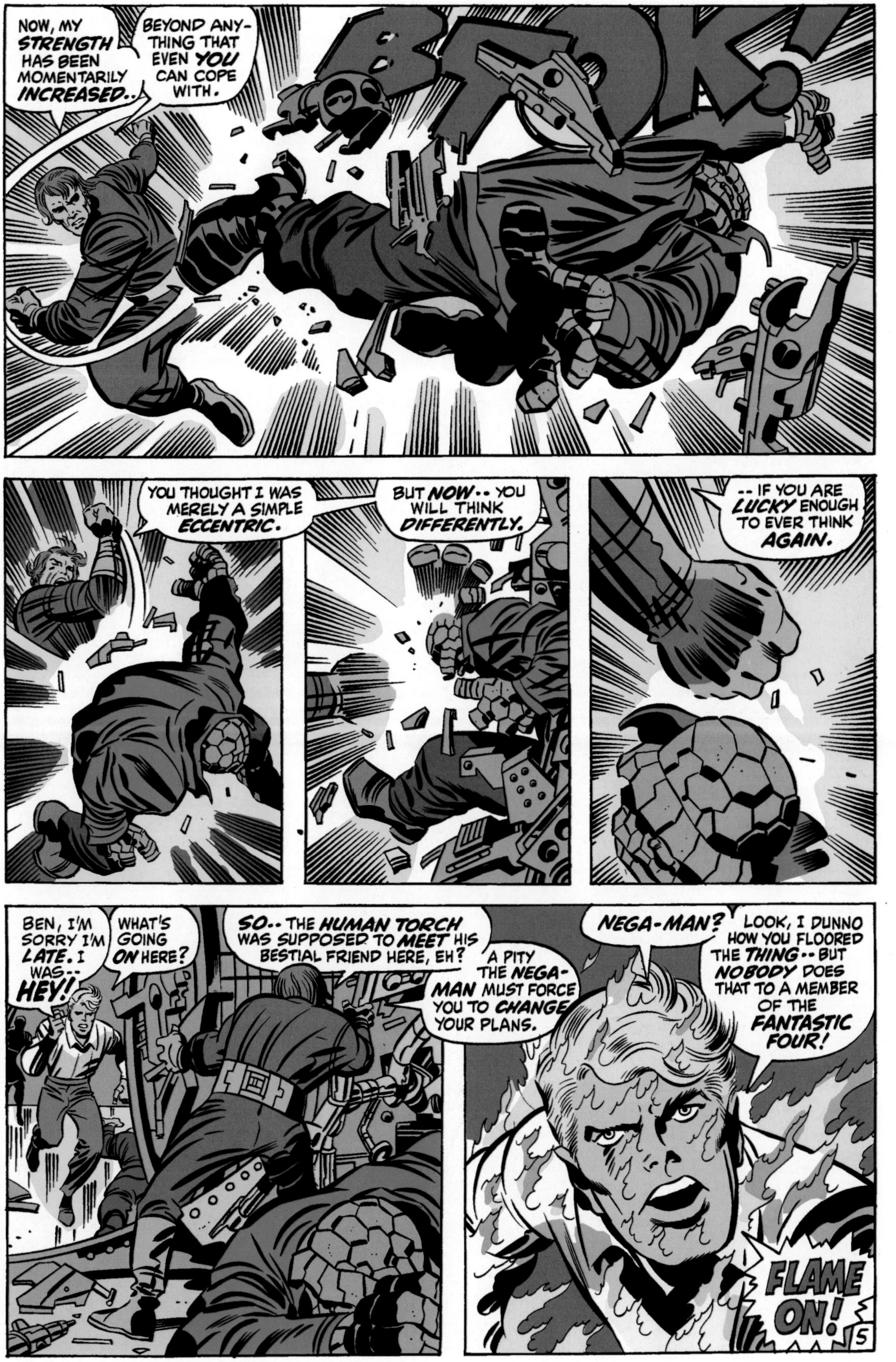
NOW, MY STRENGTH HAS BEEN MOMENTARILY INCREASED..
BEYOND ANYTHING THAT EVEN YOU CAN COPE WITH.
BTOK!
YOU THOUGHT I WAS MERELY A SIMPLE ECCENTRIC.
BUT NOW.. YOU WILL THINK DIFFERENTLY.
-- IF YOU ARE LUCKY ENOUGH TO EVER THINK AGAIN.
BEN, I'M SORRY I'M LATE. I WAS-- HEY!
WHAT'S GOING ON HERE?
SO.. THE HUMAN TORCH WAS SUPPOSED TO MEET HIS BESTIAL FRIEND HERE, EH?
A PITY THE NEGA-MAN MUST FORCE YOU TO CHANGE YOUR PLANS.
NEGA-MAN?
LOOK, I DUNNO HOW YOU FLOORED THE THING.. BUT NOBODY DOES THAT TO A MEMBER OF THE FANTASTIC FOUR!
FLAME ON!
5

A *LIVING DYNAMO!*

6.

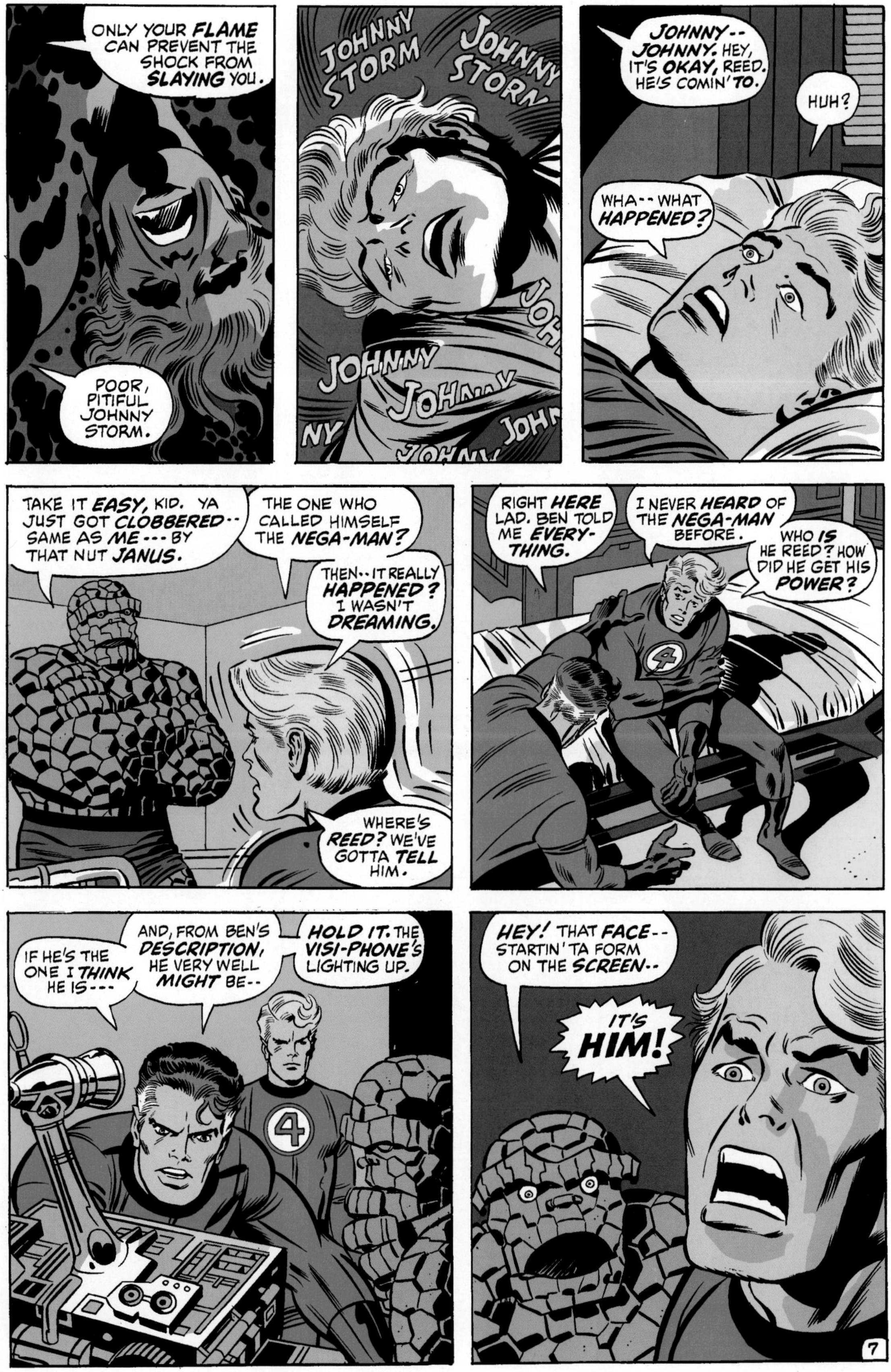
ONLY YOUR FLAME CAN PREVENT THE SHOCK FROM SLAYING YOU.
POOR, PITIFUL JOHNNY STORM.
JOHNNY STORM JOHNNY STORM
JOHNNY JOHNNY JOHN JOHN
JOHNNY-- JOHNNY. HEY, IT'S OKAY, REED. HE'S COMIN' TO.
HUH?
WHA-- WHAT HAPPENED?
TAKE IT EASY, KID. YA JUST GOT CLOBBERED-- SAME AS ME--- BY THAT NUT JANUS.
THE ONE WHO CALLED HIMSELF THE NEGA-MAN?
THEN.. IT REALLY HAPPENED? I WASN'T DREAMING.
WHERE'S REED? WE'VE GOTTA TELL HIM.
RIGHT HERE LAD. BEN TOLD ME EVERY-THING.
I NEVER HEARD OF THE NEGA-MAN BEFORE.
WHO IS HE REED? HOW DID HE GET HIS POWER?
IF HE'S THE ONE I THINK HE IS---
AND, FROM BEN'S DESCRIPTION, HE VERY WELL MIGHT BE--
HOLD IT. THE VISI-PHONE'S LIGHTING UP.
HEY! THAT FACE-- STARTIN' TA FORM ON THE SCREEN--
IT'S HIM!
7

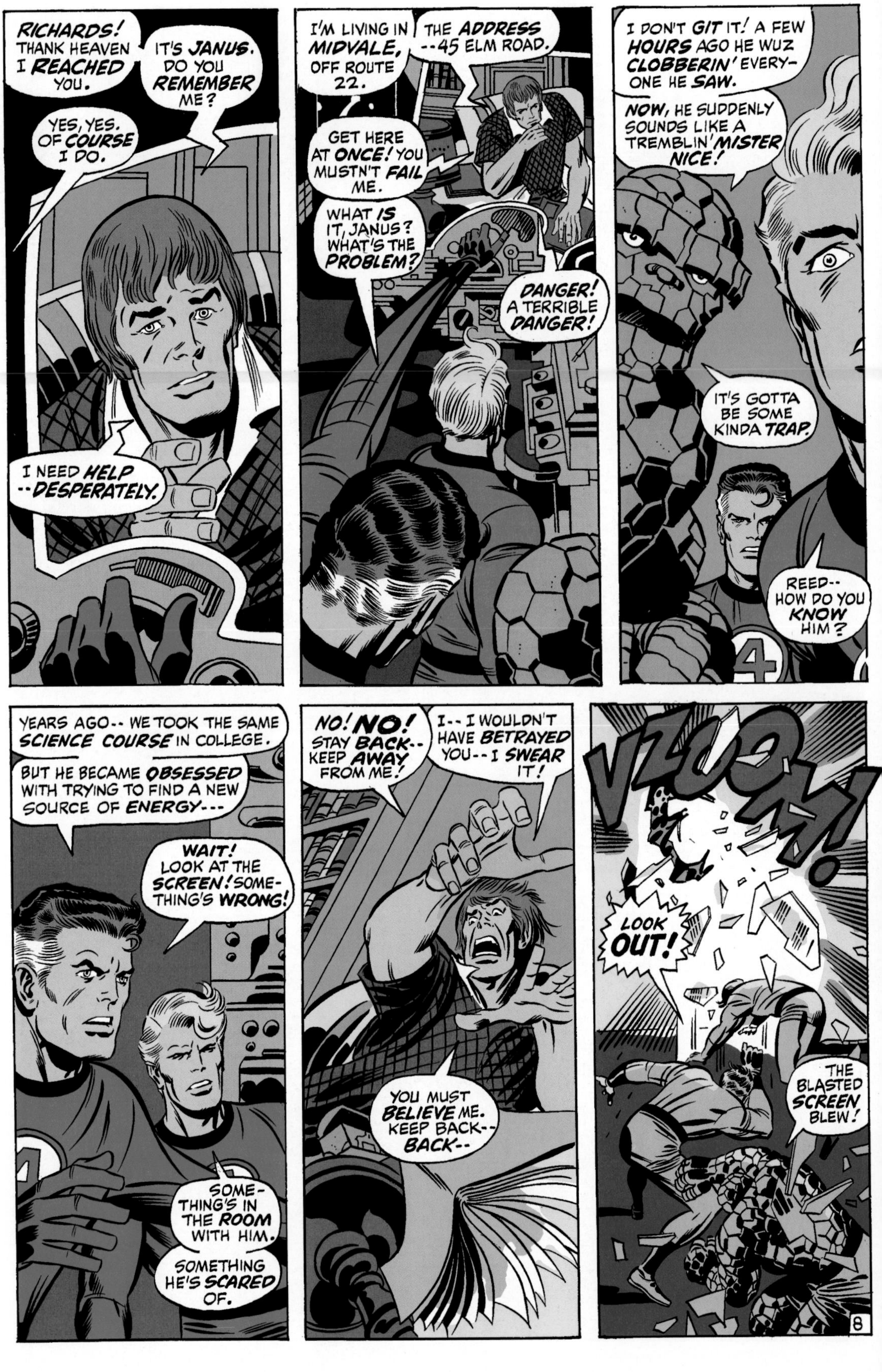
RICHARDS! THANK HEAVEN I REACHED YOU.
IT'S JANUS. DO YOU REMEMBER ME?
YES, YES. OF COURSE I DO.
I NEED HELP --DESPERATELY.
I'M LIVING IN MIDVALE, OFF ROUTE 22.
THE ADDRESS --45 ELM ROAD.
GET HERE AT ONCE! YOU MUSTN'T FAIL ME.
WHAT IS IT, JANUS? WHAT'S THE PROBLEM?
DANGER! A TERRIBLE DANGER!
I DON'T GIT IT! A FEW HOURS AGO HE WUZ CLOBBERIN' EVERY-ONE HE SAW.
NOW, HE SUDDENLY SOUNDS LIKE A TREMBLIN' MISTER NICE!
IT'S GOTTA BE SOME KINDA TRAP.
REED-- HOW DO YOU KNOW HIM?
YEARS AGO-- WE TOOK THE SAME SCIENCE COURSE IN COLLEGE.
BUT HE BECAME OBSESSED WITH TRYING TO FIND A NEW SOURCE OF ENERGY---
WAIT! LOOK AT THE SCREEN! SOME-THING'S WRONG!
SOME-THING'S IN THE ROOM WITH HIM.
SOMETHING HE'S SCARED OF.
NO! NO! STAY BACK-- KEEP AWAY FROM ME!
I-- I WOULDN'T HAVE BETRAYED YOU-- I SWEAR IT!
YOU MUST BELIEVE ME. KEEP BACK-- BACK--
VZOOM!
LOOK OUT!
THE BLASTED SCREEN BLEW!
8

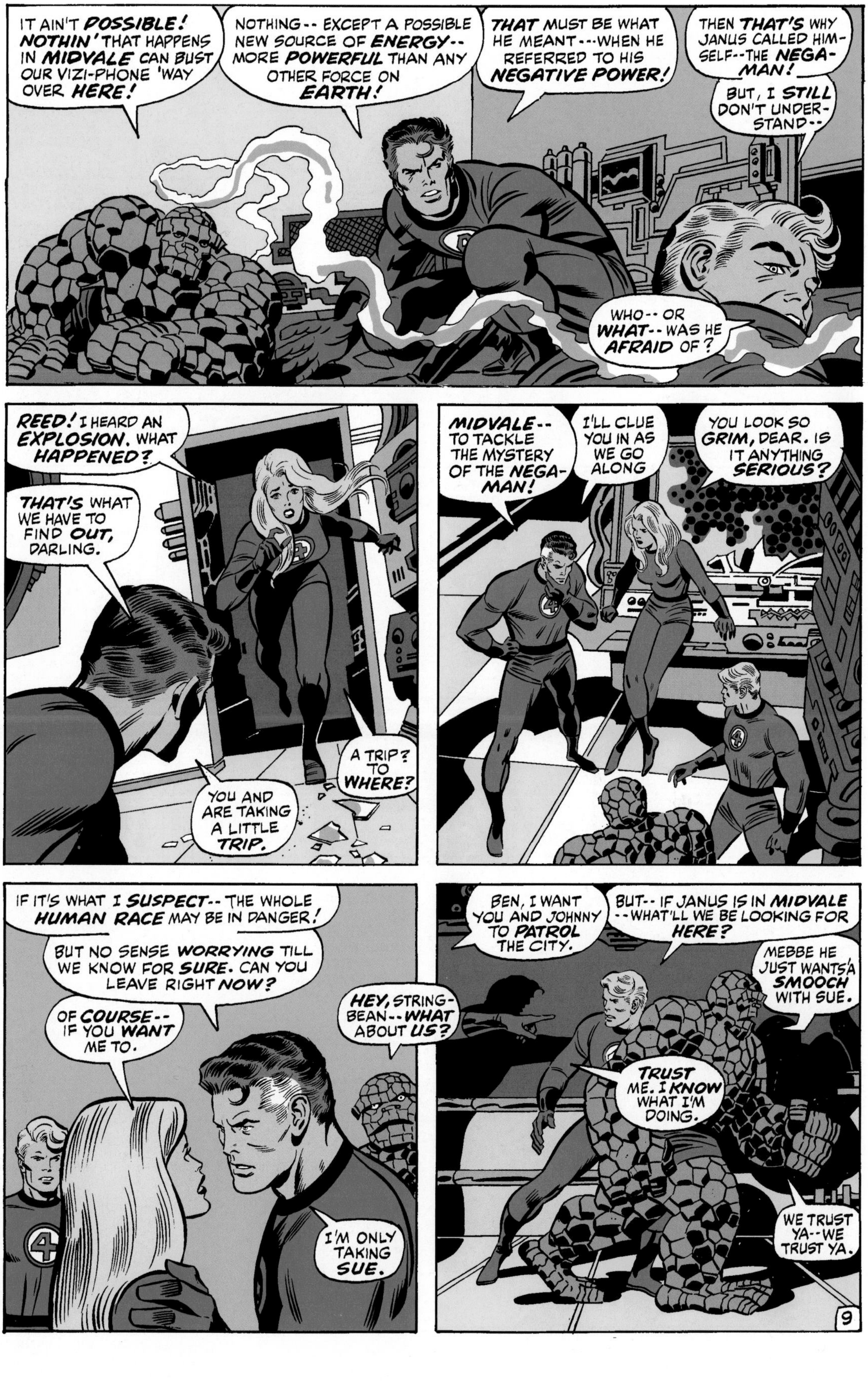
IT AIN'T POSSIBLE! NOTHIN' THAT HAPPENS IN MIDVALE CAN BUST OUR VIZI-PHONE 'WAY OVER HERE!
NOTHING -- EXCEPT A POSSIBLE NEW SOURCE OF ENERGY -- MORE POWERFUL THAN ANY OTHER FORCE ON EARTH!
THAT MUST BE WHAT HE MEANT --- WHEN HE REFERRED TO HIS NEGATIVE POWER!
THEN THAT'S WHY JANUS CALLED HIMSELF -- THE NEGA-MAN!
BUT, I STILL DON'T UNDERSTAND --
WHO -- OR WHAT -- WAS HE AFRAID OF?
REED! I HEARD AN EXPLOSION. WHAT HAPPENED?
THAT'S WHAT WE HAVE TO FIND OUT, DARLING.
YOU AND ARE TAKING A LITTLE TRIP.
A TRIP? TO WHERE?
MIDVALE -- TO TACKLE THE MYSTERY OF THE NEGA-MAN!
I'LL CLUE YOU IN AS WE GO ALONG
YOU LOOK SO GRIM, DEAR. IS IT ANYTHING SERIOUS?
IF IT'S WHAT I SUSPECT -- THE WHOLE HUMAN RACE MAY BE IN DANGER!
BUT NO SENSE WORRYING TILL WE KNOW FOR SURE. CAN YOU LEAVE RIGHT NOW?
OF COURSE -- IF YOU WANT ME TO.
HEY, STRING-BEAN -- WHAT ABOUT US?
I'M ONLY TAKING SUE.
BEN, I WANT YOU AND JOHNNY TO PATROL THE CITY.
BUT -- IF JANUS IS IN MIDVALE -- WHAT'LL WE BE LOOKING FOR HERE?
MEBBE HE JUST WANTS A SMOOCH WITH SUE.
TRUST ME. I KNOW WHAT I'M DOING.
WE TRUST YA -- WE TRUST YA.
9

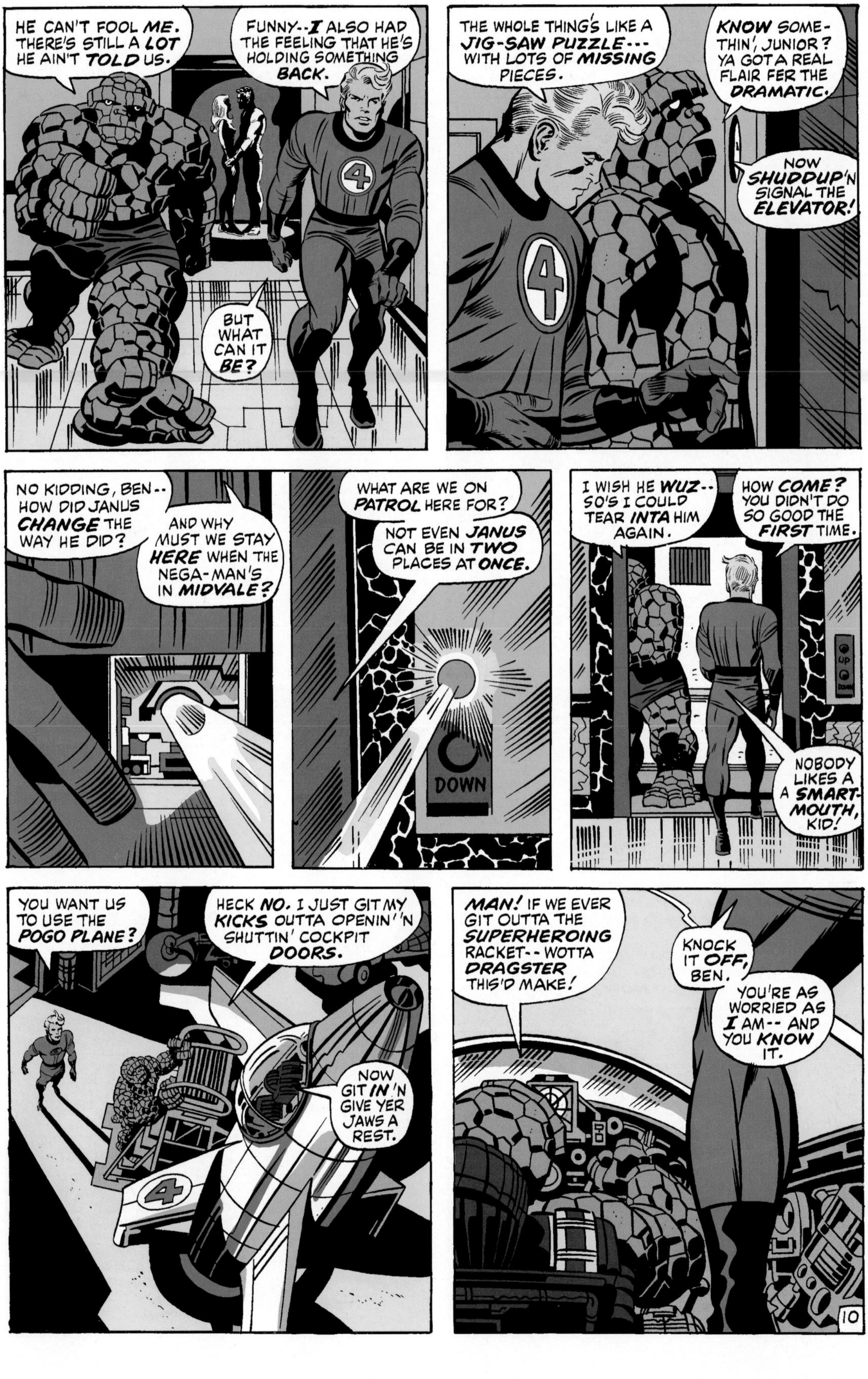
HE CAN'T FOOL ME. THERE'S STILL A LOT HE AIN'T TOLD US.
FUNNY--I ALSO HAD THE FEELING THAT HE'S HOLDING SOMETHING BACK.
BUT WHAT CAN IT BE?
THE WHOLE THING'S LIKE A JIG-SAW PUZZLE--- WITH LOTS OF MISSING PIECES.
KNOW SOMETHIN', JUNIOR? YA GOT A REAL FLAIR FER THE DRAMATIC.
NOW SHUDDUP'N SIGNAL THE ELEVATOR!
NO KIDDING, BEN-- HOW DID JANUS CHANGE THE WAY HE DID?
AND WHY MUST WE STAY HERE WHEN THE NEGA-MAN'S IN MIDVALE?
WHAT ARE WE ON PATROL HERE FOR?
NOT EVEN JANUS CAN BE IN TWO PLACES AT ONCE.
DOWN
I WISH HE WUZ-- SO'S I COULD TEAR INTA HIM AGAIN.
HOW COME? YOU DIDN'T DO SO GOOD THE FIRST TIME.
UP
DOWN
NOBODY LIKES A SMART-MOUTH, KID!
YOU WANT US TO USE THE POGO PLANE?
HECK NO. I JUST GIT MY KICKS OUTTA OPENIN' 'N SHUTTIN' COCKPIT DOORS.
NOW GIT IN 'N GIVE YER JAWS A REST.
MAN! IF WE EVER GIT OUTTA THE SUPERHEROING RACKET-- WOTTA DRAGSTER THIS'D MAKE!
KNOCK IT OFF, BEN.
YOU'RE AS WORRIED AS I AM-- AND YOU KNOW IT.
10

YEAH? WHO MADE YOU A MIND-READER ALL OF A SUDDEN?
HEY! WAIT A MINNIT--
SOMETHIN'S HAPPENIN' DOWN THERE! HANG ON, MATCH-HEAD!
I SEE IT, BEN. BUT--I CAN'T BELIEVE IT!
MEBBE THIS IS WHAT STRETCHO WUZ EXPECT-IN'?
BUT-- HOW DID HE KNOW?
A WHOLE STREET'S BEING TORN UP-- RIGHT BEFORE OUR EYES!
MUST BE MORE OF THAT BLASTED NEGA POWER--OR WHAT-EVER HE CALLED IT!
BUT HOW-- IF JANUS IS IN MIDVALE?
"AND NOW, BACK TO THE PRESENT AGAIN..."
AWRIGHT-- AWRIGHT! WHAT IS THIS-- THE THOUSAND AND ONE NIGHTS?!!
I KNOW, BEN. BUT IT'S VITAL THAT I REVIEW THE FACTS.
YOU AIN'T TELLIN' US NOTHIN' NEW, MISTER--WE WERE THERE!
I HAVE TO MAKE YOU UNDERSTAND.
THEN HOW'S ABOUT GETTIN' TO THE POINT? --IF THERE IS ONE?
THERE IS ONE, ALL RIGHT.
BUT IT'S SO INCREDIBLE-- I'M ALMOST AT A LOSS FOR WORDS.
YOU? THAT'LL BE THE DAY!
11.

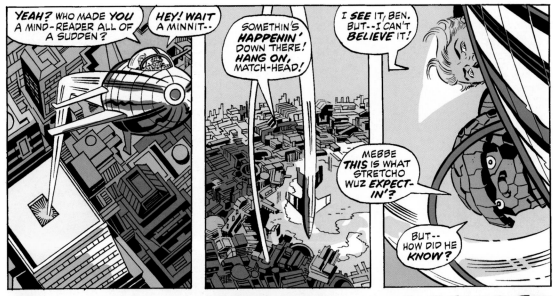

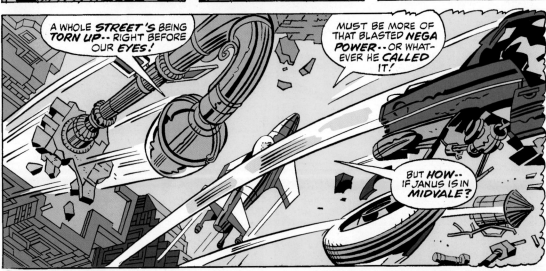

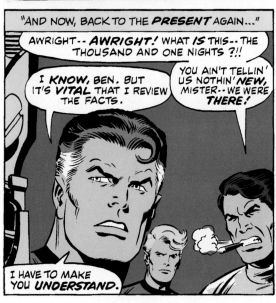

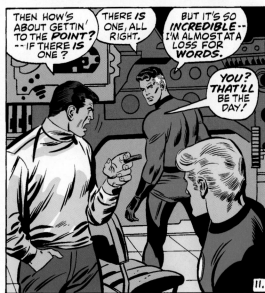

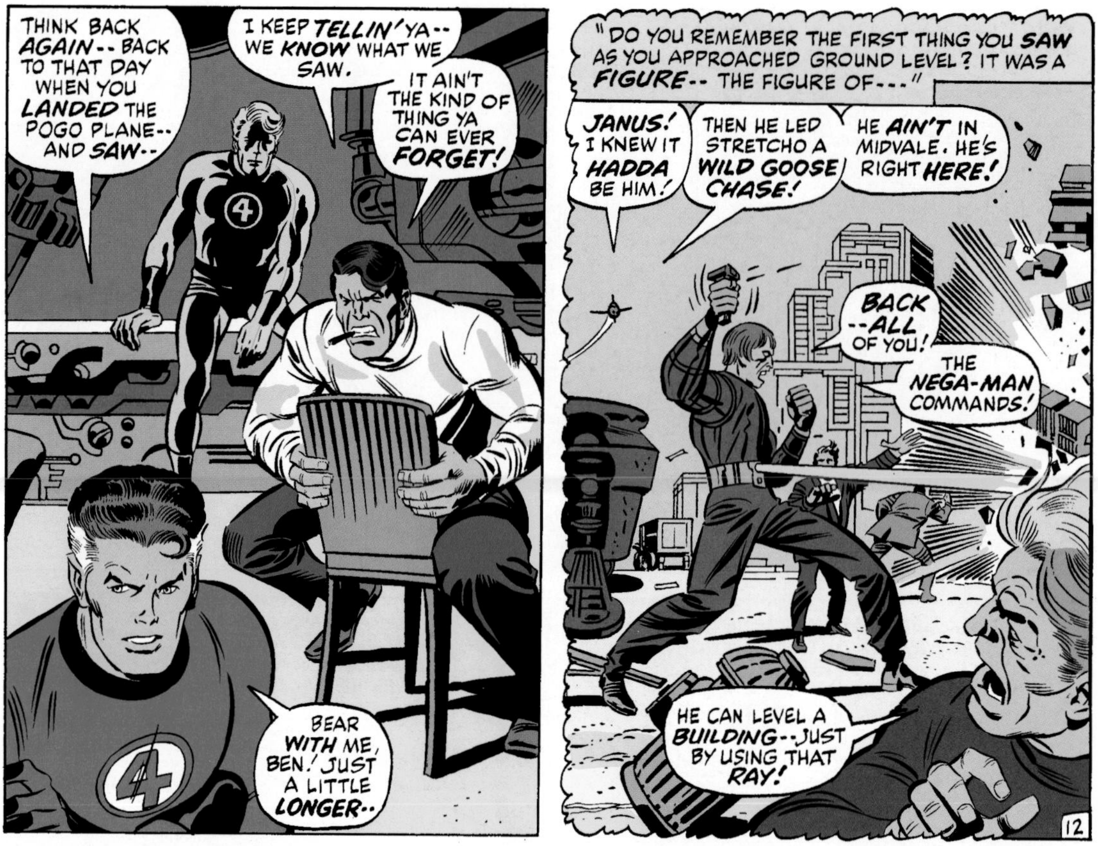
THINK BACK AGAIN-- BACK TO THAT DAY WHEN YOU LANDED THE POGO PLANE-- AND SAW--
I KEEP TELLIN' YA-- WE KNOW WHAT WE SAW.
IT AIN'T THE KIND OF THING YA CAN EVER FORGET!
BEAR WITH ME, BEN! JUST A LITTLE LONGER--
"DO YOU REMEMBER THE FIRST THING YOU SAW AS YOU APPROACHED GROUND LEVEL? IT WAS A FIGURE-- THE FIGURE OF---"
JANUS! I KNEW IT HADDA BE HIM!
THEN HE LED STRETCHO A WILD GOOSE CHASE!
HE AIN'T IN MIDVALE. HE'S RIGHT HERE!
BACK --ALL OF YOU!
THE NEGA-MAN COMMANDS!
HE CAN LEVEL A BUILDING--JUST BY USING THAT RAY!
12

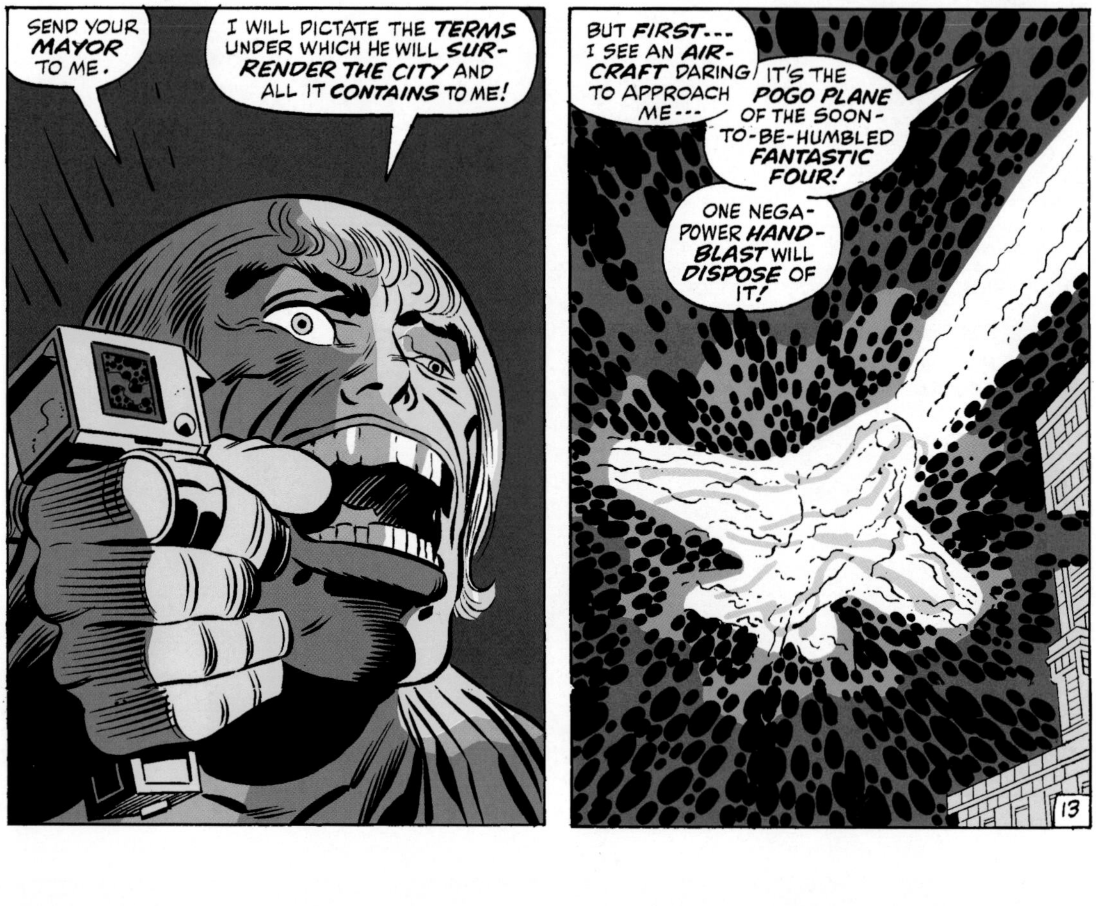
SEND YOUR MAYOR TO ME.
I WILL DICTATE THE TERMS UNDER WHICH HE WILL SURRENDER THE CITY AND ALL IT CONTAINS TO ME!
BUT FIRST--- I SEE AN AIRCRAFT DARING TO APPROACH ME---
IT'S THE POGO PLANE OF THE SOON-TO-BE-HUMBLED FANTASTIC FOUR!
ONE NEGA-POWER HAND-BLAST WILL DISPOSE OF IT!
13

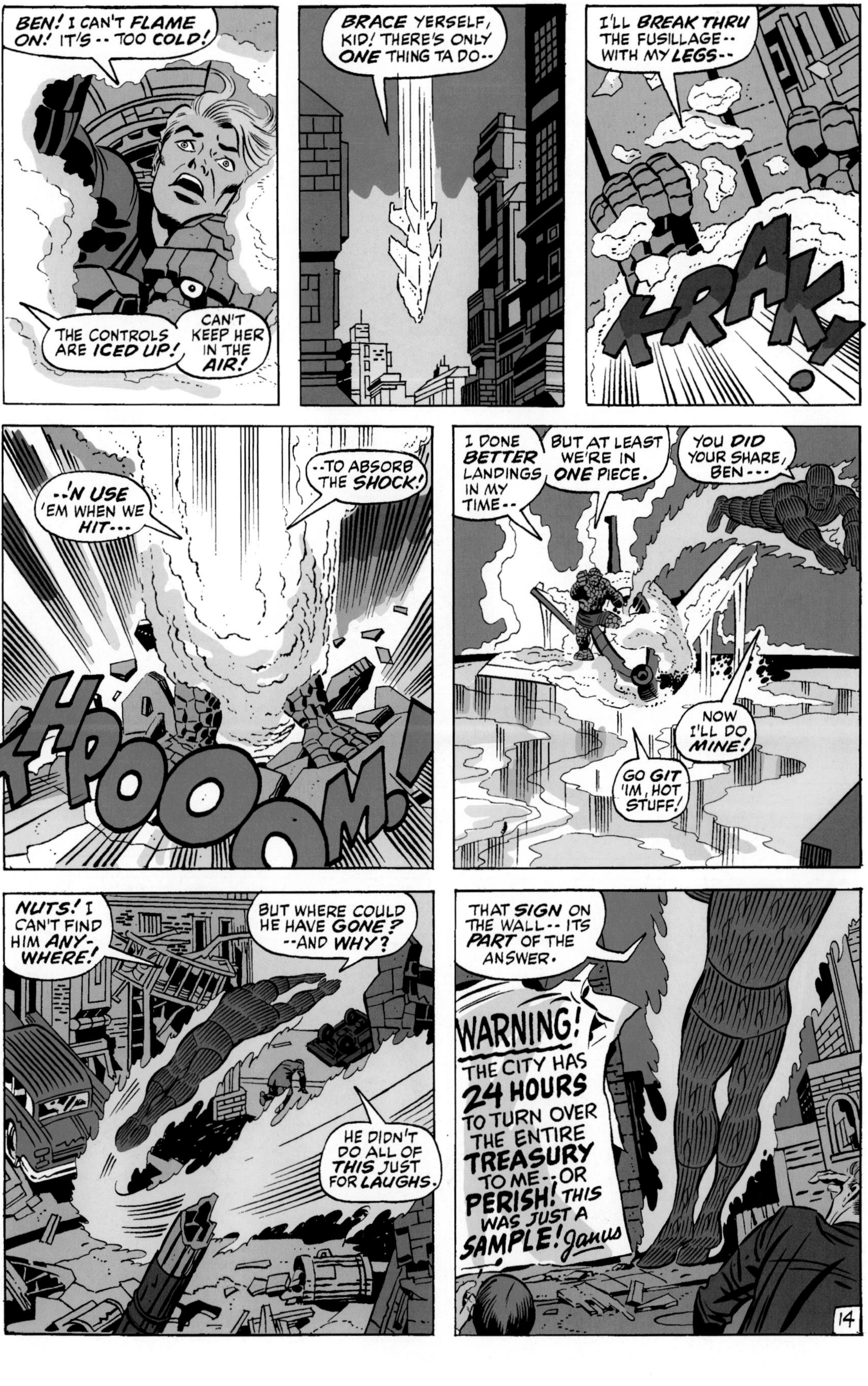

BEN! I CAN'T FLAME ON! IT'S -- TOO COLD!
THE CONTROLS ARE ICED UP!
CAN'T KEEP HER IN THE AIR!
BRACE YERSELF, KID! THERE'S ONLY ONE THING TA DO--
I'LL BREAK THRU THE FUSILLAGE-- WITH MY LEGS--
KRAK!
--'N USE 'EM WHEN WE HIT---
--TO ABSORB THE SHOCK!
THPOOOM!
I DONE BETTER LANDINGS IN MY TIME--
BUT AT LEAST WE'RE IN ONE PIECE.
YOU DID YOUR SHARE, BEN---
NOW I'LL DO MINE!
GO GIT 'IM, HOT STUFF!
NUTS! I CAN'T FIND HIM ANY-WHERE!
BUT WHERE COULD HE HAVE GONE? --AND WHY?
HE DIDN'T DO ALL OF THIS JUST FOR LAUGHS.
THAT SIGN ON THE WALL -- ITS PART OF THE ANSWER.
WARNING! THE CITY HAS 24 HOURS TO TURN OVER THE ENTIRE TREASURY TO ME--OR PERISH! THIS WAS JUST A SAMPLE! Janus

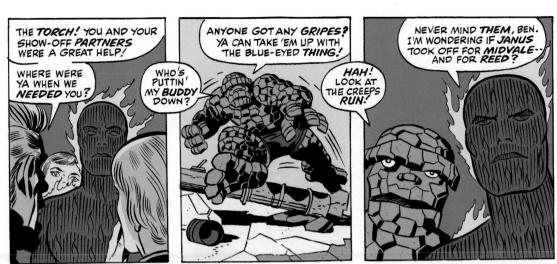

THE *TORCH!* YOU AND YOUR SHOW-OFF *PARTNERS* WERE A GREAT HELP!

WHERE WERE YA WHEN WE *NEEDED* YOU?

WHO'S PUTTIN' MY *BUDDY* DOWN?

ANYONE GOT ANY *GRIPES?* YA CAN TAKE 'EM UP WITH THE BLUE-EYED *THING!*

HAH! LOOK AT THE CREEPS *RUN!*

NEVER MIND *THEM,* BEN. I'M WONDERING IF *JANUS* TOOK OFF FOR *MIDVALE--* AND FOR *REED?*

"AND, EVEN AS JOHNNY WAS *SPEAKING--*"

THERE HE *IS,* SUE!

EXCEPT FOR HIS *LEGS,* WHICH WERE *ALWAYS AFFLICTED,* HE SEEMS *UNHARMED!*

JUST TO PLAY *SAFE,* YOU'D BETTER TURN *INVISIBLE--*

TILL WE LEARN WHAT IT'S ALL *ABOUT.*

IT WAS GOOD OF YOU TO *COME,* RICHARDS.

NEVER MIND *THAT!* THERE'S ONLY *ONE* THING THAT MATTERS--

HOW DID HE TAP THE POWER OF--- THE *NEGATIVE ZONE?*

HE-- HE *DIDN'T!*

DON'T *LIE* TO ME, JANUS!

15

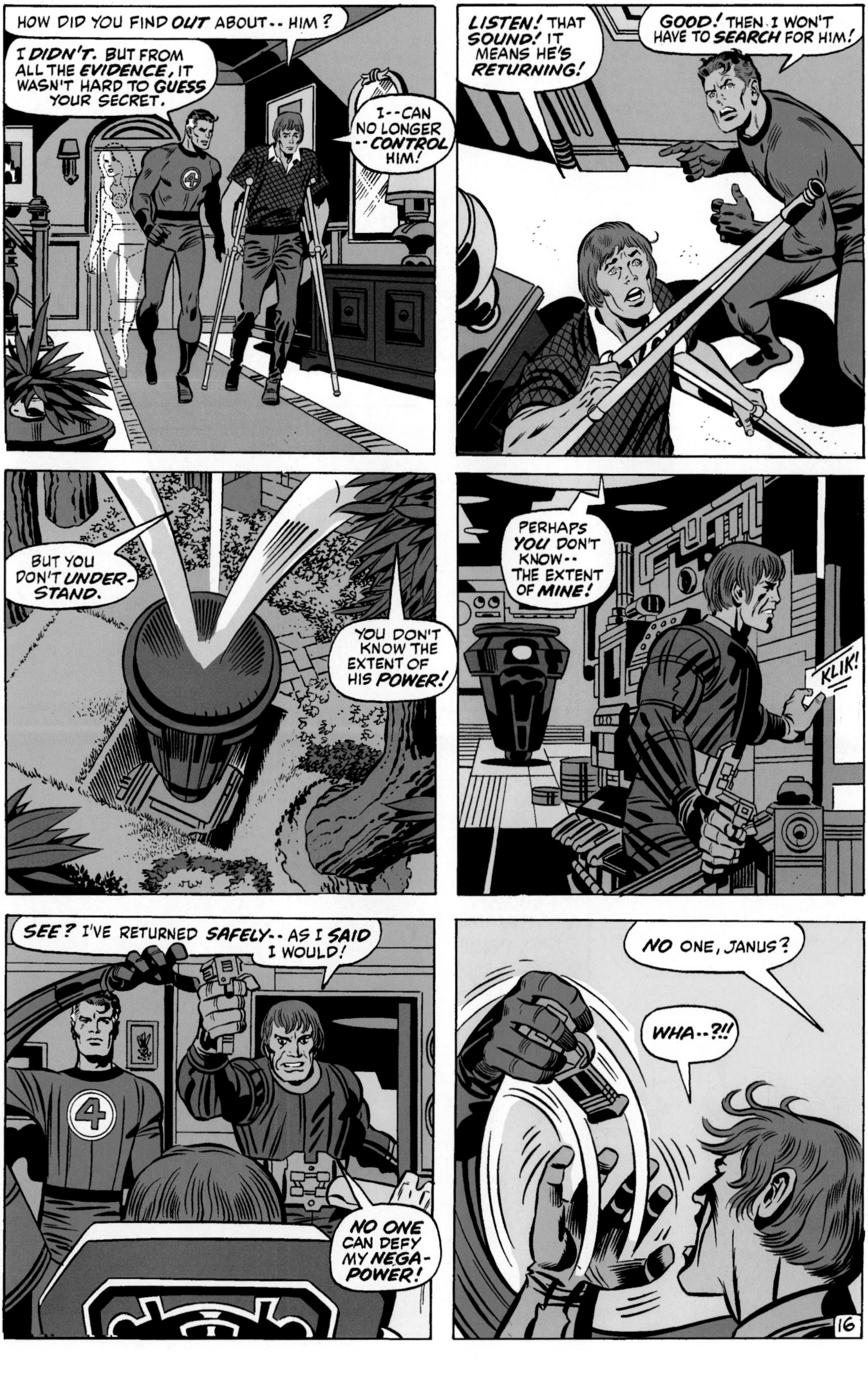

HOW DID YOU FIND OUT ABOUT -- HIM?
I DIDN'T. BUT FROM ALL THE EVIDENCE, IT WASN'T HARD TO GUESS YOUR SECRET.
I -- CAN NO LONGER -- CONTROL HIM!
LISTEN! THAT SOUND! IT MEANS HE'S RETURNING!
GOOD! THEN I WON'T HAVE TO SEARCH FOR HIM!
BUT YOU DON'T UNDER-STAND.
YOU DON'T KNOW THE EXTENT OF HIS POWER!
PERHAPS YOU DON'T KNOW -- THE EXTENT OF MINE!
KLIK!
SEE? I'VE RETURNED SAFELY -- AS I SAID I WOULD!
NO ONE CAN DEFY MY NEGA-POWER!
NO ONE, JANUS?
WHA--?!!
16

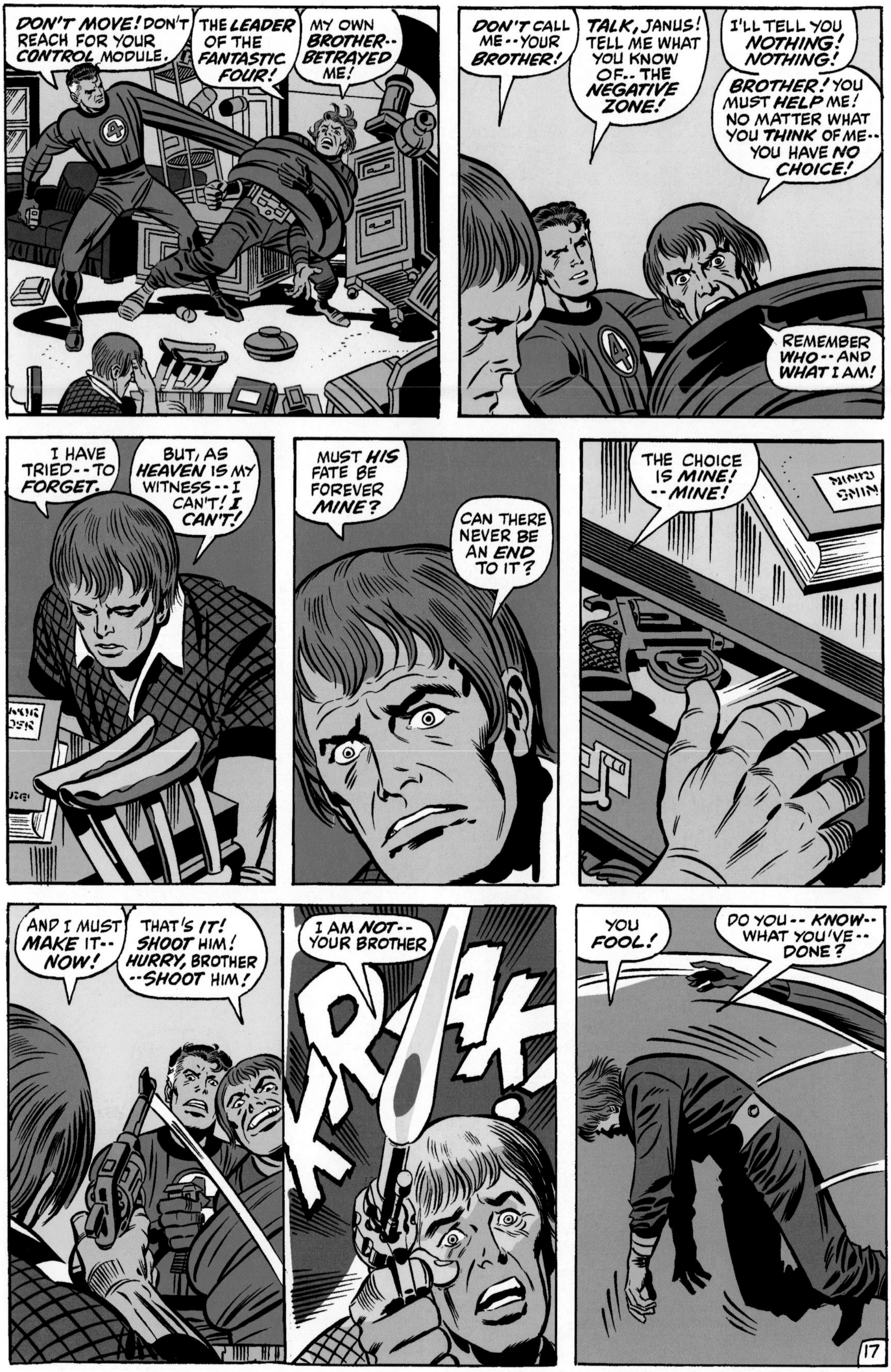
DON'T MOVE! DON'T REACH FOR YOUR CONTROL MODULE.
THE LEADER OF THE FANTASTIC FOUR!
MY OWN BROTHER-- BETRAYED ME!
DON'T CALL ME--YOUR BROTHER!
TALK, JANUS! TELL ME WHAT YOU KNOW OF-- THE NEGATIVE ZONE!
I'LL TELL YOU NOTHING! NOTHING!
BROTHER! YOU MUST HELP ME! NO MATTER WHAT YOU THINK OF ME-- YOU HAVE NO CHOICE!
REMEMBER WHO--AND WHAT I AM!
I HAVE TRIED--TO FORGET.
BUT, AS HEAVEN IS MY WITNESS--I CAN'T! I CAN'T!
MUST HIS FATE BE FOREVER MINE?
CAN THERE NEVER BE AN END TO IT?
THE CHOICE IS MINE! --MINE!
AND I MUST MAKE IT-- NOW!
THAT'S IT! SHOOT HIM! HURRY, BROTHER --SHOOT HIM!
I AM NOT-- YOUR BROTHER
KRAK
YOU FOOL!
DO YOU--KNOW-- WHAT YOU'VE-- DONE?

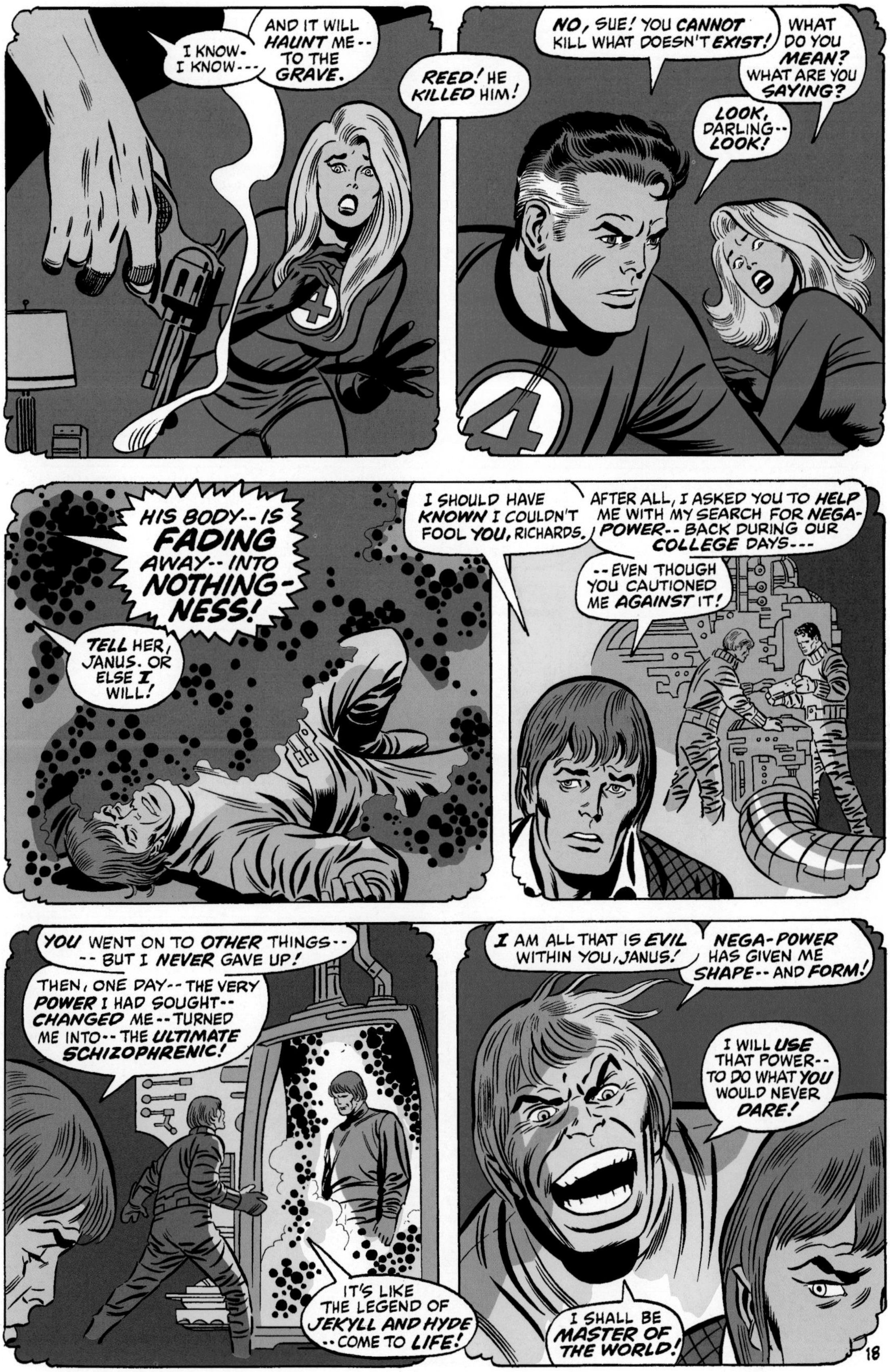
I KNOW-
I KNOW---
AND IT WILL HAUNT ME-- TO THE GRAVE.
REED! HE KILLED HIM!
NO, SUE! YOU CANNOT KILL WHAT DOESN'T EXIST!
WHAT DO YOU MEAN? WHAT ARE YOU SAYING?
LOOK, DARLING-- LOOK!
HIS BODY-- IS FADING AWAY-- INTO NOTHING-NESS!
TELL HER, JANUS. OR ELSE I WILL!
I SHOULD HAVE KNOWN I COULDN'T FOOL YOU, RICHARDS.
AFTER ALL, I ASKED YOU TO HELP ME WITH MY SEARCH FOR NEGA-POWER-- BACK DURING OUR COLLEGE DAYS---
--EVEN THOUGH YOU CAUTIONED ME AGAINST IT!
YOU WENT ON TO OTHER THINGS-- -- BUT I NEVER GAVE UP!
THEN, ONE DAY-- THE VERY POWER I HAD SOUGHT-- CHANGED ME-- TURNED ME INTO-- THE ULTIMATE SCHIZOPHRENIC!
IT'S LIKE THE LEGEND OF JEKYLL AND HYDE ..COME TO LIFE!
I AM ALL THAT IS EVIL WITHIN YOU, JANUS!
NEGA-POWER HAS GIVEN ME SHAPE-- AND FORM!
I WILL USE THAT POWER-- TO DO WHAT YOU WOULD NEVER DARE!
I SHALL BE MASTER OF THE WORLD!

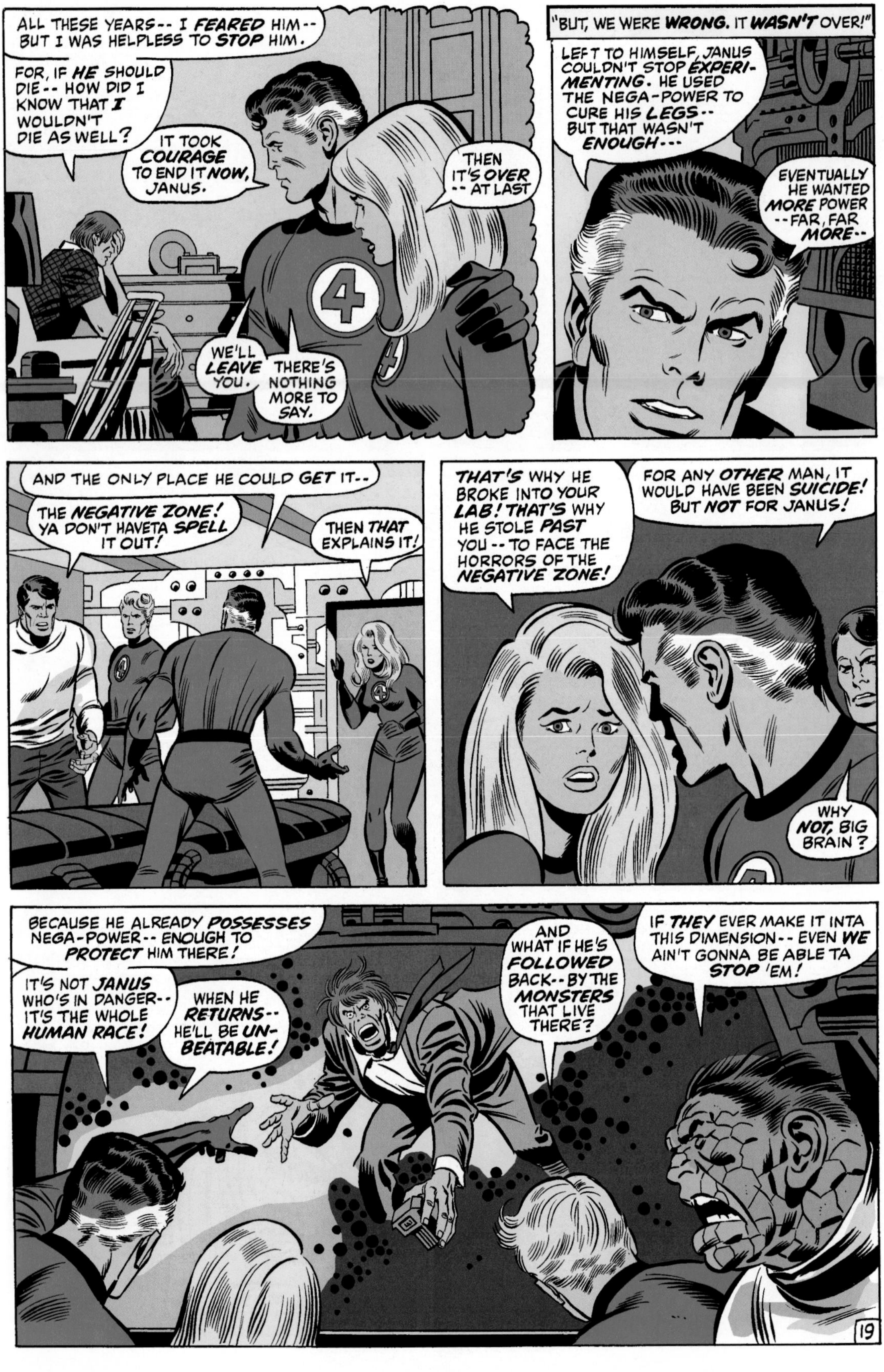
ALL THESE YEARS-- I FEARED HIM-- BUT I WAS HELPLESS TO STOP HIM.
FOR, IF HE SHOULD DIE-- HOW DID I KNOW THAT I WOULDN'T DIE AS WELL?
IT TOOK COURAGE TO END IT NOW, JANUS.
THEN IT'S OVER -- AT LAST
WE'LL LEAVE YOU.
THERE'S NOTHING MORE TO SAY.
"BUT, WE WERE WRONG. IT WASN'T OVER!"
LEFT TO HIMSELF, JANUS COULDN'T STOP EXPERIMENTING. HE USED THE NEGA-POWER TO CURE HIS LEGS-- BUT THAT WASN'T ENOUGH---
EVENTUALLY HE WANTED MORE POWER --FAR, FAR MORE--
AND THE ONLY PLACE HE COULD GET IT--
THE NEGATIVE ZONE! YA DON'T HAVETA SPELL IT OUT!
THEN THAT EXPLAINS IT!
THAT'S WHY HE BROKE INTO YOUR LAB! THAT'S WHY HE STOLE PAST YOU -- TO FACE THE HORRORS OF THE NEGATIVE ZONE!
FOR ANY OTHER MAN, IT WOULD HAVE BEEN SUICIDE! BUT NOT FOR JANUS!
WHY NOT, BIG BRAIN?
BECAUSE HE ALREADY POSSESSES NEGA-POWER-- ENOUGH TO PROTECT HIM THERE!
IT'S NOT JANUS WHO'S IN DANGER-- IT'S THE WHOLE HUMAN RACE!
WHEN HE RETURNS-- HE'LL BE UNBEATABLE!
AND WHAT IF HE'S FOLLOWED BACK-- BY THE MONSTERS THAT LIVE THERE?
IF THEY EVER MAKE IT INTA THIS DIMENSION-- EVEN WE AIN'T GONNA BE ABLE TA STOP 'EM!

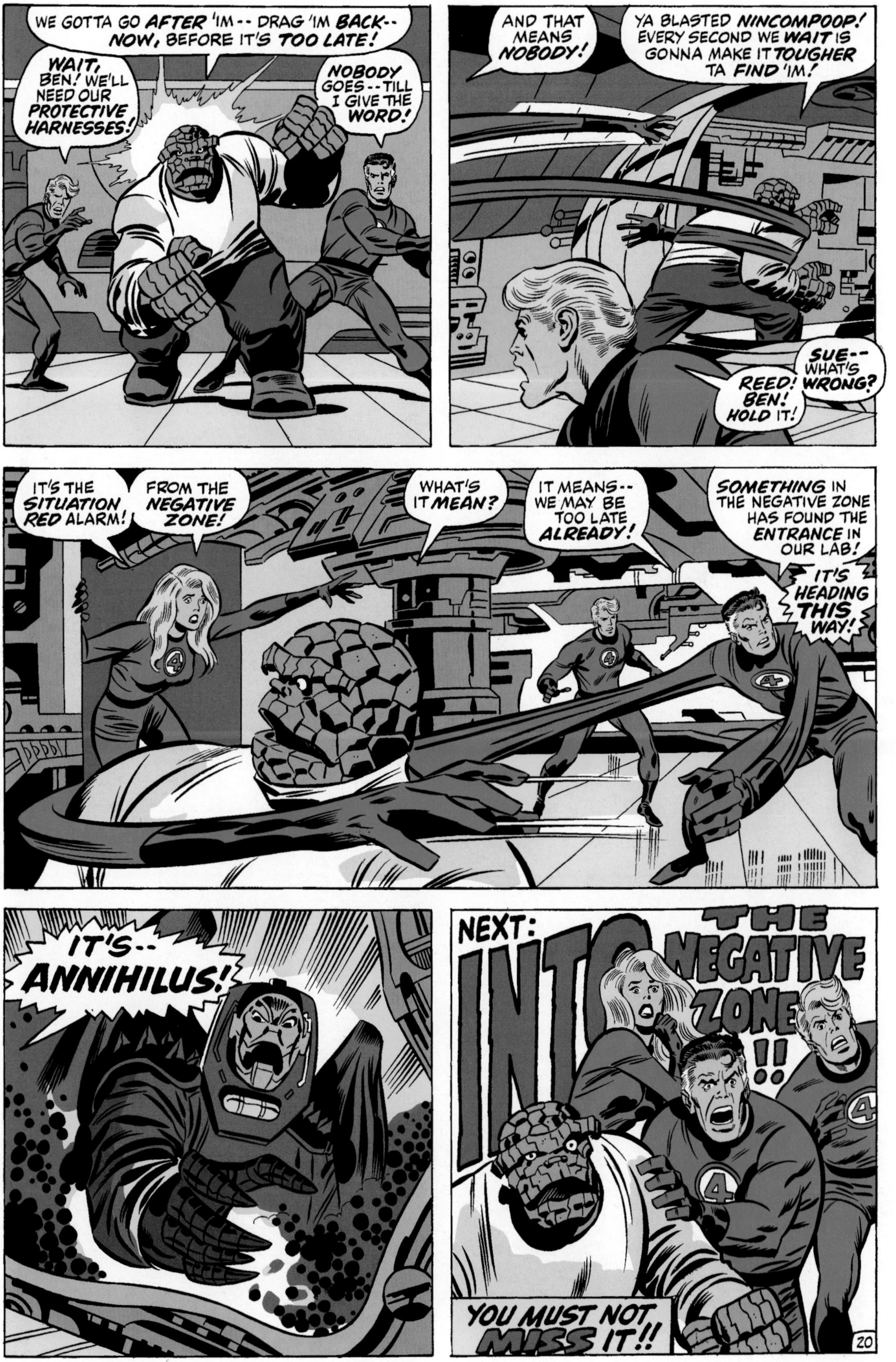
WE GOTTA GO AFTER 'IM -- DRAG 'IM BACK-- NOW, BEFORE IT'S TOO LATE!
WAIT, BEN! WE'LL NEED OUR PROTECTIVE HARNESSES!
NOBODY GOES -- TILL I GIVE THE WORD!
AND THAT MEANS NOBODY!
YA BLASTED NINCOMPOOP! EVERY SECOND WE WAIT IS GONNA MAKE IT TOUGHER TA FIND 'IM!
REED! BEN! HOLD IT!
SUE-- WHAT'S WRONG?
IT'S THE SITUATION RED ALARM!
FROM THE NEGATIVE ZONE!
WHAT'S IT MEAN?
IT MEANS-- WE MAY BE TOO LATE ALREADY!
SOMETHING IN THE NEGATIVE ZONE HAS FOUND THE ENTRANCE IN OUR LAB!
IT'S HEADING THIS WAY!
IT'S-- ANNIHILUS!
NEXT:
INTO THE NEGATIVE ZONE!!
YOU MUST NOT MISS IT!!
20

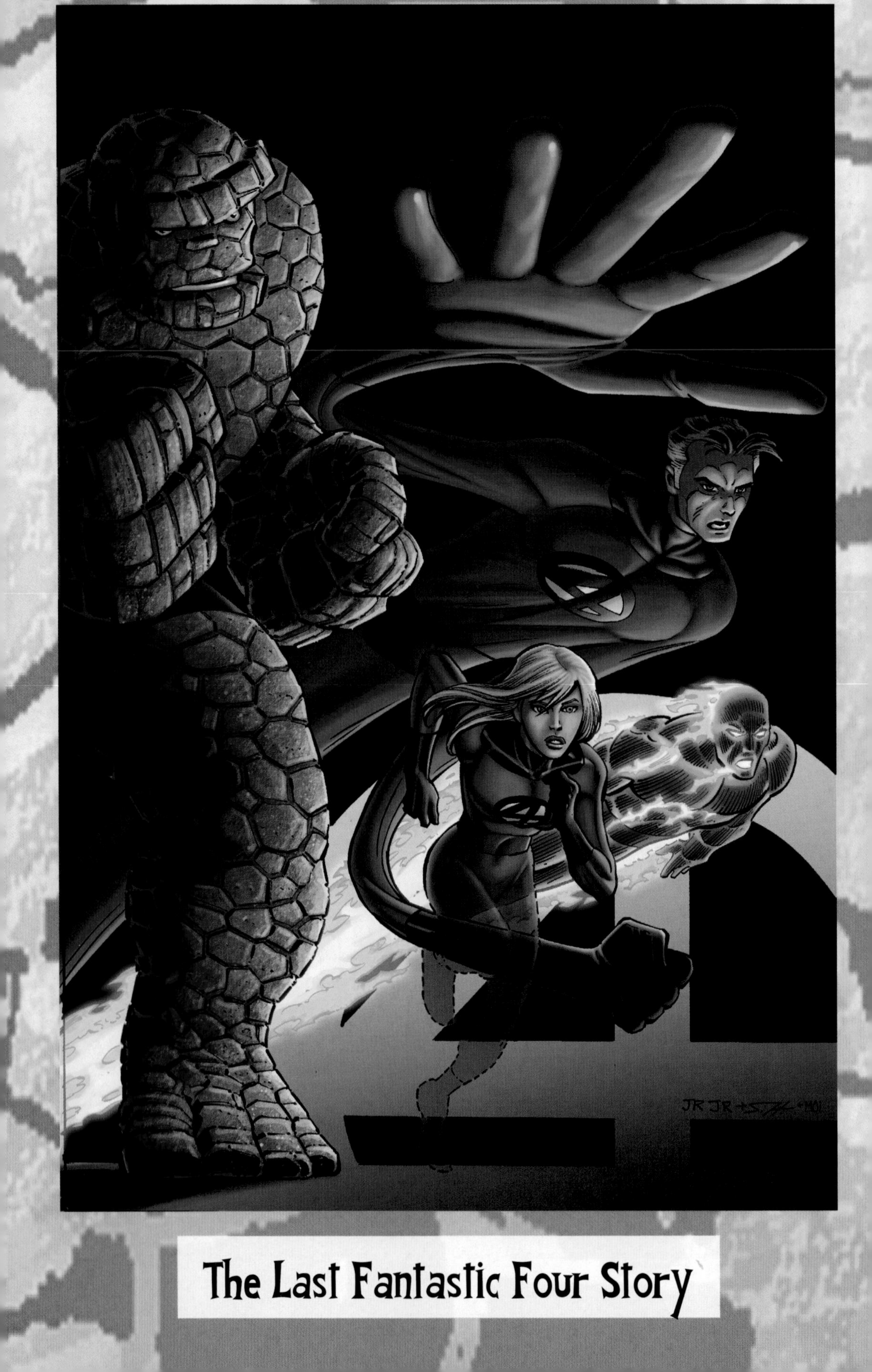

The Last Fantastic Four Story

THE LAST
FANTASTIC FOUR STORY

A brilliant scientist--his best friend--the woman he loves--and her fiery-tempered kid brother! Together, they braved the unknown terrors of outer space, and were changed by cosmic rays into something more than human! Mr. Fantastic! The Thing! The Invisible Girl! The Human Torch! Now they are the Fantastic Four--and the world will never be the same again!

"WORLD'S END"

STAN LEE – WRITER
JOHN ROMITA, JR. – PENCILER
SCOTT HANNA – INKER
MORRY HOLLOWELL – COLORIST
VC'S JOE CARAMAGNA – LETTERER

MOLLY LAZER & AUBREY SITTERSON – ASSISTANT EDITORS
TOM BREVOORT – EDITOR
JOE QUESADA – EDITOR IN CHIEF
DAN BUCKLEY – PUBLISHER

Special thanks to Jeff Youngquist, Marc Sumerak and Andy Schmidt

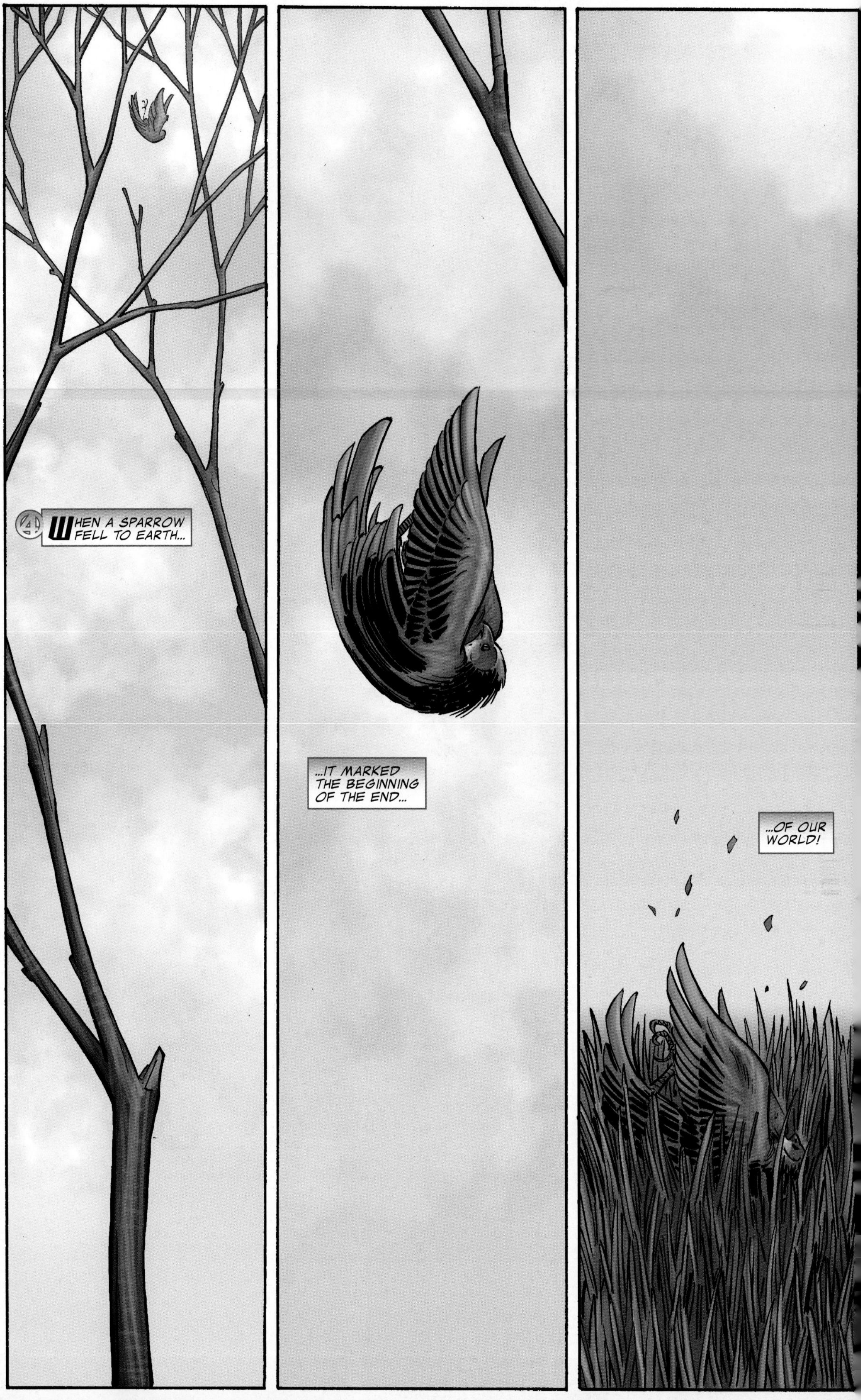
WHEN A SPARROW FELL TO EARTH...
...IT MARKED THE BEGINNING OF THE END...
...OF OUR WORLD!

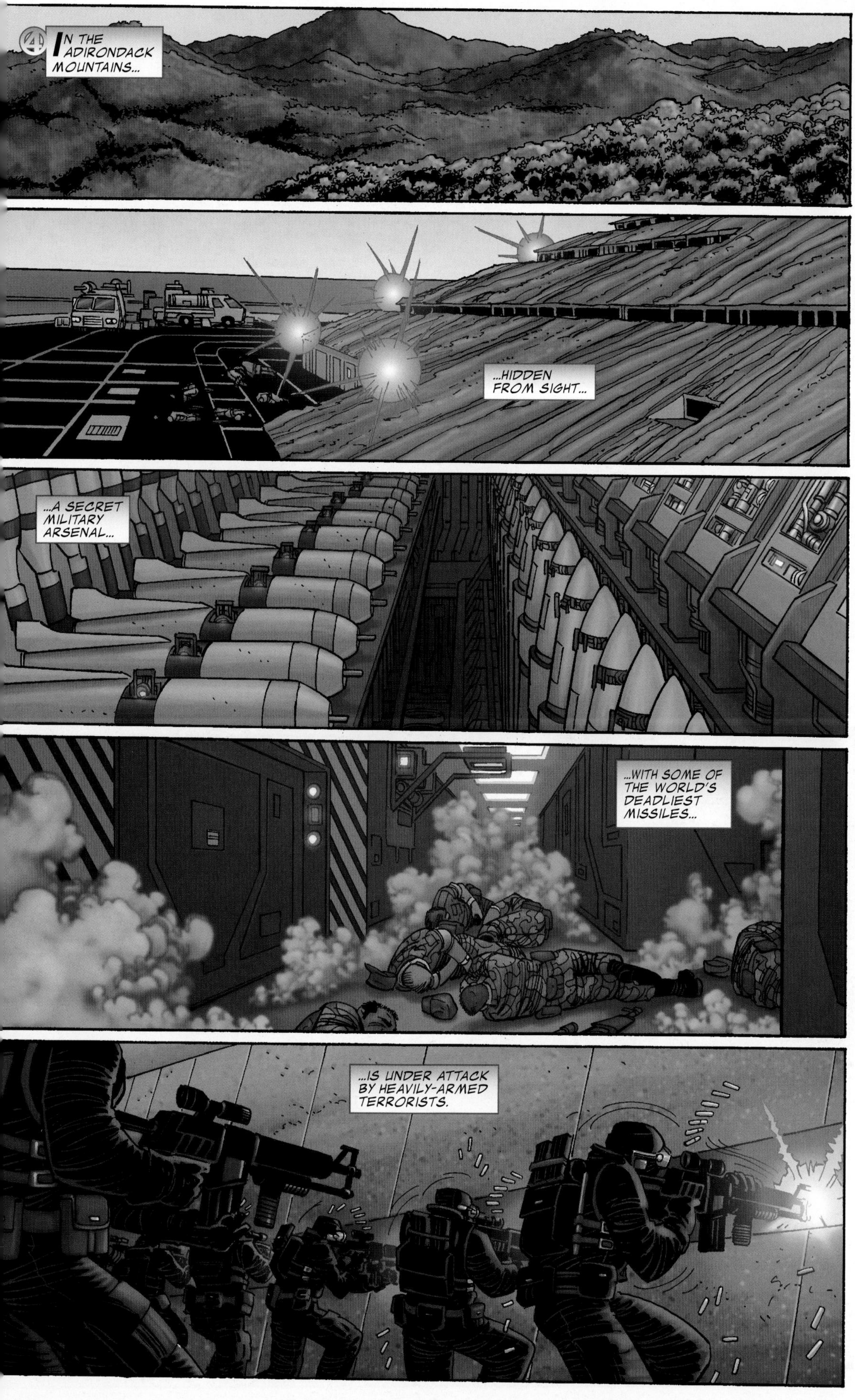
IN THE ADIRONDACK MOUNTAINS...
...HIDDEN FROM SIGHT...
...A SECRET MILITARY ARSENAL...
...WITH SOME OF THE WORLD'S DEADLIEST MISSILES...
...IS UNDER ATTACK BY HEAVILY-ARMED TERRORISTS.

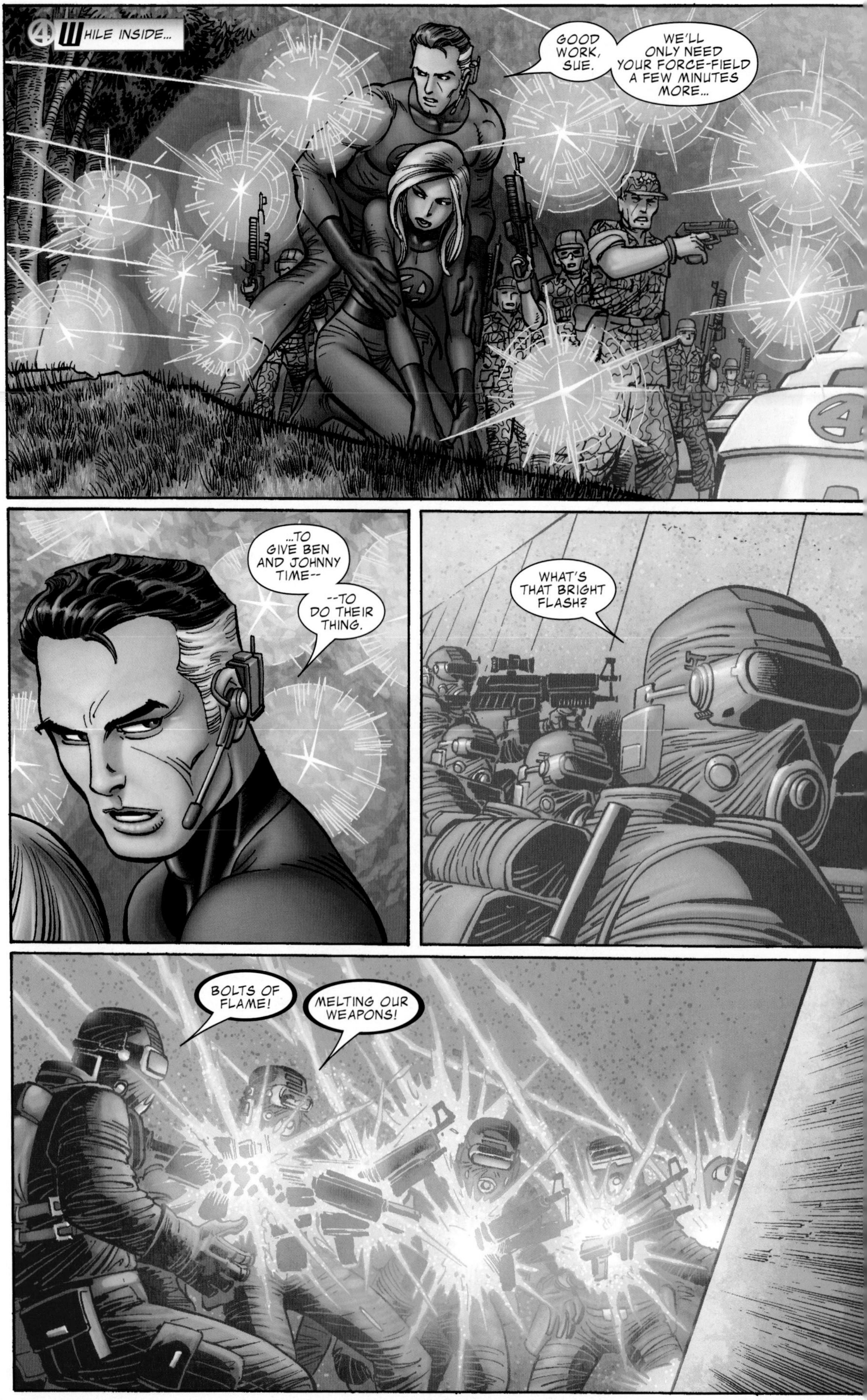
WHILE INSIDE...
GOOD WORK, SUE.
WE'LL ONLY NEED YOUR FORCE-FIELD A FEW MINUTES MORE...
...TO GIVE BEN AND JOHNNY TIME--
--TO DO THEIR THING.
WHAT'S THAT BRIGHT FLASH?
BOLTS OF FLAME!
MELTING OUR WEAPONS!

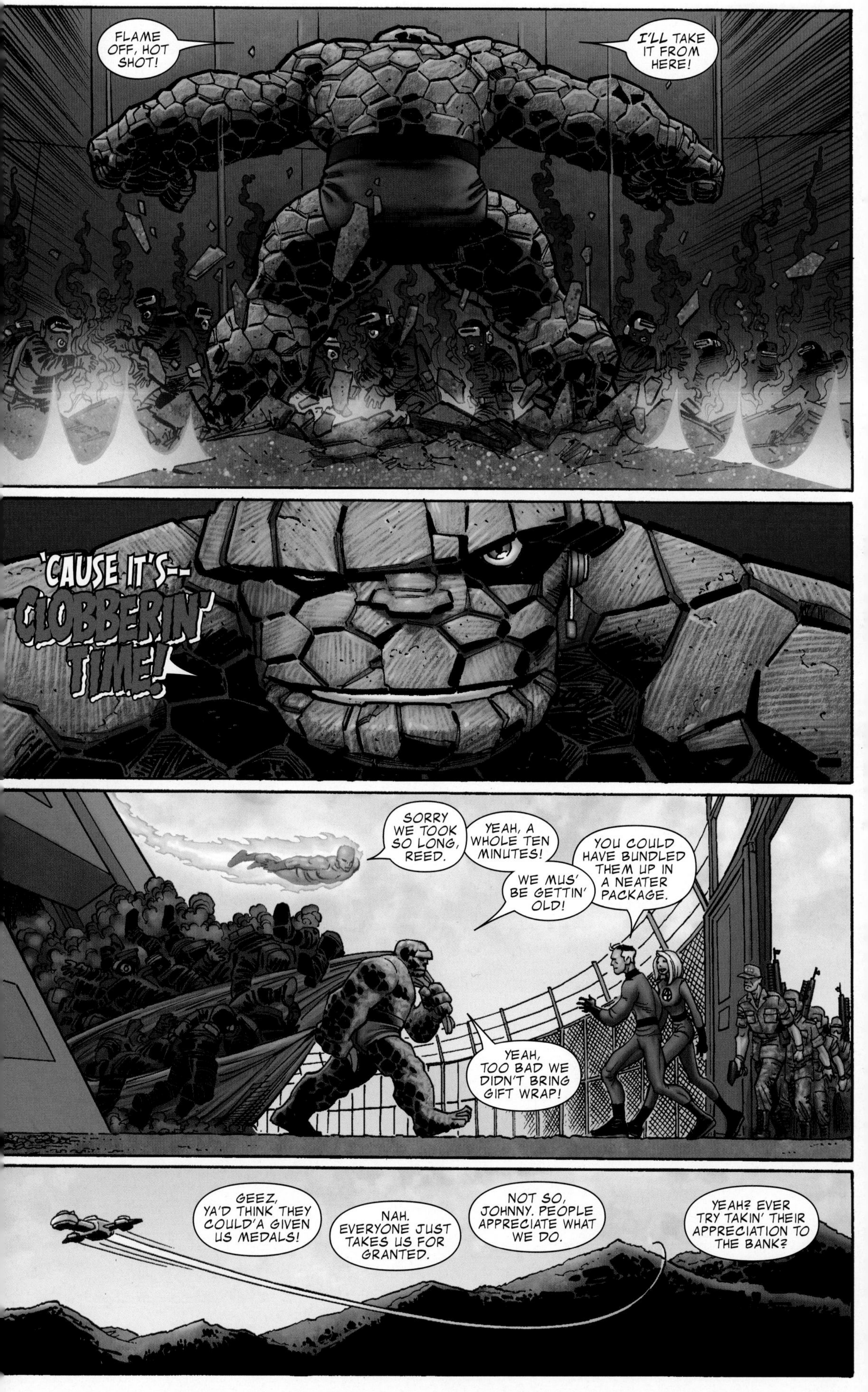
FLAME OFF, HOT SHOT!
I'LL TAKE IT FROM HERE!
'CAUSE IT'S-- CLOBBERIN' TIME!
SORRY WE TOOK SO LONG, REED.
YEAH, A WHOLE TEN MINUTES!
WE MUS' BE GETTIN' OLD!
YOU COULD HAVE BUNDLED THEM UP IN A NEATER PACKAGE.
YEAH, TOO BAD WE DIDN'T BRING GIFT WRAP!
GEEZ, YA'D THINK THEY COULD'A GIVEN US MEDALS!
NAH. EVERYONE JUST TAKES US FOR GRANTED.
NOT SO, JOHNNY. PEOPLE APPRECIATE WHAT WE DO.
YEAH? EVER TRY TAKIN' THEIR APPRECIATION TO THE BANK?

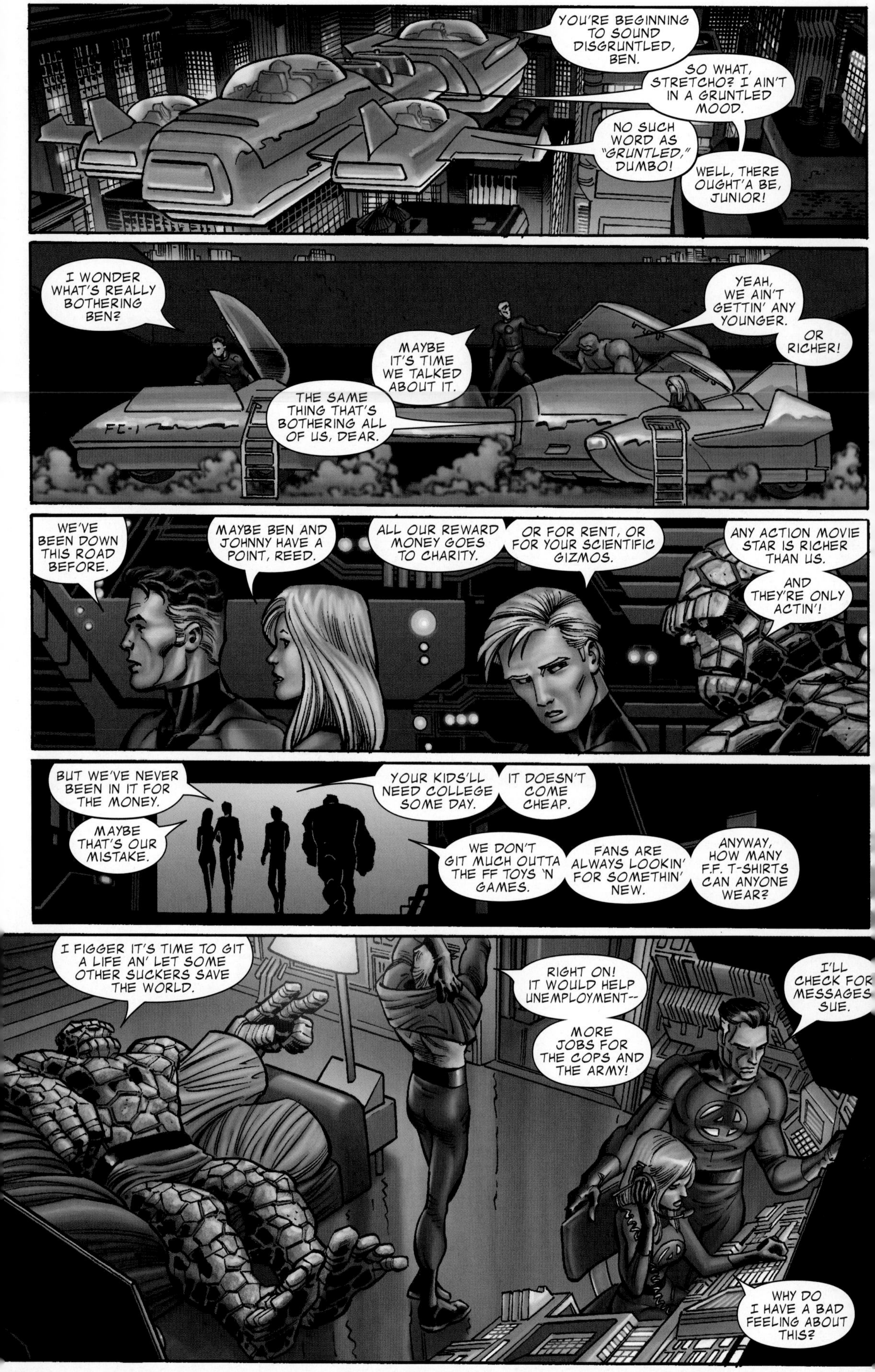
YOU'RE BEGINNING TO SOUND DISGRUNTLED, BEN.
SO WHAT, STRETCHO? I AIN'T IN A GRUNTLED MOOD.
NO SUCH WORD AS "GRUNTLED," DUMBO!
WELL, THERE OUGHT'A BE, JUNIOR!
I WONDER WHAT'S REALLY BOTHERING BEN?
THE SAME THING THAT'S BOTHERING ALL OF US, DEAR.
MAYBE IT'S TIME WE TALKED ABOUT IT.
YEAH, WE AIN'T GETTIN' ANY YOUNGER.
OR RICHER!
FC-1
WE'VE BEEN DOWN THIS ROAD BEFORE.
MAYBE BEN AND JOHNNY HAVE A POINT, REED.
ALL OUR REWARD MONEY GOES TO CHARITY.
OR FOR RENT, OR FOR YOUR SCIENTIFIC GIZMOS.
ANY ACTION MOVIE STAR IS RICHER THAN US.
AND THEY'RE ONLY ACTIN'!
BUT WE'VE NEVER BEEN IN IT FOR THE MONEY.
MAYBE THAT'S OUR MISTAKE.
YOUR KIDS'LL NEED COLLEGE SOME DAY.
IT DOESN'T COME CHEAP.
WE DON'T GIT MUCH OUTTA THE FF TOYS 'N GAMES.
FANS ARE ALWAYS LOOKIN' FOR SOMETHIN' NEW.
ANYWAY, HOW MANY F.F. T-SHIRTS CAN ANYONE WEAR?
I FIGGER IT'S TIME TO GIT A LIFE AN' LET SOME OTHER SUCKERS SAVE THE WORLD.
RIGHT ON! IT WOULD HELP UNEMPLOYMENT--
MORE JOBS FOR THE COPS AND THE ARMY!
I'LL CHECK FOR MESSAGES, SUE.
WHY DO I HAVE A BAD FEELING ABOUT THIS?

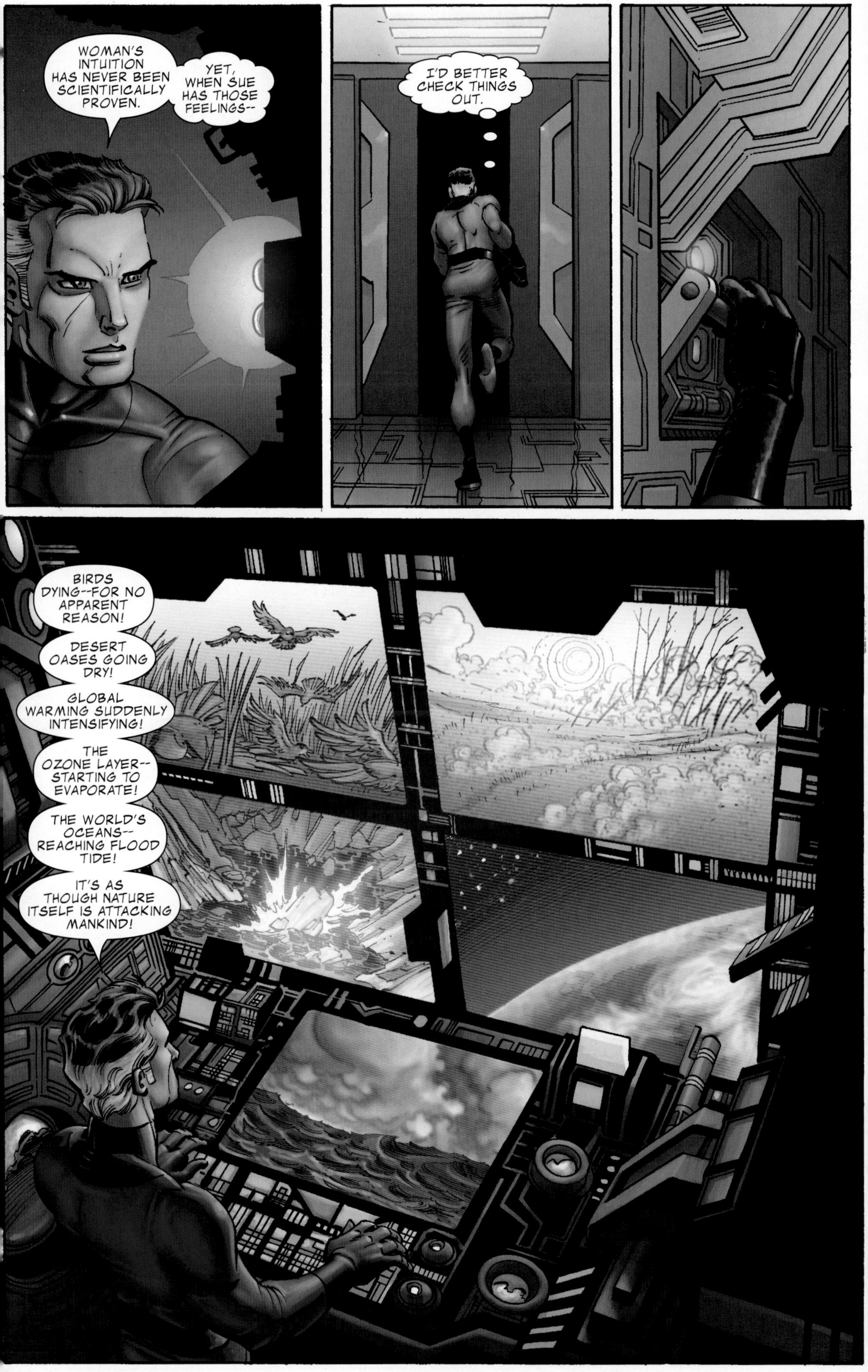
WOMAN'S INTUITION HAS NEVER BEEN SCIENTIFICALLY PROVEN.
YET, WHEN SUE HAS THOSE FEELINGS--
I'D BETTER CHECK THINGS OUT.
BIRDS DYING--FOR NO APPARENT REASON!
DESERT OASES GOING DRY!
GLOBAL WARMING SUDDENLY INTENSIFYING!
THE OZONE LAYER--STARTING TO EVAPORATE!
THE WORLD'S OCEANS--REACHING FLOOD TIDE!
IT'S AS THOUGH NATURE ITSELF IS ATTACKING MANKIND!

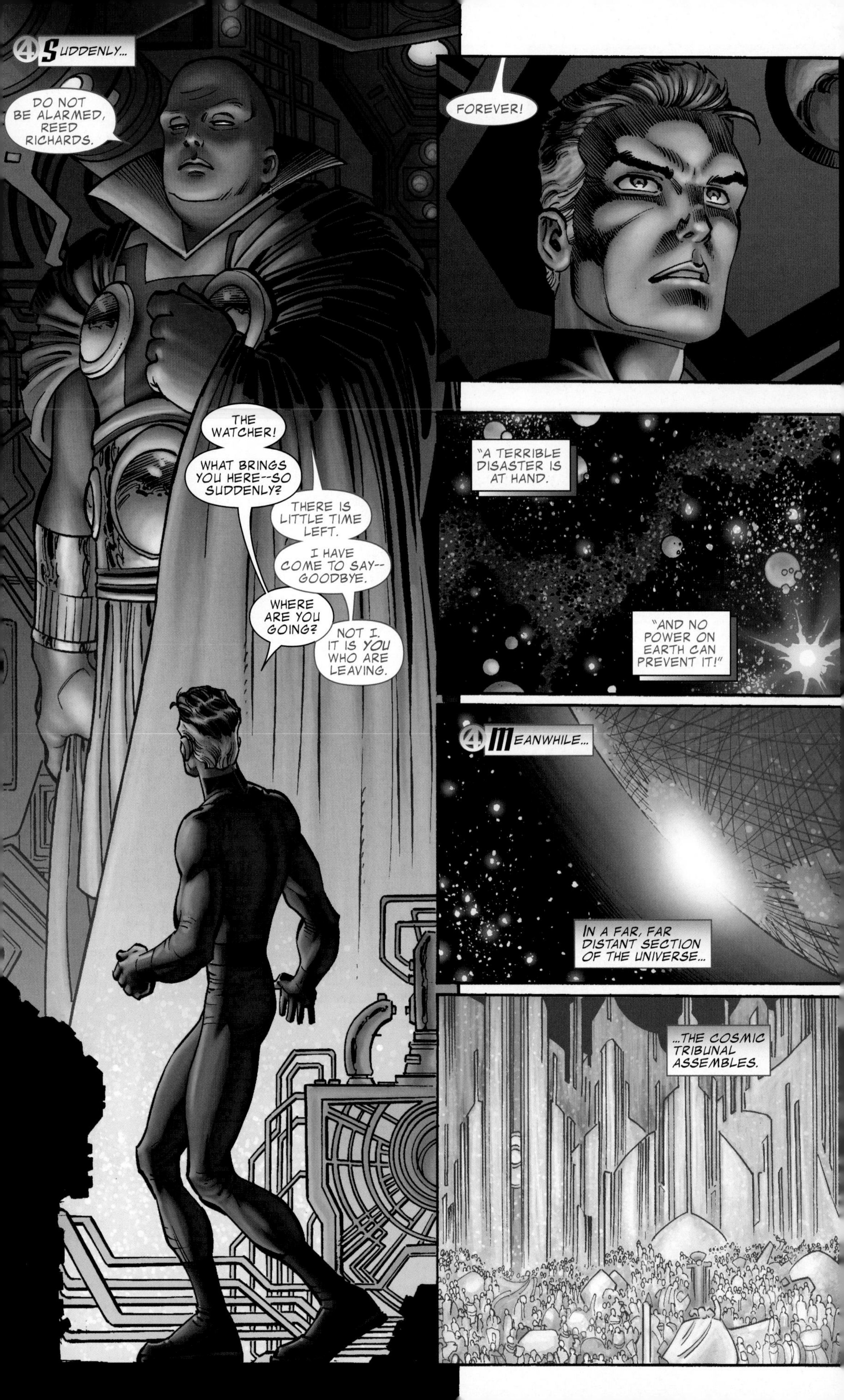
SUDDENLY...
DO NOT BE ALARMED, REED RICHARDS.
THE WATCHER!
WHAT BRINGS YOU HERE--SO SUDDENLY?
THERE IS LITTLE TIME LEFT.
I HAVE COME TO SAY--GOODBYE.
WHERE ARE YOU GOING?
NOT I. IT IS YOU WHO ARE LEAVING.
FOREVER!
"A TERRIBLE DISASTER IS AT HAND.
"AND NO POWER ON EARTH CAN PREVENT IT!"
MEANWHILE...
IN A FAR, FAR DISTANT SECTION OF THE UNIVERSE...
...THE COSMIC TRIBUNAL ASSEMBLES.

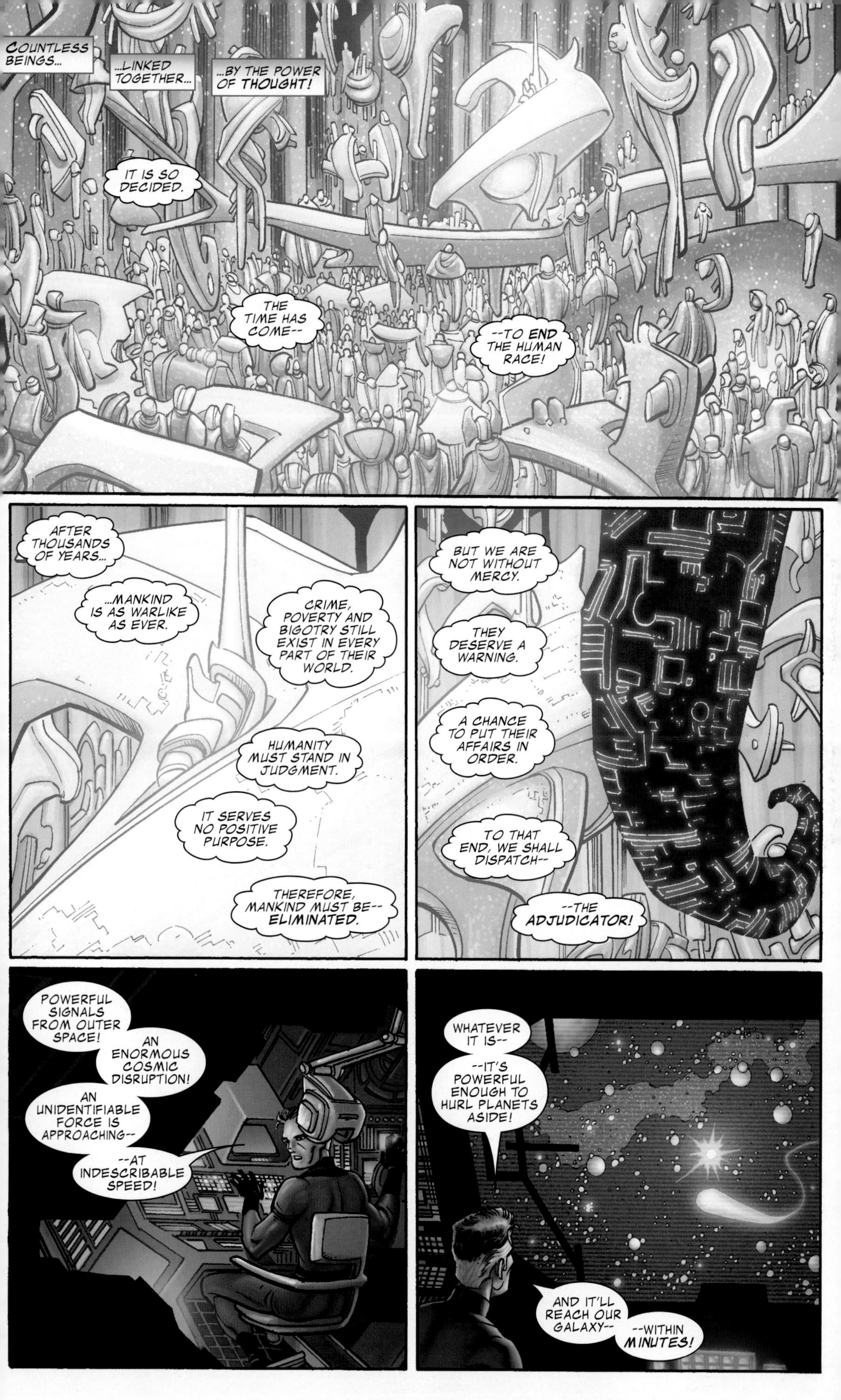
COUNTLESS BEINGS...
...LINKED TOGETHER...
...BY THE POWER OF THOUGHT!
IT IS SO DECIDED.
THE TIME HAS COME--
--TO END THE HUMAN RACE!
AFTER THOUSANDS OF YEARS...
...MANKIND IS AS WARLIKE AS EVER.
CRIME, POVERTY AND BIGOTRY STILL EXIST IN EVERY PART OF THEIR WORLD.
HUMANITY MUST STAND IN JUDGMENT.
IT SERVES NO POSITIVE PURPOSE.
THEREFORE, MANKIND MUST BE-- ELIMINATED.
BUT WE ARE NOT WITHOUT MERCY.
THEY DESERVE A WARNING.
A CHANCE TO PUT THEIR AFFAIRS IN ORDER.
TO THAT END, WE SHALL DISPATCH--
--THE ADJUDICATOR!
POWERFUL SIGNALS FROM OUTER SPACE!
AN ENORMOUS COSMIC DISRUPTION!
AN UNIDENTIFIABLE FORCE IS APPROACHING--
--AT INDESCRIBABLE SPEED!
WHATEVER IT IS--
--IT'S POWERFUL ENOUGH TO HURL PLANETS ASIDE!
AND IT'LL REACH OUR GALAXY--
--WITHIN MINUTES!

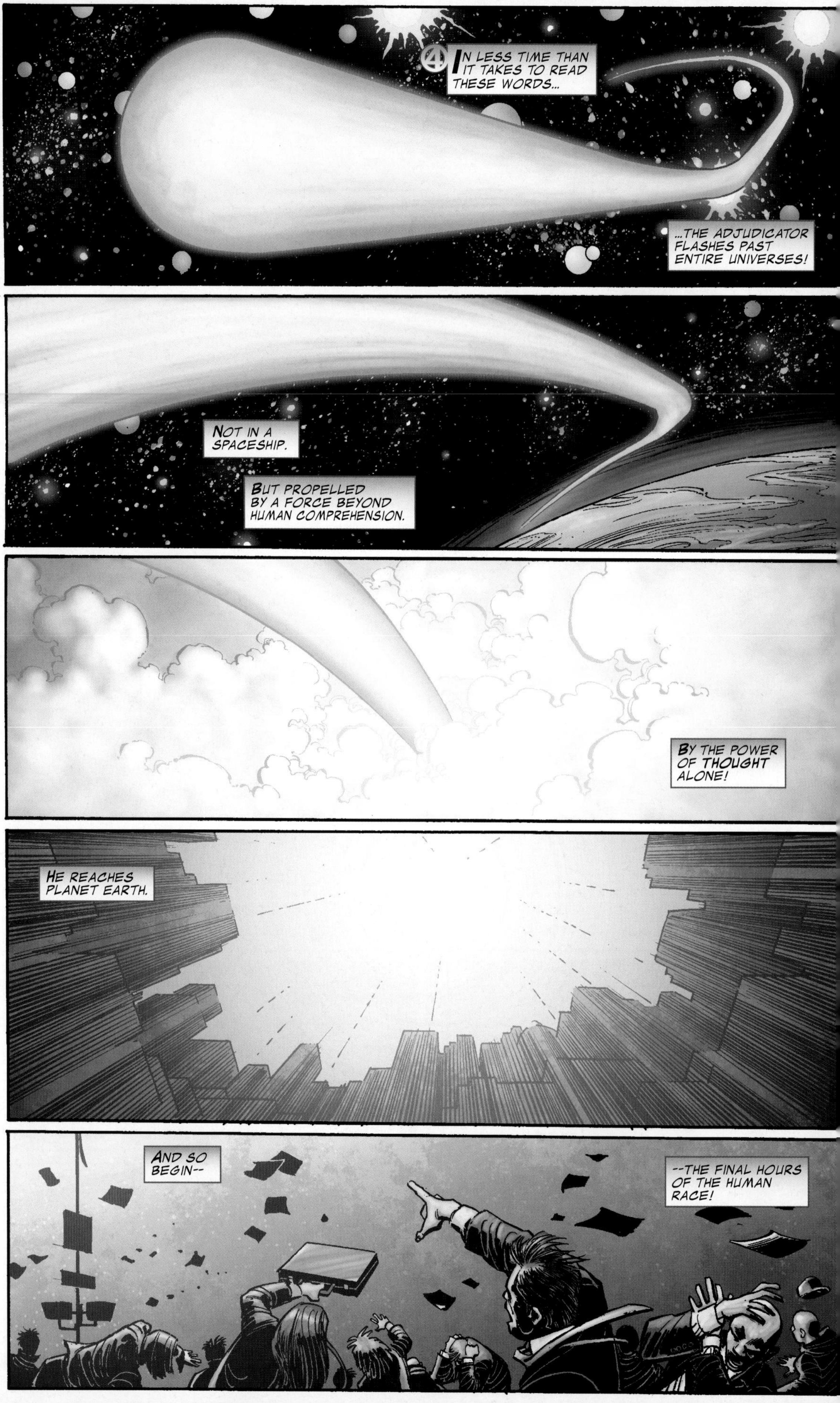
IN LESS TIME THAN IT TAKES TO READ THESE WORDS...
...THE ADJUDICATOR FLASHES PAST ENTIRE UNIVERSES!
NOT IN A SPACESHIP.
BUT PROPELLED BY A FORCE BEYOND HUMAN COMPREHENSION.
BY THE POWER OF THOUGHT ALONE!
HE REACHES PLANET EARTH.
AND SO BEGIN--
--THE FINAL HOURS OF THE HUMAN RACE!

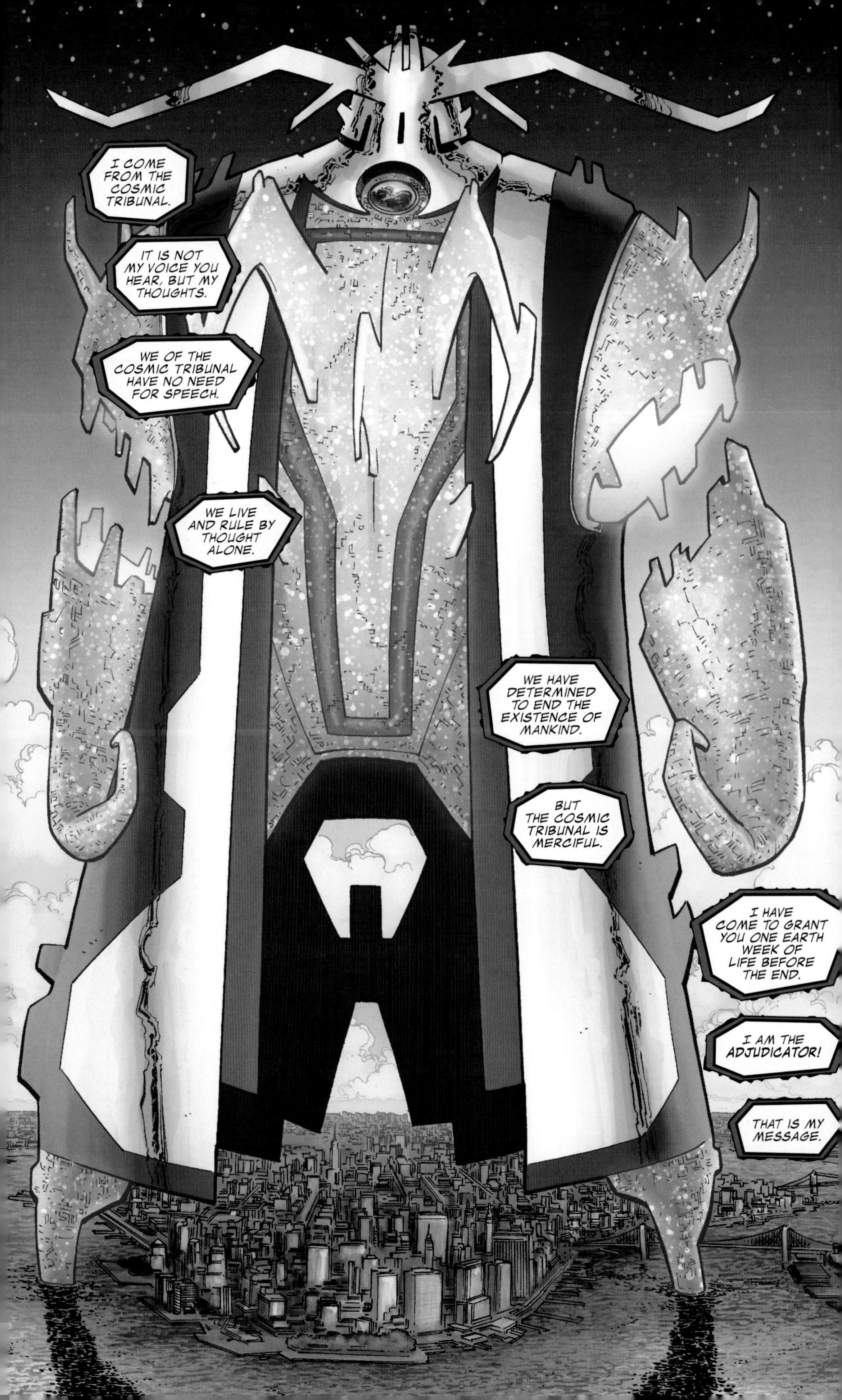
I COME FROM THE COSMIC TRIBUNAL.
IT IS NOT MY VOICE YOU HEAR, BUT MY THOUGHTS.
WE OF THE COSMIC TRIBUNAL HAVE NO NEED FOR SPEECH.
WE LIVE AND RULE BY THOUGHT ALONE.
WE HAVE DETERMINED TO END THE EXISTENCE OF MANKIND.
BUT THE COSMIC TRIBUNAL IS MERCIFUL.
I HAVE COME TO GRANT YOU ONE EARTH WEEK OF LIFE BEFORE THE END.
I AM THE ADJUDICATOR!
THAT IS MY MESSAGE.

As if to punctuate the adjudicator's words...

...the coastal waters start rising over the nation's highways.

Inundating piers and docks on every coast.

He also appears off the coast of Los Angeles.

And issues an incredible edict...

By the power of thought, I can will myself to be in any number of places...

...at the same time!

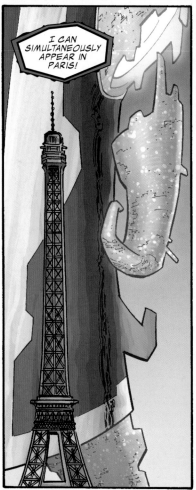

I can simultaneously appear in Paris!

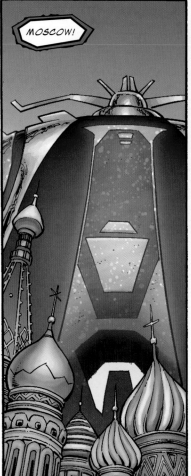

Moscow!

Even the Himalayas!

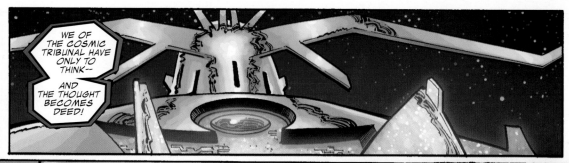

WE OF THE COSMIC TRIBUNAL HAVE ONLY TO THINK--

AND THE THOUGHT BECOMES DEED!

BUT I WISH NOT TO INTRUDE UPON YOUR FINAL HOURS.

SURELY YOU HAVE MANY FAREWELLS TO UTTER.

AND MANY FINAL DEEDS TO PERFORM.

WHO'S THAT OVERGROWN WEIRDO KIDDIN'?

HE'S THREATENIN' TO WASTE THE WHOLE BLAMED PLANET--

--AN' TRYIN' TO SOUND LIKE A GOOD GUY AT THE SAME TIME!

"GOOD" AND "BAD" MAY BE ALIEN CONCEPTS TO HIM, BEN.

HEY! LOOK WHAT HE'S DOIN' NOW!

I WAS NOT PREPARED FOR HOW SMALL HUMANS ARE.

THERE IS NO NEED FOR ME TO BE SO LARGE.

HE'S SHRINKING DOWN RIGHT BEFORE OUR EYES!

BUT HE'S STILL LIKE SOME HORROR MOVIE GIANT!

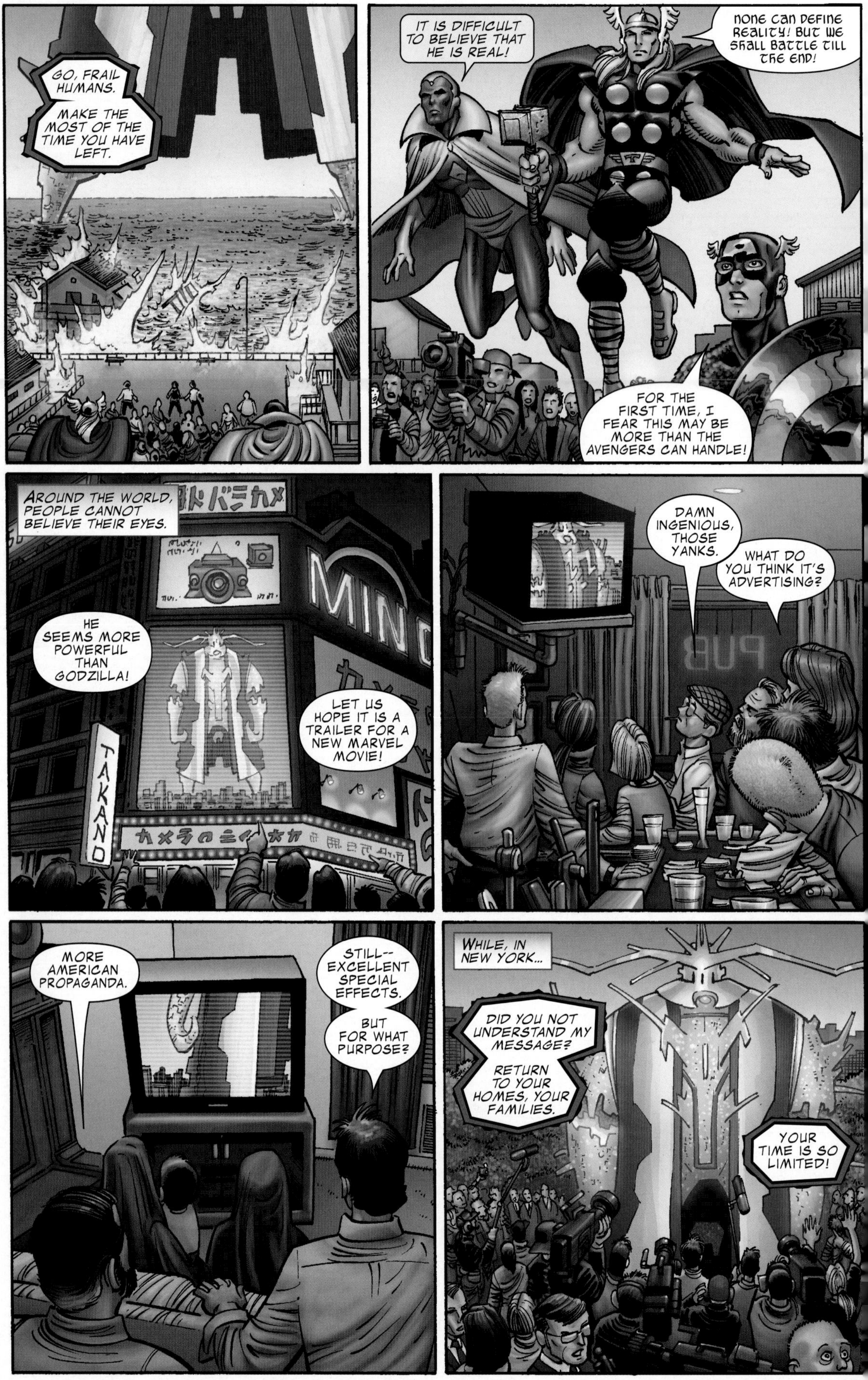
GO, FRAIL HUMANS.
MAKE THE MOST OF THE TIME YOU HAVE LEFT.
IT IS DIFFICULT TO BELIEVE THAT HE IS REAL!
NONE CAN DEFINE REALITY! BUT WE SHALL BATTLE TILL THE END!
FOR THE FIRST TIME, I FEAR THIS MAY BE MORE THAN THE AVENGERS CAN HANDLE!
AROUND THE WORLD, PEOPLE CANNOT BELIEVE THEIR EYES.
MINO
HE SEEMS MORE POWERFUL THAN GODZILLA!
LET US HOPE IT IS A TRAILER FOR A NEW MARVEL MOVIE!
TAKANO
DAMN INGENIOUS, THOSE YANKS.
WHAT DO YOU THINK IT'S ADVERTISING?
PUB
MORE AMERICAN PROPAGANDA.
STILL-- EXCELLENT SPECIAL EFFECTS.
BUT FOR WHAT PURPOSE?
WHILE, IN NEW YORK...
DID YOU NOT UNDERSTAND MY MESSAGE?
RETURN TO YOUR HOMES, YOUR FAMILIES.
YOUR TIME IS SO LIMITED!

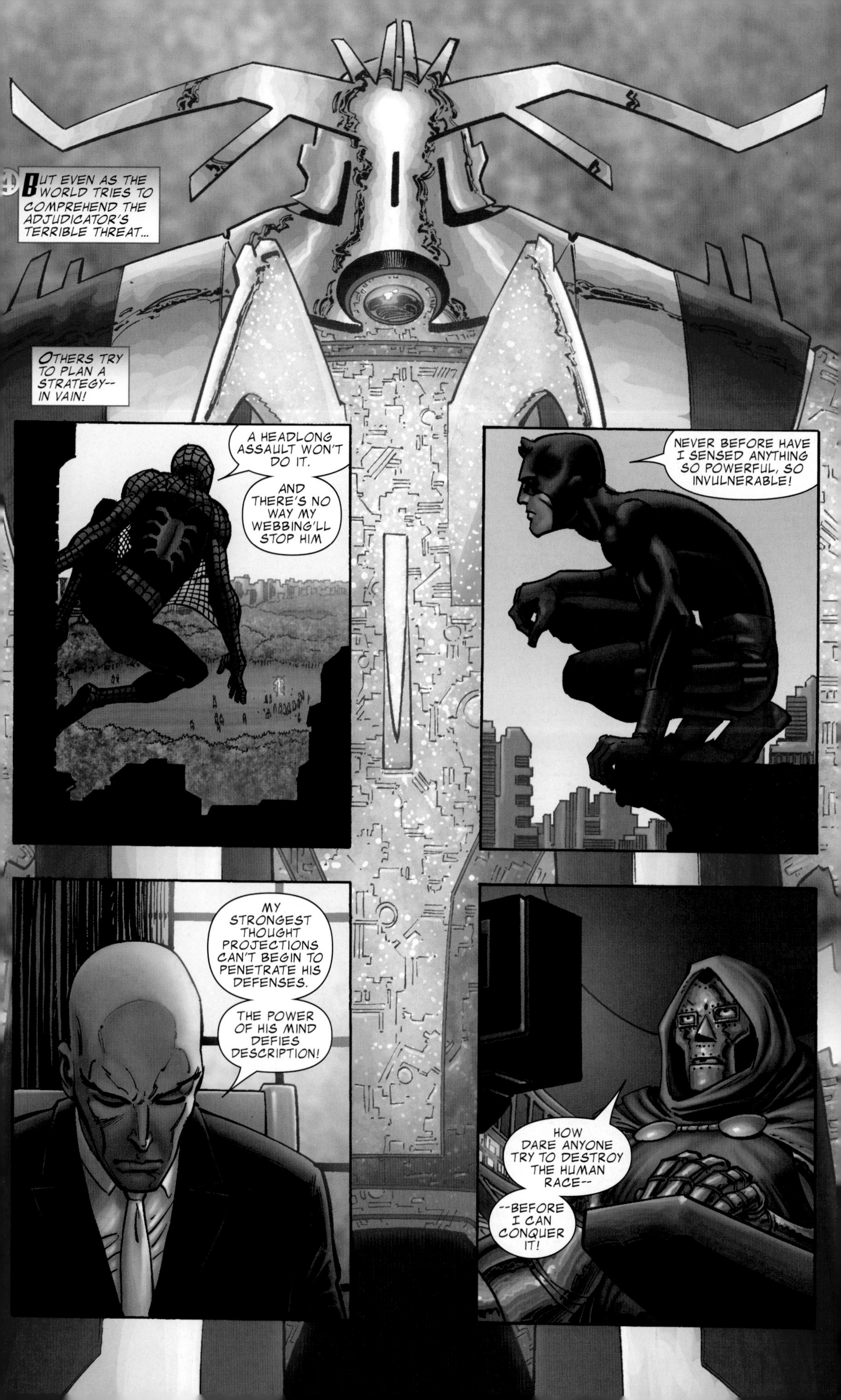
BUT EVEN AS THE WORLD TRIES TO COMPREHEND THE ADJUDICATOR'S TERRIBLE THREAT...
OTHERS TRY TO PLAN A STRATEGY-- IN VAIN!
A HEADLONG ASSAULT WON'T DO IT.
AND THERE'S NO WAY MY WEBBING'LL STOP HIM
NEVER BEFORE HAVE I SENSED ANYTHING SO POWERFUL, SO INVULNERABLE!
MY STRONGEST THOUGHT PROJECTIONS CAN'T BEGIN TO PENETRATE HIS DEFENSES.
THE POWER OF HIS MIND DEFIES DESCRIPTION!
HOW DARE ANYONE TRY TO DESTROY THE HUMAN RACE--
--BEFORE I CAN CONQUER IT!

SUDDENLY, A SPECTACULAR DISRUPTION AT NEW YORK'S BATTERY PARK--

--AS A MIGHTY WARRIOR LEGION OF ATLANTIS BREAKS THROUGH TO THE SURFACE--

--AND IS MET BY NEW YORK'S BATTLE-WISE SWAT TEAMS!

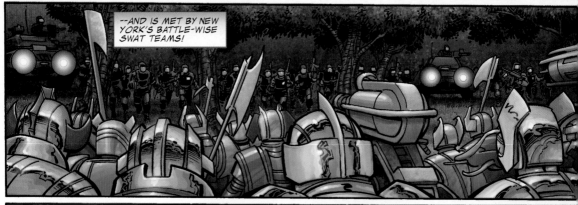

THEN, A RAGING PRINCE NAMOR HURLS HIMSELF INTO THE FRAY!

FOR ATLANTIS-- AND VICTORY!

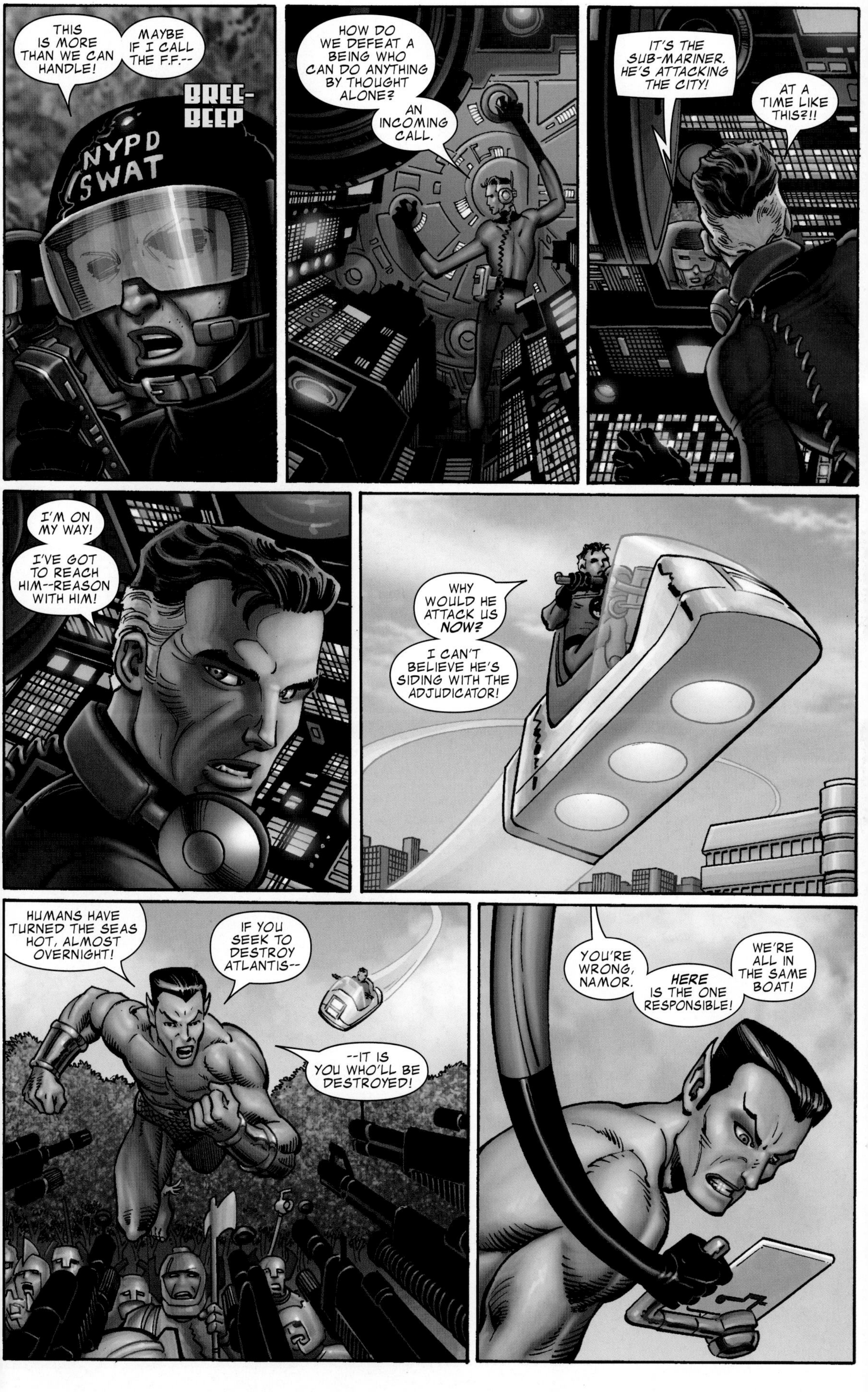
THIS IS MORE THAN WE CAN HANDLE!
MAYBE IF I CALL THE F.F.--
BREE-BEEP
NYPD SWAT
HOW DO WE DEFEAT A BEING WHO CAN DO ANYTHING BY THOUGHT ALONE?
AN INCOMING CALL.
IT'S THE SUB-MARINER. HE'S ATTACKING THE CITY!
AT A TIME LIKE THIS?!!
I'M ON MY WAY!
I'VE GOT TO REACH HIM--REASON WITH HIM!
WHY WOULD HE ATTACK US NOW?
I CAN'T BELIEVE HE'S SIDING WITH THE ADJUDICATOR!
HUMANS HAVE TURNED THE SEAS HOT, ALMOST OVERNIGHT!
IF YOU SEEK TO DESTROY ATLANTIS--
--IT IS YOU WHO'LL BE DESTROYED!
YOU'RE WRONG, NAMOR.
HERE IS THE ONE RESPONSIBLE!
WE'RE ALL IN THE SAME BOAT!

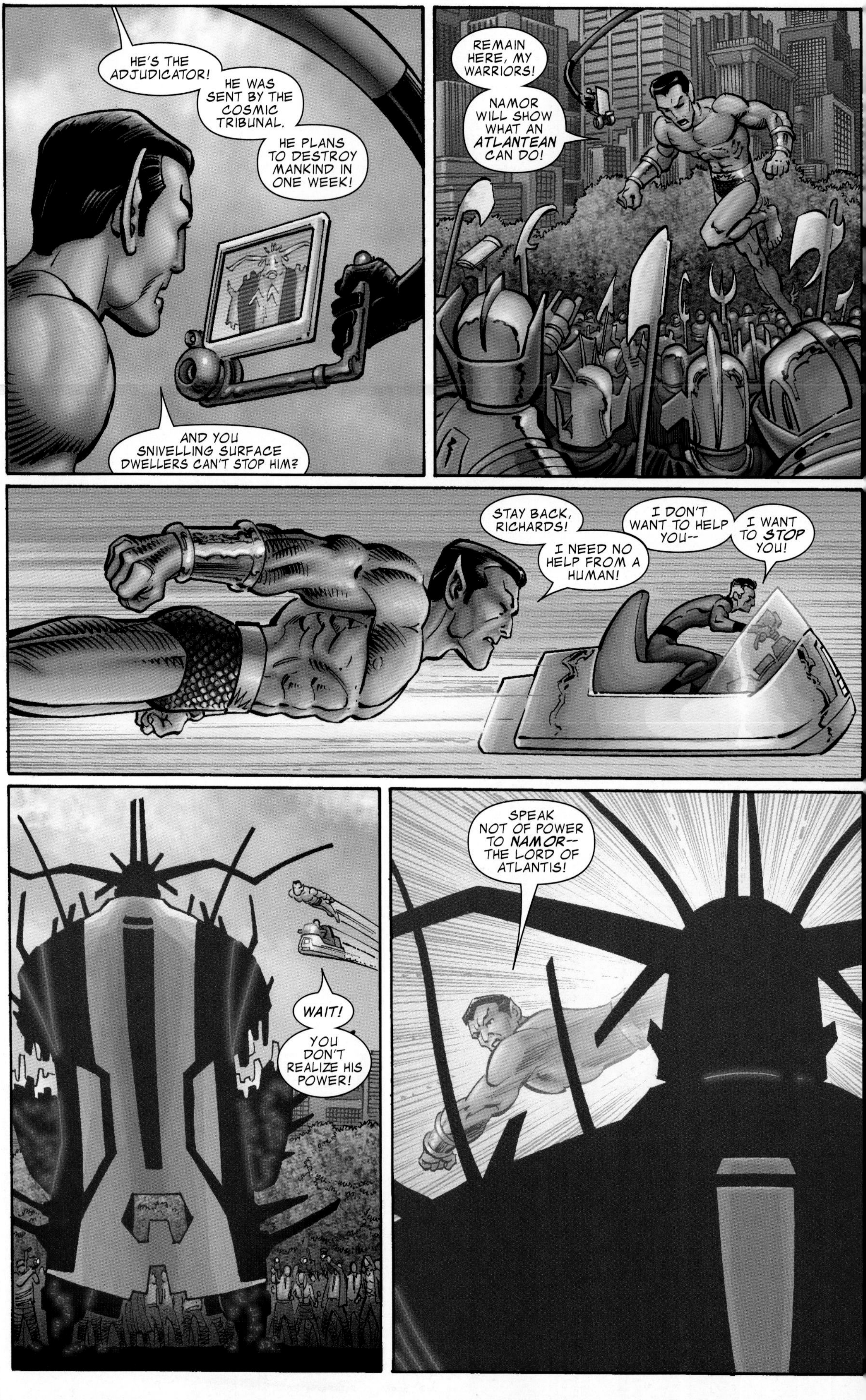
HE'S THE ADJUDICATOR!
HE WAS SENT BY THE COSMIC TRIBUNAL.
HE PLANS TO DESTROY MANKIND IN ONE WEEK!
AND YOU SNIVELLING SURFACE DWELLERS CAN'T STOP HIM?
REMAIN HERE, MY WARRIORS!
NAMOR WILL SHOW WHAT AN ATLANTEAN CAN DO!
STAY BACK, RICHARDS!
I NEED NO HELP FROM A HUMAN!
I DON'T WANT TO HELP YOU--
I WANT TO STOP YOU!
WAIT!
YOU DON'T REALIZE HIS POWER!
SPEAK NOT OF POWER TO NAMOR-- THE LORD OF ATLANTIS!

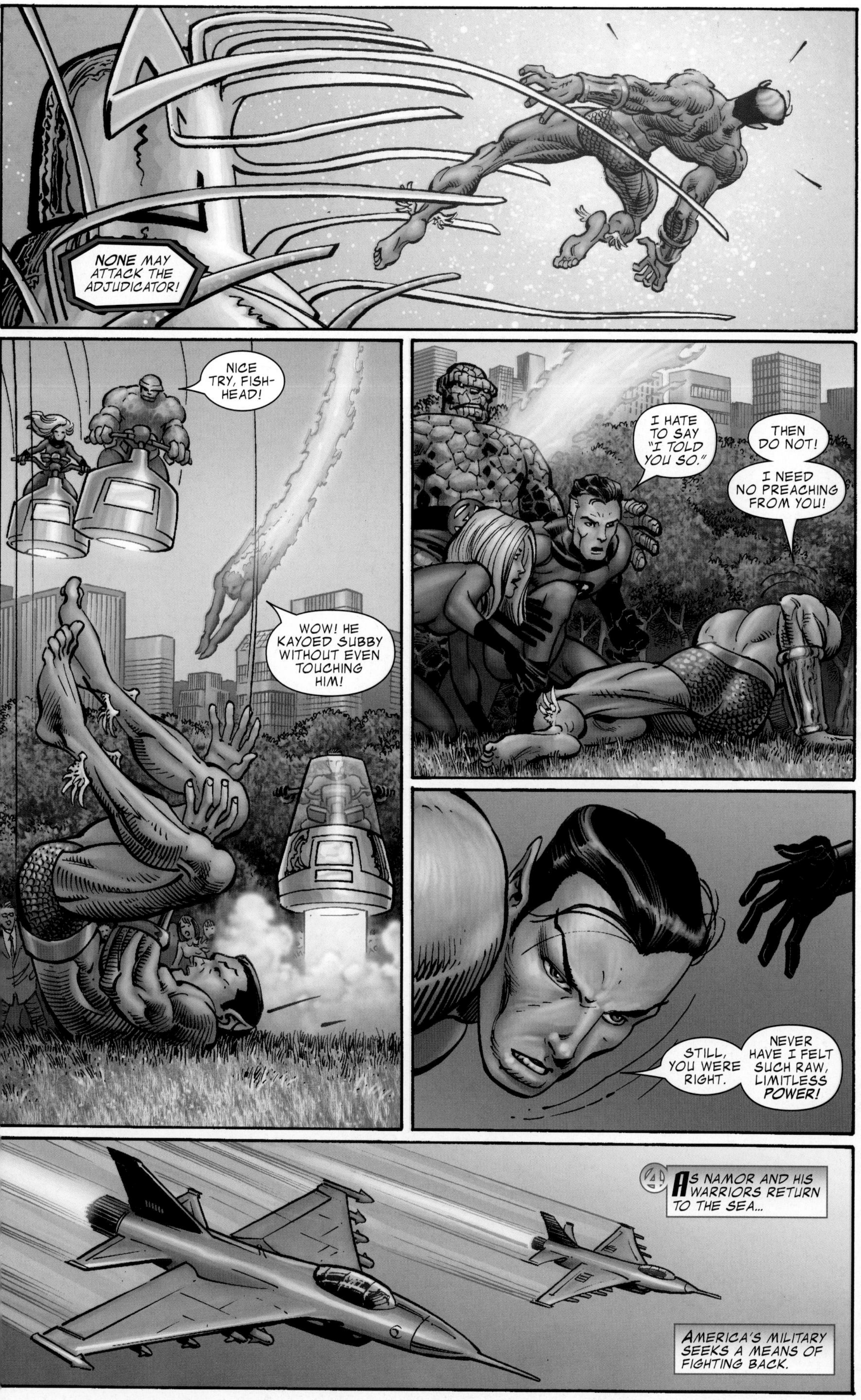
NONE MAY ATTACK THE ADJUDICATOR!
NICE TRY, FISH-HEAD!
WOW! HE KAYOED SUBBY WITHOUT EVEN TOUCHING HIM!
I HATE TO SAY "I TOLD YOU SO."
THEN DO NOT!
I NEED NO PREACHING FROM YOU!
STILL, YOU WERE RIGHT.
NEVER HAVE I FELT SUCH RAW, LIMITLESS POWER!
AS NAMOR AND HIS WARRIORS RETURN TO THE SEA...
AMERICA'S MILITARY SEEKS A MEANS OF FIGHTING BACK.

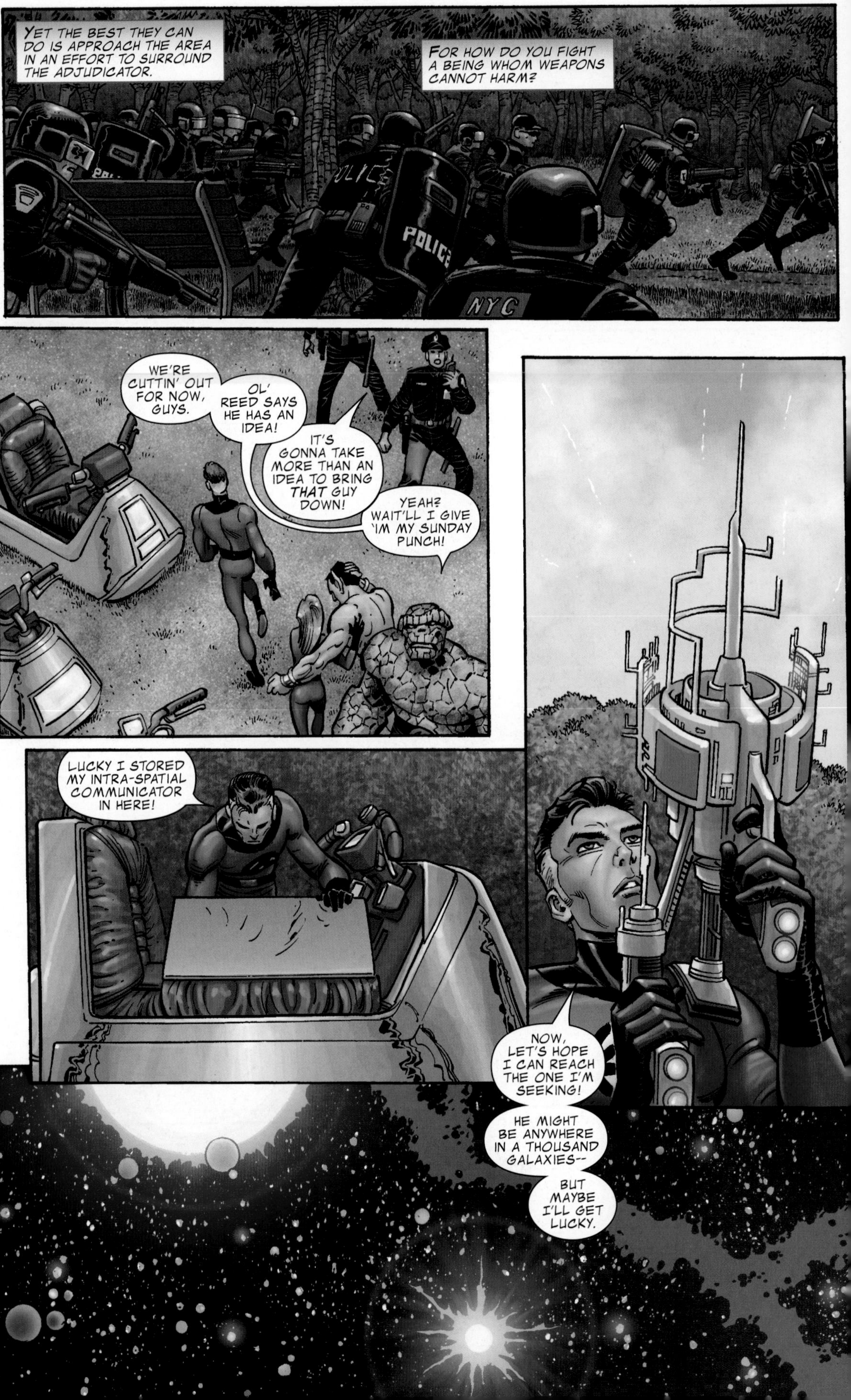
YET THE BEST THEY CAN DO IS APPROACH THE AREA IN AN EFFORT TO SURROUND THE ADJUDICATOR.
FOR HOW DO YOU FIGHT A BEING WHOM WEAPONS CANNOT HARM?
POLICE
POLICE
NYC
WE'RE CUTTIN' OUT FOR NOW, GUYS.
OL' REED SAYS HE HAS AN IDEA!
IT'S GONNA TAKE MORE THAN AN IDEA TO BRING THAT GUY DOWN!
YEAH? WAIT'LL I GIVE 'IM MY SUNDAY PUNCH!
LUCKY I STORED MY INTRA-SPATIAL COMMUNICATOR IN HERE!
NOW, LET'S HOPE I CAN REACH THE ONE I'M SEEKING!
HE MIGHT BE ANYWHERE IN A THOUSAND GALAXIES--
BUT MAYBE I'LL GET LUCKY.

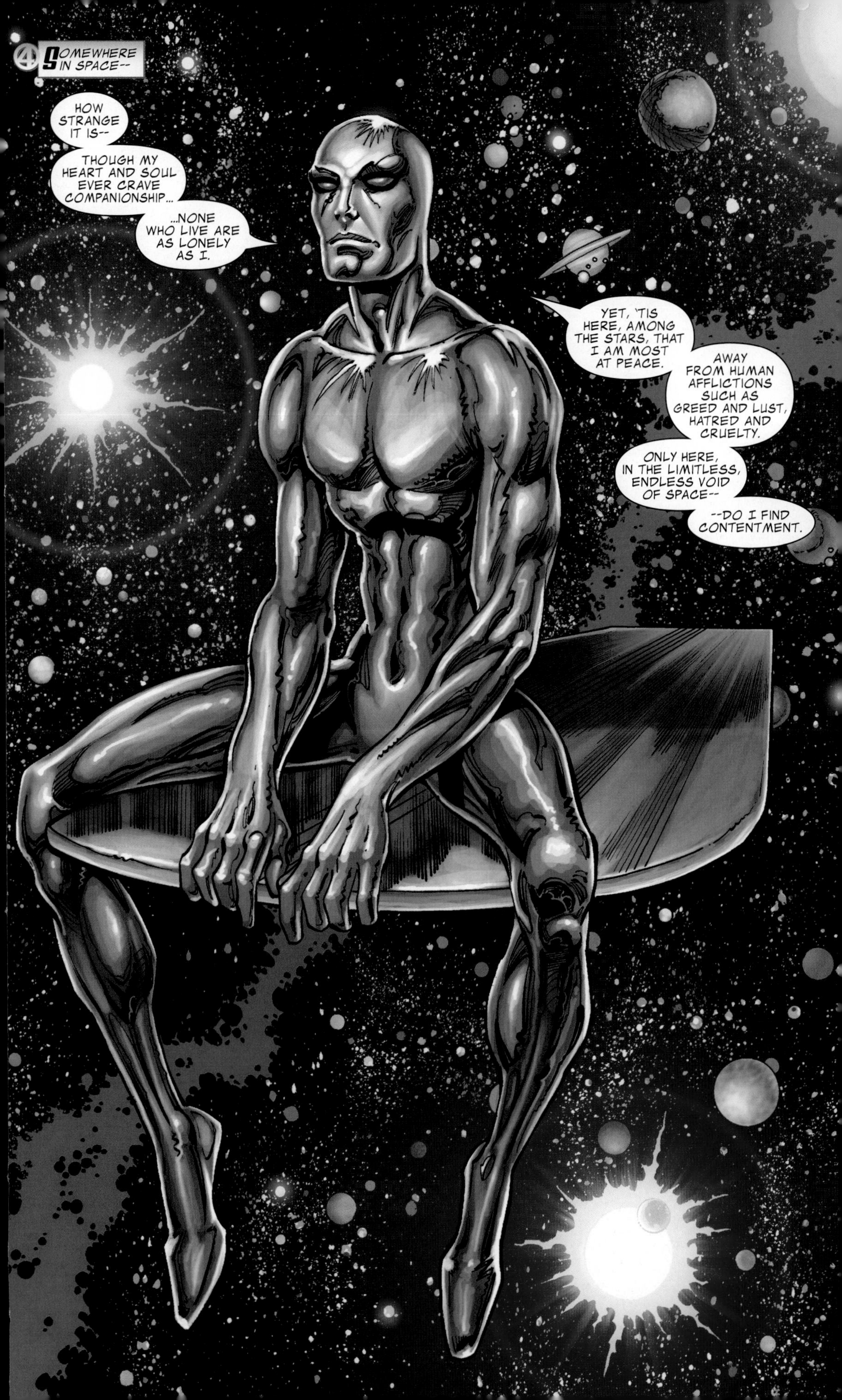
SOMEWHERE IN SPACE--
HOW STRANGE IT IS--
THOUGH MY HEART AND SOUL EVER CRAVE COMPANIONSHIP...
...NONE WHO LIVE ARE AS LONELY AS I.
YET, 'TIS HERE, AMONG THE STARS, THAT I AM MOST AT PEACE.
AWAY FROM HUMAN AFFLICTIONS SUCH AS GREED AND LUST, HATRED AND CRUELTY.
ONLY HERE, IN THE LIMITLESS, ENDLESS VOID OF SPACE--
--DO I FIND CONTENTMENT.

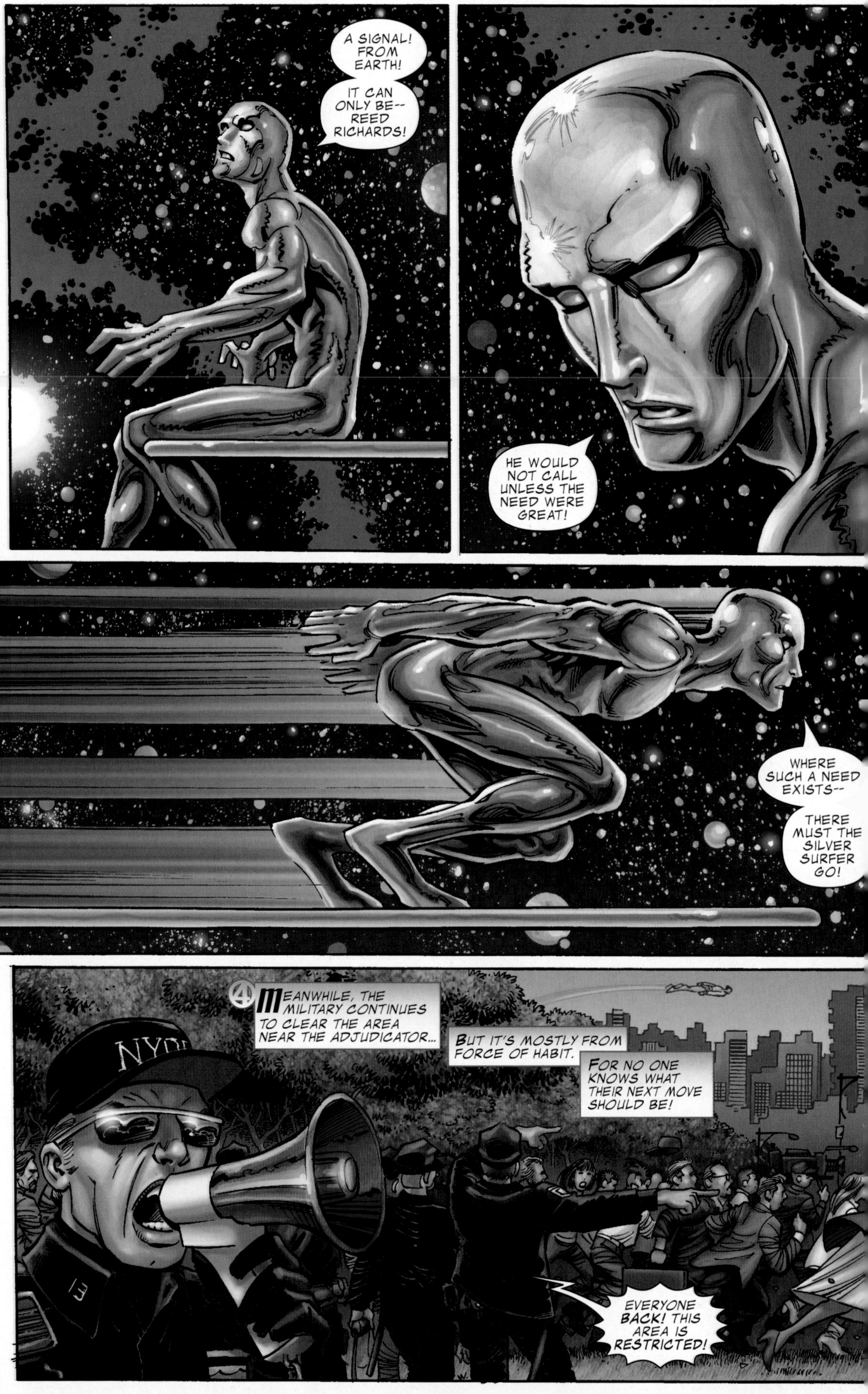
A SIGNAL! FROM EARTH!
IT CAN ONLY BE-- REED RICHARDS!
HE WOULD NOT CALL UNLESS THE NEED WERE GREAT!
WHERE SUCH A NEED EXISTS--
THERE MUST THE SILVER SURFER GO!
MEANWHILE, THE MILITARY CONTINUES TO CLEAR THE AREA NEAR THE ADJUDICATOR...
BUT IT'S MOSTLY FROM FORCE OF HABIT.
FOR NO ONE KNOWS WHAT THEIR NEXT MOVE SHOULD BE!
EVERYONE BACK! THIS AREA IS RESTRICTED!

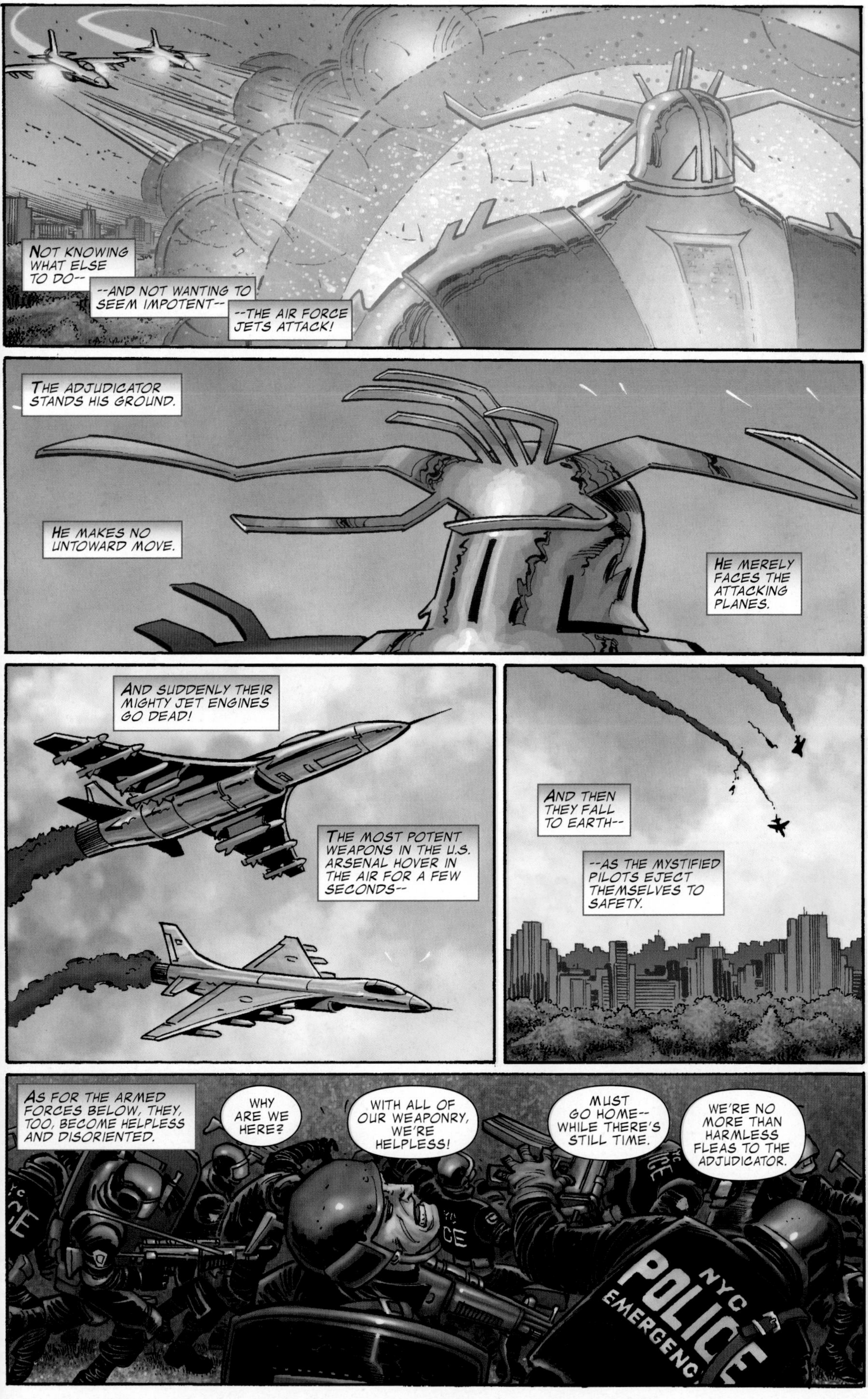
NOT KNOWING WHAT ELSE TO DO--
--AND NOT WANTING TO SEEM IMPOTENT--
--THE AIR FORCE JETS ATTACK!
THE ADJUDICATOR STANDS HIS GROUND.
HE MAKES NO UNTOWARD MOVE.
HE MERELY FACES THE ATTACKING PLANES.
AND SUDDENLY THEIR MIGHTY JET ENGINES GO DEAD!
THE MOST POTENT WEAPONS IN THE U.S. ARSENAL HOVER IN THE AIR FOR A FEW SECONDS--
AND THEN THEY FALL TO EARTH--
--AS THE MYSTIFIED PILOTS EJECT THEMSELVES TO SAFETY.
AS FOR THE ARMED FORCES BELOW, THEY, TOO, BECOME HELPLESS AND DISORIENTED.
WHY ARE WE HERE?
WITH ALL OF OUR WEAPONRY, WE'RE HELPLESS!
MUST GO HOME-- WHILE THERE'S STILL TIME.
WE'RE NO MORE THAN HARMLESS FLEAS TO THE ADJUDICATOR.
NYC POLICE EMERGENCY

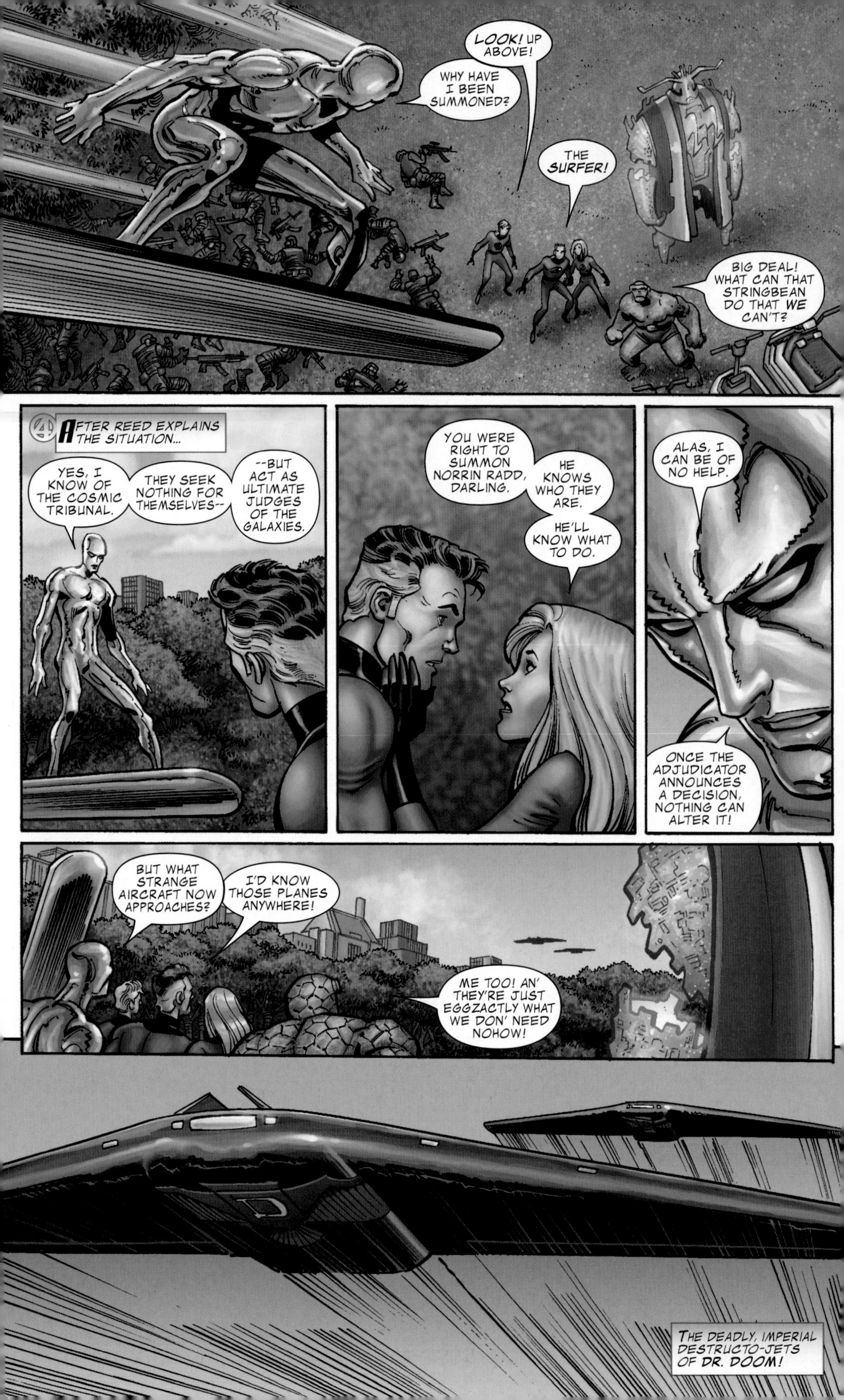
LOOK! UP ABOVE!
WHY HAVE I BEEN SUMMONED?
THE SURFER!
BIG DEAL! WHAT CAN THAT STRINGBEAN DO THAT WE CAN'T?
AFTER REED EXPLAINS THE SITUATION...
YES, I KNOW OF THE COSMIC TRIBUNAL.
THEY SEEK NOTHING FOR THEMSELVES--
--BUT ACT AS ULTIMATE JUDGES OF THE GALAXIES.
YOU WERE RIGHT TO SUMMON NORRIN RADD, DARLING.
HE KNOWS WHO THEY ARE.
HE'LL KNOW WHAT TO DO.
ALAS, I CAN BE OF NO HELP.
ONCE THE ADJUDICATOR ANNOUNCES A DECISION, NOTHING CAN ALTER IT!
BUT WHAT STRANGE AIRCRAFT NOW APPROACHES?
I'D KNOW THOSE PLANES ANYWHERE!
ME TOO! AN' THEY'RE JUST EGGZACTLY WHAT WE DON' NEED NOHOW!
THE DEADLY, IMPERIAL DESTRUCTO-JETS OF DR. DOOM!

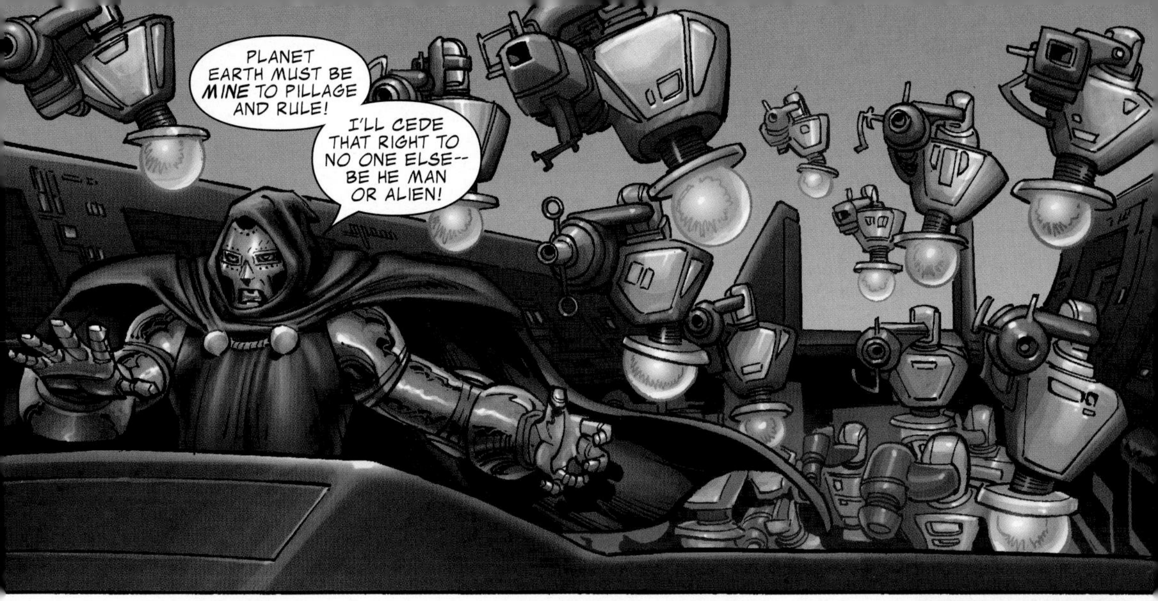
PLANET EARTH MUST BE MINE TO PILLAGE AND RULE!
I'LL CEDE THAT RIGHT TO NO ONE ELSE-- BE HE MAN OR ALIEN!

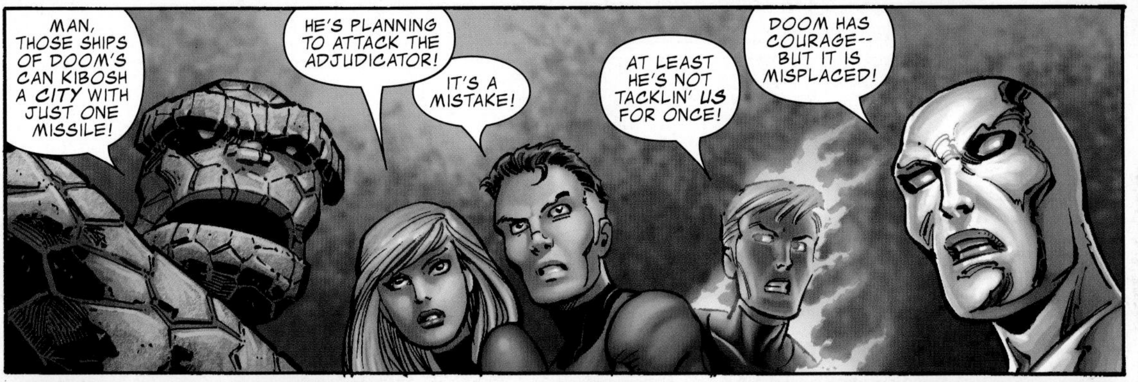
MAN, THOSE SHIPS OF DOOM'S CAN KIBOSH A CITY WITH JUST ONE MISSILE!
HE'S PLANNING TO ATTACK THE ADJUDICATOR!
IT'S A MISTAKE!
AT LEAST HE'S NOT TACKLIN' US FOR ONCE!
DOOM HAS COURAGE-- BUT IT IS MISPLACED!

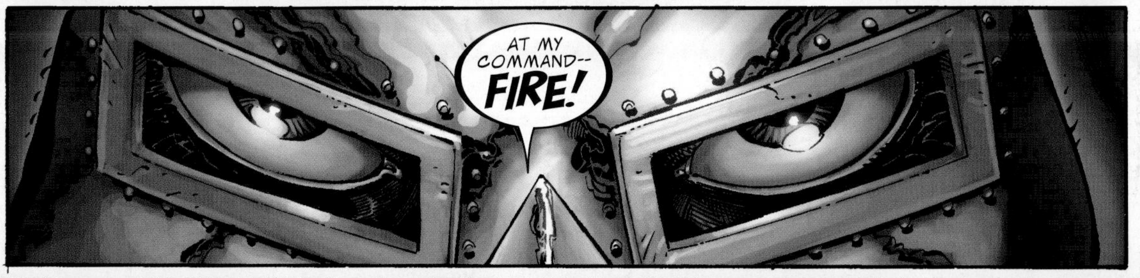
AT MY COMMAND-- FIRE!

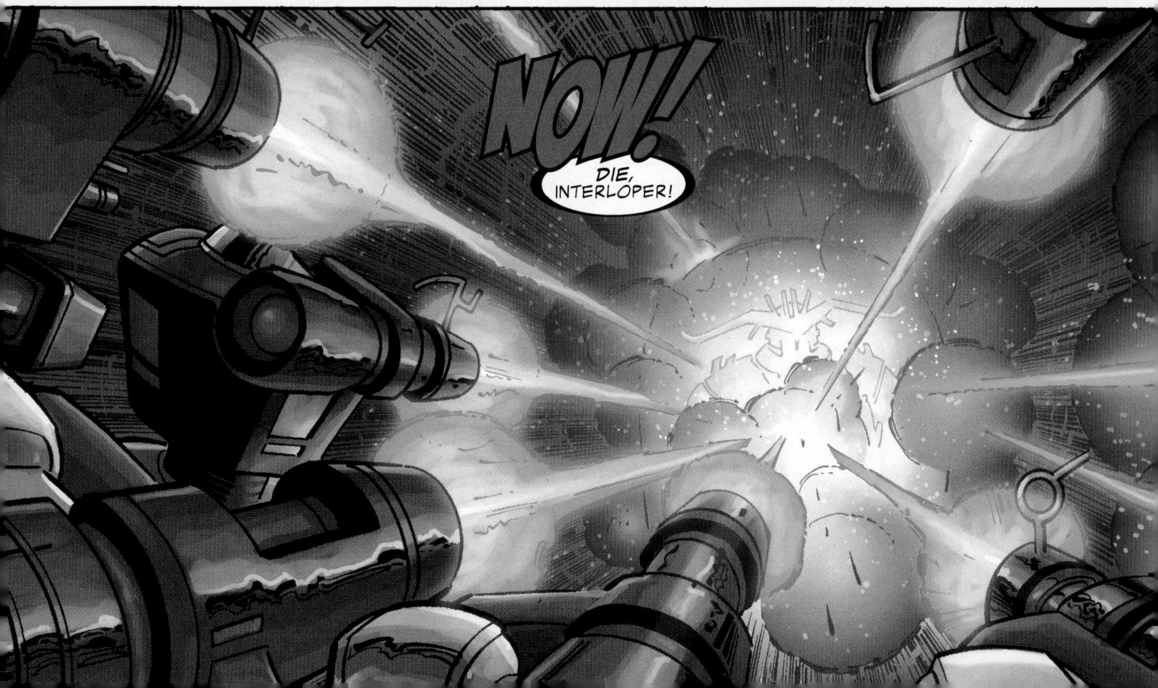
NOW!
DIE, INTERLOPER!

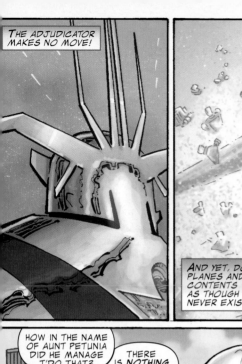

THE ADJUDICATOR MAKES NO MOVE!

AND YET, DOOM'S PLANES AND THEIR CONTENTS VANISH AS THOUGH THEY NEVER EXISTED!

HOW IN THE NAME OF AUNT PETUNIA DID HE MANAGE T'DO THAT?

THERE IS *NOTHING* THEY CANNOT DO!

REMEMBER, THEIRS IS THE POWER OF THOUGHT.

WHATEVER THEY THINK-- COMES TO PASS!

THEN-- WE'RE ALL DONE FOR!

HAVING SEEN THE PREVIOUS INCIDENTS ON WORLDWIDE TV, ALL ACROSS PLANET EARTH PEOPLE REALIZE--

--THE HUMAN RACE IS DOOMED!

PERHAPS THERE IS STILL A CHANCE!

TO ME, MY BOARD!

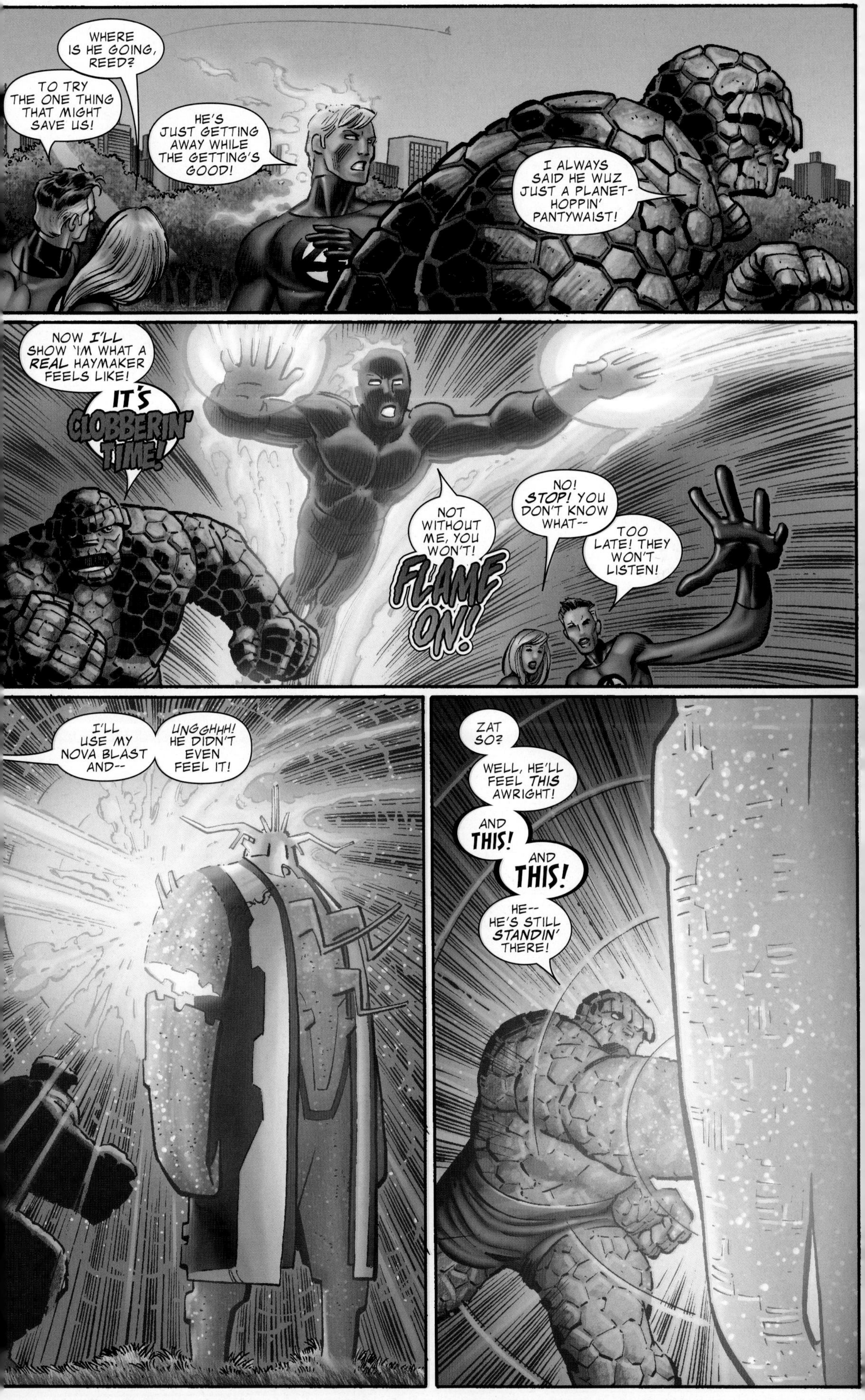
WHERE IS HE GOING, REED?
TO TRY THE ONE THING THAT MIGHT SAVE US!
HE'S JUST GETTING AWAY WHILE THE GETTING'S GOOD!
I ALWAYS SAID HE WUZ JUST A PLANET-HOPPIN' PANTYWAIST!
NOW I'LL SHOW 'IM WHAT A REAL HAYMAKER FEELS LIKE!
IT'S CLOBBERIN' TIME!
NOT WITHOUT ME, YOU WON'T!
FLAME ON!
NO! STOP! YOU DON'T KNOW WHAT--
TOO LATE! THEY WON'T LISTEN!
I'LL USE MY NOVA BLAST AND--
UNGGHHH! HE DIDN'T EVEN FEEL IT!
ZAT SO?
WELL, HE'LL FEEL THIS AWRIGHT!
AND THIS!
AND THIS!
HE-- HE'S STILL STANDIN' THERE!

UNABLE TO STAY BEHIND, DESPITE THE SEEMING HOPELESSNESS OF THE SITUATION, OTHER SUPER HEROES JOIN THE ATTACK...

THE TRUE TEST OF A WARRIOR IS FIGHTING WHEN THERE SEEMS TO BE NO HOPE!

THERE IS EVER HOPE WHILST LIFE ENDURES!

WHAT BETTER WAY TO DIE THAN TO DO SO FOR A CAUSE!

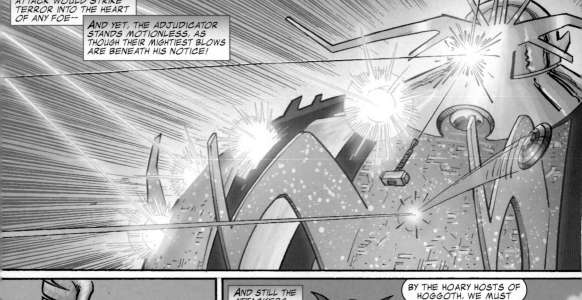

THREE HEROES WHOSE ATTACK WOULD STRIKE TERROR INTO THE HEART OF ANY FOE--

AND YET, THE ADJUDICATOR STANDS MOTIONLESS, AS THOUGH THEIR MIGHTIEST BLOWS ARE BENEATH HIS NOTICE!

WHAT MANNER OF BEING IS HE WHO CAN WITHSTAND THE ONSLAUGHT OF MIGHTY MJOLNIR?!

DON'T SWEAT IT, THOR. MY SHIELD DIDN'T EVEN TICKLE HIM, EITHER!

AND STILL THE ATTACKERS COME!

BY THE HOARY HOSTS OF HOGGOTH, WE MUST PREVAIL!

PERSONALLY, I'M BANKING ON MY ARMOR!

PERHAPS MY THOUGHTS CAN COUNTERACT HIS!

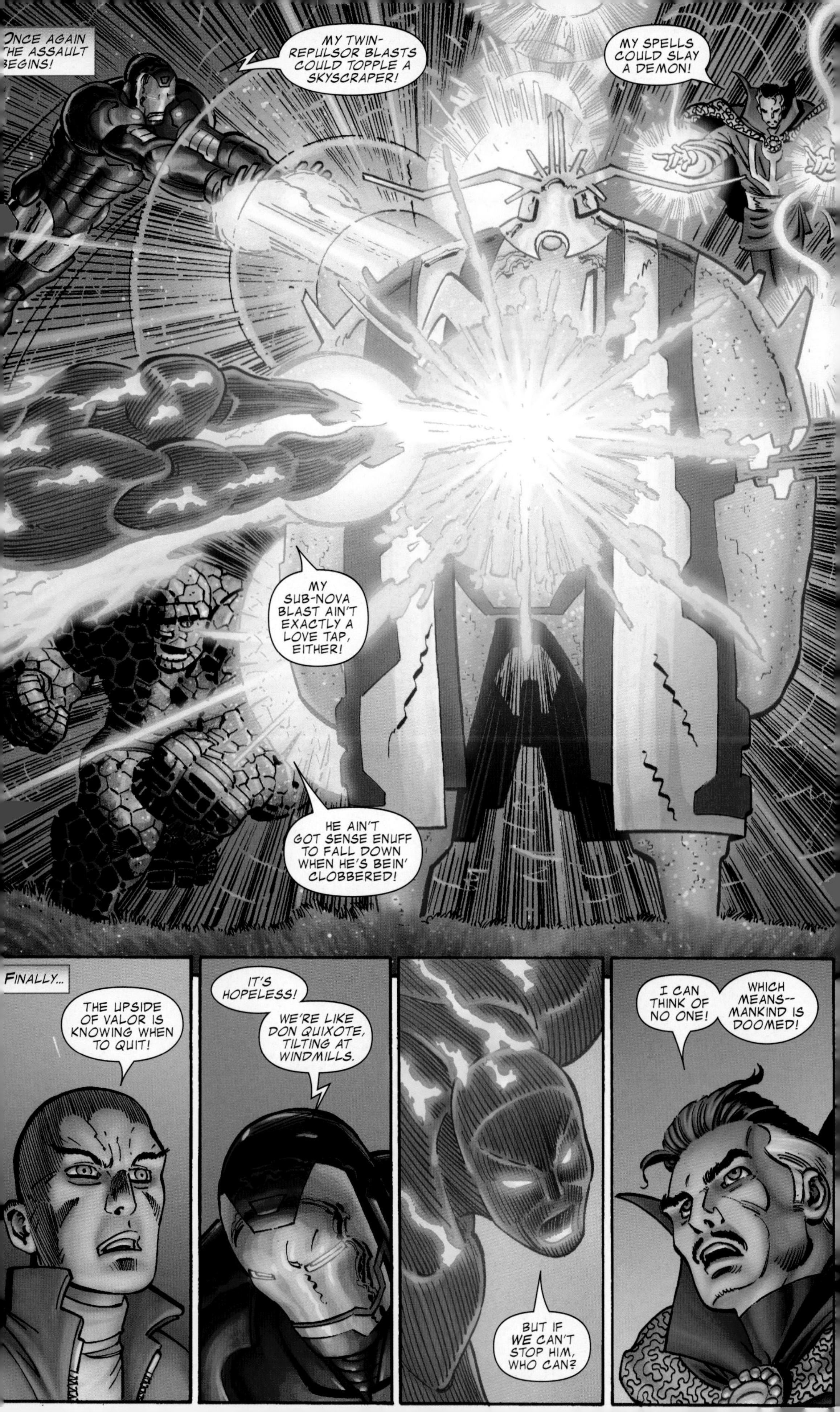

ONCE AGAIN THE ASSAULT BEGINS!
MY TWIN-REPULSOR BLASTS COULD TOPPLE A SKYSCRAPER!
MY SPELLS COULD SLAY A DEMON!
MY SUB-NOVA BLAST AIN'T EXACTLY A LOVE TAP, EITHER!
HE AIN'T GOT SENSE ENUFF TO FALL DOWN WHEN HE'S BEIN' CLOBBERED!
FINALLY...
THE UPSIDE OF VALOR IS KNOWING WHEN TO QUIT!
IT'S HOPELESS!
WE'RE LIKE DON QUIXOTE, TILTING AT WINDMILLS.
BUT IF WE CAN'T STOP HIM, WHO CAN?
I CAN THINK OF NO ONE!
WHICH MEANS-- MANKIND IS DOOMED!

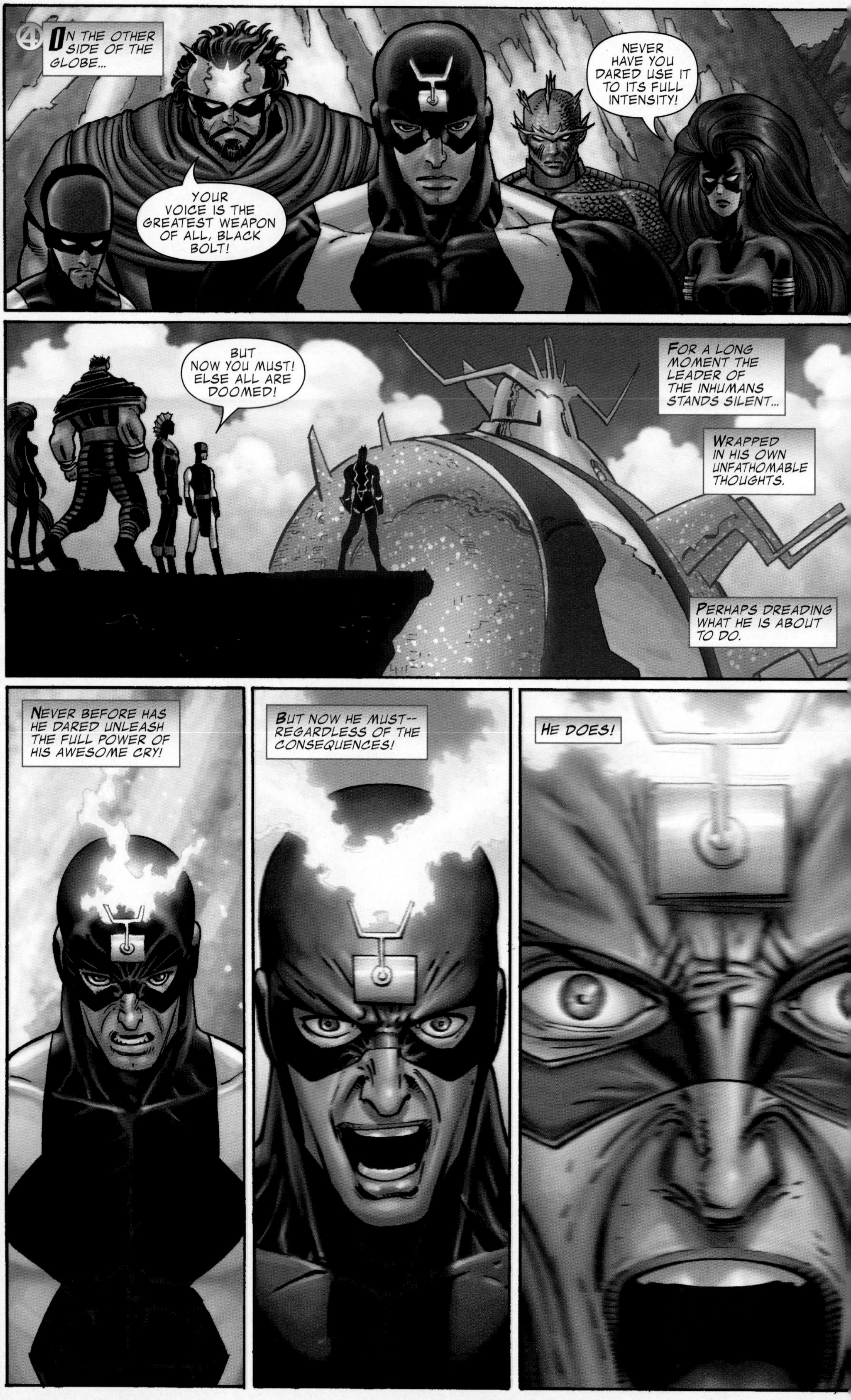
ON THE OTHER SIDE OF THE GLOBE...
YOUR VOICE IS THE GREATEST WEAPON OF ALL, BLACK BOLT!
NEVER HAVE YOU DARED USE IT TO ITS FULL INTENSITY!
BUT NOW YOU MUST! ELSE ALL ARE DOOMED!
FOR A LONG MOMENT THE LEADER OF THE INHUMANS STANDS SILENT...
WRAPPED IN HIS OWN UNFATHOMABLE THOUGHTS.
PERHAPS DREADING WHAT HE IS ABOUT TO DO.
NEVER BEFORE HAS HE DARED UNLEASH THE FULL POWER OF HIS AWESOME CRY!
BUT NOW HE MUST-- REGARDLESS OF THE CONSEQUENCES!
HE DOES!

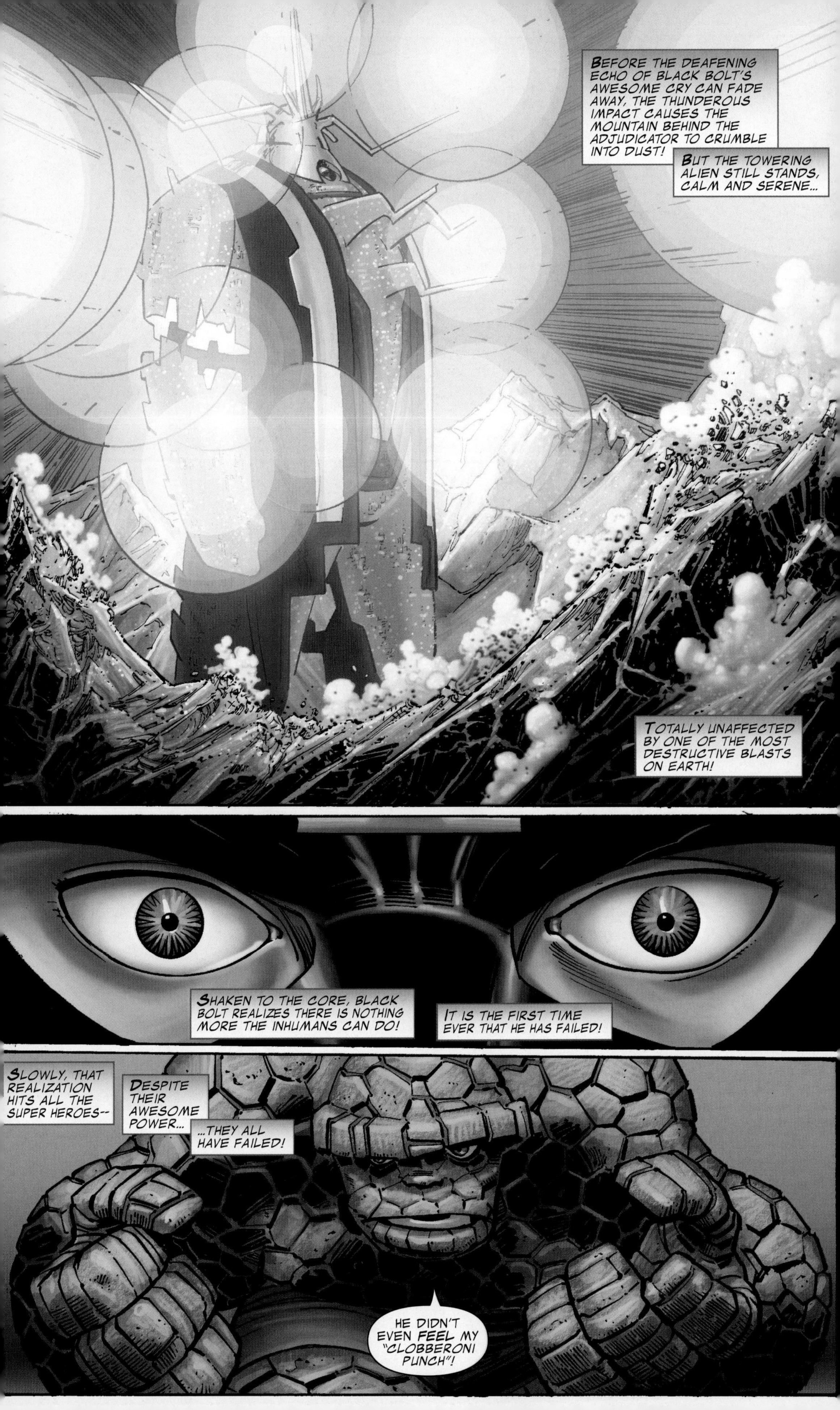

BEFORE THE DEAFENING ECHO OF BLACK BOLT'S AWESOME CRY CAN FADE AWAY, THE THUNDEROUS IMPACT CAUSES THE MOUNTAIN BEHIND THE ADJUDICATOR TO CRUMBLE INTO DUST!
BUT THE TOWERING ALIEN STILL STANDS, CALM AND SERENE...
TOTALLY UNAFFECTED BY ONE OF THE MOST DESTRUCTIVE BLASTS ON EARTH!
SHAKEN TO THE CORE, BLACK BOLT REALIZES THERE IS NOTHING MORE THE INHUMANS CAN DO!
IT IS THE FIRST TIME EVER THAT HE HAS FAILED!
SLOWLY, THAT REALIZATION HITS ALL THE SUPER HEROES--
DESPITE THEIR AWESOME POWER...
...THEY ALL HAVE FAILED!
HE DIDN'T EVEN **FEEL** MY "CLOBBERONI PUNCH"!

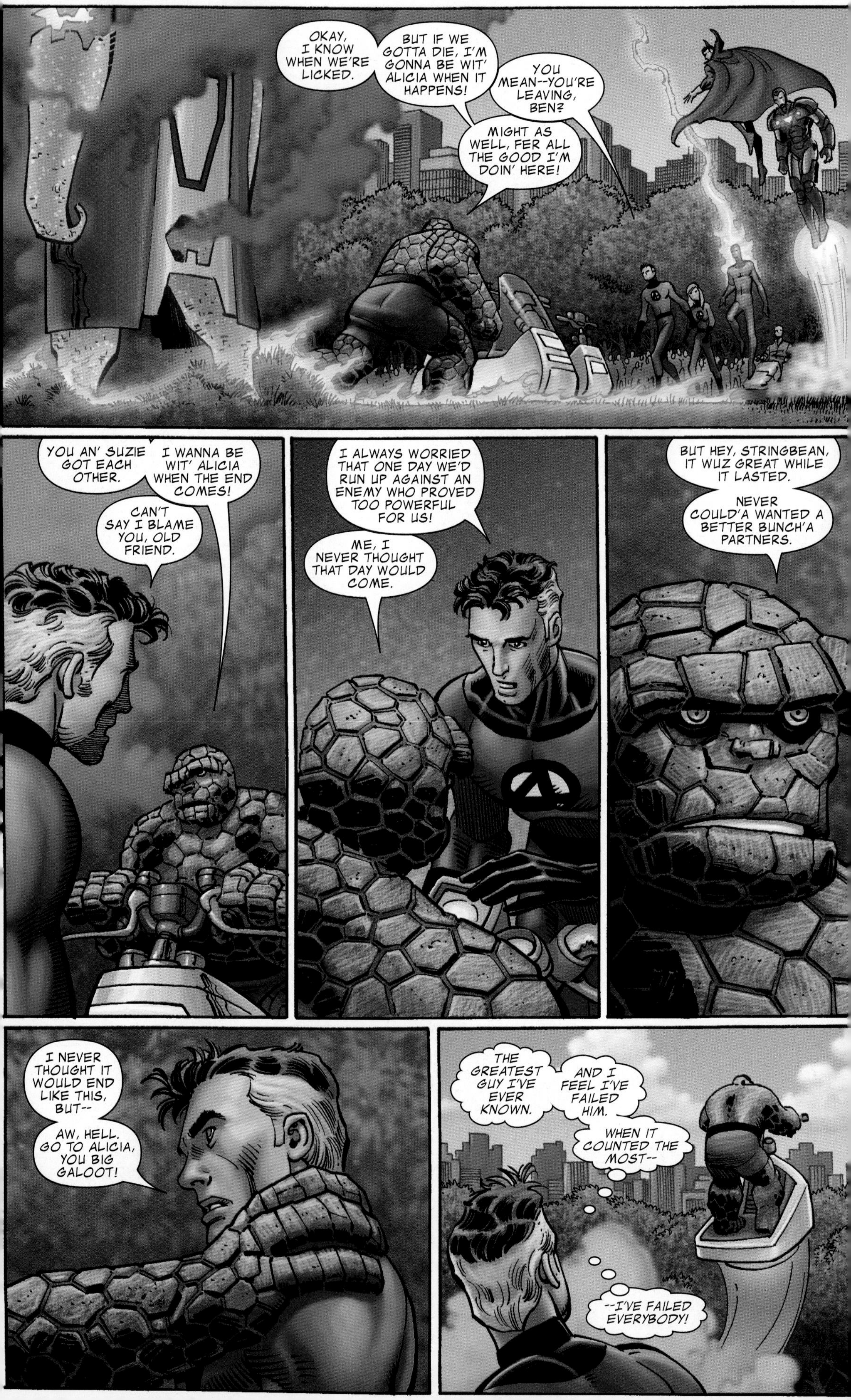

OKAY, I KNOW WHEN WE'RE LICKED.
BUT IF WE GOTTA DIE, I'M GONNA BE WIT' ALICIA WHEN IT HAPPENS!
YOU MEAN--YOU'RE LEAVING, BEN?
MIGHT AS WELL, FER ALL THE GOOD I'M DOIN' HERE!
YOU AN' SUZIE GOT EACH OTHER.
I WANNA BE WIT' ALICIA WHEN THE END COMES!
CAN'T SAY I BLAME YOU, OLD FRIEND.
I ALWAYS WORRIED THAT ONE DAY WE'D RUN UP AGAINST AN ENEMY WHO PROVED TOO POWERFUL FOR US!
ME, I NEVER THOUGHT THAT DAY WOULD COME.
BUT HEY, STRINGBEAN, IT WUZ GREAT WHILE IT LASTED.
NEVER COULD'A WANTED A BETTER BUNCH'A PARTNERS.
I NEVER THOUGHT IT WOULD END LIKE THIS, BUT--
AW, HELL. GO TO ALICIA, YOU BIG GALOOT!
THE GREATEST GUY I'VE EVER KNOWN.
AND I FEEL I'VE FAILED HIM.
WHEN IT COUNTED THE MOST--
--I'VE FAILED EVERYBODY!

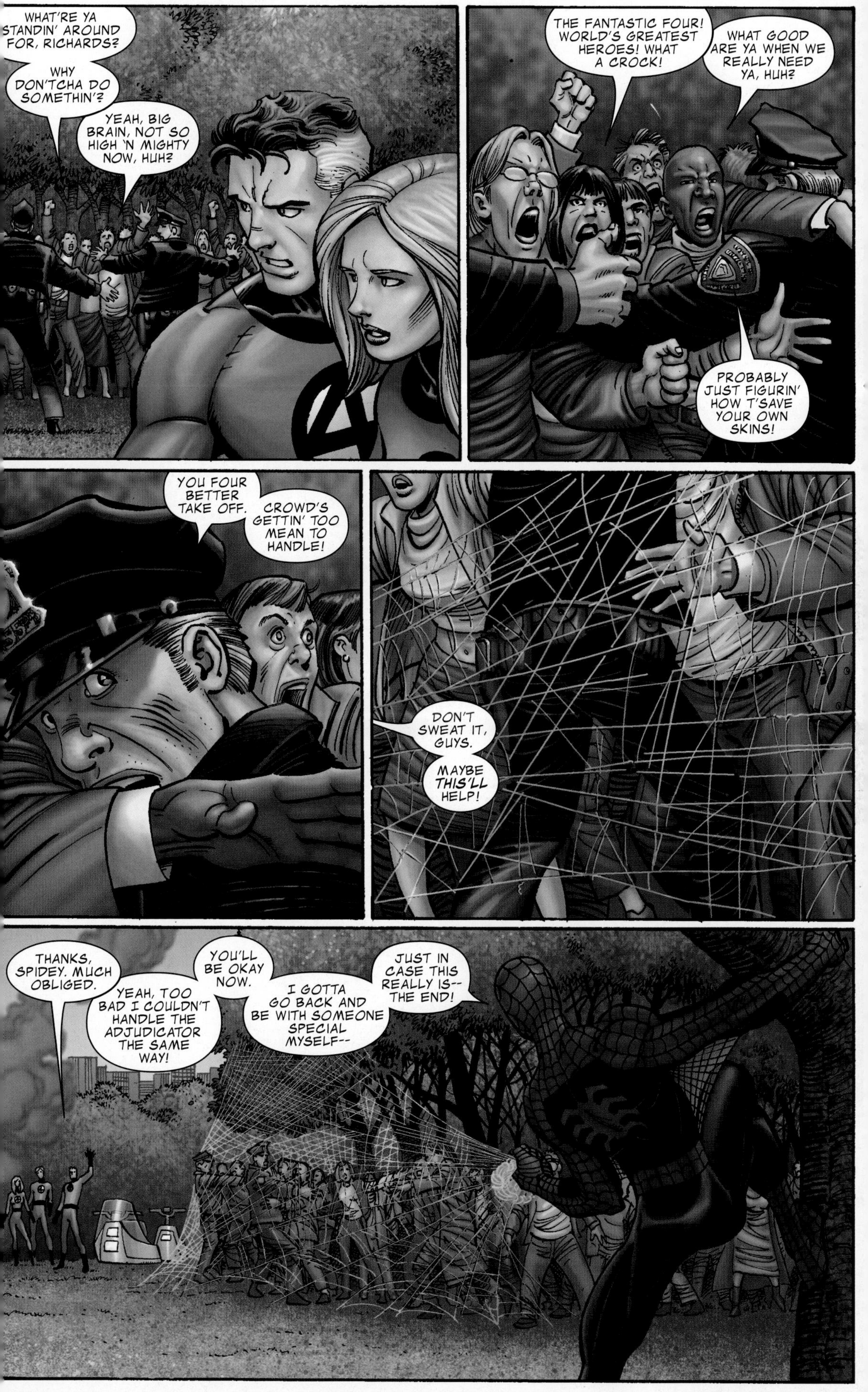
WHAT'RE YA STANDIN' AROUND FOR, RICHARDS?
WHY DON'TCHA DO SOMETHIN'?
YEAH, BIG BRAIN, NOT SO HIGH 'N MIGHTY NOW, HUH?
THE FANTASTIC FOUR! WORLD'S GREATEST HEROES! WHAT A CROCK!
WHAT GOOD ARE YA WHEN WE REALLY NEED YA, HUH?
PROBABLY JUST FIGURIN' HOW T'SAVE YOUR OWN SKINS!
YOU FOUR BETTER TAKE OFF.
CROWD'S GETTIN' TOO MEAN TO HANDLE!
DON'T SWEAT IT, GUYS.
MAYBE *THIS'LL* HELP!
THANKS, SPIDEY. MUCH OBLIGED.
YEAH, TOO BAD I COULDN'T HANDLE THE ADJUDICATOR THE SAME WAY!
YOU'LL BE OKAY NOW.
I GOTTA GO BACK AND BE WITH SOMEONE SPECIAL MYSELF--
JUST IN CASE THIS REALLY IS-- THE END!

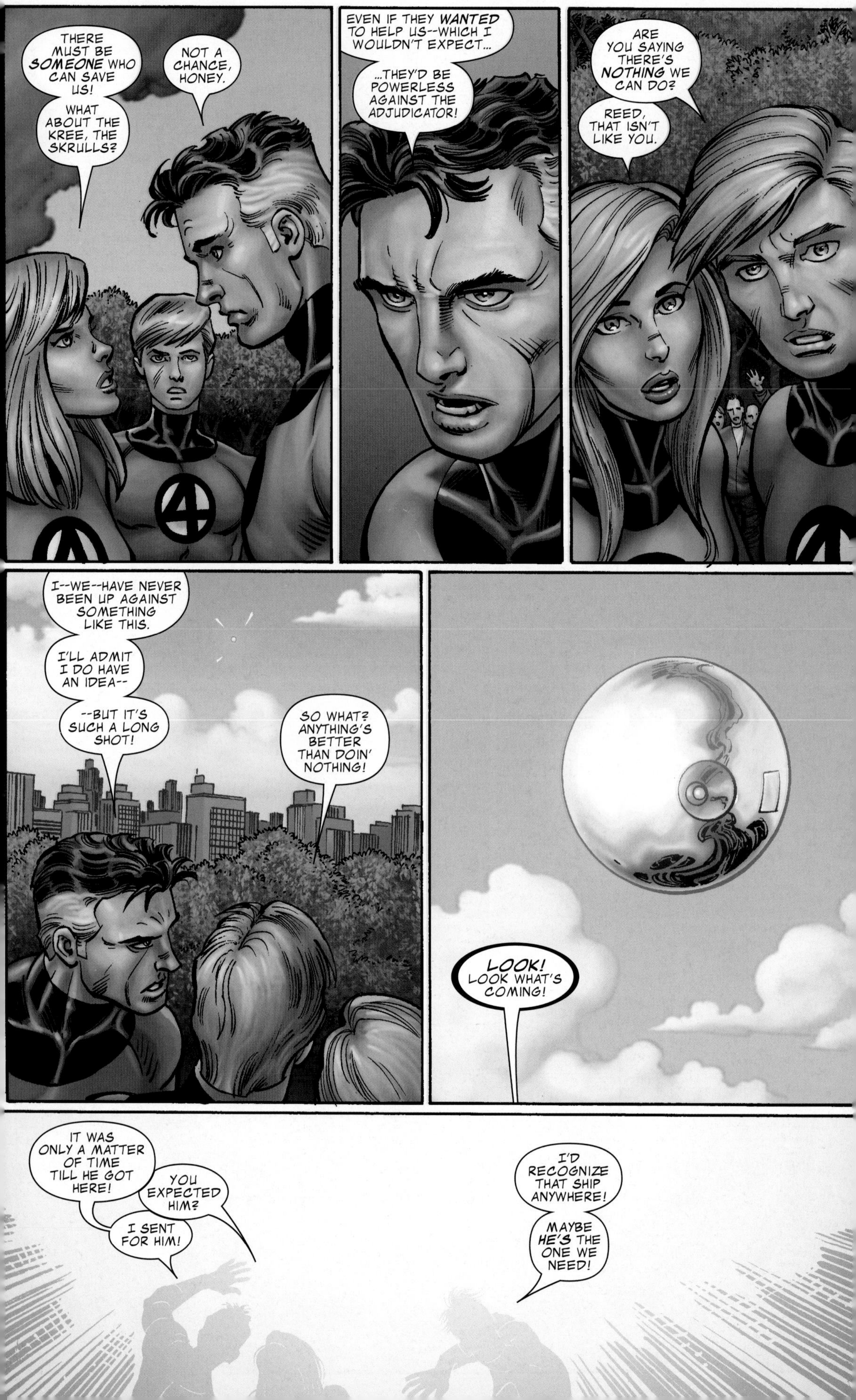
THERE MUST BE SOMEONE WHO CAN SAVE US!
WHAT ABOUT THE KREE, THE SKRULLS?
NOT A CHANCE, HONEY.
EVEN IF THEY WANTED TO HELP US--WHICH I WOULDN'T EXPECT...
...THEY'D BE POWERLESS AGAINST THE ADJUDICATOR!
ARE YOU SAYING THERE'S NOTHING WE CAN DO?
REED, THAT ISN'T LIKE YOU.
I--WE--HAVE NEVER BEEN UP AGAINST SOMETHING LIKE THIS.
I'LL ADMIT I DO HAVE AN IDEA--
--BUT IT'S SUCH A LONG SHOT!
SO WHAT? ANYTHING'S BETTER THAN DOIN' NOTHING!
LOOK! LOOK WHAT'S COMING!
IT WAS ONLY A MATTER OF TIME TILL HE GOT HERE!
YOU EXPECTED HIM?
I SENT FOR HIM!
I'D RECOGNIZE THAT SHIP ANYWHERE!
MAYBE HE'S THE ONE WE NEED!

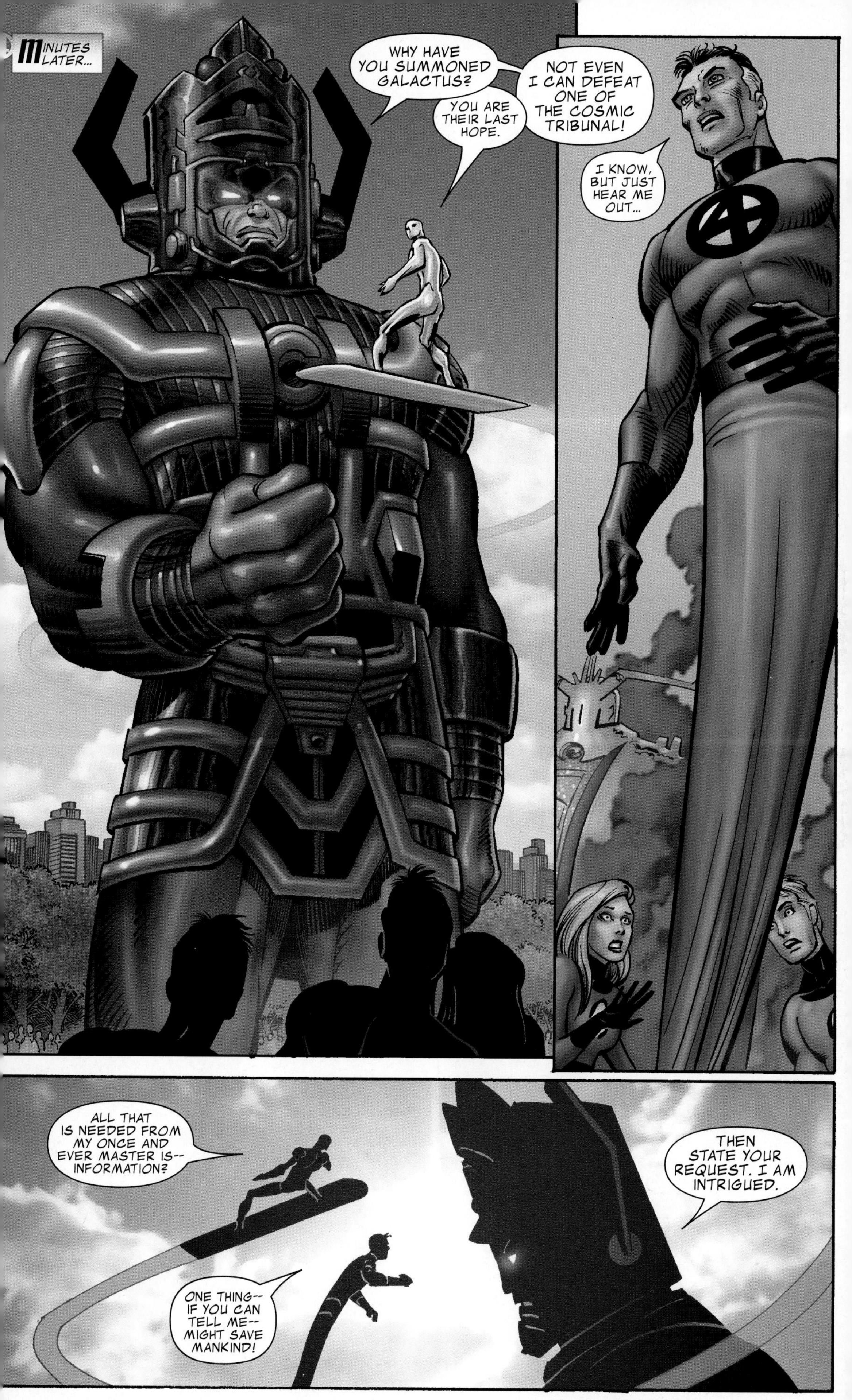
MINUTES LATER...
WHY HAVE YOU SUMMONED GALACTUS?
YOU ARE THEIR LAST HOPE.
NOT EVEN I CAN DEFEAT ONE OF THE COSMIC TRIBUNAL!
I KNOW, BUT JUST HEAR ME OUT...
ALL THAT IS NEEDED FROM MY ONCE AND EVER MASTER IS-- INFORMATION?
THEN STATE YOUR REQUEST. I AM INTRIGUED.
ONE THING-- IF YOU CAN TELL ME-- MIGHT SAVE MANKIND!

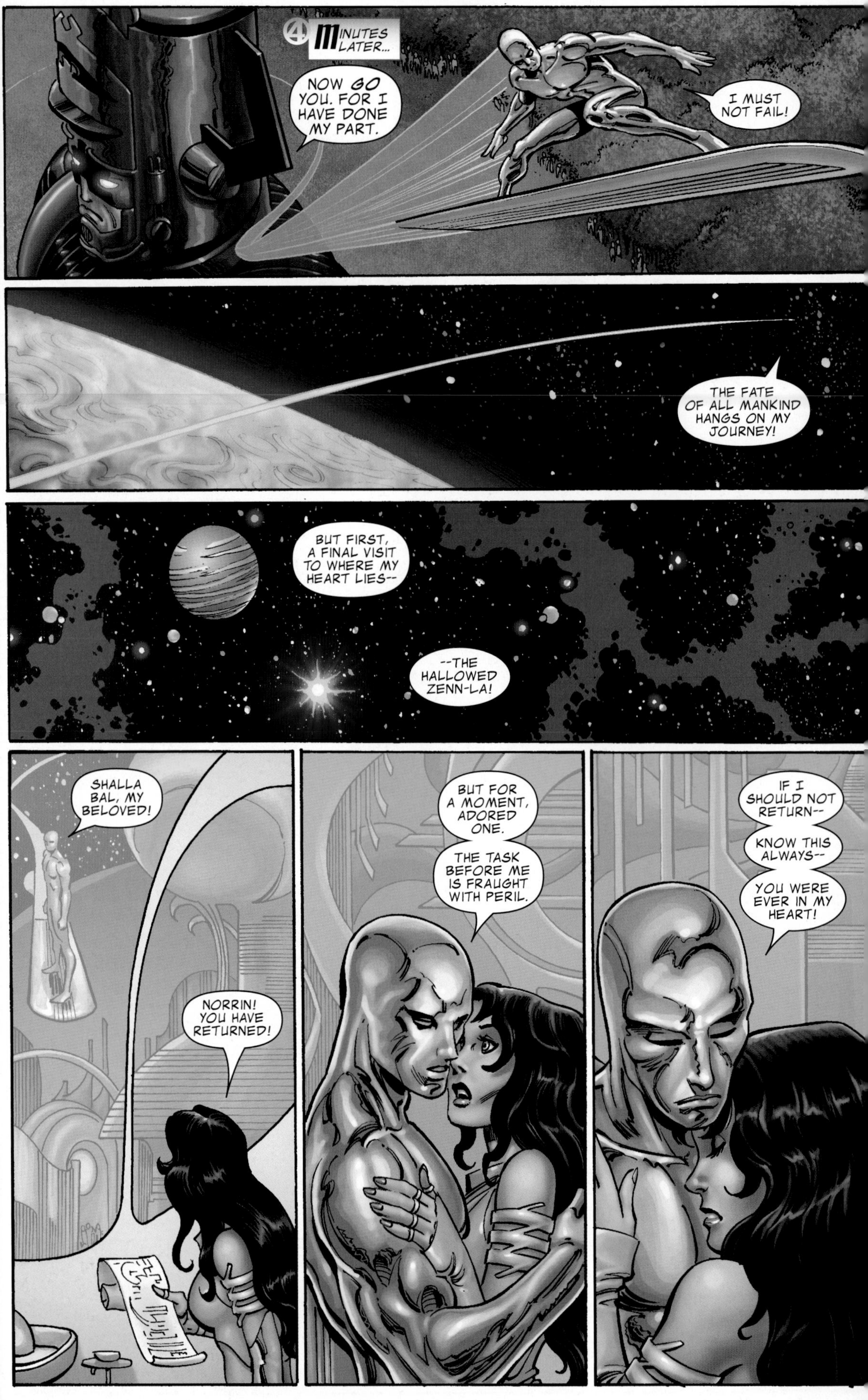

MINUTES LATER...
NOW GO YOU. FOR I HAVE DONE MY PART.
I MUST NOT FAIL!
THE FATE OF ALL MANKIND HANGS ON MY JOURNEY!
BUT FIRST, A FINAL VISIT TO WHERE MY HEART LIES--
--THE HALLOWED ZENN-LA!
SHALLA BAL, MY BELOVED!
NORRIN! YOU HAVE RETURNED!
BUT FOR A MOMENT, ADORED ONE.
THE TASK BEFORE ME IS FRAUGHT WITH PERIL.
IF I SHOULD NOT RETURN--
KNOW THIS ALWAYS--
YOU WERE EVER IN MY HEART!

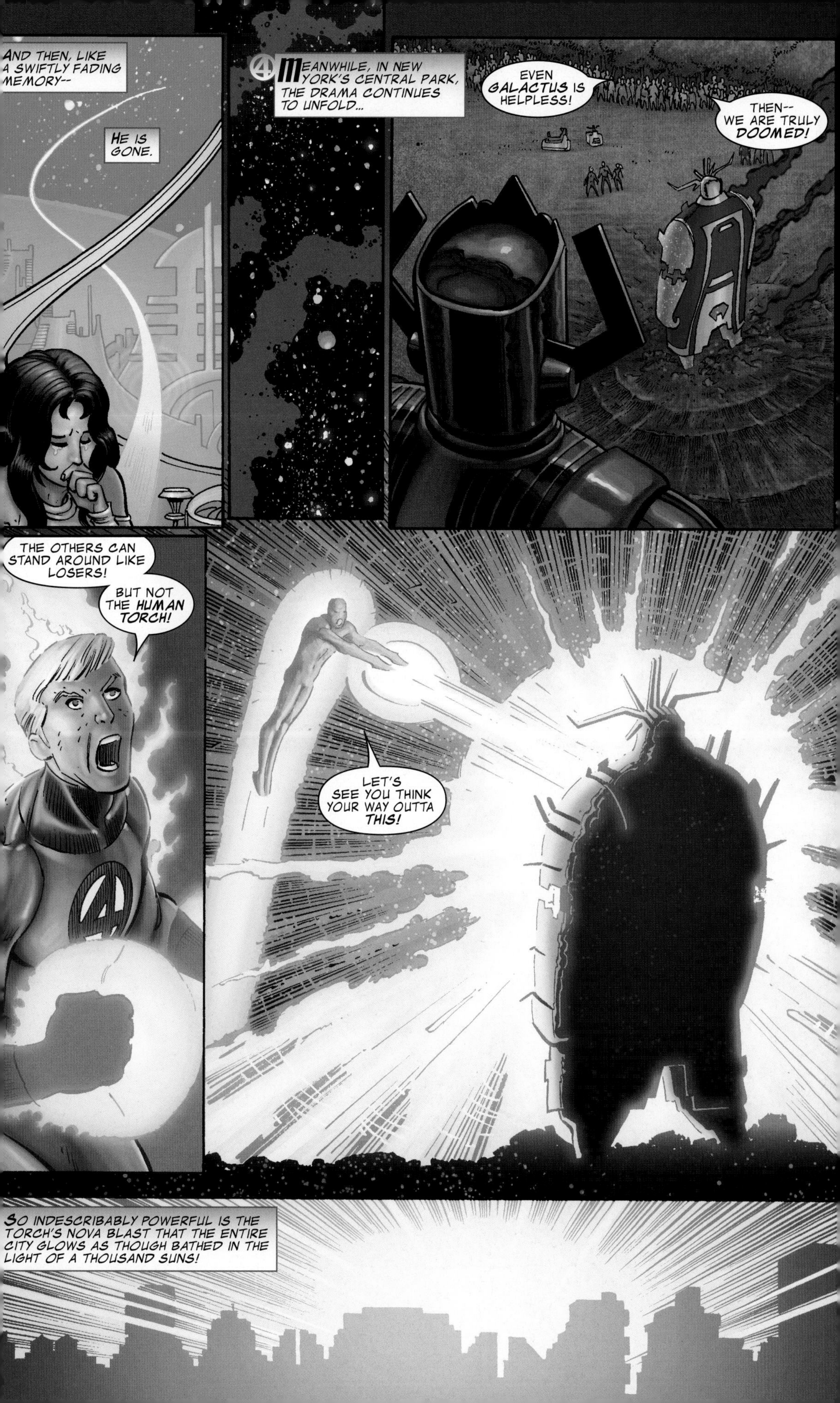

AND THEN, LIKE A SWIFTLY FADING MEMORY--
HE IS GONE.
MEANWHILE, IN NEW YORK'S CENTRAL PARK, THE DRAMA CONTINUES TO UNFOLD...
EVEN GALACTUS IS HELPLESS!
THEN-- WE ARE TRULY DOOMED!
THE OTHERS CAN STAND AROUND LIKE LOSERS!
BUT NOT THE HUMAN TORCH!
LET'S SEE YOU THINK YOUR WAY OUTTA THIS!
SO INDESCRIBABLY POWERFUL IS THE TORCH'S NOVA BLAST THAT THE ENTIRE CITY GLOWS AS THOUGH BATHED IN THE LIGHT OF A THOUSAND SUNS!

BUT, SECONDS LATER, ALL IS BACK TO NORMAL.

AND THE ADJUDICATOR STILL STANDS.

I-I FAILED!

MY STRONGEST BLAST--HE DIDN'T EVEN FEEL IT.

JOHNNY!

WHY DID YOU DO IT, SON?

YOU KNEW HE WAS INVULNERABLE.

I--WANTED-- TO DROWN OUT--ONE THOUGHT--

YOU HAVE EACH OTHER. BEN HAS ALICIA.

EVEN THE SURFER HAS SHALLA BAL.

BUT I'VE WASTED MY TIME PLAYING THE FIELD.

NOW, WITH THE END SO NEAR--

I'VE NO ONE TO TURN TO!

NO LOVE OF MY OWN!

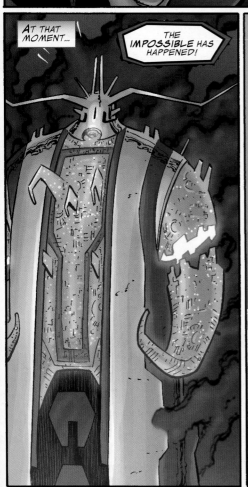

AT THAT MOMENT...

THE IMPOSSIBLE HAS HAPPENED!

UNEXPECTEDLY, THE ADJUDICATOR BEGINS TO GROW TO HIS ORIGINAL SIZE!

DWARFING EVEN THE GIANT GALACTUS!

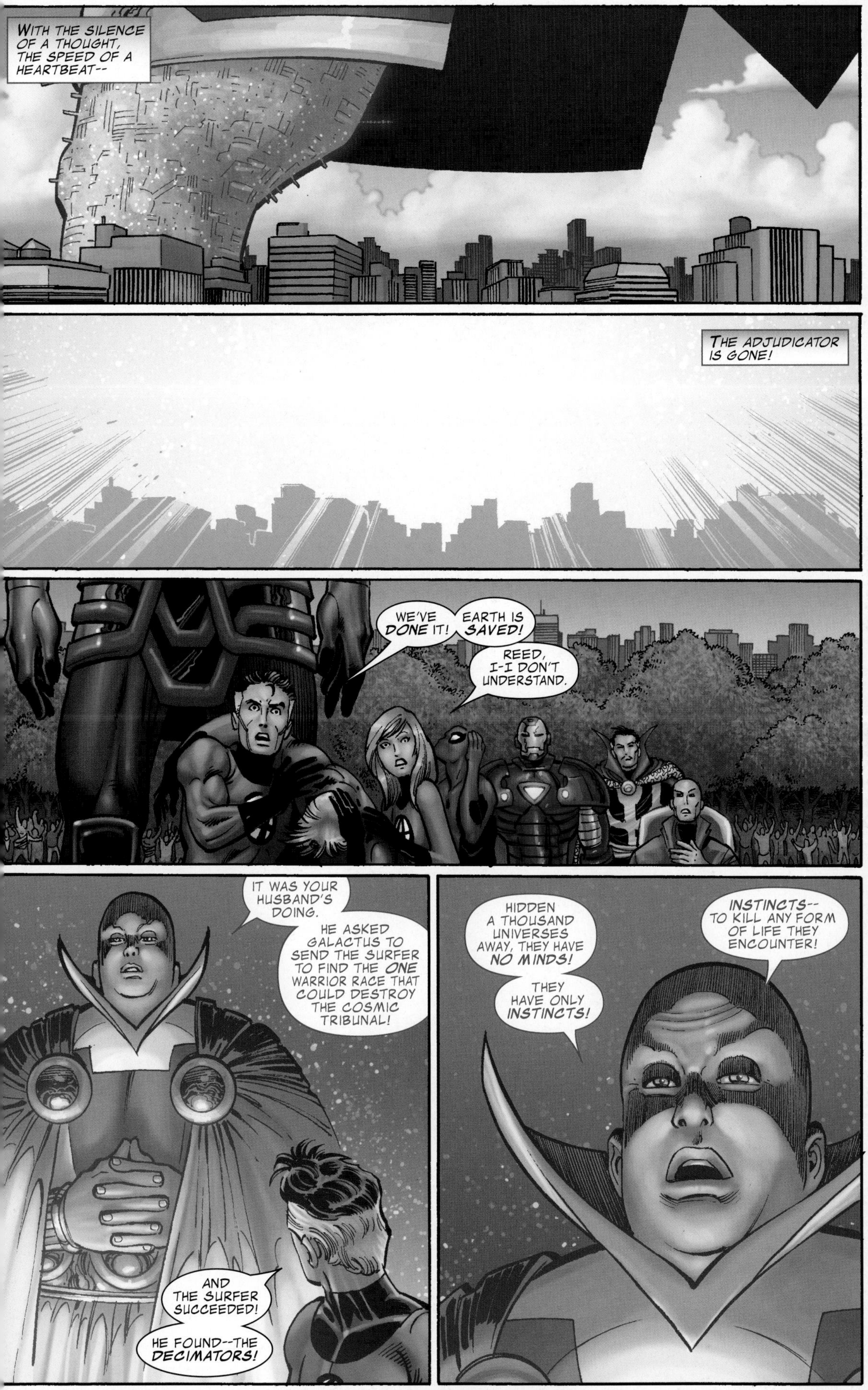
WITH THE SILENCE OF A THOUGHT, THE SPEED OF A HEARTBEAT--
THE ADJUDICATOR IS GONE!
WE'VE DONE IT!
EARTH IS SAVED!
REED, I-I DON'T UNDERSTAND.
IT WAS YOUR HUSBAND'S DOING.
HE ASKED GALACTUS TO SEND THE SURFER TO FIND THE ONE WARRIOR RACE THAT COULD DESTROY THE COSMIC TRIBUNAL!
AND THE SURFER SUCCEEDED!
HE FOUND--THE DECIMATORS!
HIDDEN A THOUSAND UNIVERSES AWAY, THEY HAVE NO MINDS!
THEY HAVE ONLY INSTINCTS!
INSTINCTS-- TO KILL ANY FORM OF LIFE THEY ENCOUNTER!

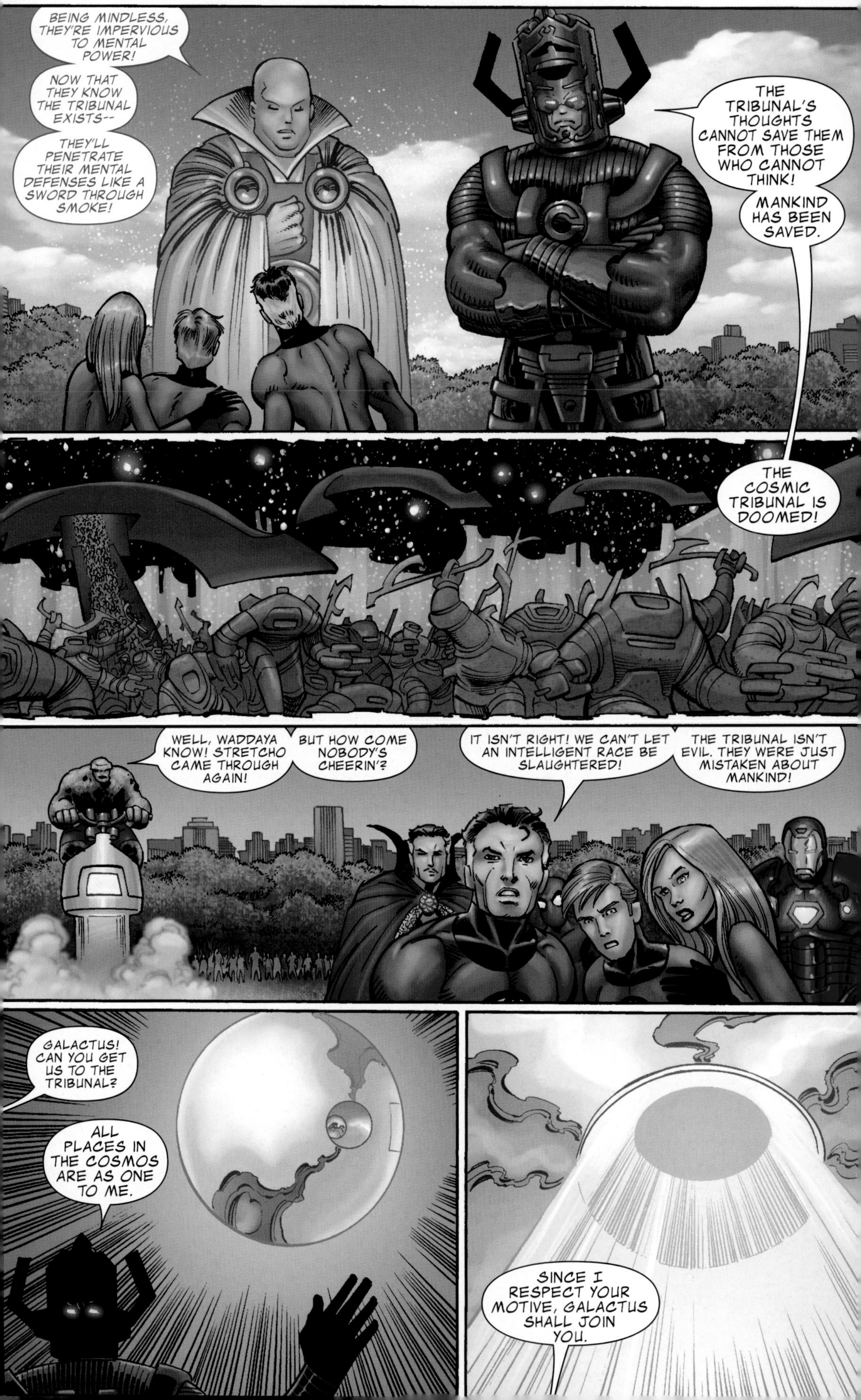
BEING MINDLESS, THEY'RE IMPERVIOUS TO MENTAL POWER!
NOW THAT THEY KNOW THE TRIBUNAL EXISTS--
THEY'LL PENETRATE THEIR MENTAL DEFENSES LIKE A SWORD THROUGH SMOKE!
THE TRIBUNAL'S THOUGHTS CANNOT SAVE THEM FROM THOSE WHO CANNOT THINK!
MANKIND HAS BEEN SAVED.
THE COSMIC TRIBUNAL IS DOOMED!
WELL, WADDAYA KNOW! STRETCHO CAME THROUGH AGAIN!
BUT HOW COME NOBODY'S CHEERIN'?
IT ISN'T RIGHT! WE CAN'T LET AN INTELLIGENT RACE BE SLAUGHTERED!
THE TRIBUNAL ISN'T EVIL. THEY WERE JUST MISTAKEN ABOUT MANKIND!
GALACTUS! CAN YOU GET US TO THE TRIBUNAL?
ALL PLACES IN THE COSMOS ARE AS ONE TO ME.
SINCE I RESPECT YOUR MOTIVE, GALACTUS SHALL JOIN YOU.

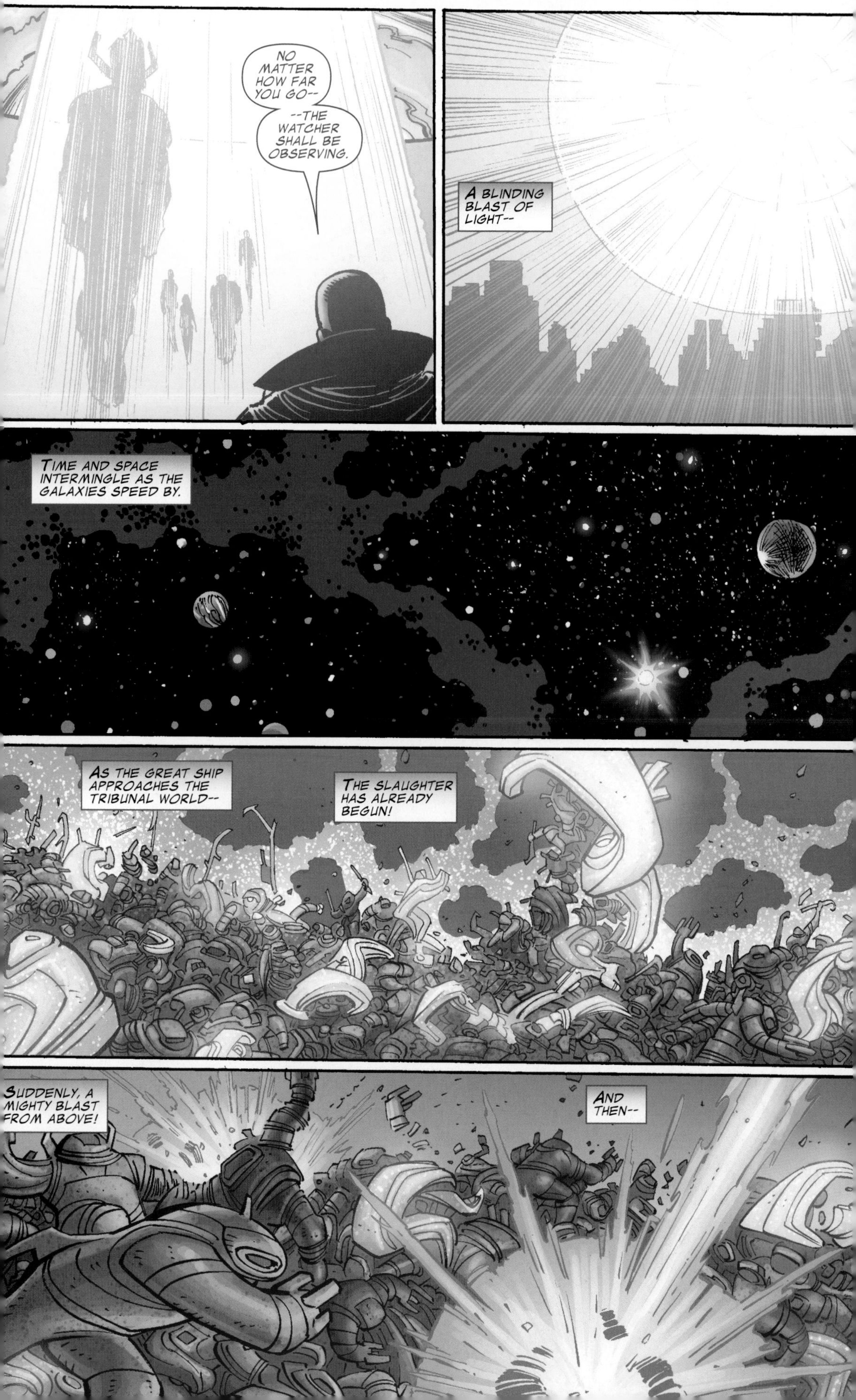

NO MATTER HOW FAR YOU GO--
--THE WATCHER SHALL BE OBSERVING.
A BLINDING BLAST OF LIGHT--
TIME AND SPACE INTERMINGLE AS THE GALAXIES SPEED BY.
AS THE GREAT SHIP APPROACHES THE TRIBUNAL WORLD--
THE SLAUGHTER HAS ALREADY BEGUN!
SUDDENLY, A MIGHTY BLAST FROM ABOVE!
AND THEN--

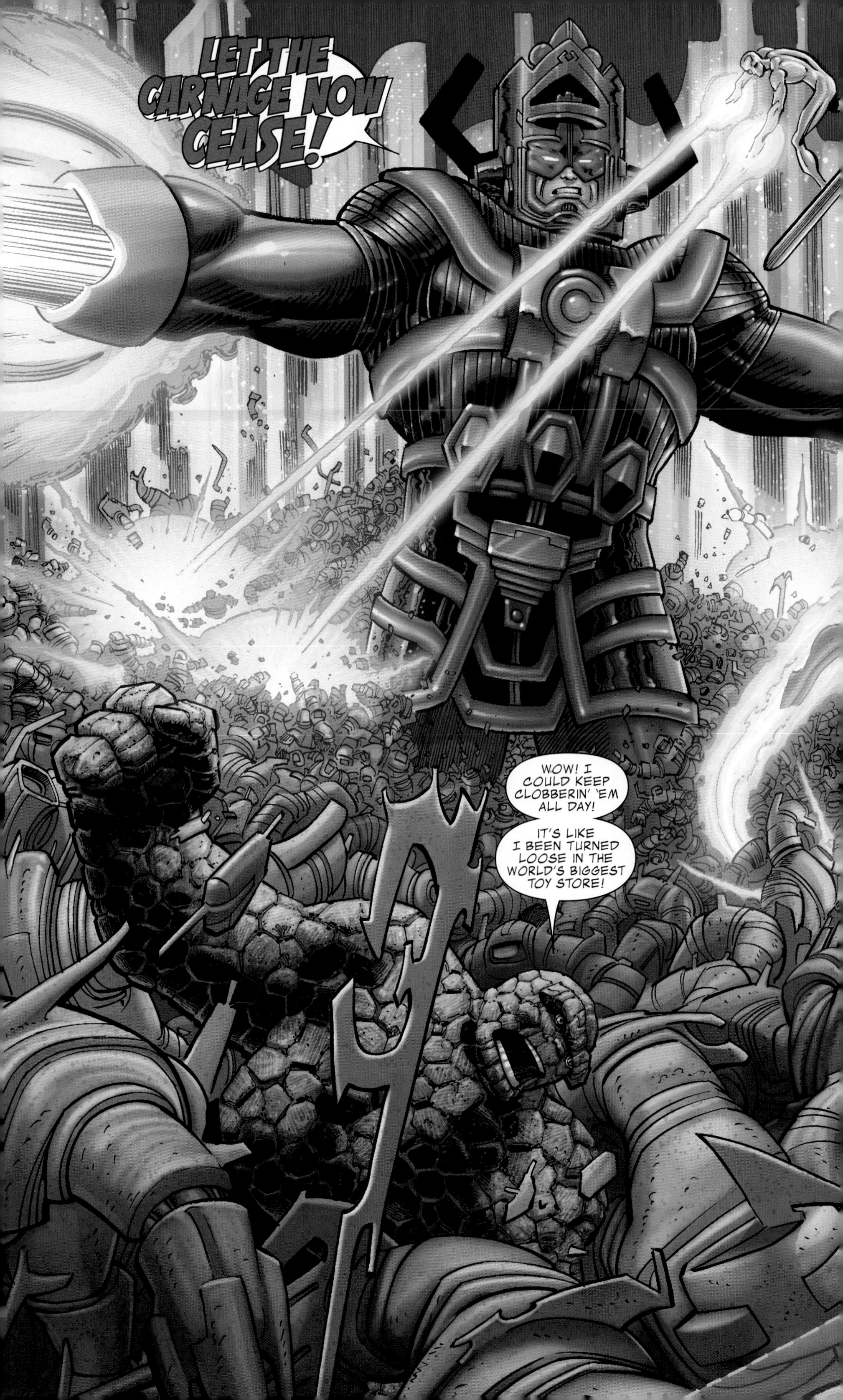
LET THE CARNAGE NOW CEASE!
WOW! I COULD KEEP CLOBBERIN' 'EM ALL DAY!
IT'S LIKE I BEEN TURNED LOOSE IN THE WORLD'S BIGGEST TOY STORE!

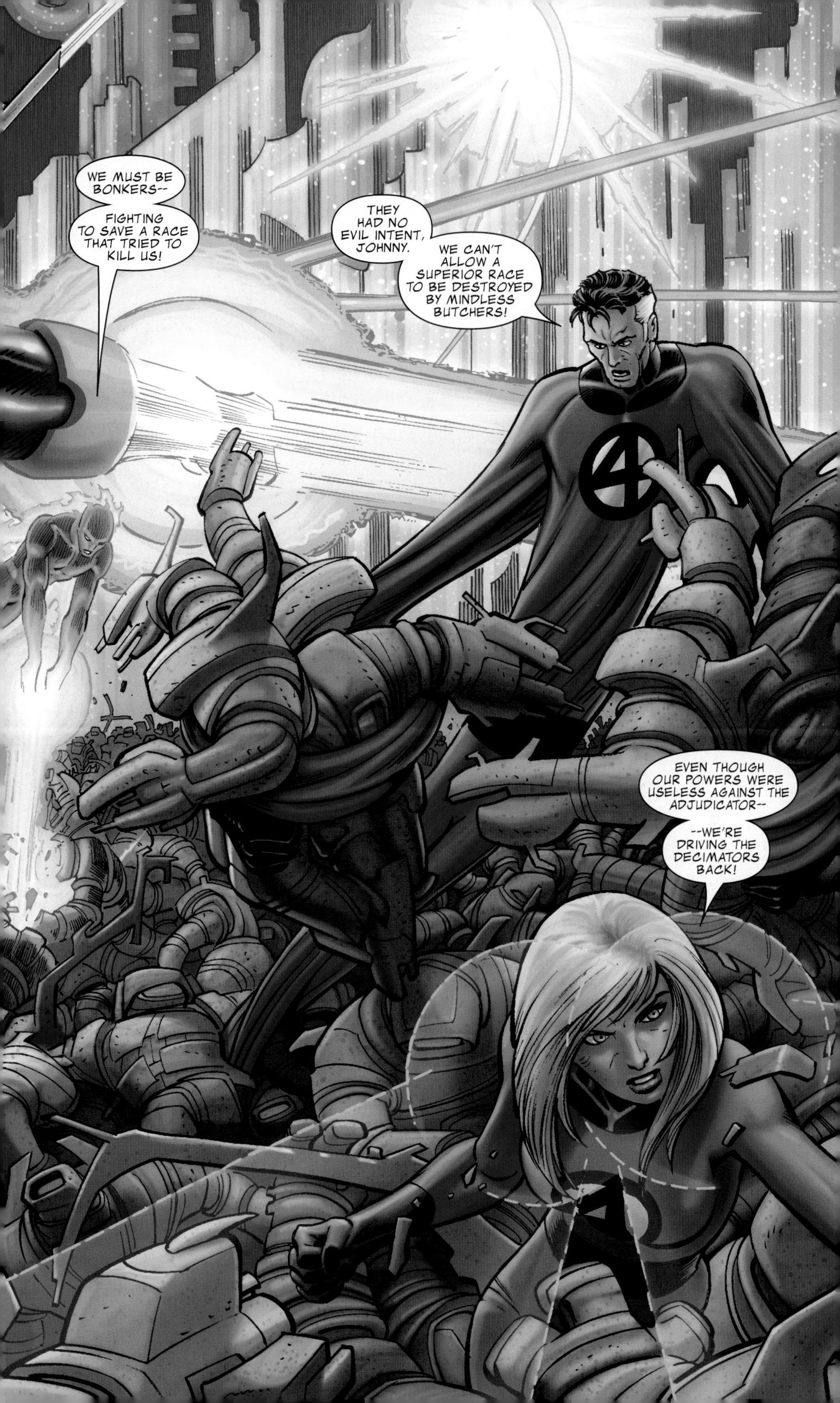
WE MUST BE BONKERS--
FIGHTING TO SAVE A RACE THAT TRIED TO KILL US!
THEY HAD NO EVIL INTENT, JOHNNY.
WE CAN'T ALLOW A SUPERIOR RACE TO BE DESTROYED BY MINDLESS BUTCHERS!
EVEN THOUGH OUR POWERS WERE USELESS AGAINST THE ADJUDICATOR--
--WE'RE DRIVING THE DECIMATORS BACK!

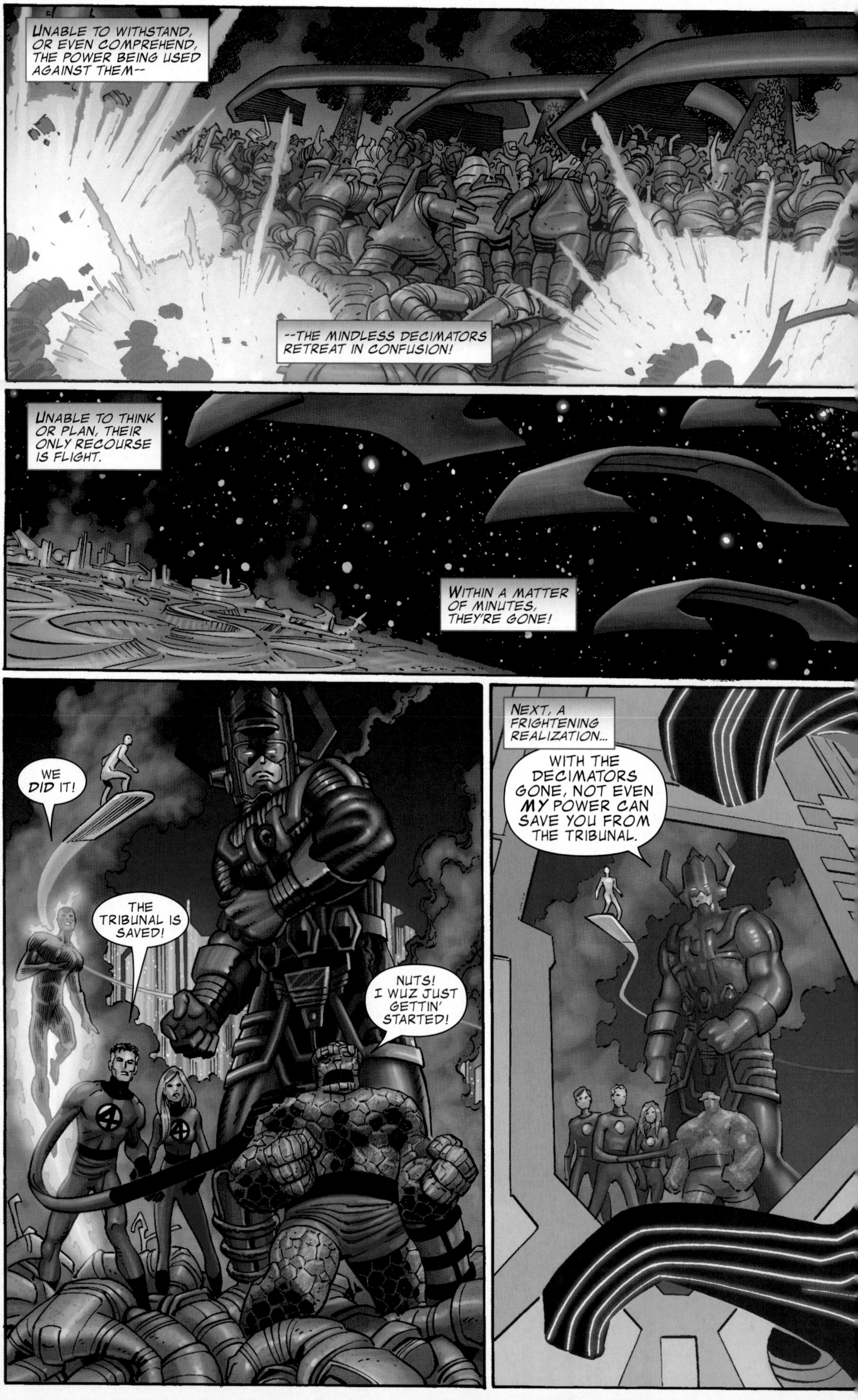
UNABLE TO WITHSTAND, OR EVEN COMPREHEND, THE POWER BEING USED AGAINST THEM--
--THE MINDLESS DECIMATORS RETREAT IN CONFUSION!
UNABLE TO THINK OR PLAN, THEIR ONLY RECOURSE IS FLIGHT.
WITHIN A MATTER OF MINUTES, THEY'RE GONE!
WE DID IT!
THE TRIBUNAL IS SAVED!
NUTS! I WUZ JUST GETTIN' STARTED!
NEXT, A FRIGHTENING REALIZATION...
WITH THE DECIMATORS GONE, NOT EVEN MY POWER CAN SAVE YOU FROM THE TRIBUNAL.

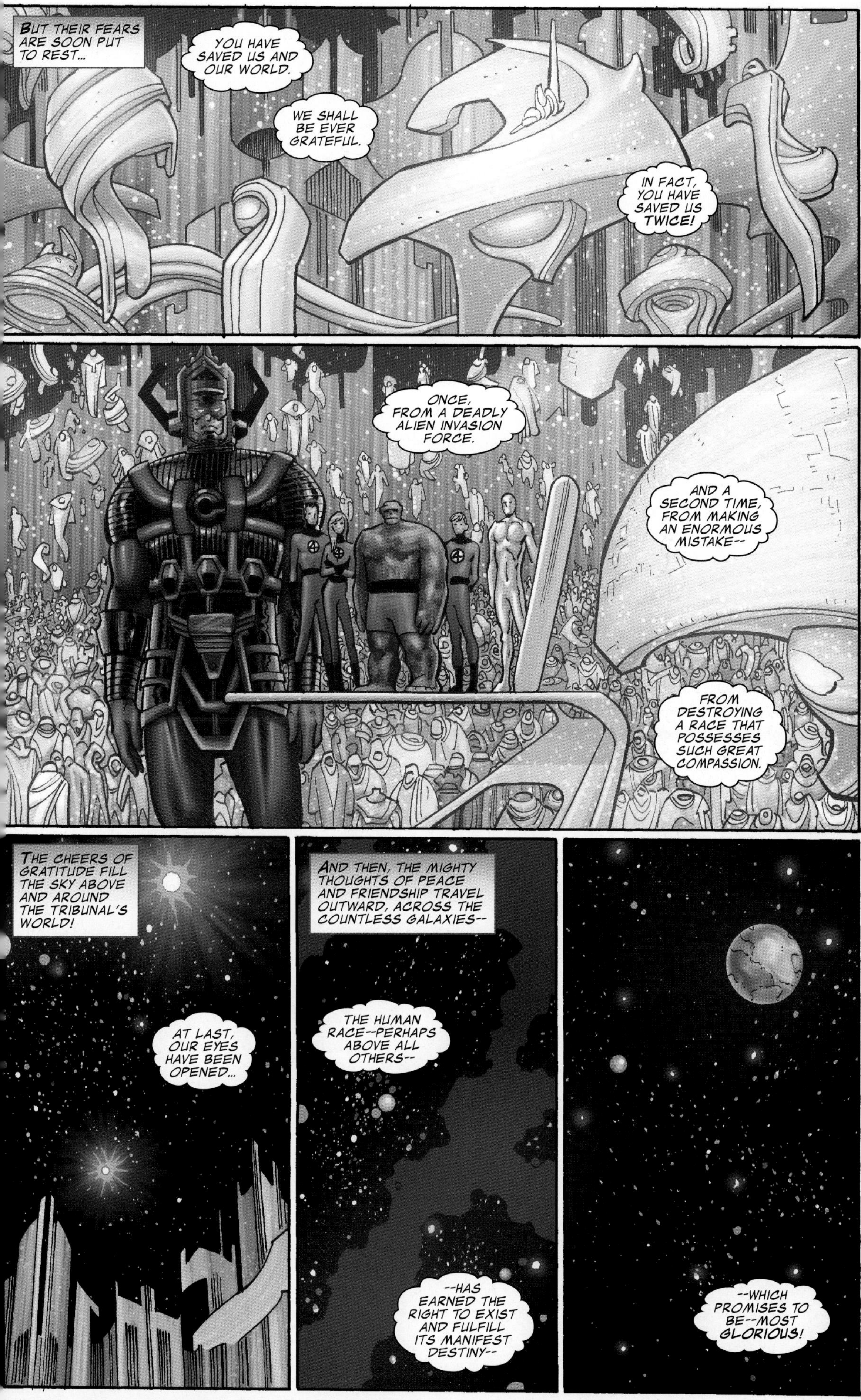
BUT THEIR FEARS ARE SOON PUT TO REST...
YOU HAVE SAVED US AND OUR WORLD.
WE SHALL BE EVER GRATEFUL.
IN FACT, YOU HAVE SAVED US TWICE!
ONCE, FROM A DEADLY ALIEN INVASION FORCE.
AND A SECOND TIME, FROM MAKING AN ENORMOUS MISTAKE--
FROM DESTROYING A RACE THAT POSSESSES SUCH GREAT COMPASSION.
THE CHEERS OF GRATITUDE FILL THE SKY ABOVE AND AROUND THE TRIBUNAL'S WORLD!
AT LAST, OUR EYES HAVE BEEN OPENED...
AND THEN, THE MIGHTY THOUGHTS OF PEACE AND FRIENDSHIP TRAVEL OUTWARD, ACROSS THE COUNTLESS GALAXIES--
THE HUMAN RACE--PERHAPS ABOVE ALL OTHERS--
--HAS EARNED THE RIGHT TO EXIST AND FULFILL ITS MANIFEST DESTINY--
--WHICH PROMISES TO BE--MOST GLORIOUS!

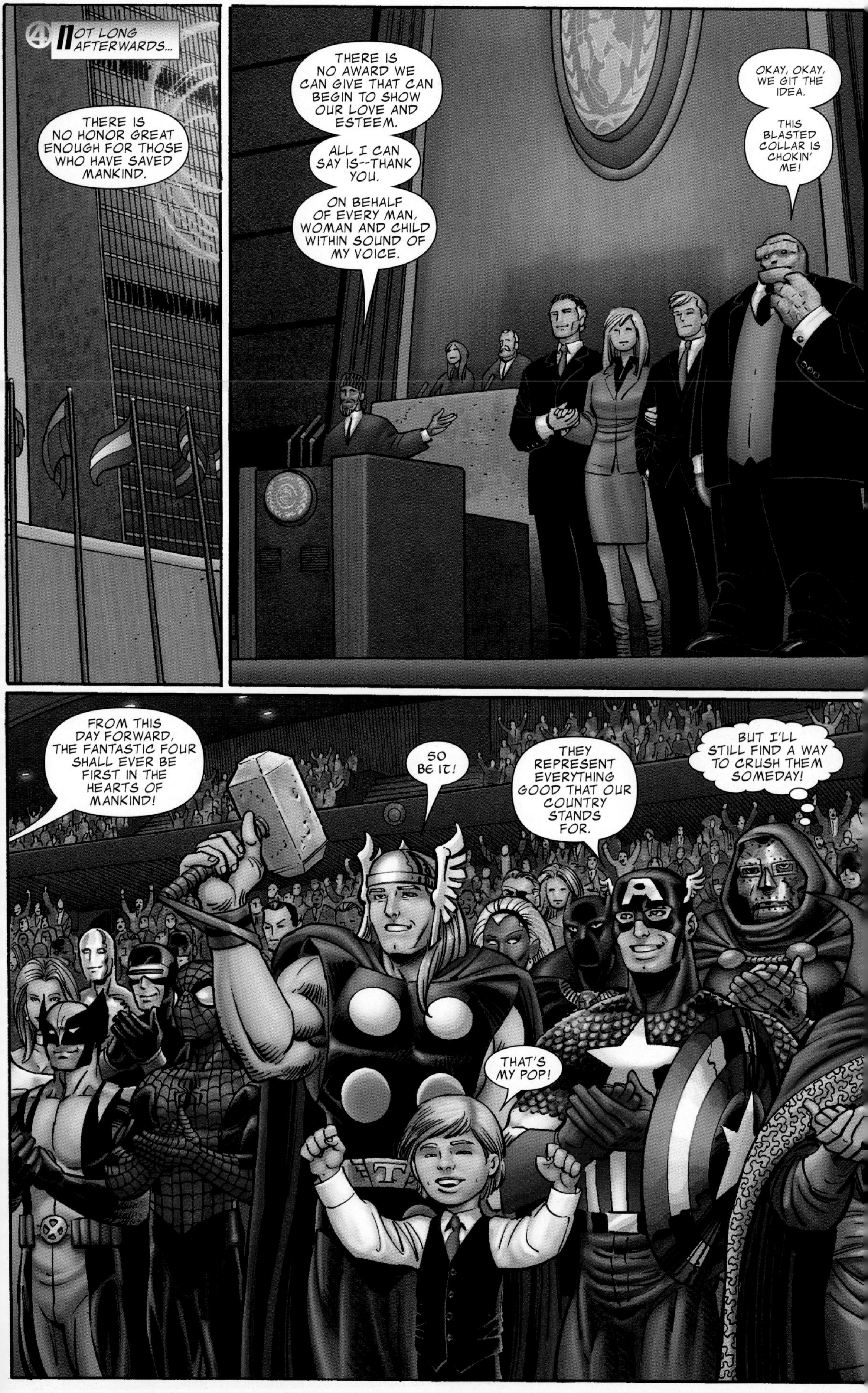
NOT LONG AFTERWARDS...
THERE IS NO HONOR GREAT ENOUGH FOR THOSE WHO HAVE SAVED MANKIND.
THERE IS NO AWARD WE CAN GIVE THAT CAN BEGIN TO SHOW OUR LOVE AND ESTEEM.
ALL I CAN SAY IS--THANK YOU.
ON BEHALF OF EVERY MAN, WOMAN AND CHILD WITHIN SOUND OF MY VOICE.
OKAY, OKAY, WE GIT THE IDEA.
THIS BLASTED COLLAR IS CHOKIN' ME!
FROM THIS DAY FORWARD, THE FANTASTIC FOUR SHALL EVER BE FIRST IN THE HEARTS OF MANKIND!
SO BE IT!
THEY REPRESENT EVERYTHING GOOD THAT OUR COUNTRY STANDS FOR.
BUT I'LL STILL FIND A WAY TO CRUSH THEM SOMEDAY!
THAT'S MY POP!

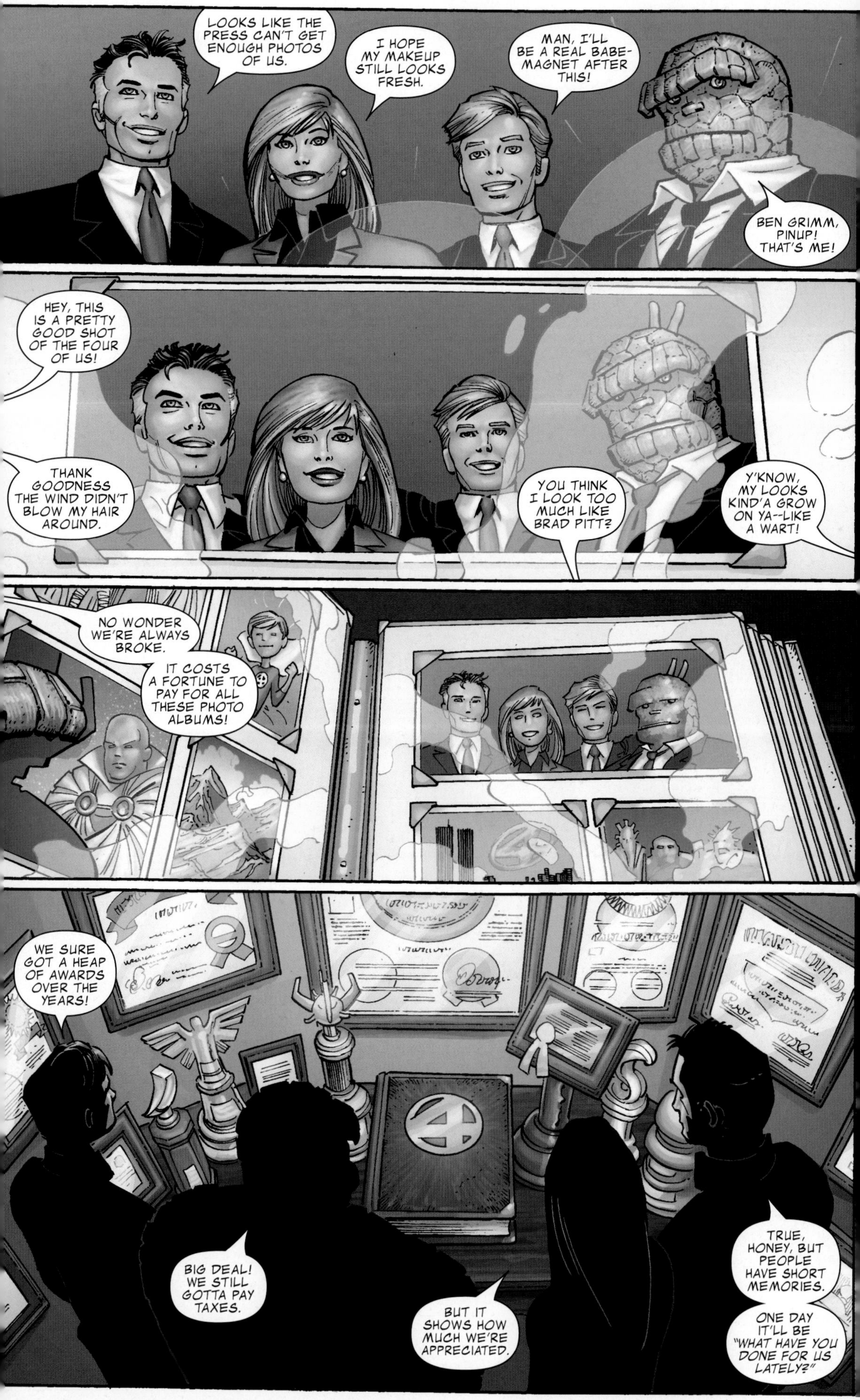
LOOKS LIKE THE PRESS CAN'T GET ENOUGH PHOTOS OF US.
I HOPE MY MAKEUP STILL LOOKS FRESH.
MAN, I'LL BE A REAL BABE-MAGNET AFTER THIS!
BEN GRIMM, PINUP! THAT'S ME!
HEY, THIS IS A PRETTY GOOD SHOT OF THE FOUR OF US!
THANK GOODNESS THE WIND DIDN'T BLOW MY HAIR AROUND.
YOU THINK I LOOK TOO MUCH LIKE BRAD PITT?
Y'KNOW, MY LOOKS KIND'A GROW ON YA--LIKE A WART!
NO WONDER WE'RE ALWAYS BROKE.
IT COSTS A FORTUNE TO PAY FOR ALL THESE PHOTO ALBUMS!
WE SURE GOT A HEAP OF AWARDS OVER THE YEARS!
BIG DEAL! WE STILL GOTTA PAY TAXES.
BUT IT SHOWS HOW MUCH WE'RE APPRECIATED.
TRUE, HONEY, BUT PEOPLE HAVE SHORT MEMORIES.
ONE DAY IT'LL BE "WHAT HAVE YOU DONE FOR US LATELY?"

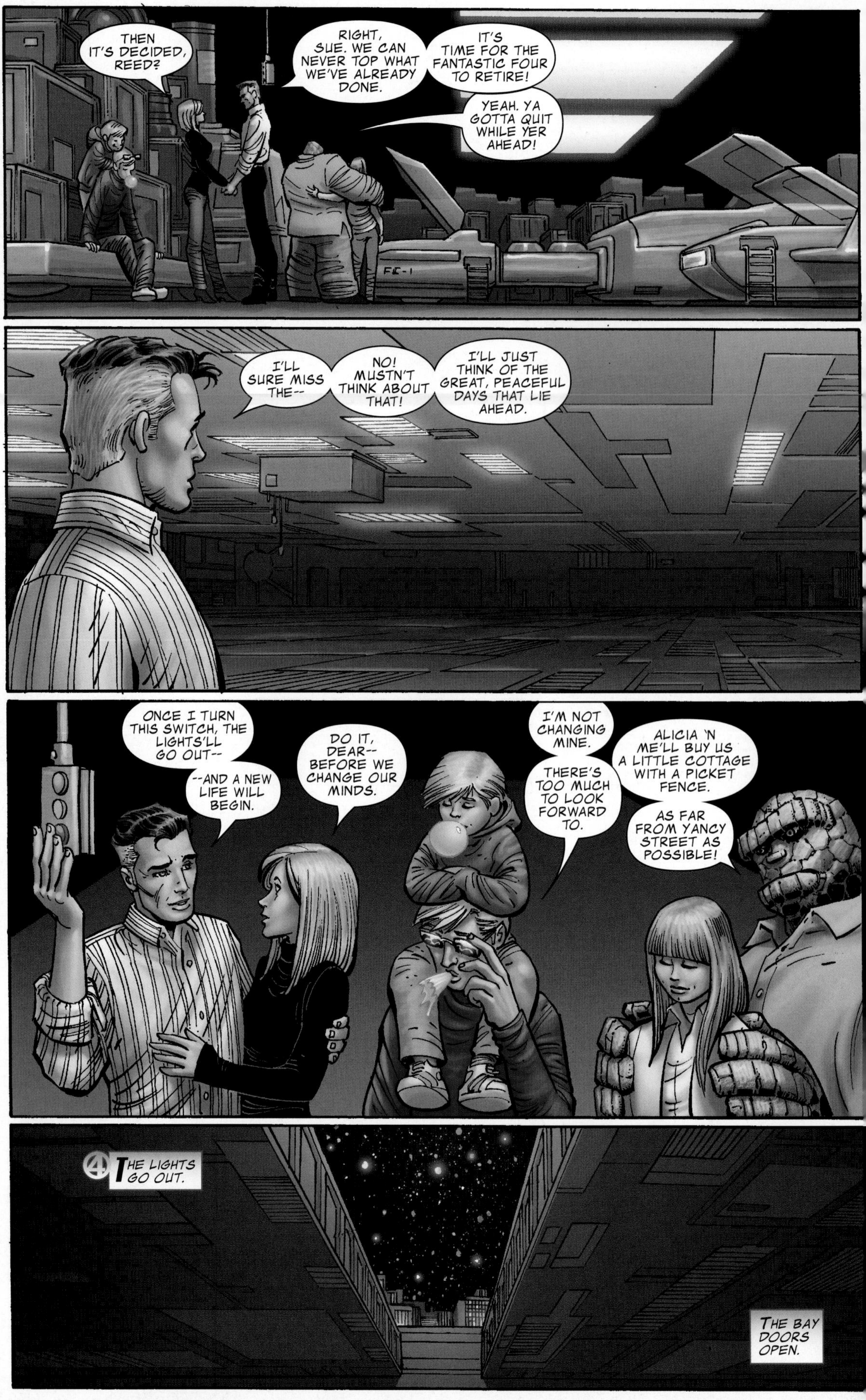
THEN IT'S DECIDED, REED?
RIGHT, SUE. WE CAN NEVER TOP WHAT WE'VE ALREADY DONE.
IT'S TIME FOR THE FANTASTIC FOUR TO RETIRE!
YEAH. YA GOTTA QUIT WHILE YER AHEAD!
FF-1
I'LL SURE MISS THE--
NO! MUSTN'T THINK ABOUT THAT!
I'LL JUST THINK OF THE GREAT, PEACEFUL DAYS THAT LIE AHEAD.
ONCE I TURN THIS SWITCH, THE LIGHTS'LL GO OUT--
--AND A NEW LIFE WILL BEGIN.
DO IT, DEAR-- BEFORE WE CHANGE OUR MINDS.
I'M NOT CHANGING MINE.
THERE'S TOO MUCH TO LOOK FORWARD TO.
ALICIA 'N ME'LL BUY US A LITTLE COTTAGE WITH A PICKET FENCE.
AS FAR FROM YANCY STREET AS POSSIBLE!
THE LIGHTS GO OUT.
THE BAY DOORS OPEN.

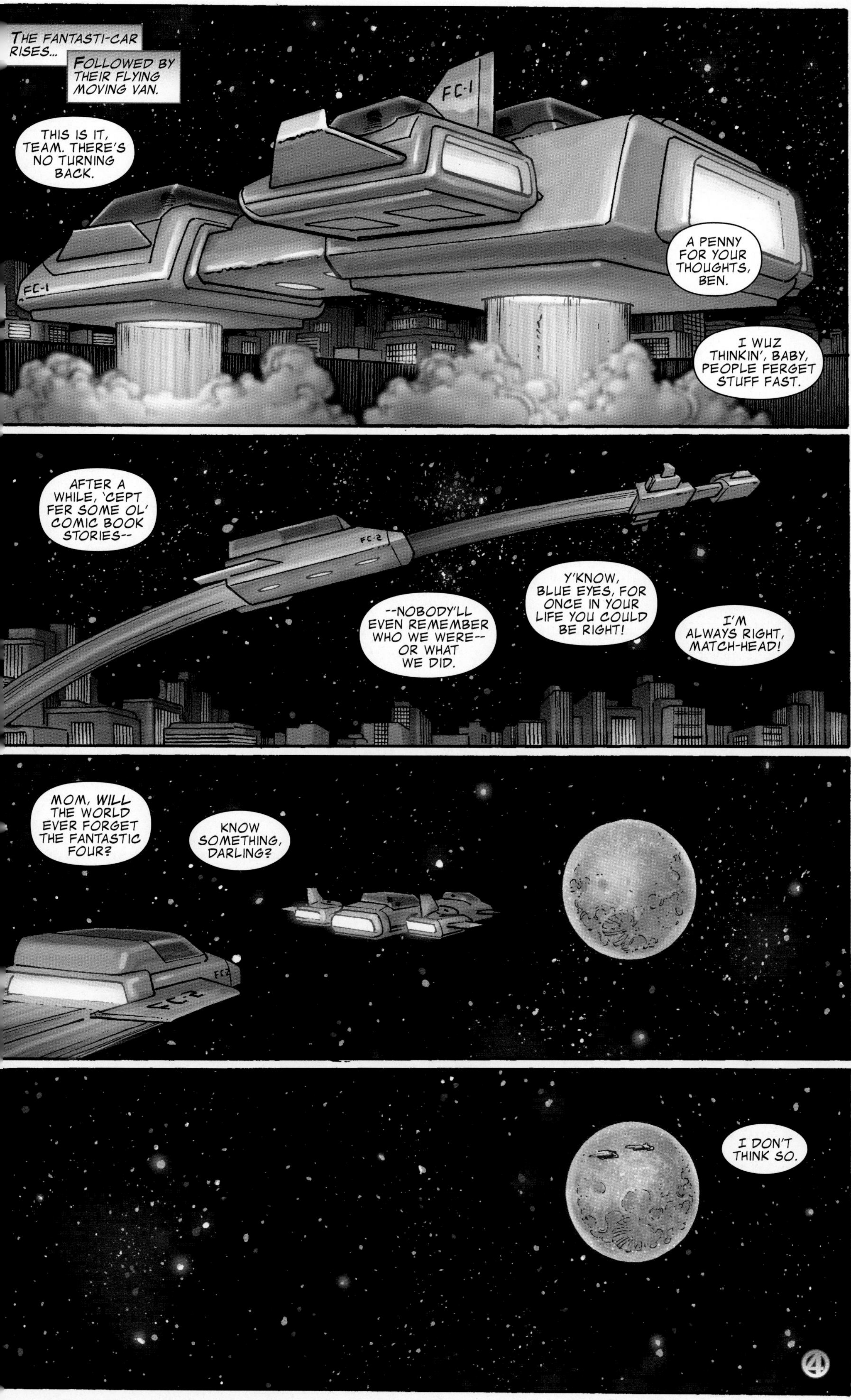

THE FANTASTI-CAR RISES...
FOLLOWED BY THEIR FLYING MOVING VAN.
FC-1
THIS IS IT, TEAM. THERE'S NO TURNING BACK.
A PENNY FOR YOUR THOUGHTS, BEN.
I WUZ THINKIN', BABY, PEOPLE FERGET STUFF FAST.
AFTER A WHILE, 'CEPT FER SOME OL' COMIC BOOK STORIES--
FC-2
--NOBODY'LL EVEN REMEMBER WHO WE WERE-- OR WHAT WE DID.
Y'KNOW, BLUE EYES, FOR ONCE IN YOUR LIFE YOU COULD BE RIGHT!
I'M ALWAYS RIGHT, MATCH-HEAD!
MOM, WILL THE WORLD EVER FORGET THE FANTASTIC FOUR?
KNOW SOMETHING, DARLING?
I DON'T THINK SO.

FANTASTIC FOUR
Final Issue

(JOHN: I've incorporated my notes and suggestions into this document in this font. All of this stuff has been run past Stan, and he didn't seem to have any real problem with it. Once you've had a chance to read this over, Stan would like to have a conversation with you before we get started.—Tom B.)

"SO ENDS THE WORLD!"

Open with a dead sparrow falling to earth.

The caption will read: "When a sparrow fell to earth... it was the beginning of the end of the world!"

The FF finish mopping up some terrorists who tried to take over an arsenal. When they return to FF headquarters, the Thing and the Torch are griping about the fact that they aren't getting any younger and they're not getting anywhere financially. The dough they get paid as rewards usually goes to charity and the rest to taxes. Their expenses at the headquarters keep mounting, what with the cost of maintaining the Fantasti-Car, the Pogo Plane and all Reed's equipment while their rent keeps going up. They're making hardly anything anymore from endorsing products or FF toys and games, etc., because there's always some new fad coming along and people always want to buy the latest stuff. After all, how many FF T-shirts can people wear?

Susan says, "What if we all just retire?" Reed says they're needed. Johnny says that nobody's indispensable. Thing says, "Yeah, it might help employment if we quit. There'll be more jobs for the army and the police." And so it goes, until...

Reed, using his scientific instruments, sees ever-increasing signs of impending disaster. Other birds are dying—in the deserts, oases are drying up and the ozone layer is dissipating faster than normal; global warming has speeded up; versions of El Nino are appearing in all the oceans, etc.

Reed realizes these events aren't normal. Some terrible power is causing them to happen. (This is why the sparrow died in the beginning.)

The Watcher appears. He has come to say farewell.

Reed asks him where he's going. The Watcher says "Nowhere. It is you who shall be leaving—forever."

A terrible disaster is about to befall Earth and the Watcher is powerless to do anything about it.

In another sector of the universe, further than we have ever gone or even discovered, the Cosmic Tribunal is trying to figure out how to eliminate all human life without destroying the entire planet.

The Cosmic Tribunal has determined that the human race has been on Earth for thousands of years and, despite technical progress, nothing in the social scheme of things has improved. There is as much crime, poverty, hatred and war as ever. Therefore, the Cosmic Tribunal has determined that it's time for the human race to be eliminated since it serves no useful purpose.

The Cosmic Tribunal plans to end life on Earth in as natural a manner as possible, as though it's being caused by natural forces. They themselves can't directly kill anything or take a life. They don't believe in violence. But they can affect nature so that nature will eliminate the human race!

They send one member of the Tribunal, "The Adjudicator" (the judge) to Earth to tell us what our fate will be. They feel we're entitled to know.

The unique thing about the Cosmic Tribunal, the most powerful foe the FF have ever faced, is that they really aren't evil. Their only purpose is to keep peace and tranquility in the Universe and they feel that the human race is a threat to that peace.

The Tribunal want no personal gain for themselves. They just feel they're helping to protect the Universe.

So, for the first time, the FF will have to find a way to defeat super-powerful good guys!

In his lab, Reed is the first to notice something incredible happening out in space. A disturbance in the cosmos. A gigantic object is approaching our galaxy at unbelievable speed.

The Adjudicator arrives on Earth. He's gigantic. He has a head, two arms and two legs, but aside from that he looks very alien, not like a normal human. He's not grotesque. He looks somewhat godlike, in the way that Galactus does, but still larger and far more impressive. He's so huge that he straddles Manhatten Island, with one of his legs in the East River and one in the Hudson! (That's so we can get some fantastic illos!) His head and torso are high above the clouds.

He has no spaceship. The Cosmic Tribunal travel (and do everything) by thought alone.

All over the world the sight of him causes panic—some people even think he's an incredible special effect created for a movie.

But they soon learn he's for real.

(It's both a little bit convenient and a little bit standard that the Adjudicator lands in Manhattan to deliver his address—again, we've seen this sort of thing before with Galactus and others. So what if, given that the Adjudicator is a cosmic being unfathomable to the minds of men, the giant form of the Adjudicator lands in several different places on Earth. That is to say that there are giant Adjudicators strategically positioned all across the globe, but that they're all facets of a single entity rather than a number of individual Adjudicators—there's only one being, but he manifests in several places at once (in a manner that our limited human minds cannot fathom.) This would help to make the Adjudicator distinctive from all of the other cosmic world-beaters in an immediate, visual way. This would also limit the need to bring all of the other characters to New York one by one. The Inhumans, for example, could battle the Adjudicator in the area around their Himalayan Great Refuge—and Black Bolt's mighty scream could level the Himalayas themselves for miles around without us having to worry about all of the innocent bystanders were he to do the same thing in New York.)

He communicates with us, without speaking. He has the ability to simply send out his thoughts, which are received and understood all over the globe.

His thoughts tell us that, for want of a better name, we can call him "The Adjudicator." He lets us know that we are far smaller than the Cosmic Tribunal thought we were. He will make it easier for us to relate to him and so he causes himself to shrink down to human size—well, almost human size. We see him continuing to shrink until he stands in Central Park—ten feet tall, surrounded by the news media.

Everything stops, all around Earth. Every TV camera is focused on the Adjudicator. Every human within sight or sound of a television set or radio is breathlessly following this incredible event.

The Adjudicator tells us (actually he "thinks" rather than "tells" because his thoughts can be understood by everyone no matter what language they speak. However, I'll use the word "tells" or "speaks" from now on because it's a simpler way to convey what's happening) –he's come to announce the end of human life on Earth, to give us a short time to make our final farewells.
(The Adjudicator doesn't think of himself as a villain, or the Cosmic Tribunal as being evil. They're just doing what they feel they have to do.)
The Adjudicator says we have one week (Earth time) to prepare for our final fate before he will signal the Cosmic Tribunal to destroy mankind...

The Sub-Mariner, suddenly aware that the oceans are getting dangerously warm, thinks Reed Richards is responsible, thinking it's Reed's way of attacking Namor and destroying Atlantis.
So the Sub-Mariner attacks the FF in their headquarters.
During the battle, Reed tries to make Namor look at a videotape he took of the Adjudicator when the Adjudicator was gigantic. He wants Namor to realize that the Adjudicator is the enemy. But Namor won't stop fighting.
Suddenly, the Black Panther appears. He has flown from Wakanda to help. He tells Reed that he'll battle Namor—Reed must return to his lab because it will take all his scientific knowledge to find a way to save humanity.
We have an interesting Black Panther/Sub-Mariner battle until the Panther makes Namor look at the video and Namor realizes who the real enemy is.
Before he can be warned, Namor leaps out of the FF's window to dive down and attack the Adjudicator. The Adjudicator just gestures at Namor and Namor falls to the ground, injured.
Sue sees that he's hurt. She gets the Pogo Plane and she and the Black Panther go down and pick Namor up.
When he comes to, it's decided that Namor must return to his people and look after them in this time of crisis. The Black Panther will do the same for his people. It will require more than mere battle skills to defeat the Adjudicator. It's up to Reed to find the way.

(I didn't entirely buy into the notion of the Sub-Mariner moving to attack Reed and company because the oceans are beginning to heat up and boil. The Adjudicator addresses all life on Earth—I'd expect that this would include the Atlanteans. What if, instead, as the world reacts to the Adjudicator's pronouncement, a horde of Atlanteans appears on the coastline, marching out of the sea. At first, Reed and everybody else think it's another invasion—just what they need at a time like this!—but it turns out that it's instead an exodus, that the entirety of the Atlantean population is leaving the seas, which have become inhospitable to them due to what the Tribunal is doing to the biosphere. They're a nation of refugees, and Namor attacks the human authorities and military who've come out to meet and stop them, thinking that they're an invading army. What we should do with the Black Panther in this case, I'm not quite sure.)

Johnny asks Reed if he wants to get little Franklin and put him in a safe place. Reed says, "No. There will be no safe place on Earth unless we can find a way to stop the Adjudicator. We can only save those we love by staying in the battle."

Many people on Earth still think it's all a gigantic hoax. Perhaps the setup for a new, big-budget movie. Besides, with all the super heroes around there can't be anything to worry about.

Reed sends out an emergency call to the Silver Surfer.
The Surfer is resting on his surfboard as it idly drifts along the currents of space while he muses to himself about the grandeur of the Universe.
That's when he gets the call. He hates to tear himself away but he knows Reed wouldn't call unless it was imperative.
We see the Surfer zooming through space towards our galaxy.

Meanwhile, on Earth, the law enforcement agencies try to apprehend the Adjudicator. No matter who or what he is, nobody can make threats against mankind the way he did. We've had it up to here with terrorists.
That's when we learn of his incredible power. With just a thought he creates a force field around himself that nothing can penetrate. In addition, he can cause almost anything he wishes for to happen. By just waving his arm, he can make a battalion of heavily-armed soldiers crumble helplessly into a heap. He can wave at planes that might be attacking him and their engines stall and they have to try to glide to Earth, or the pilots simply have to bail out. Nothing can harm him.

And Reed learns that the Cosmic Tribunal has even more power. They will only have to think it and all human life on Earth will come to an end. And there are only so many hours left!
Now a brief romantic interlude between Sue and Reed. They profess their love for each other and Reed swears to do his best to save mankind for Sue's sake, for little Franklin's sake and for the sake of the whole human race.

Suddenly, Dr. Doom shows up at FF headquarters in one of his incredibly powerful flying battle cruisers, loaded with heavily armed robots, and followed by many other flying cruisers of his Latverian air force. Doom himself is in the flagship of Latveria's battle fleet and the Thing and Torch think Doom has taken this moment to launch a surprise attack on the FF.
But it turns out that Doom wants to help in the battle against the Adjudicator. He says he has devoted his life to conquering the human race and putting all humanity under the rule of Latveria, and he won't let any alien, no matter how powerful, keep him from his goal.

Doom and his robots try to down the Adjudicator, but when the Adjudicator finally takes notice of them, he dispatches them with a simple wave of his hand—and they land back in Latveria!

When the Surfer arrives he tells Reed he knows of the Cosmic Tribunal. No power can stand against them. They have no weapons because they need none. Their thoughts are the most potent weapons in the universe. Stunned, Reed asks, "You mean—we have no hope?"

FANTASTIC FOUR: Final Issue Plot By Stan Lee

The Inhumans arrive on the scene. Though they want nothing to do with the human race, they feel it's their duty to try their powers against the Adjudicator.

Gorgon kicks out at the Adjudicator. His kick actually causes a point 4 earthquake, but doesn't affect the Adjudicator at all. The others are equally helpless. Then Black Bolt decides to unleash the greatest power he possesses—his unimaginably lethal shout, deadlier than a hundred H-bombs. He focuses his shout directly at the Adjudicator so no one else will be shattered. It hits him head-on, although a small portion of his shout passes beyond the Adjudicator and causes a mountaintop in the Adirondacks to topple. But again, the Adjudicator is totally unhurt. Protected by his force field, the Adjudicator doesn't even feel it. (Sue Storm wishes her force field was one-thousandth as powerful.)

We see the Surfer flying off into the heavens. People think he's getting out while the getting is good.

The Cosmic Tribunal people actually are weaponless themselves, feeling they need no weapons except the power of their minds; and they seem to be right.

The Torch and the Thing and even Sue try everything they can to defeat the Adjudicator, to capture and render him helpless so he won't be able to signal the Tribunal at the end of the week. (The clock keeps ticking!) But they are unable to accomplish anything.

(This paragraph is optional. In case you're worried that readers will wonder what happened to the rest of Marvel's heroes, we can show as many as you have room for: Thor, the X-Men, the Hulk, Spider-Man, Capt. America, Iron Man, Daredevil, Dr. Strange, Ghost Rider—etc.

They all try to topple The Adjudicator, but can't. Not even Thor's hammer or Dr. Strange's magic can do the trick. Professor X sends his thoughts as far out into the Universe as possible, but can't reach the home of the Cosmic Tribunal—it's too far away. The Adjudicator is totally invulnerable!)

(JOHN: I think I'd cut the above sequence, particularly if we're pressed for space. However, if you think it's important that we see everybody else take their swing at the Adjudicator and fail, feel free to go ahead.)

Finally, the Thing says at least there's one thing he can accomplish. He'll be damned if he'll let the girl he loves die alone and unprotected.

He races out of FF headquarters and smashes his way through the traffic jam which is crowding the street, due to the people's panic. He shoves cars and trucks aside, letting nothing stand in his way until he reaches Alicia.

He embraces her and says if the world's gotta end, then they'll face the end together.

I like the scene where Ben runs off to find Alicia again—I'd even suggest that he do so despite Reed needing his help for some facet of his research or other. That in this time of extreme crisis, when it looks like things are absolutely hopeless, Ben realizes what's more important to him. (Maybe we could also include a touching scene between Ben and Reed, where Ben says that he knows Reed's always been trying to find a cure for his being the Thing, and that he wants Reed to know that he doesn't blame him for what happened—a scene that really gets across the bond between these two old friends in what they think may be their final moments.)

The world wonders why Reed doesn't do anything. He's the greatest brain on Earth. He has scientific apparatus that even Einstein wouldn't understand. Why does he just stay locked in his lab? Is he afraid?

The other members of the FF ask if he's trying to contact the Kree or the Skrulls for help (or any other group Marvel has encountered that I don't know about) but Reed says "No, The Adjudicator could destroy them with a shrug!"

Keep up the mystery. What is it that Reed is doing, and why? Not even Sue, Ben or Johnny know.

Meanwhile, angry, raging crowds gather in the street below, demanding that Reed do something. The crowd grows ever bigger, threatening to become violent, preparing to storm the Baxter Building.

This is a chance to show more action with Sue and the Torch. They have to stop the huge, angry crowd which has gathered below from storming the FF building. The crowd is shouting that Reed and the FF are traitors for doing nothing. Sue and Johnny have to keep the crowds at bay without actually hurting any of the innocent people who are mad with fear and panic.

A new, startling, dramatic event suddenly occurs.

Down from the sky above, Galactus arrives in his mighty ship, with the Surfer flying alongside.

At first we think he's a new threat to Earth, but then it develops Reed sent for him. That's what he was doing in his lab with the Surfer, trying to find out where Galactus was and then sending the Surfer to get him.

Galactus hasn't come to harm us. He'll be true to his oath to never harm Earth. He's come to help. But even he hasn't the power to defeat the Adjudicator. However, Reed has an idea. He feels there is one way Galactus can help.

Nobody knows more about the unfolding cosmos than Galactus, who has been everywhere and done everything. If he can tell Reed one special thing, the human race may be saved. Can Galactus do it? Will Galactus do it? And—what is that special thing?

Galactus says he can—and he does. (We don't yet know what he tells Reed.) Now it's up to the Surfer. Only he has the speed to reach a certain place in the Universe in time.

The Surfer leaves the lab and heads straight for Shalla-Bal in Zenn-La. A tender moment as he says he has to leave. If he fails, he'll never see her again, so he had to tell her that he loves her. She admits she loves him, too, and always will. A passionate embrace and then she tearfully watches him streak into the heavens, going—where?

Back at FF headquarters Johnny flames on, mad as hell, and personally attacks the Adjudicator—but to no avail. He attacks again and again, hurling all sorts of potent fireballs, hurling his own flaming body—attacking almost like a madman, but it's all useless.

Finally, spent and exhausted, he barely has enough flame left to make it back to Reed who asks him why he knocked himself out in such a futile attempt. Johnny, almost tearfully, says it was just a mood of rage, of anger—and of self-pity. He had to do something to drown out the thought that Ben has Alicia, the Surfer has Shalla- Bal, Reed has Sue and he, Johnny, has no one. He's wasted all those years playing the field, and now, during the greatest crisis in the world, he has no one to turn to.

Sue and Reed sympathize when suddenly—

The Adjudicator looks towards the sky and says, "The impossible has happened!"
He becomes his original gigantic size and zooms up into the sky, vanishing within a microsecond as he apparently returns to his own cosmos.

The Watcher returns and tells us, "Fate has saved the human race! The world of the Cosmic Tribunal is being attacked by another enemy race, the only race that can destroy them."
When asked how anything can destroy those whose mental powers can protect them from anything, the Watcher replies, "There is one warlike race, a thousand universes away, who have no minds—they act only on instinct, and their instinct is to kill any other race they encounter. Therefore, having no minds themselves, they are impervious to mental power, and can penetrate the Tribunal's force fields like a sword can go through smoke."

We learn that it was Galactus' doing. He, summoned by Reed, has saved us. Only he knew of the one race that could stop the Tribunal. It was he who dispatched the heroic Silver Surfer to go to that race and direct them to the quadrant of the Universe where they could find the Tribunal.
We might get some great illustrations by showing a deadly, savage, heavily armed armada attacking the Tribunal's world.

 This is when Reed proves what heroes the FF really are. He says they've got to go and help the Tribunal, to save them from that other race. He says that the Tribunal aren't basically bad, they just were mistaken about mankind.
But, he adds, the FF can't stand idly by and see such a superior race destroyed by mindless butchers. He say even though their own super-powers were helpless against the Tribunal, they just might be able to stop that savage invading force.

So, the FF get into Galactus' mighty starship and, led by the Silver Surfer, they head for the Cosmic Tribunal's world. This is where we see the final battle, as Galactus, the Surfer and the FF, with all their cosmic and scientific power, defeat the savage but primitive invading force of the other aliens and drive them back to their own galaxy in defeat.

The Cosmic Tribunal are suddenly aware of the fact that our heroes were noble enough to save the very ones who had tried to destroy them.
The Tribunal realize they have been saved twice—once from the invading alien force, and the second time from making the enormous mistake of destroying a race that had so much compassion in it.
They're grateful that their eyes have been opened. They now feel that the human race, perhaps above all others, has earned the right to exist and to eventually fulfill its manifest destiny-- one which promises to be a most glorious destiny!

Now we see things getting back to normal on Earth...

The U.N. holds a colorful ceremony attended by representatives of all nations in which they give the FF a special award for saving the planet. It's the most prestigious award in the world, never before given to anyone. Little Franklin is in the audience, sitting with the Black Panther, Surfer, Namor and the Inhumans.

Even Dr. Doom, who is in attendance, applauds them.

(NOTE: If you think we should, you might include Marvel's other super heroes in the audience, as well. Your option.)

End with the FF back in their headquarters, together with Alicia and little Franklin.

They look over their scrapbook and all the awards they've gotten during their career. They feel there's nothing they can ever do to top this achievement, the fact that they saved the human race from annihilation, and they saved the world of the Cosmic Tribunal, as well.

They look at each other thoughtfully and come up with the same decision after some discussion…

It's the perfect time for them to retire.

(You might devote a full two pages to the following conclusion of our tale…
If there's no room for two pages, then at least one complete page)

It's evening. We see them taking a last sentimental look around their quarters in the Baxter Building.

They talk as they lock the place up

It's hard for them to tear themselves away, but they know it's time.

Johnny mentions that he'll now stop playing the field and try to find the right female for himself and settle down to a normal life.

Sue, holding Franklin lovingly, with Reed's arm around her, adds, "A normal life. It sounds like a dream come true."

The Thing grunts his approval. He has one arm around Alicia and carries a ton of their luggage in his other arm as they go up to the roof. It's obvious they don't intend to return.

They get into the Fantasti-Car.

They start to fly away from us, towards the full moon over the Hudson on the horizon, getting smaller and smaller in each succeeding panel.

Their dialogue will be in the following vein (as they get further and further away from us):

THING: "People forget stuff fast. 'Cept for some old comic-book stories, after a while no one'll even remember who we were or what we did."

JOHNNY: "For once in your life you could be right, Blue Eyes."

FRANKLIN: "You mean—someday the world will forget the Fantastic Four?"

SUE: "Know something?

REED: "What?"

SUE: "I- don't- think- so."

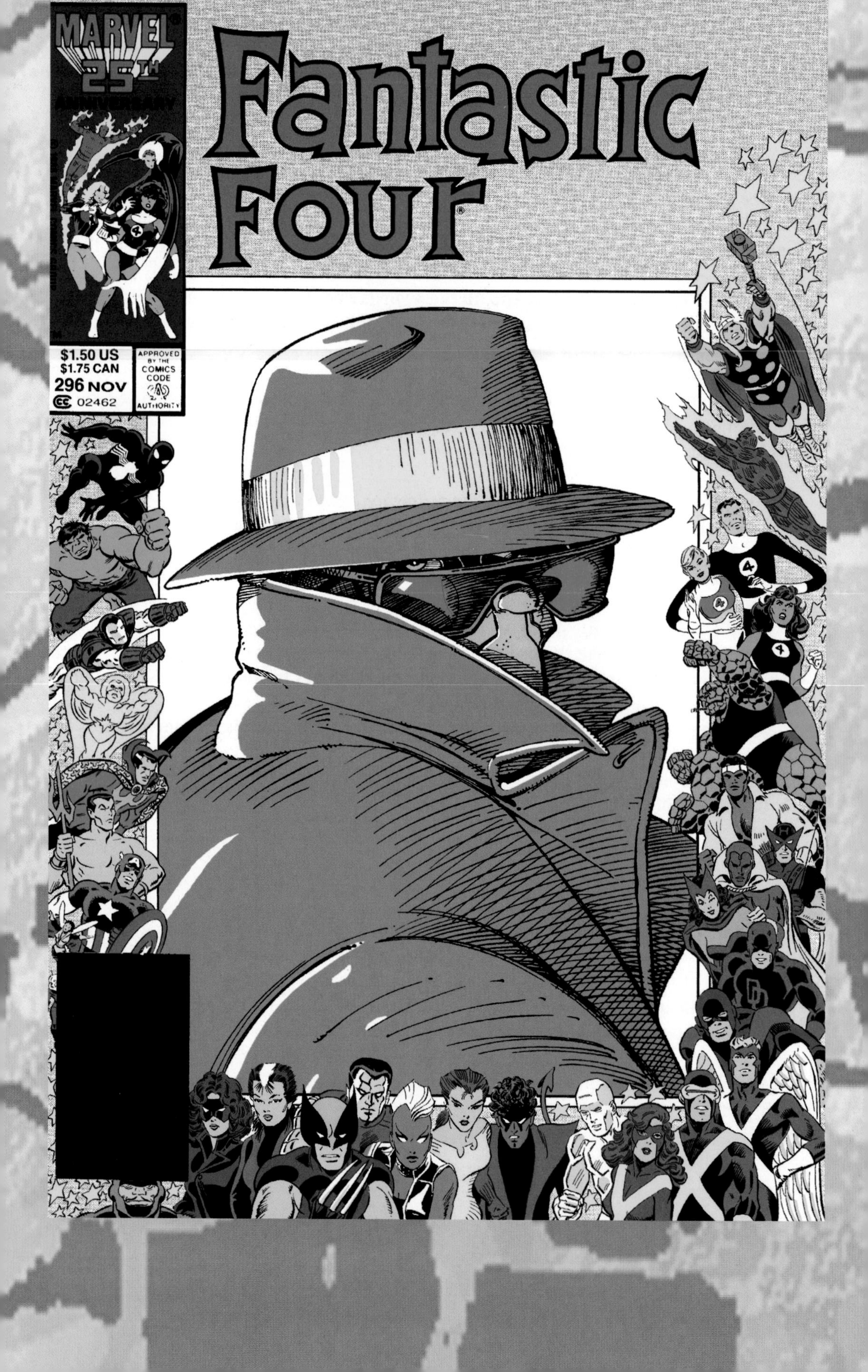
MARVEL
25TH
ANNIVERSARY
Fantastic Four
$1.50 US
$1.75 CAN
296 NOV
02462
APPROVED BY THE COMICS CODE AUTHORITY

Fantastic Four

FROM THE VAST POOL OF MARVEL TALENT WAS DRAWN A HANDFUL OF ARTISTS WHOSE NOBLE TASK IT THEN BECAME TO COMMEMORATE 25 YEARS OF CHRONICLING THE EXPLOITS, THE LOVES AND THE LIVES OF THAT MOST VENERABLE QUARTET, THE FANTASTIC FOUR.

PAGES	PENCILS	INKS
1–5	BARRY WINDSOR-SMITH	BARRY WINDSOR-SMITH
6–10	BARRY WINDSOR-SMITH & KERRY GAMMILL	VINCE COLLETTA & BARRY WINDSOR-SMITH
11–20	RON FRENZ	BOB WIACEK
21–30	AL MILGROM	KLAUS JANSON
31–40	JOHN BUSCEMA	STEVE LEIALOHA
41–49	MARC SILVESTRI	JOE RUBENSTEIN
50	JERRY ORDWAY	JOE SINNOTT
51–57	JERRY ORDWAY	BOB WIACEK
58–64	JERRY ORDWAY	JOE SINNOTT

PLOTTER—JIM SHOOTER
SCRIPT—STAN LEE
LETTERER—JOHN WORKMAN
COLORIST—GLYNIS OLIVER
EDITOR—MIKE CARLIN
EDITOR IN CHIEF—JIM SHOOTER

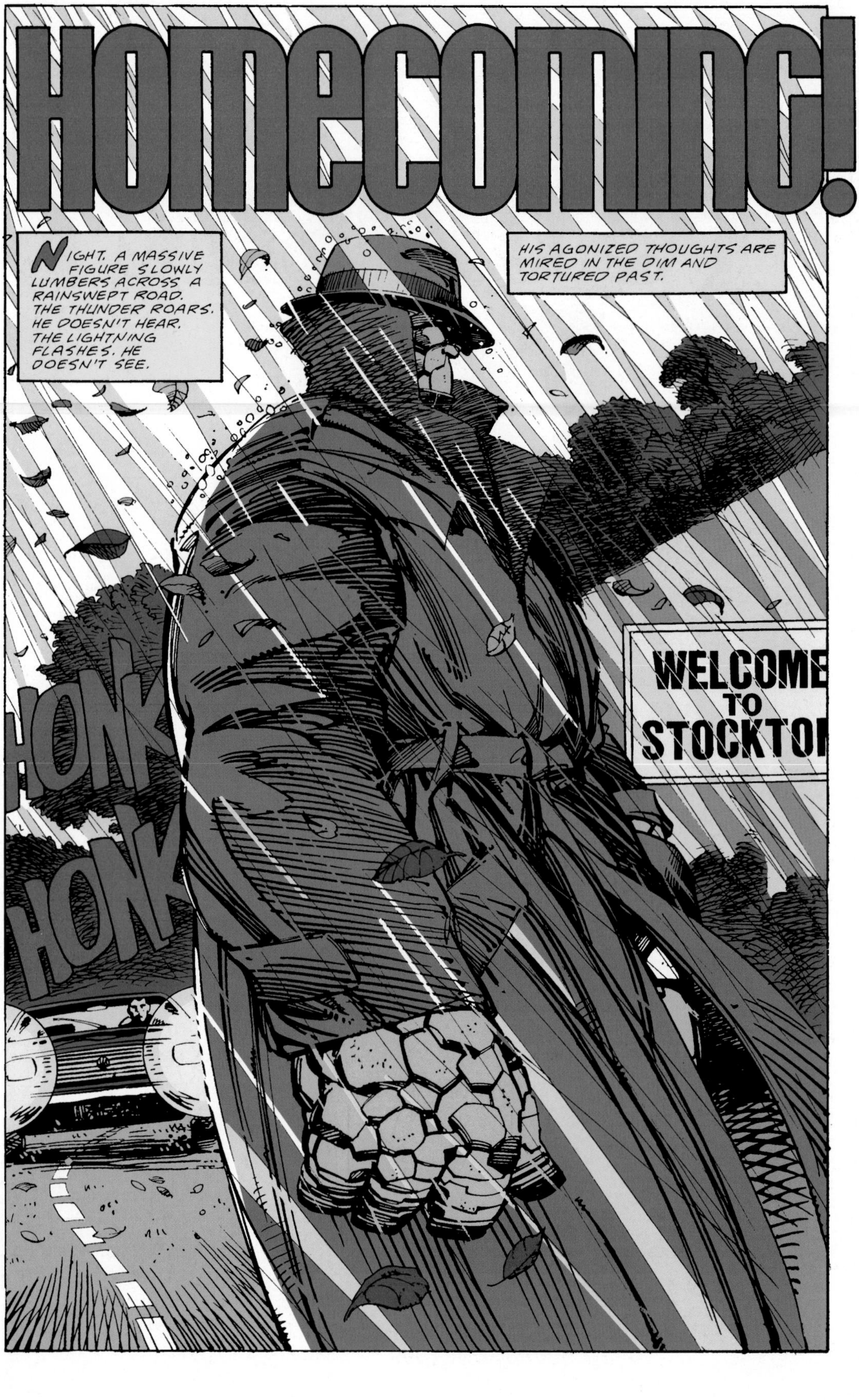
HOMECOMING!
NIGHT. A MASSIVE FIGURE SLOWLY LUMBERS ACROSS A RAINSWEPT ROAD. THE THUNDER ROARS. HE DOESN'T HEAR. THE LIGHTNING FLASHES. HE DOESN'T SEE.
HIS AGONIZED THOUGHTS ARE MIRED IN THE DIM AND TORTURED PAST.
WELCOME TO STOCKTON
HONK
HONK

CAN'T *STOP* IN TIME! THE ROAD'S TOO *WET!*

MOVE! WHY DON'T YOU *UNHHHH!*

SSSCRRREEEEE THUMP!! TISH!!

YOU--YOU'RE NOT *HURT!* THANK HEAV--

YOUR *FACE!* WHAT --?!

WH-WHO *ARE* YOU? WHERE ARE YOU *FROM?*

YOU GOT SOME-PLACE T'GO?

GO THERE.

I...I CAN'T! THE FRONT WHEEL IS TWISTED! IT'S HITTING THE FENDER!

YEAH....

WH-WHAT ARE YOU *DOING?*

FIXIN' IT.

KRRK RUNCH!

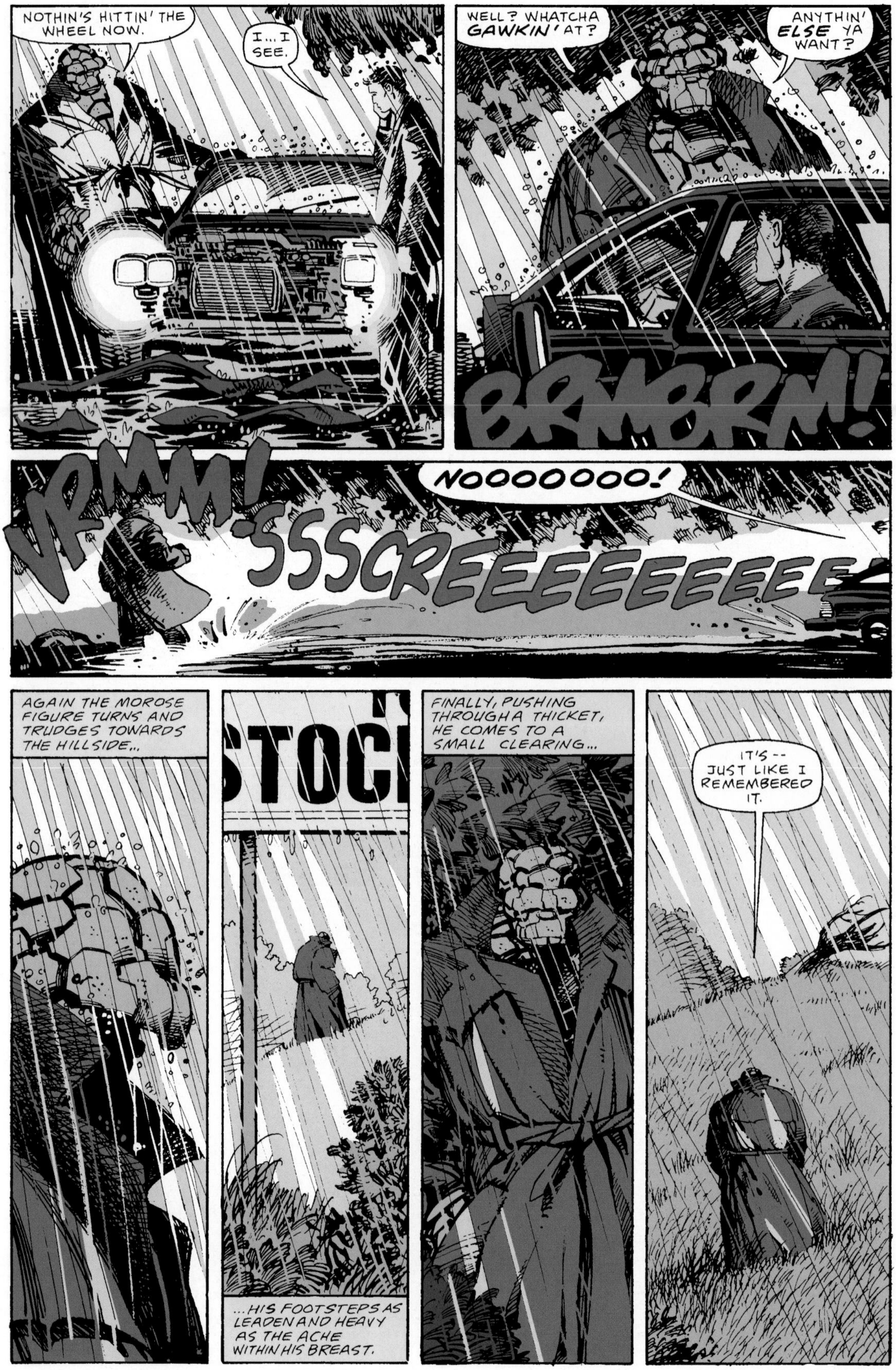
NOTHIN'S HITTIN' THE WHEEL NOW.
I... I SEE.
WELL? WHATCHA GAWKIN' AT?
ANYTHIN' ELSE YA WANT?
BRMBRM!
VRMMM!
NOOOOOOO!
SSSCREEEEEEEEEE
AGAIN THE MOROSE FIGURE TURNS AND TRUDGES TOWARDS THE HILLSIDE...
STOC
...HIS FOOTSTEPS AS LEADEN AND HEAVY AS THE ACHE WITHIN HIS BREAST.
FINALLY, PUSHING THROUGH A THICKET, HE COMES TO A SMALL CLEARING...
IT'S -- JUST LIKE I REMEMBERED IT.

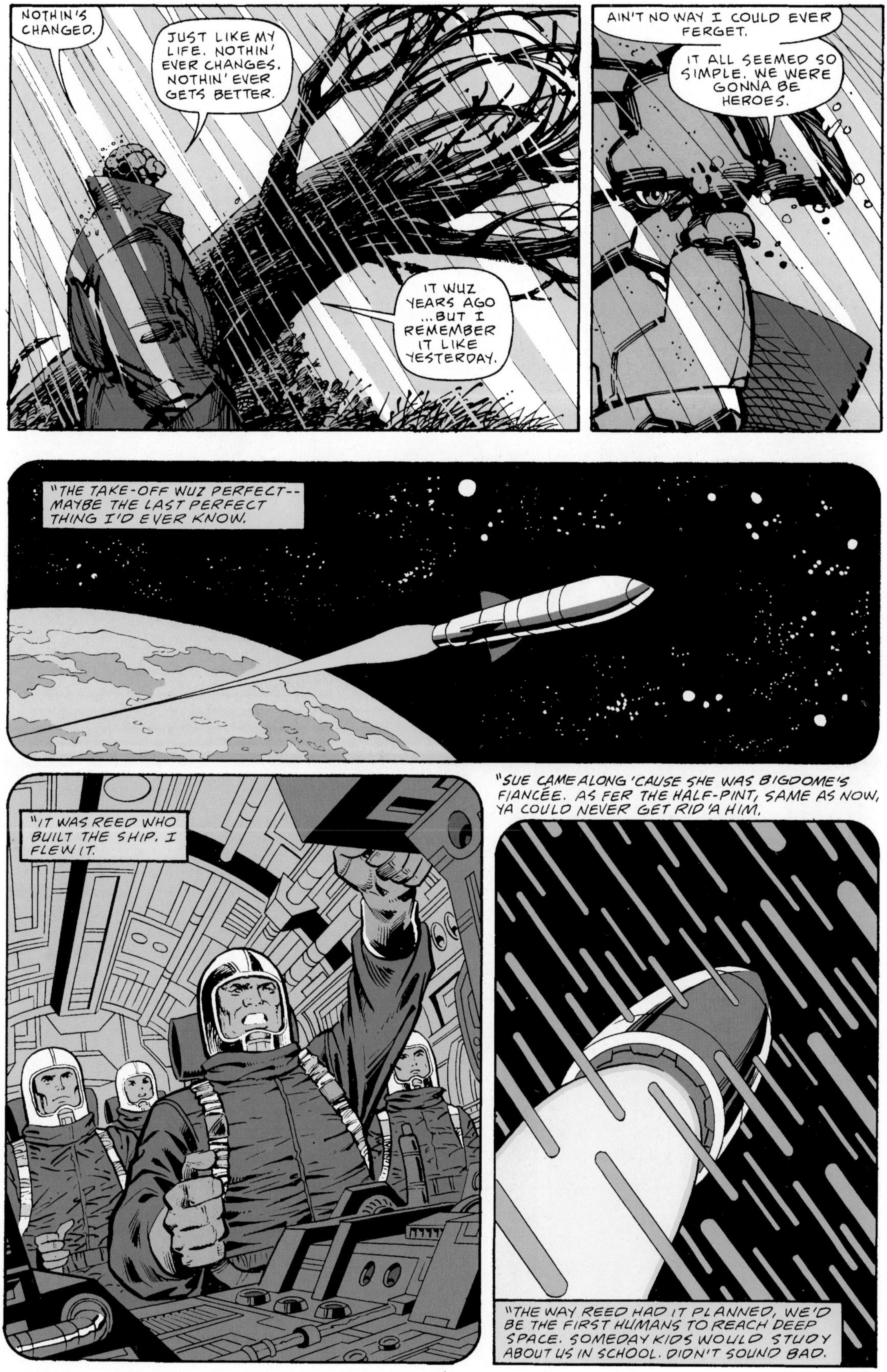
NOTHIN'S CHANGED.
JUST LIKE MY LIFE. NOTHIN' EVER CHANGES. NOTHIN' EVER GETS BETTER.
IT WUZ YEARS AGO ...BUT I REMEMBER IT LIKE YESTERDAY.
AIN'T NO WAY I COULD EVER FERGET.
IT ALL SEEMED SO SIMPLE. WE WERE GONNA BE HEROES.
"THE TAKE-OFF WUZ PERFECT-- MAYBE THE LAST PERFECT THING I'D EVER KNOW.
"IT WAS REED WHO BUILT THE SHIP. I FLEW IT.
"SUE CAME ALONG 'CAUSE SHE WAS BIGDOME'S FIANCÉE. AS FER THE HALF-PINT, SAME AS NOW, YA COULD NEVER GET RID 'A HIM.
"THE WAY REED HAD IT PLANNED, WE'D BE THE FIRST HUMANS TO REACH DEEP SPACE. SOMEDAY KIDS WOULD STUDY ABOUT US IN SCHOOL. DIDN'T SOUND BAD.

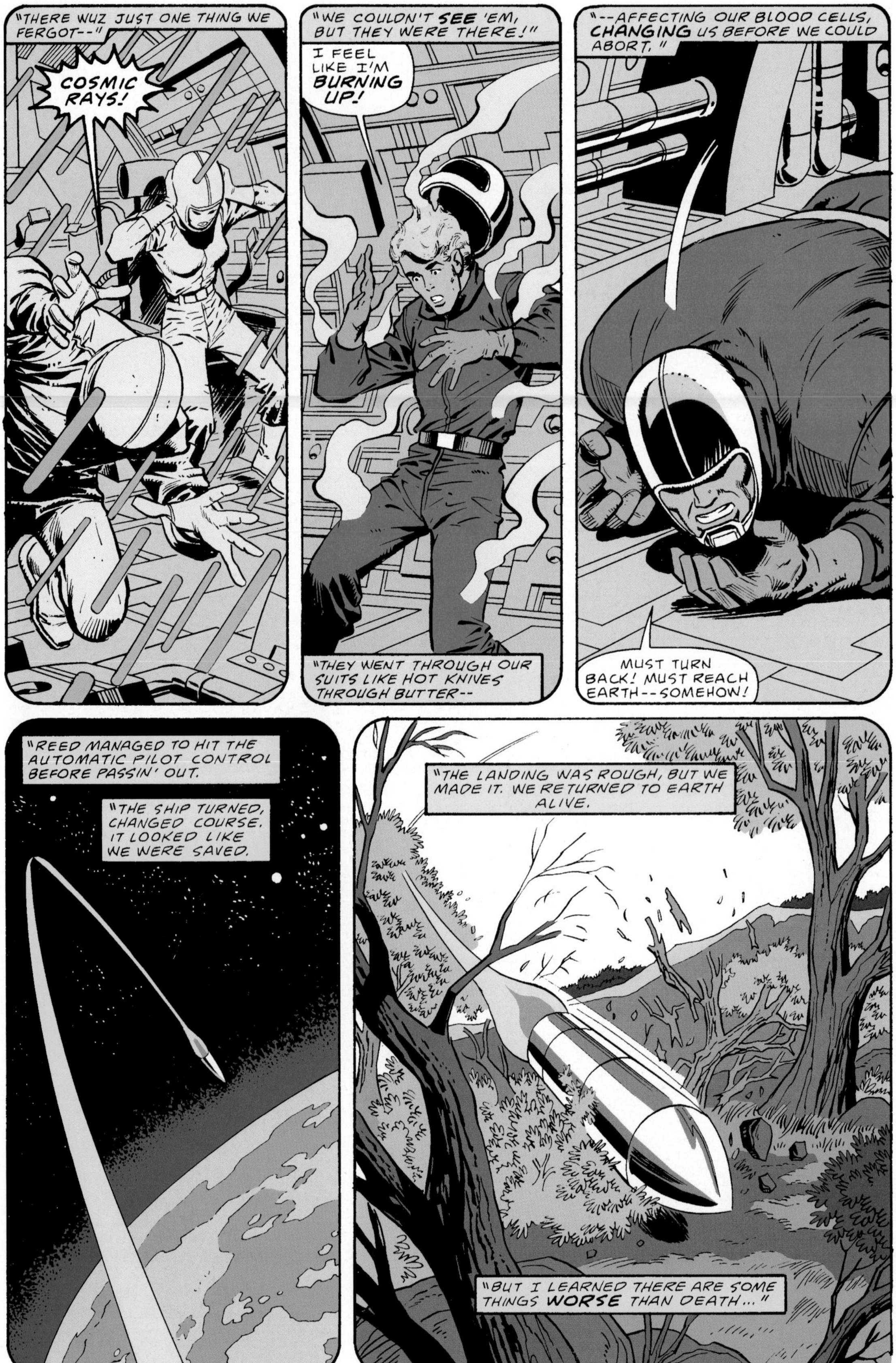

"THERE WUZ JUST ONE THING WE FERGOT--"
COSMIC RAYS!
"WE COULDN'T **SEE** 'EM, BUT THEY WERE THERE!"
I FEEL LIKE I'M **BURNING** UP!
"THEY WENT THROUGH OUR SUITS LIKE HOT KNIVES THROUGH BUTTER--
"--AFFECTING OUR BLOOD CELLS, **CHANGING** US BEFORE WE COULD ABORT."
MUST TURN BACK! MUST REACH EARTH--SOMEHOW!
"REED MANAGED TO HIT THE AUTOMATIC PILOT CONTROL BEFORE PASSIN' OUT.
"THE SHIP TURNED, CHANGED COURSE. IT LOOKED LIKE WE WERE SAVED.
"THE LANDING WAS ROUGH, BUT WE MADE IT. WE RETURNED TO EARTH ALIVE.
"BUT I LEARNED THERE ARE SOME THINGS **WORSE** THAN DEATH..."

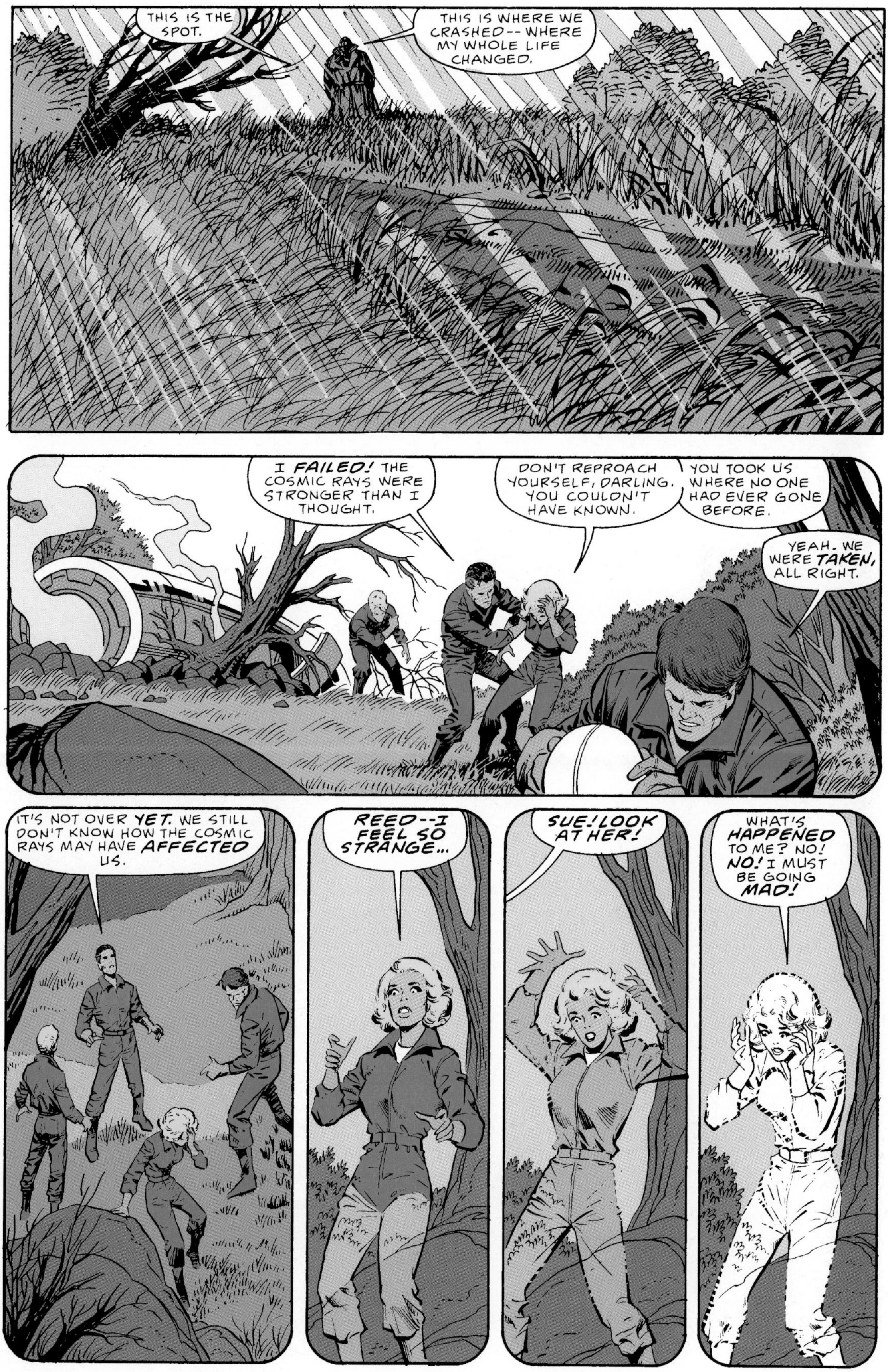
THIS IS THE SPOT.
THIS IS WHERE WE CRASHED-- WHERE MY WHOLE LIFE CHANGED.
I FAILED! THE COSMIC RAYS WERE STRONGER THAN I THOUGHT.
DON'T REPROACH YOURSELF, DARLING. YOU COULDN'T HAVE KNOWN.
YOU TOOK US WHERE NO ONE HAD EVER GONE BEFORE.
YEAH. WE WERE TAKEN, ALL RIGHT.
IT'S NOT OVER YET. WE STILL DON'T KNOW HOW THE COSMIC RAYS MAY HAVE AFFECTED US.
REED--I FEEL SO STRANGE...
SUE! LOOK AT HER!
WHAT'S HAPPENED TO ME? NO! NO! I MUST BE GOING MAD!

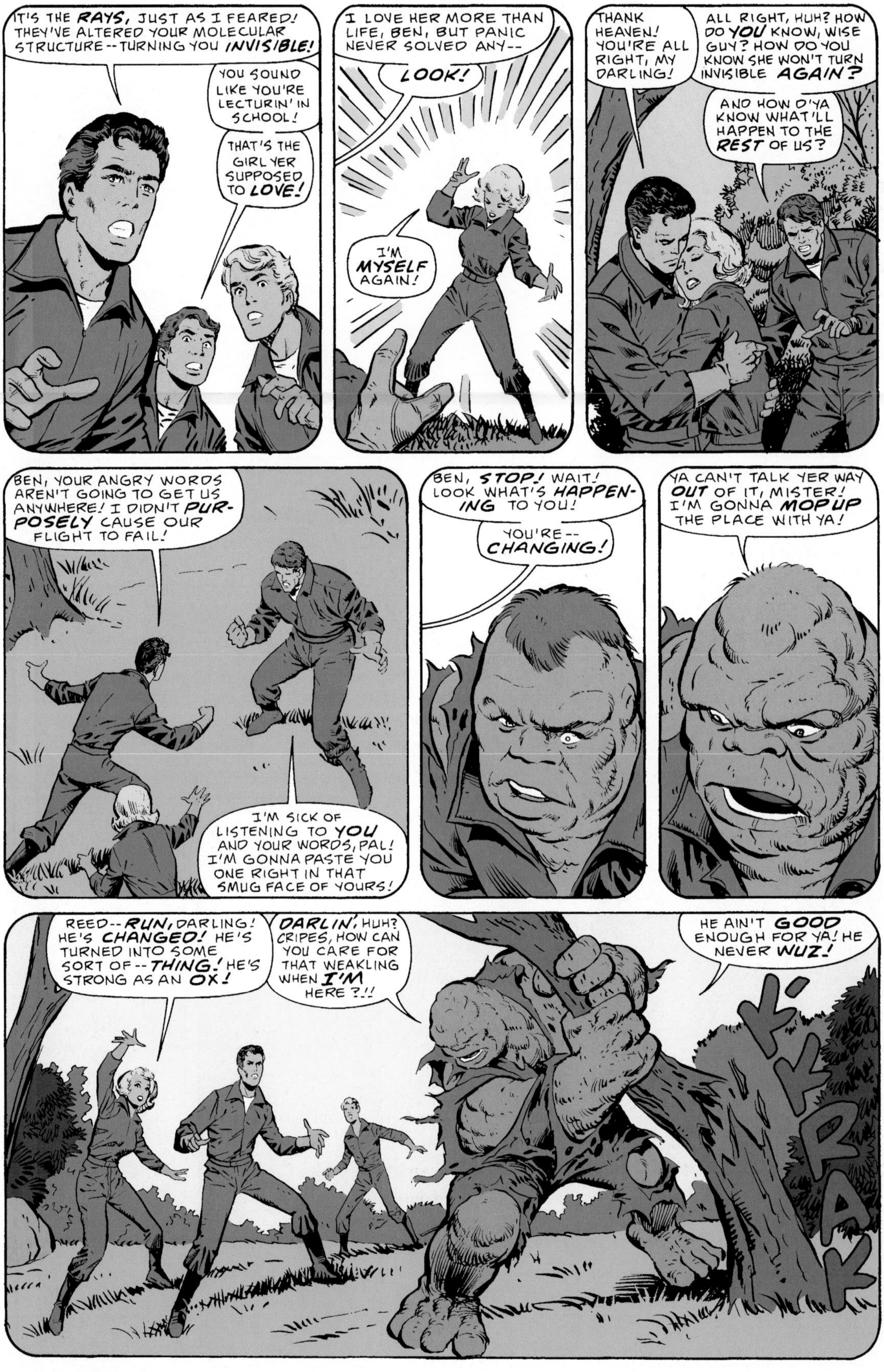
IT'S THE RAYS, JUST AS I FEARED! THEY'VE ALTERED YOUR MOLECULAR STRUCTURE--TURNING YOU INVISIBLE!
YOU SOUND LIKE YOU'RE LECTURIN' IN SCHOOL!
THAT'S THE GIRL YER SUPPOSED TO LOVE!
I LOVE HER MORE THAN LIFE, BEN, BUT PANIC NEVER SOLVED ANY--
LOOK!
I'M MYSELF AGAIN!
THANK HEAVEN! YOU'RE ALL RIGHT, MY DARLING!
ALL RIGHT, HUH? HOW DO YOU KNOW, WISE GUY? HOW DO YOU KNOW SHE WON'T TURN INVISIBLE AGAIN?
AND HOW D'YA KNOW WHAT'LL HAPPEN TO THE REST OF US?
BEN, YOUR ANGRY WORDS AREN'T GOING TO GET US ANYWHERE! I DIDN'T PURPOSELY CAUSE OUR FLIGHT TO FAIL!
I'M SICK OF LISTENING TO YOU AND YOUR WORDS, PAL! I'M GONNA PASTE YOU ONE RIGHT IN THAT SMUG FACE OF YOURS!
BEN, STOP! WAIT! LOOK WHAT'S HAPPENING TO YOU!
YOU'RE--CHANGING!
YA CAN'T TALK YER WAY OUT OF IT, MISTER! I'M GONNA MOP UP THE PLACE WITH YA!
REED--RUN, DARLING! HE'S CHANGED! HE'S TURNED INTO SOME SORT OF--THING! HE'S STRONG AS AN OX!
DARLIN', HUH? CRIPES, HOW CAN YOU CARE FOR THAT WEAKLING WHEN I'M HERE?!!
HE AIN'T GOOD ENOUGH FOR YA! HE NEVER WUZ!
K'KRAK

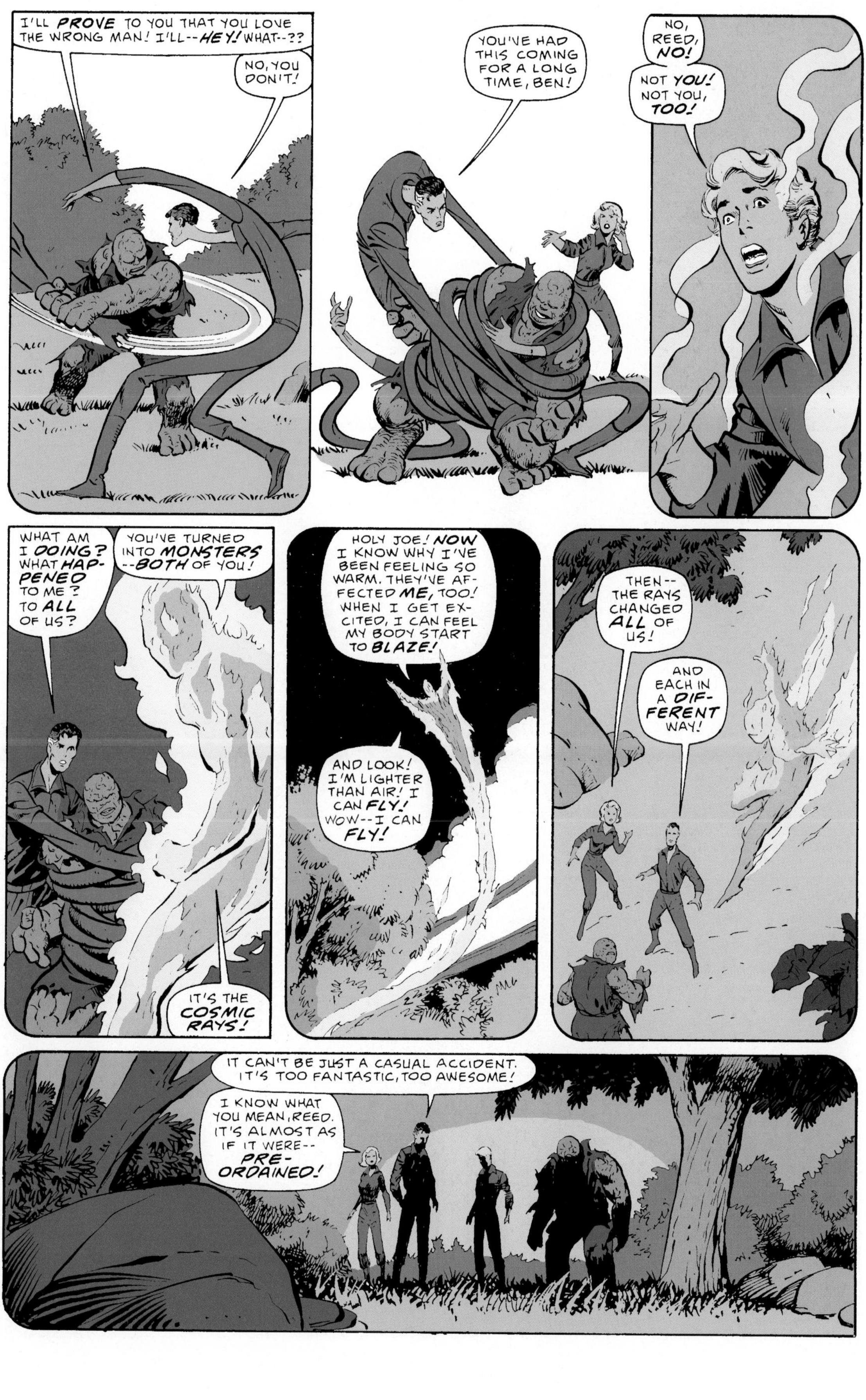
I'LL PROVE TO YOU THAT YOU LOVE THE WRONG MAN! I'LL--HEY! WHAT--??
NO, YOU DON'T!
YOU'VE HAD THIS COMING FOR A LONG TIME, BEN!
NO, REED, NO!
NOT YOU! NOT YOU, TOO!
WHAT AM I DOING? WHAT HAPPENED TO ME? TO ALL OF US?
YOU'VE TURNED INTO MONSTERS --BOTH OF YOU!
IT'S THE COSMIC RAYS!
HOLY JOE! NOW I KNOW WHY I'VE BEEN FEELING SO WARM. THEY'VE AFFECTED ME, TOO! WHEN I GET EXCITED, I CAN FEEL MY BODY START TO BLAZE!
AND LOOK! I'M LIGHTER THAN AIR! I CAN FLY! WOW--I CAN FLY!
THEN--THE RAYS CHANGED ALL OF US!
AND EACH IN A DIFFERENT WAY!
IT CAN'T BE JUST A CASUAL ACCIDENT. IT'S TOO FANTASTIC, TOO AWESOME!
I KNOW WHAT YOU MEAN, REED. IT'S ALMOST AS IF IT WERE--PRE-ORDAINED!

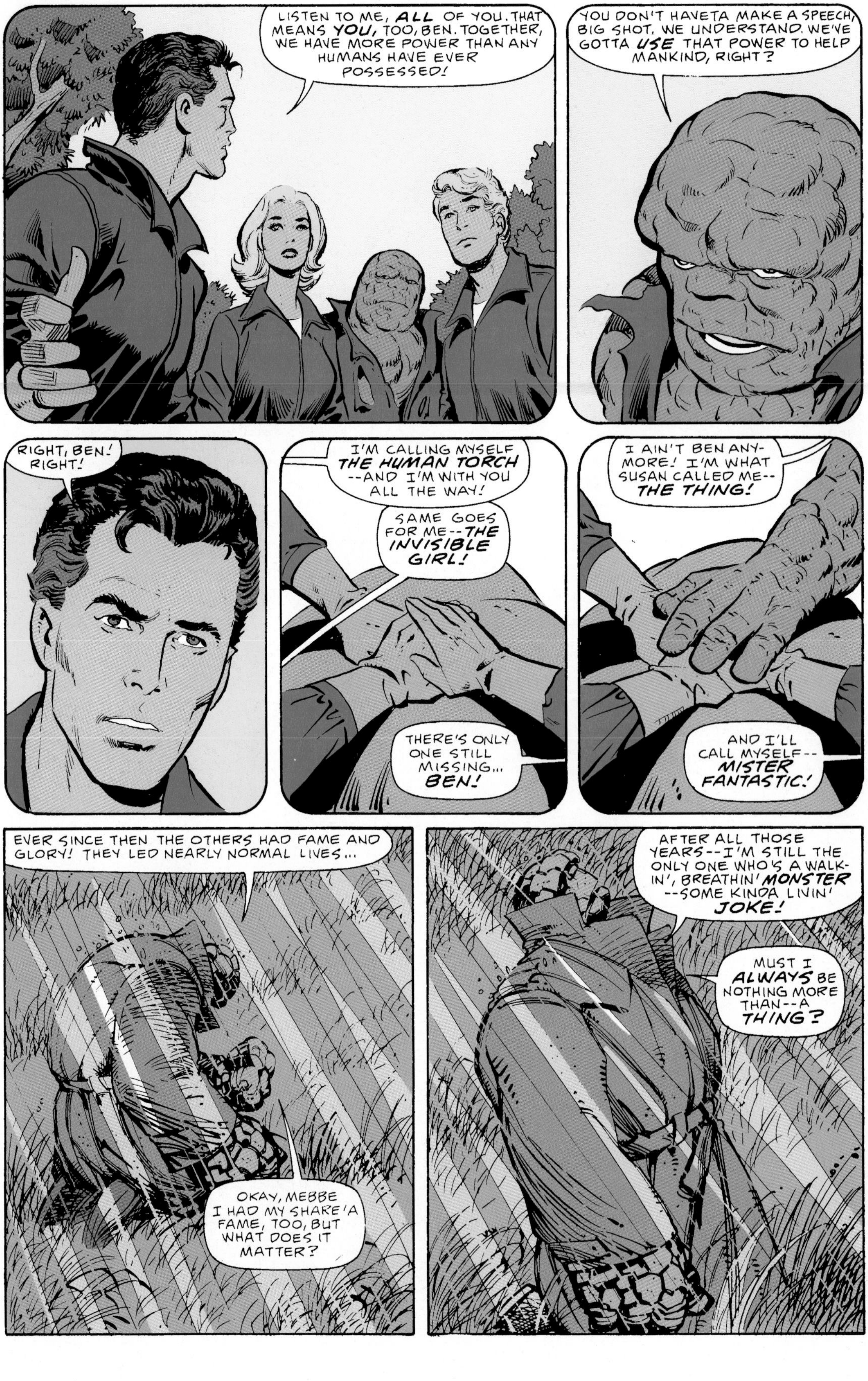
LISTEN TO ME, ALL OF YOU. THAT MEANS YOU, TOO, BEN. TOGETHER, WE HAVE MORE POWER THAN ANY HUMANS HAVE EVER POSSESSED!
YOU DON'T HAVETA MAKE A SPEECH, BIG SHOT. WE UNDERSTAND. WE'VE GOTTA USE THAT POWER TO HELP MANKIND, RIGHT?
RIGHT, BEN! RIGHT!
I'M CALLING MYSELF THE HUMAN TORCH --AND I'M WITH YOU ALL THE WAY!
SAME GOES FOR ME--THE INVISIBLE GIRL!
THERE'S ONLY ONE STILL MISSING... BEN!
I AIN'T BEN ANY-MORE! I'M WHAT SUSAN CALLED ME-- THE THING!
AND I'LL CALL MYSELF-- MISTER FANTASTIC!
EVER SINCE THEN THE OTHERS HAD FAME AND GLORY! THEY LED NEARLY NORMAL LIVES...
OKAY, MEBBE I HAD MY SHARE 'A FAME, TOO, BUT WHAT DOES IT MATTER?
AFTER ALL THOSE YEARS--I'M STILL THE ONLY ONE WHO'S A WALK-IN', BREATHIN' MONSTER --SOME KINDA LIVIN' JOKE!
MUST I ALWAYS BE NOTHING MORE THAN--A THING?

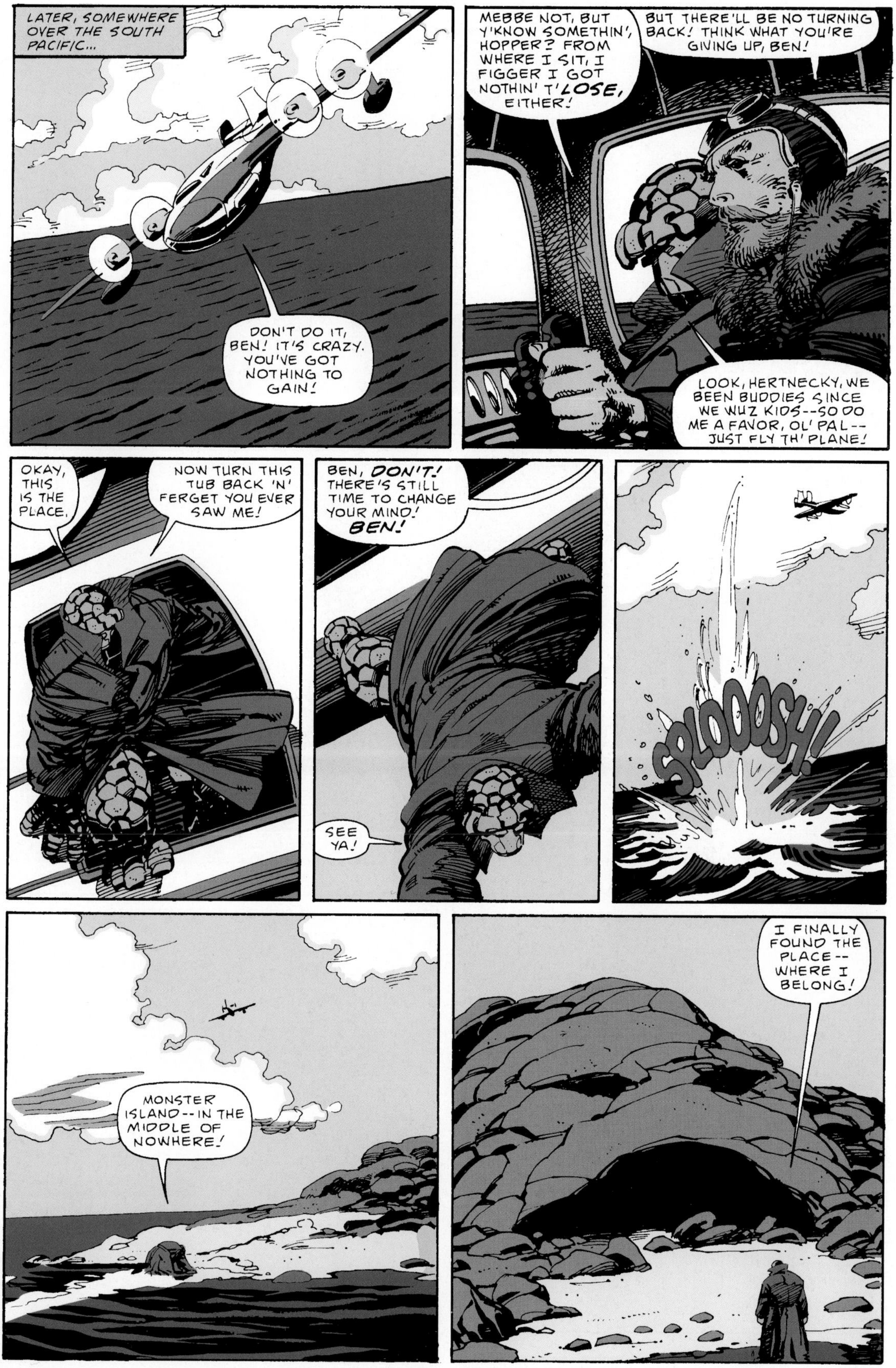
LATER, SOMEWHERE OVER THE SOUTH PACIFIC...
DON'T DO IT, BEN! IT'S CRAZY. YOU'VE GOT NOTHING TO GAIN!
MEBBE NOT, BUT Y'KNOW SOMETHIN', HOPPER? FROM WHERE I SIT, I FIGGER I GOT NOTHIN' T'LOSE, EITHER!
BUT THERE'LL BE NO TURNING BACK! THINK WHAT YOU'RE GIVING UP, BEN!
LOOK, HERTNECKY, WE BEEN BUDDIES SINCE WE WUZ KIDS--SO DO ME A FAVOR, OL' PAL-- JUST FLY TH' PLANE!
OKAY, THIS IS THE PLACE.
NOW TURN THIS TUB BACK 'N' FERGET YOU EVER SAW ME!
BEN, DON'T! THERE'S STILL TIME TO CHANGE YOUR MIND! BEN!
SEE YA!
SPLOOOSH!
MONSTER ISLAND--IN THE MIDDLE OF NOWHERE!
I FINALLY FOUND THE PLACE-- WHERE I BELONG!

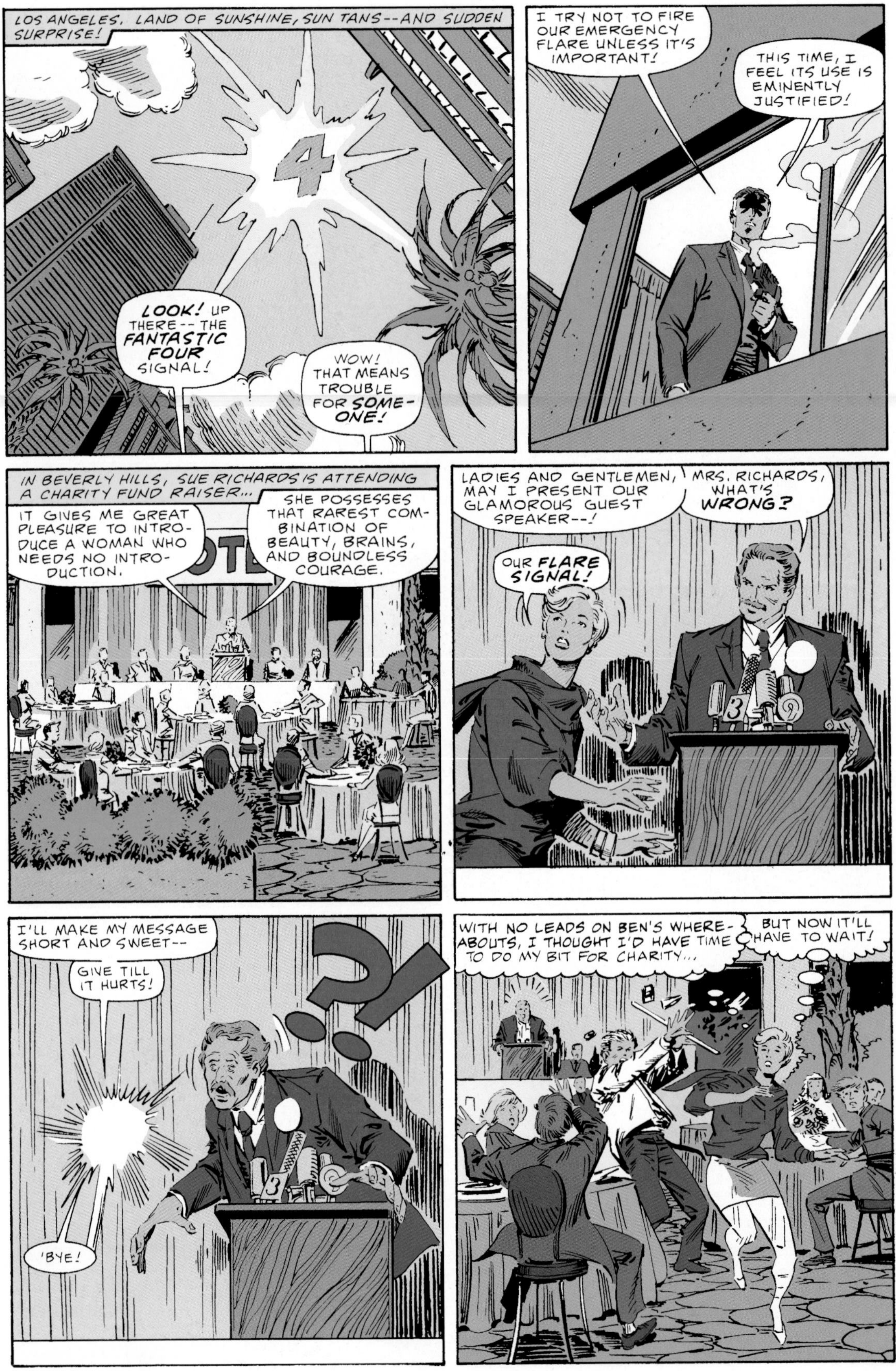
LOS ANGELES. LAND OF SUNSHINE, SUN TANS--AND SUDDEN SURPRISE!
LOOK! UP THERE-- THE FANTASTIC FOUR SIGNAL!
WOW! THAT MEANS TROUBLE FOR SOME-ONE!
I TRY NOT TO FIRE OUR EMERGENCY FLARE UNLESS IT'S IMPORTANT!
THIS TIME, I FEEL ITS USE IS EMINENTLY JUSTIFIED!
IN BEVERLY HILLS, SUE RICHARDS IS ATTENDING A CHARITY FUND RAISER...
IT GIVES ME GREAT PLEASURE TO INTRO-DUCE A WOMAN WHO NEEDS NO INTRO-DUCTION.
SHE POSSESSES THAT RAREST COM-BINATION OF BEAUTY, BRAINS, AND BOUNDLESS COURAGE.
LADIES AND GENTLEMEN, MAY I PRESENT OUR GLAMOROUS GUEST SPEAKER--!
MRS. RICHARDS, WHAT'S WRONG?
OUR FLARE SIGNAL!
I'LL MAKE MY MESSAGE SHORT AND SWEET--
GIVE TILL IT HURTS!
'BYE!
WITH NO LEADS ON BEN'S WHERE-ABOUTS, I THOUGHT I'D HAVE TIME TO DO MY BIT FOR CHARITY...
BUT NOW IT'LL HAVE TO WAIT!

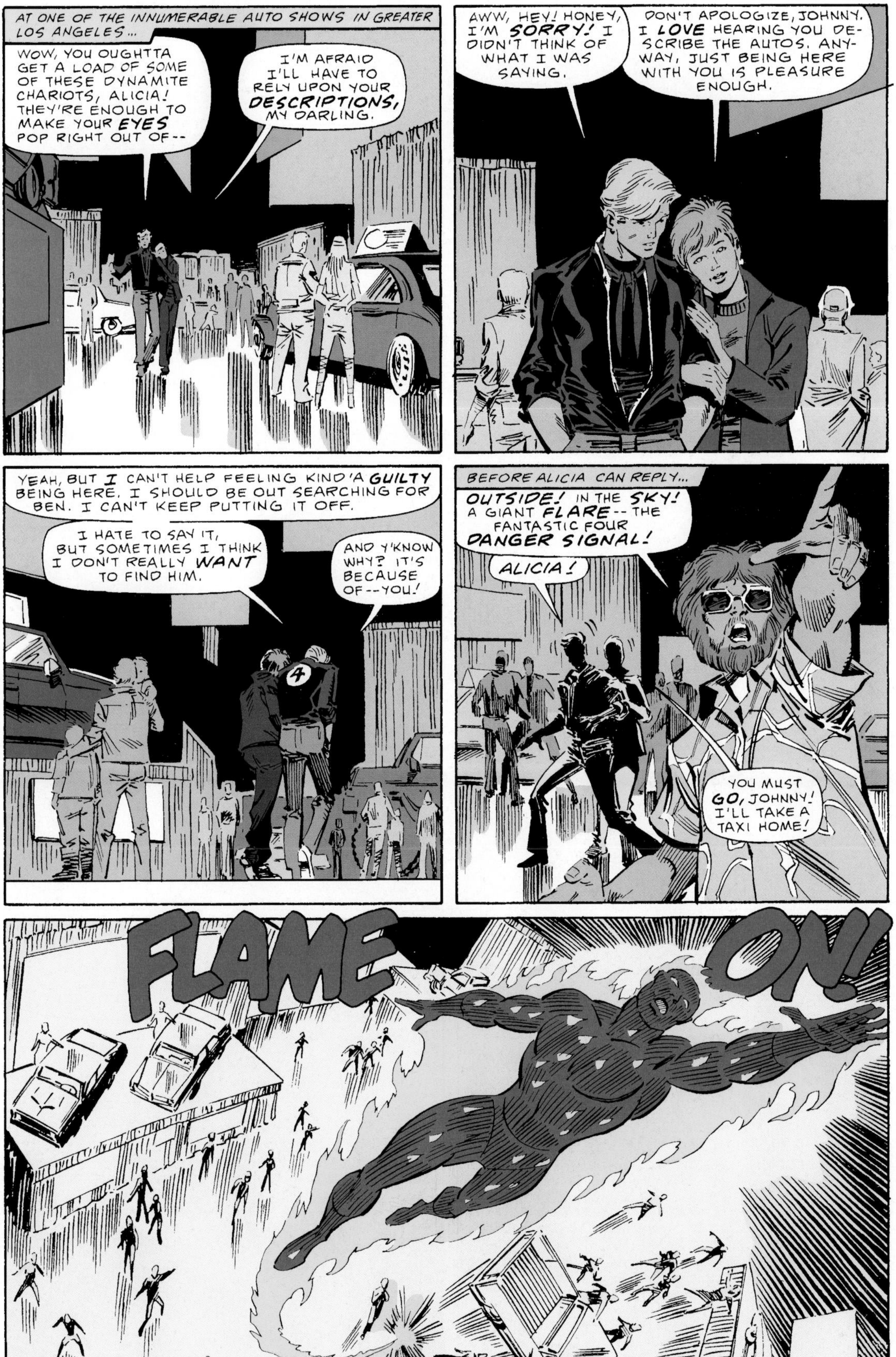
AT ONE OF THE INNUMERABLE AUTO SHOWS IN GREATER LOS ANGELES...
WOW, YOU OUGHTTA GET A LOAD OF SOME OF THESE DYNAMITE CHARIOTS, ALICIA! THEY'RE ENOUGH TO MAKE YOUR EYES POP RIGHT OUT OF--
I'M AFRAID I'LL HAVE TO RELY UPON YOUR DESCRIPTIONS, MY DARLING.
AWW, HEY! HONEY, I'M SORRY! I DIDN'T THINK OF WHAT I WAS SAYING.
DON'T APOLOGIZE, JOHNNY. I LOVE HEARING YOU DESCRIBE THE AUTOS. ANYWAY, JUST BEING HERE WITH YOU IS PLEASURE ENOUGH.
YEAH, BUT I CAN'T HELP FEELING KIND'A GUILTY BEING HERE. I SHOULD BE OUT SEARCHING FOR BEN. I CAN'T KEEP PUTTING IT OFF.
I HATE TO SAY IT, BUT SOMETIMES I THINK I DON'T REALLY WANT TO FIND HIM.
AND Y'KNOW WHY? IT'S BECAUSE OF--YOU!
BEFORE ALICIA CAN REPLY...
OUTSIDE! IN THE SKY! A GIANT FLARE-- THE FANTASTIC FOUR DANGER SIGNAL!
ALICIA!
YOU MUST GO, JOHNNY! I'LL TAKE A TAXI HOME!
FLAME ON!

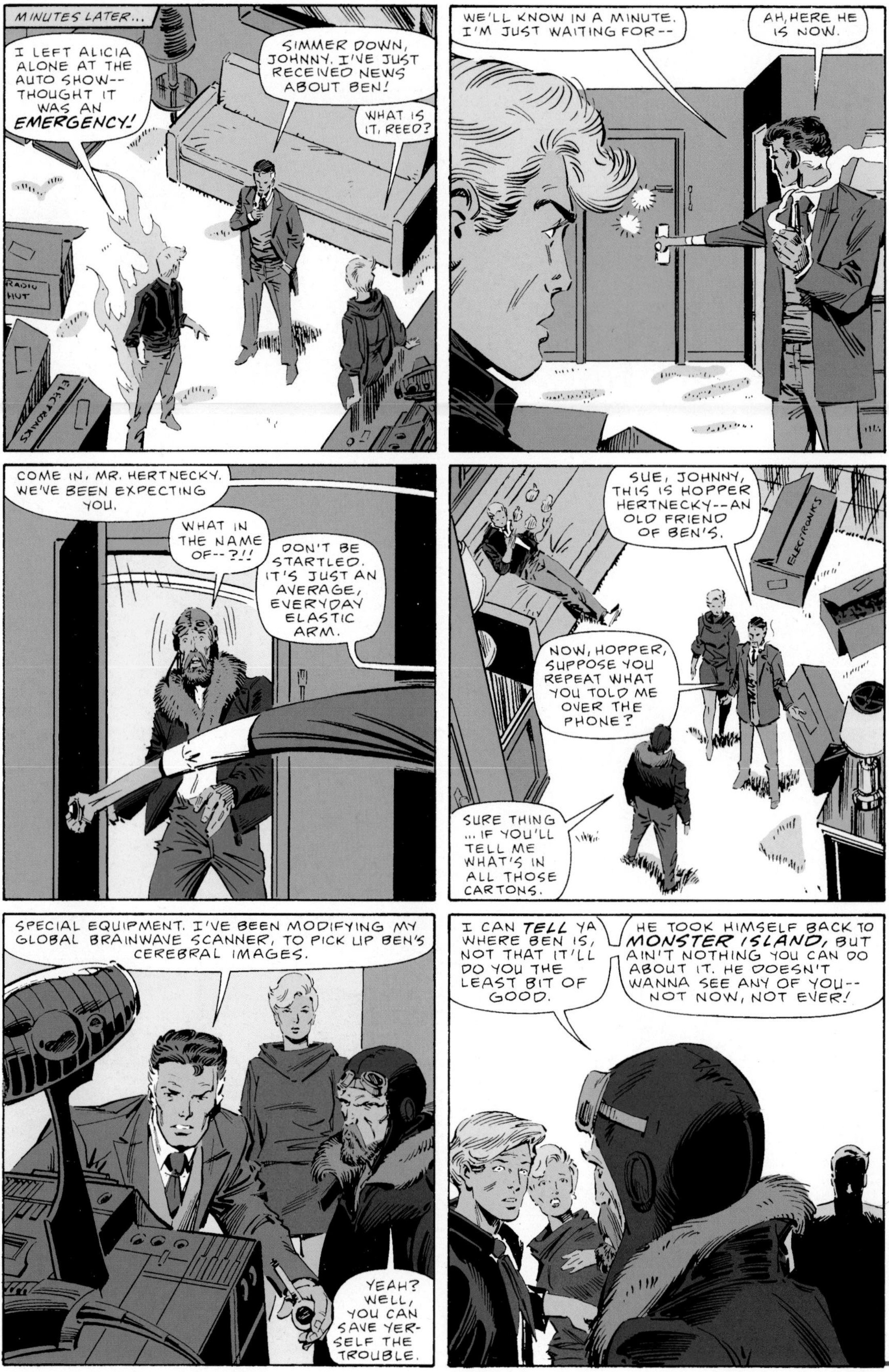
MINUTES LATER...
I LEFT ALICIA ALONE AT THE AUTO SHOW-- THOUGHT IT WAS AN EMERGENCY!
SIMMER DOWN, JOHNNY. I'VE JUST RECEIVED NEWS ABOUT BEN!
WHAT IS IT, REED?
RADIO HUT
ELECTRONICS
WE'LL KNOW IN A MINUTE. I'M JUST WAITING FOR--
AH, HERE HE IS NOW.
COME IN, MR. HERTNECKY. WE'VE BEEN EXPECTING YOU.
WHAT IN THE NAME OF--?!!
DON'T BE STARTLED. IT'S JUST AN AVERAGE, EVERYDAY ELASTIC ARM.
SUE, JOHNNY, THIS IS HOPPER HERTNECKY--AN OLD FRIEND OF BEN'S.
ELECTRONICS
NOW, HOPPER, SUPPOSE YOU REPEAT WHAT YOU TOLD ME OVER THE PHONE?
SURE THING ...IF YOU'LL TELL ME WHAT'S IN ALL THOSE CARTONS.
SPECIAL EQUIPMENT. I'VE BEEN MODIFYING MY GLOBAL BRAINWAVE SCANNER, TO PICK UP BEN'S CEREBRAL IMAGES.
YEAH? WELL, YOU CAN SAVE YER-SELF THE TROUBLE.
I CAN TELL YA WHERE BEN IS, NOT THAT IT'LL DO YOU THE LEAST BIT OF GOOD.
HE TOOK HIMSELF BACK TO MONSTER ISLAND, BUT AIN'T NOTHING YOU CAN DO ABOUT IT. HE DOESN'T WANNA SEE ANY OF YOU-- NOT NOW, NOT EVER!

HE KNEW YOU WOULD FIGURE OUT A WAY TO FIND 'IM SOONER OR LATER, RICHARDS, SO HE TOLD ME TO TELL YOU TO *LAY OFF.*

HE SAID HE'S GONE BACK WHERE HE BELONGS-- WITH THE OTHER MONSTERS!

FACE IT, MISTER, IT'S *YOUR* FAULT BEN'S THE WAY HE IS! YOU'VE DONE *ENOUGH* TO HIM! HE'S BEEN HURT ENOUGH!

THE THREE OF YOU, WITH ALL YOUR BIG TALK AND YOUR FANCY TRAPPINGS. LIFE'S BEEN PRETTY GOOD TO YOU, HASN'T IT?

YOU TWO, YOU'VE GOT EACH OTHER, AND A KID. AND THE TORCH HAS A GIRL FRIEND-- WHO USED TO BE BEN'S!

BUT DIDJA EVER STOP 'N' THINK WHAT IT'S BEEN LIKE FOR BEN? WHAT IT'S LIKE TO BE--A *THING?*

HE'S WHERE HE *WANTS* TO BE NOW, WHERE HE FIGURES HE BELONGS. SO LEAVE HIM ALONE.

DON'T *HURT* HIM ANY MORE.

HEY, WHAT DID OL' RIP VAN WINKLE WANT? DON'T TELL ME, LET ME GUESS, HE'S WORKING HIS WAY THROUGH COLLEGE SELLING SUBSCRIPTIONS, RIGHT?

LOOKS LIKE I'M WRONG.

OKAY, SO JOAN RIVERS I'M NOT! I'M STILL JUST THE PLAIN OLD SHE-HULK, BUT WHY THE LONG FACES?

SOMETHING'S WRONG, REALLY WRONG. I'VE NEVER SEEN THEM LIKE THIS!

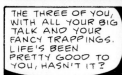

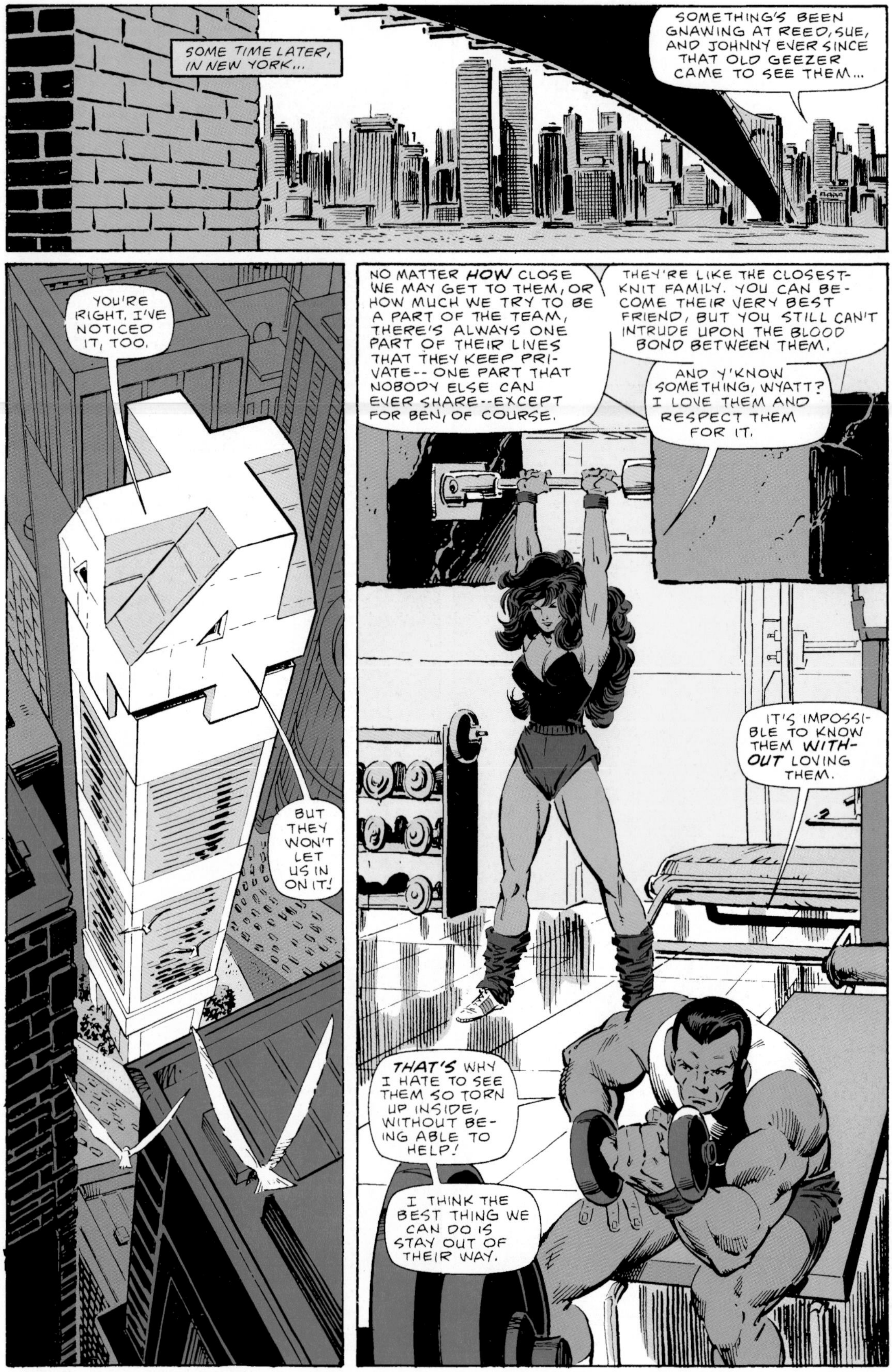
SOME TIME LATER, IN NEW YORK...
SOMETHING'S BEEN GNAWING AT REED, SUE, AND JOHNNY EVER SINCE THAT OLD GEEZER CAME TO SEE THEM...
YOU'RE RIGHT. I'VE NOTICED IT, TOO.
BUT THEY WON'T LET US IN ON IT!
NO MATTER HOW CLOSE WE MAY GET TO THEM, OR HOW MUCH WE TRY TO BE A PART OF THE TEAM, THERE'S ALWAYS ONE PART OF THEIR LIVES THAT THEY KEEP PRIVATE-- ONE PART THAT NOBODY ELSE CAN EVER SHARE--EXCEPT FOR BEN, OF COURSE.
THEY'RE LIKE THE CLOSEST-KNIT FAMILY. YOU CAN BECOME THEIR VERY BEST FRIEND, BUT YOU STILL CAN'T INTRUDE UPON THE BLOOD BOND BETWEEN THEM.
AND Y'KNOW SOMETHING, WYATT? I LOVE THEM AND RESPECT THEM FOR IT.
IT'S IMPOSSIBLE TO KNOW THEM WITHOUT LOVING THEM.
THAT'S WHY I HATE TO SEE THEM SO TORN UP INSIDE, WITHOUT BEING ABLE TO HELP!
I THINK THE BEST THING WE CAN DO IS STAY OUT OF THEIR WAY.

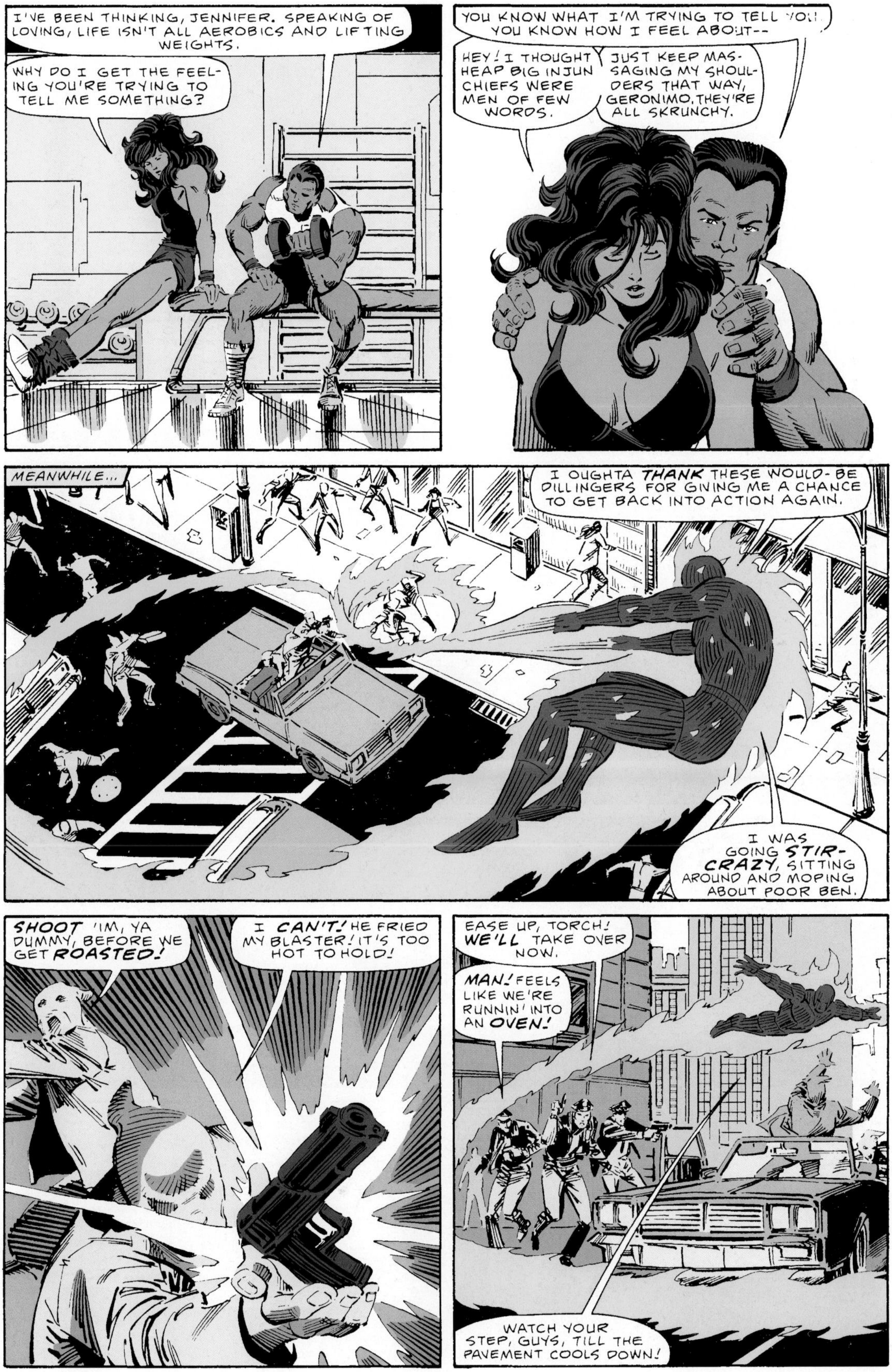
I'VE BEEN THINKING, JENNIFER. SPEAKING OF LOVING, LIFE ISN'T ALL AEROBICS AND LIFTING WEIGHTS.
WHY DO I GET THE FEELING YOU'RE TRYING TO TELL ME SOMETHING?
YOU KNOW WHAT I'M TRYING TO TELL YOU. YOU KNOW HOW I FEEL ABOUT--
HEY! I THOUGHT HEAP BIG INJUN CHIEFS WERE MEN OF FEW WORDS.
JUST KEEP MASSAGING MY SHOULDERS THAT WAY, GERONIMO. THEY'RE ALL SKRUNCHY.
MEANWHILE...
I OUGHTA THANK THESE WOULD-BE DILLINGERS FOR GIVING ME A CHANCE TO GET BACK INTO ACTION AGAIN.
I WAS GOING STIR-CRAZY, SITTING AROUND AND MOPING ABOUT POOR BEN.
SHOOT 'IM, YA DUMMY, BEFORE WE GET ROASTED!
I CAN'T! HE FRIED MY BLASTER! IT'S TOO HOT TO HOLD!
EASE UP, TORCH! WE'LL TAKE OVER NOW.
MAN! FEELS LIKE WE'RE RUNNIN' INTO AN OVEN!
WATCH YOUR STEP, GUYS, TILL THE PAVEMENT COOLS DOWN!

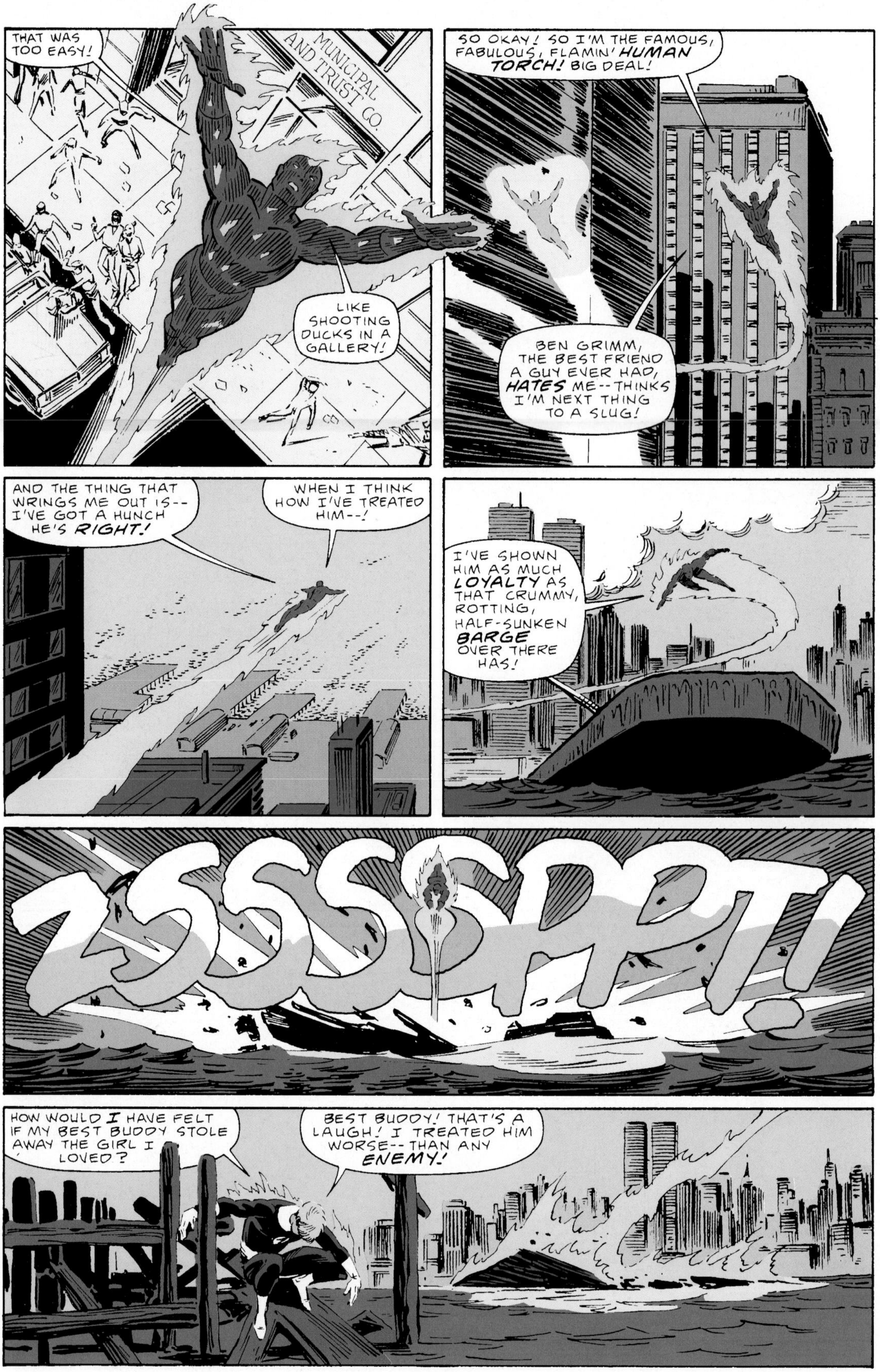

THAT WAS TOO EASY!
MUNICIPAL AND TRUST CO.
LIKE SHOOTING DUCKS IN A GALLERY!
SO OKAY! SO I'M THE FAMOUS, FABULOUS, FLAMIN' HUMAN TORCH! BIG DEAL!
BEN GRIMM, THE BEST FRIEND A GUY EVER HAD, HATES ME--THINKS I'M NEXT THING TO A SLUG!
AND THE THING THAT WRINGS ME OUT IS--I'VE GOT A HUNCH HE'S RIGHT!
WHEN I THINK HOW I'VE TREATED HIM--!
I'VE SHOWN HIM AS MUCH LOYALTY AS THAT CRUMMY, ROTTING, HALF-SUNKEN BARGE OVER THERE HAS!
ZSSSPPT!!
HOW WOULD I HAVE FELT IF MY BEST BUDDY STOLE AWAY THE GIRL I LOVED?
BEST BUDDY! THAT'S A LAUGH! I TREATED HIM WORSE--THAN ANY ENEMY!

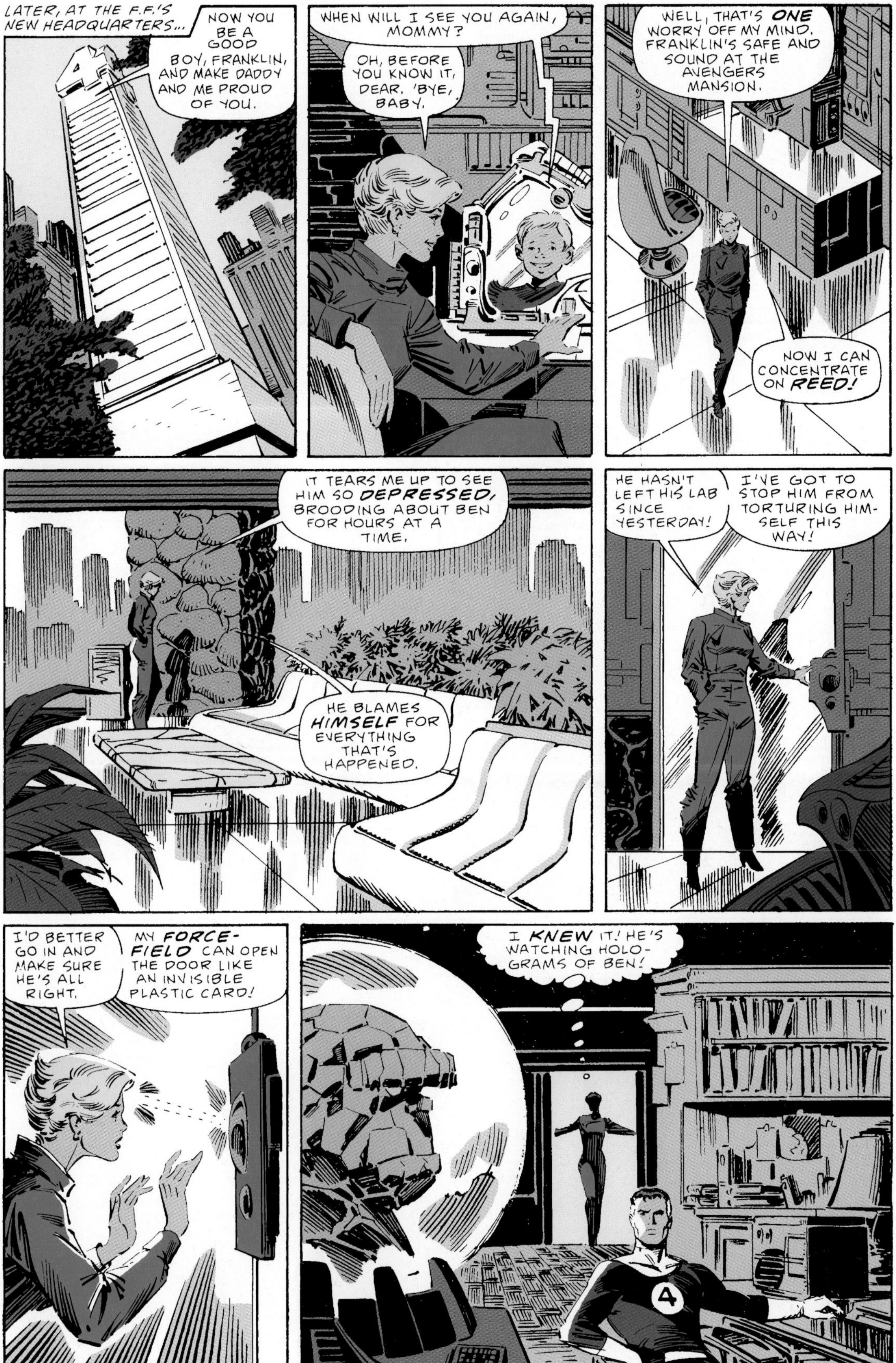
LATER, AT THE F.F.'S NEW HEADQUARTERS...
NOW YOU BE A GOOD BOY, FRANKLIN, AND MAKE DADDY AND ME PROUD OF YOU.
WHEN WILL I SEE YOU AGAIN, MOMMY?
OH, BEFORE YOU KNOW IT, DEAR. 'BYE, BABY.
WELL, THAT'S ONE WORRY OFF MY MIND. FRANKLIN'S SAFE AND SOUND AT THE AVENGERS MANSION.
NOW I CAN CONCENTRATE ON REED!
IT TEARS ME UP TO SEE HIM SO DEPRESSED, BROODING ABOUT BEN FOR HOURS AT A TIME.
HE BLAMES HIMSELF FOR EVERYTHING THAT'S HAPPENED.
HE HASN'T LEFT HIS LAB SINCE YESTERDAY!
I'VE GOT TO STOP HIM FROM TORTURING HIMSELF THIS WAY!
I'D BETTER GO IN AND MAKE SURE HE'S ALL RIGHT.
MY FORCE-FIELD CAN OPEN THE DOOR LIKE AN INVISIBLE PLASTIC CARD!
I KNEW IT! HE'S WATCHING HOLOGRAMS OF BEN!

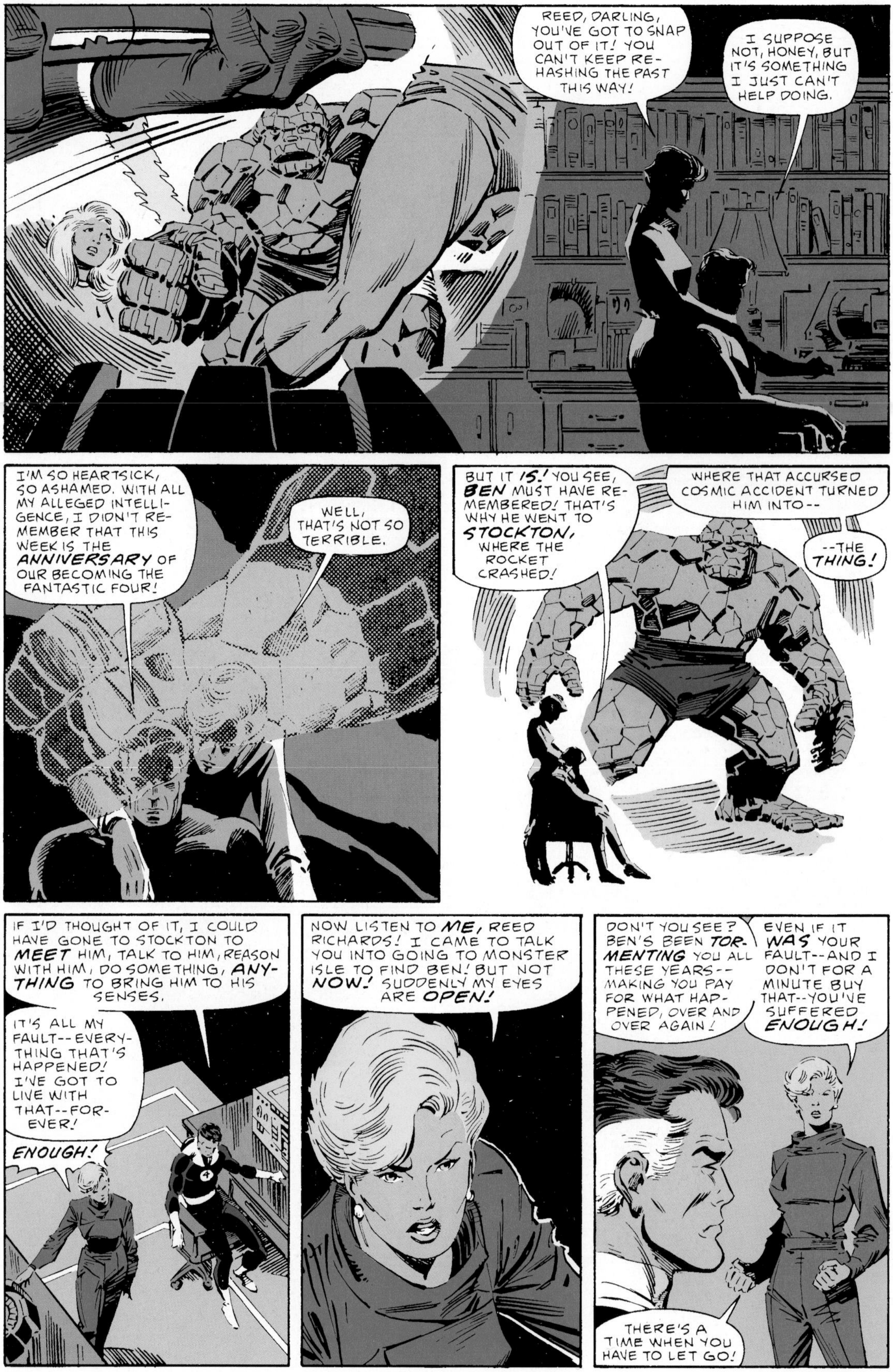

REED, DARLING, YOU'VE GOT TO SNAP OUT OF IT! YOU CAN'T KEEP RE-HASHING THE PAST THIS WAY!
I SUPPOSE NOT, HONEY, BUT IT'S SOMETHING I JUST CAN'T HELP DOING.
I'M SO HEARTSICK, SO ASHAMED. WITH ALL MY ALLEGED INTELLIGENCE, I DIDN'T REMEMBER THAT THIS WEEK IS THE ANNIVERSARY OF OUR BECOMING THE FANTASTIC FOUR!
WELL, THAT'S NOT SO TERRIBLE.
BUT IT IS! YOU SEE, BEN MUST HAVE REMEMBERED! THAT'S WHY HE WENT TO STOCKTON, WHERE THE ROCKET CRASHED!
WHERE THAT ACCURSED COSMIC ACCIDENT TURNED HIM INTO--
--THE THING!
IF I'D THOUGHT OF IT, I COULD HAVE GONE TO STOCKTON TO MEET HIM, TALK TO HIM, REASON WITH HIM, DO SOMETHING, ANYTHING TO BRING HIM TO HIS SENSES.
IT'S ALL MY FAULT--EVERYTHING THAT'S HAPPENED! I'VE GOT TO LIVE WITH THAT--FOREVER!
ENOUGH!
NOW LISTEN TO ME, REED RICHARDS! I CAME TO TALK YOU INTO GOING TO MONSTER ISLE TO FIND BEN! BUT NOT NOW! SUDDENLY MY EYES ARE OPEN!
DON'T YOU SEE? BEN'S BEEN TORMENTING YOU ALL THESE YEARS--MAKING YOU PAY FOR WHAT HAPPENED, OVER AND OVER AGAIN!
EVEN IF IT WAS YOUR FAULT--AND I DON'T FOR A MINUTE BUY THAT--YOU'VE SUFFERED ENOUGH!
THERE'S A TIME WHEN YOU HAVE TO LET GO!

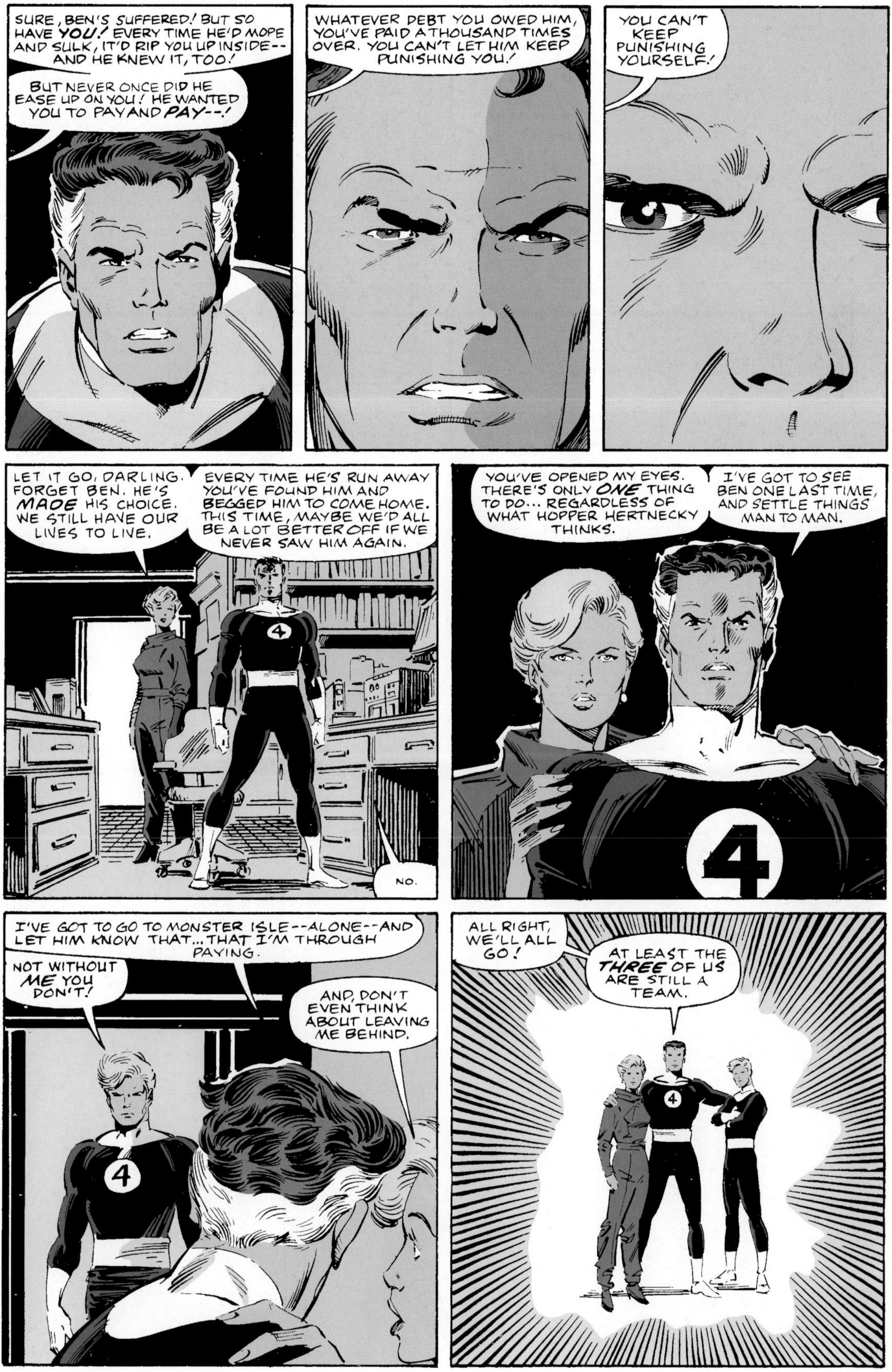

SURE, BEN'S SUFFERED! BUT SO HAVE YOU! EVERY TIME HE'D MOPE AND SULK, IT'D RIP YOU UP INSIDE-- AND HE KNEW IT, TOO!
BUT NEVER ONCE DID HE EASE UP ON YOU! HE WANTED YOU TO PAY AND PAY--!
WHATEVER DEBT YOU OWED HIM, YOU'VE PAID A THOUSAND TIMES OVER. YOU CAN'T LET HIM KEEP PUNISHING YOU!
YOU CAN'T KEEP PUNISHING YOURSELF!
LET IT GO, DARLING. FORGET BEN. HE'S MADE HIS CHOICE. WE STILL HAVE OUR LIVES TO LIVE.
EVERY TIME HE'S RUN AWAY YOU'VE FOUND HIM AND BEGGED HIM TO COME HOME. THIS TIME, MAYBE WE'D ALL BE A LOT BETTER OFF IF WE NEVER SAW HIM AGAIN.
NO.
YOU'VE OPENED MY EYES. THERE'S ONLY ONE THING TO DO... REGARDLESS OF WHAT HOPPER HERTNECKY THINKS.
I'VE GOT TO SEE BEN ONE LAST TIME, AND SETTLE THINGS MAN TO MAN.
I'VE GOT TO GO TO MONSTER ISLE--ALONE--AND LET HIM KNOW THAT... THAT I'M THROUGH PAYING.
NOT WITHOUT ME YOU DON'T!
AND, DON'T EVEN THINK ABOUT LEAVING ME BEHIND.
ALL RIGHT, WE'LL ALL GO!
AT LEAST THE THREE OF US ARE STILL A TEAM.

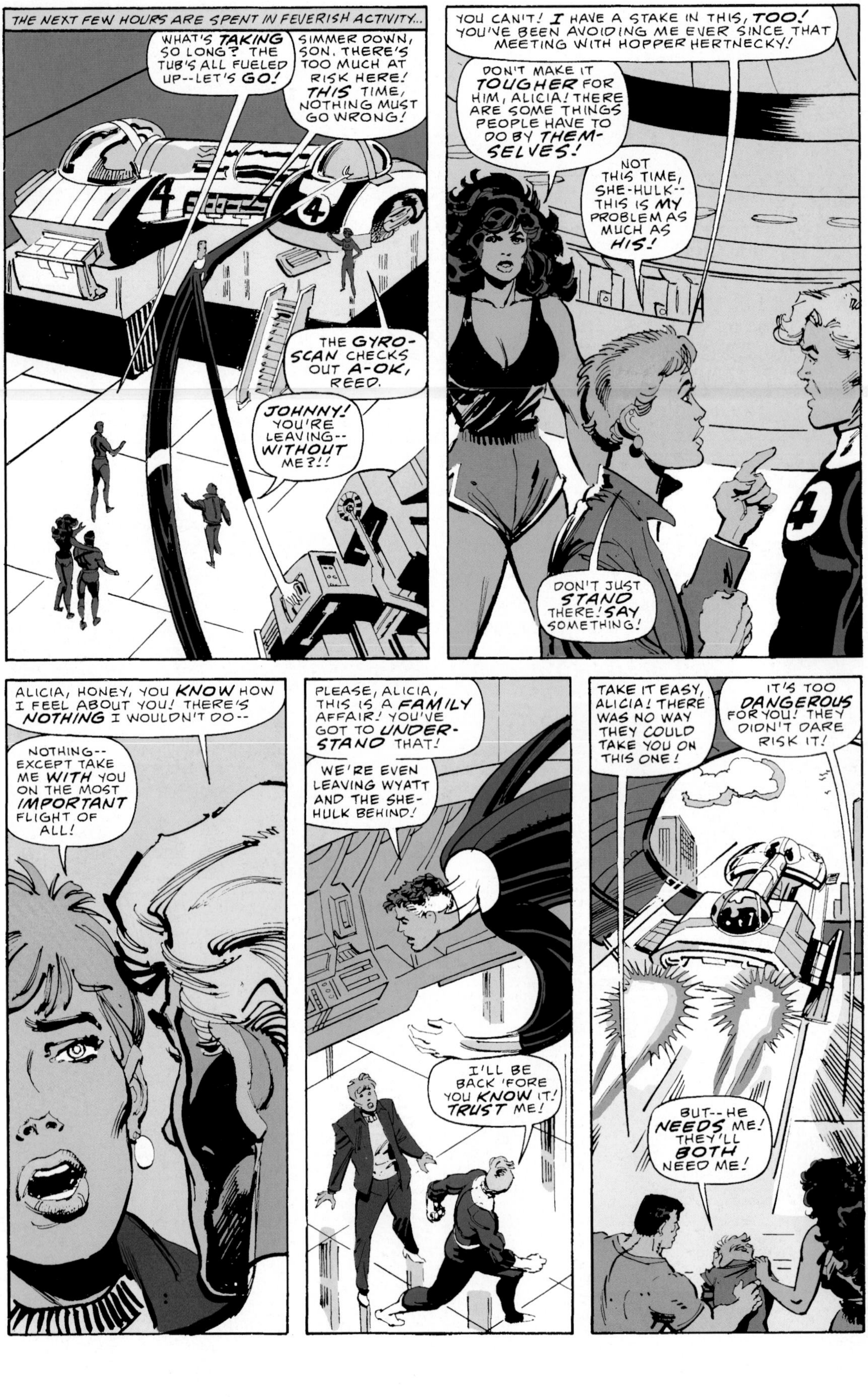
THE NEXT FEW HOURS ARE SPENT IN FEVERISH ACTIVITY...
WHAT'S TAKING SO LONG? THE TUB'S ALL FUELED UP--LET'S GO!
SIMMER DOWN, SON. THERE'S TOO MUCH AT RISK HERE! THIS TIME, NOTHING MUST GO WRONG!
THE GYRO-SCAN CHECKS OUT A-OK, REED.
JOHNNY! YOU'RE LEAVING-- WITHOUT ME?!!
YOU CAN'T! I HAVE A STAKE IN THIS, TOO! YOU'VE BEEN AVOIDING ME EVER SINCE THAT MEETING WITH HOPPER HERTNECKY!
DON'T MAKE IT TOUGHER FOR HIM, ALICIA! THERE ARE SOME THINGS PEOPLE HAVE TO DO BY THEM-SELVES!
NOT THIS TIME, SHE-HULK-- THIS IS MY PROBLEM AS MUCH AS HIS!
DON'T JUST STAND THERE! SAY SOMETHING!
ALICIA, HONEY, YOU KNOW HOW I FEEL ABOUT YOU! THERE'S NOTHING I WOULDN'T DO--
NOTHING-- EXCEPT TAKE ME WITH YOU ON THE MOST IMPORTANT FLIGHT OF ALL!
PLEASE, ALICIA, THIS IS A FAMILY AFFAIR! YOU'VE GOT TO UNDER-STAND THAT!
WE'RE EVEN LEAVING WYATT AND THE SHE-HULK BEHIND!
I'LL BE BACK 'FORE YOU KNOW IT! TRUST ME!
TAKE IT EASY, ALICIA! THERE WAS NO WAY THEY COULD TAKE YOU ON THIS ONE!
IT'S TOO DANGEROUS FOR YOU! THEY DIDN'T DARE RISK IT!
BUT--HE NEEDS ME! THEY'LL BOTH NEED ME!

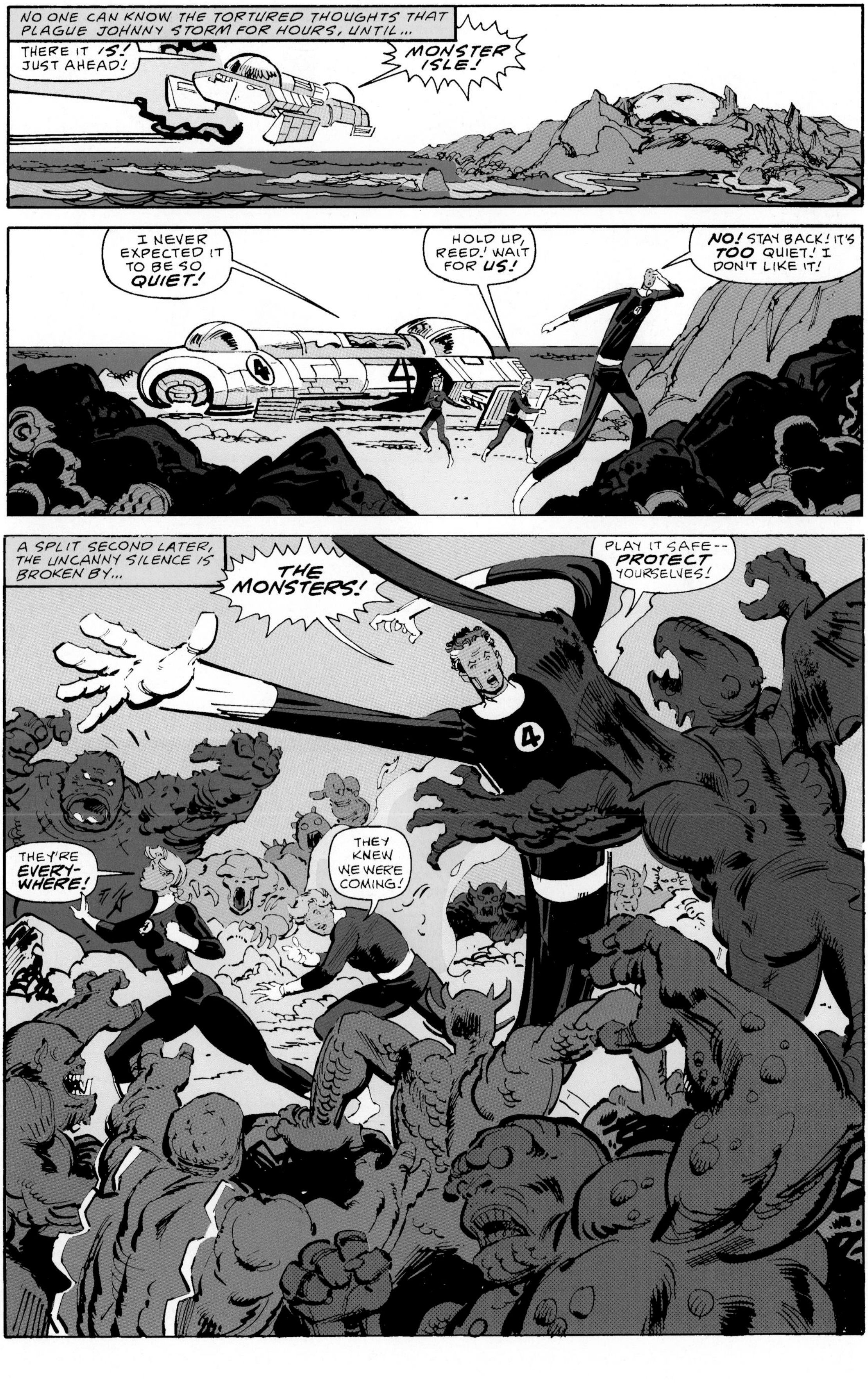
NO ONE CAN KNOW THE TORTURED THOUGHTS THAT PLAGUE JOHNNY STORM FOR HOURS, UNTIL...
THERE IT IS! JUST AHEAD!
MONSTER ISLE!
I NEVER EXPECTED IT TO BE SO QUIET!
HOLD UP, REED! WAIT FOR US!
NO! STAY BACK! IT'S TOO QUIET! I DON'T LIKE IT!
A SPLIT SECOND LATER, THE UNCANNY SILENCE IS BROKEN BY...
THE MONSTERS!
PLAY IT SAFE-- PROTECT YOURSELVES!
THEY'RE EVERY-WHERE!
THEY KNEW WE WERE COMING!

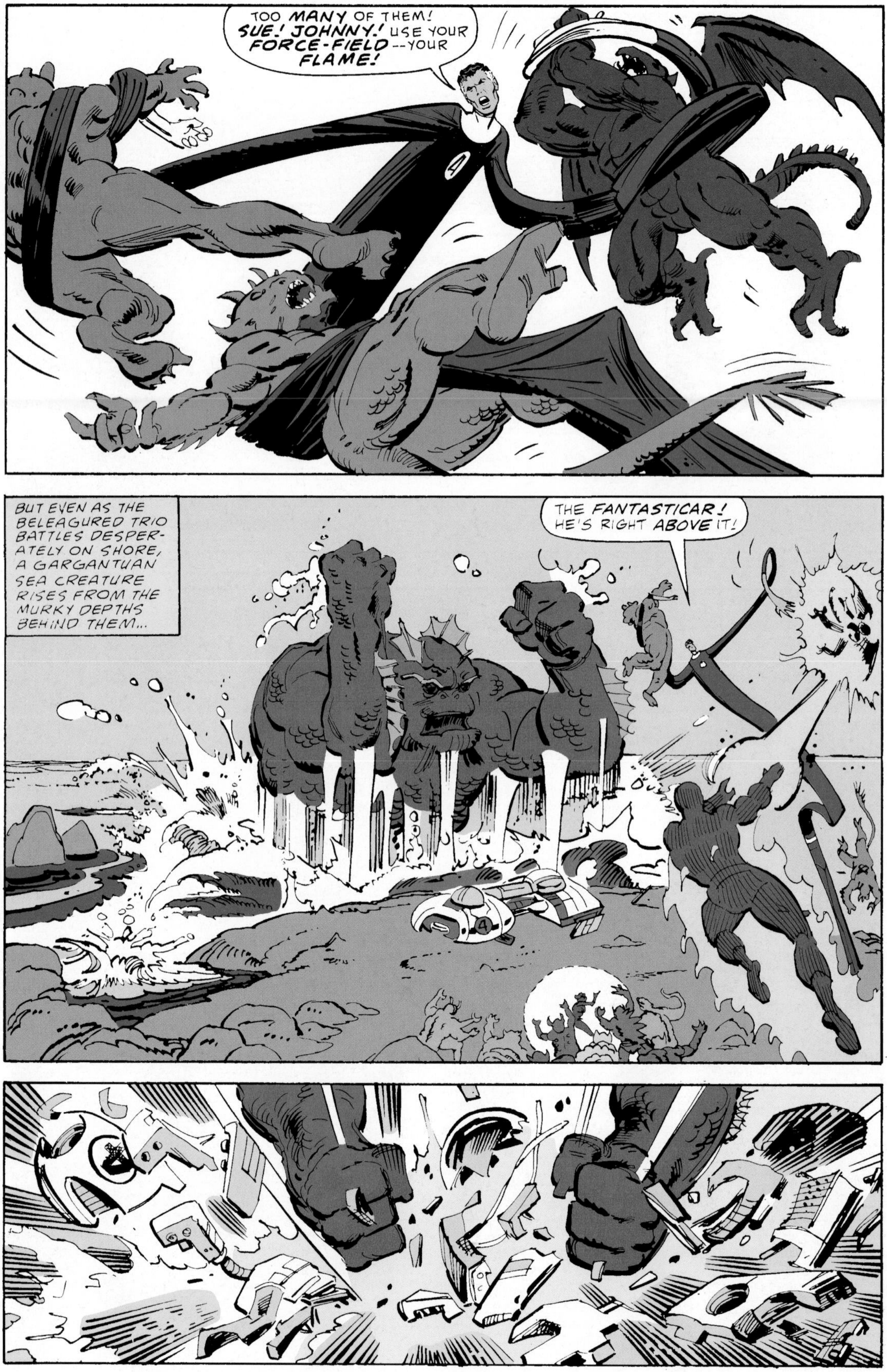

TOO MANY OF THEM! SUE! JOHNNY! USE YOUR FORCE-FIELD--YOUR FLAME!
BUT EVEN AS THE BELEAGURED TRIO BATTLES DESPERATELY ON SHORE, A GARGANTUAN SEA CREATURE RISES FROM THE MURKY DEPTHS BEHIND THEM...
THE FANTASTICAR! HE'S RIGHT ABOVE IT!

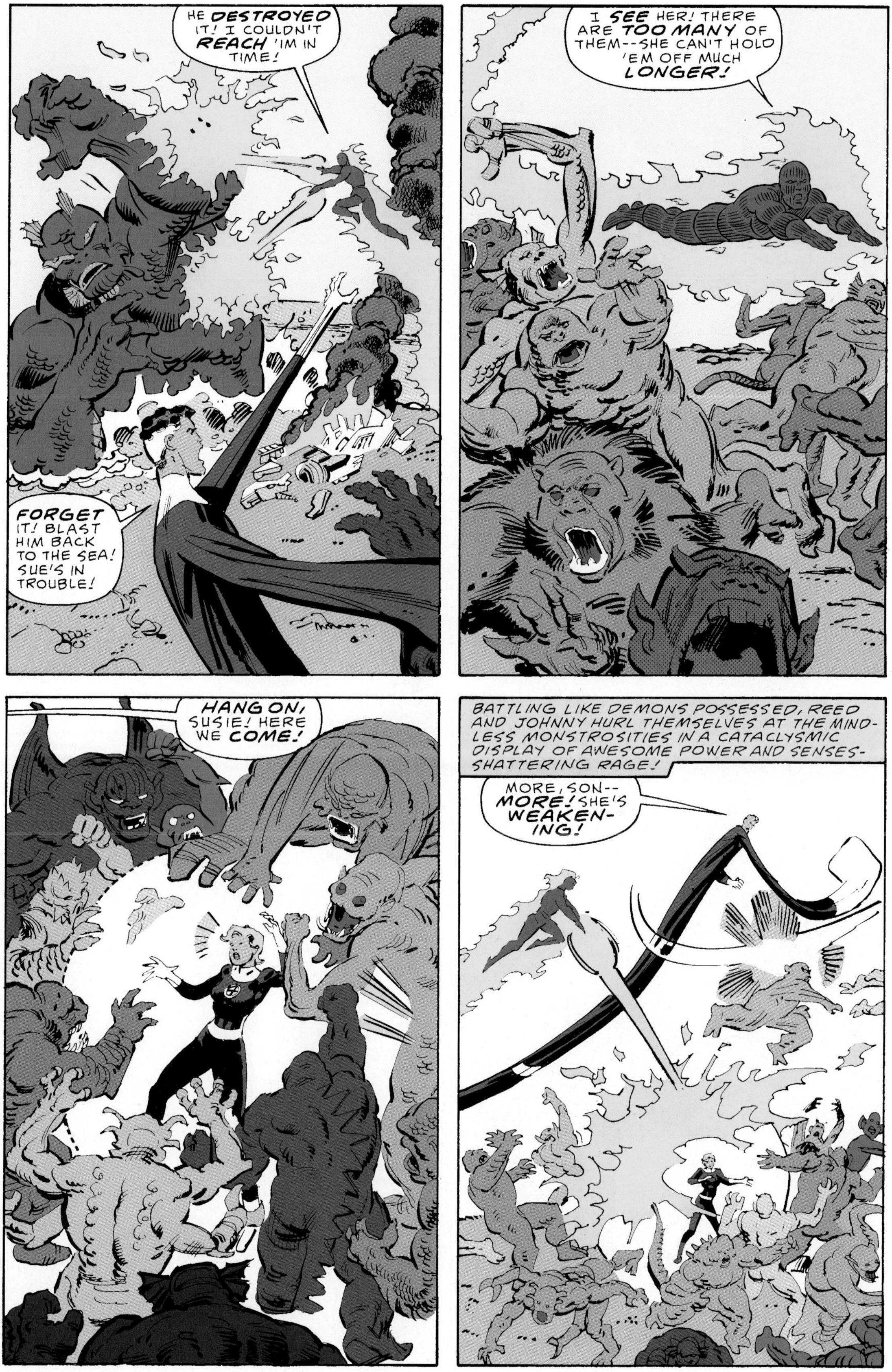
HE DESTROYED IT! I COULDN'T REACH 'IM IN TIME!
FORGET IT! BLAST HIM BACK TO THE SEA! SUE'S IN TROUBLE!
I SEE HER! THERE ARE TOO MANY OF THEM--SHE CAN'T HOLD 'EM OFF MUCH LONGER!
HANG ON, SUSIE! HERE WE COME!
BATTLING LIKE DEMONS POSSESSED, REED AND JOHNNY HURL THEMSELVES AT THE MINDLESS MONSTROSITIES IN A CATACLYSMIC DISPLAY OF AWESOME POWER AND SENSES-SHATTERING RAGE!
MORE, SON--MORE! SHE'S WEAKENING!

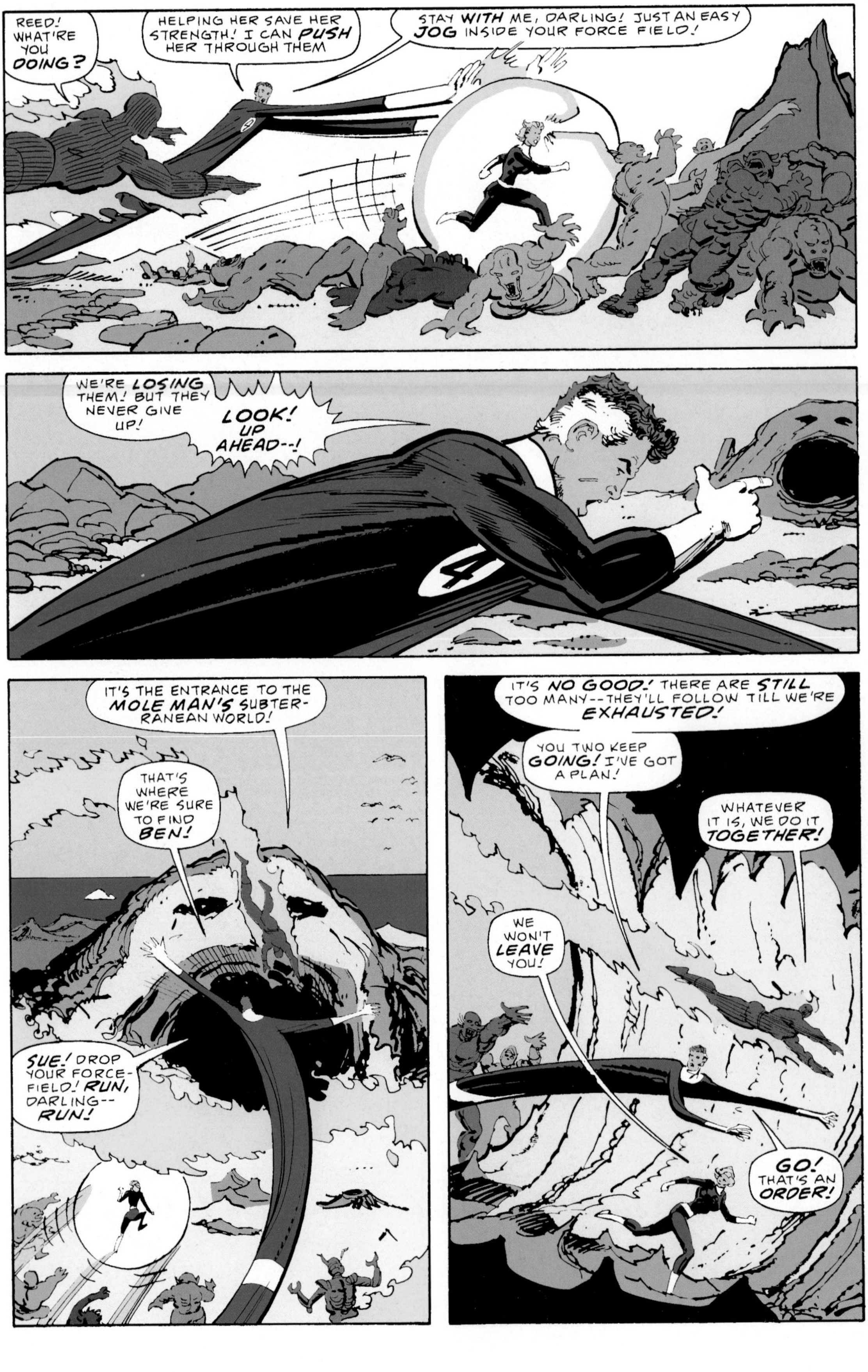

REED! WHAT'RE YOU DOING?
HELPING HER SAVE HER STRENGTH! I CAN PUSH HER THROUGH THEM
STAY WITH ME, DARLING! JUST AN EASY JOG INSIDE YOUR FORCE FIELD!
WE'RE LOSING THEM! BUT THEY NEVER GIVE UP!
LOOK! UP AHEAD--!
IT'S THE ENTRANCE TO THE MOLE MAN'S SUBTERRANEAN WORLD!
THAT'S WHERE WE'RE SURE TO FIND BEN!
SUE! DROP YOUR FORCE-FIELD! RUN, DARLING-- RUN!
IT'S NO GOOD! THERE ARE STILL TOO MANY--THEY'LL FOLLOW TILL WE'RE EXHAUSTED!
YOU TWO KEEP GOING! I'VE GOT A PLAN!
WHATEVER IT IS, WE DO IT TOGETHER!
WE WON'T LEAVE YOU!
GO! THAT'S AN ORDER!

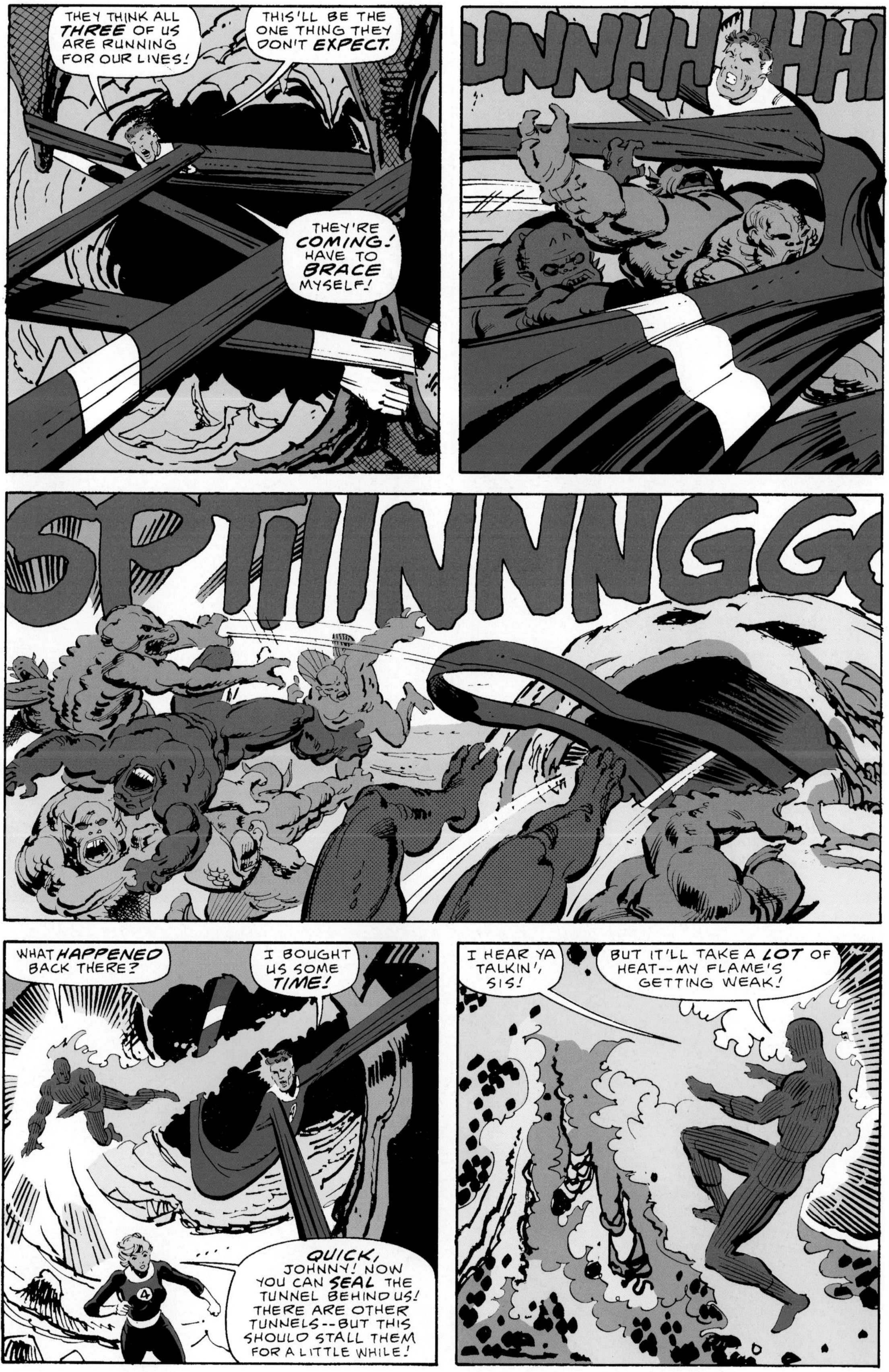

THEY THINK ALL THREE OF US ARE RUNNING FOR OUR LIVES!
THIS'LL BE THE ONE THING THEY DON'T EXPECT.
THEY'RE COMING! HAVE TO BRACE MYSELF!
UNNHHHHHH
SPTIIINNNGG
WHAT HAPPENED BACK THERE?
I BOUGHT US SOME TIME!
QUICK, JOHNNY! NOW YOU CAN SEAL THE TUNNEL BEHIND US! THERE ARE OTHER TUNNELS--BUT THIS SHOULD STALL THEM FOR A LITTLE WHILE!
I HEAR YA TALKIN', SIS!
BUT IT'LL TAKE A LOT OF HEAT--MY FLAME'S GETTING WEAK!

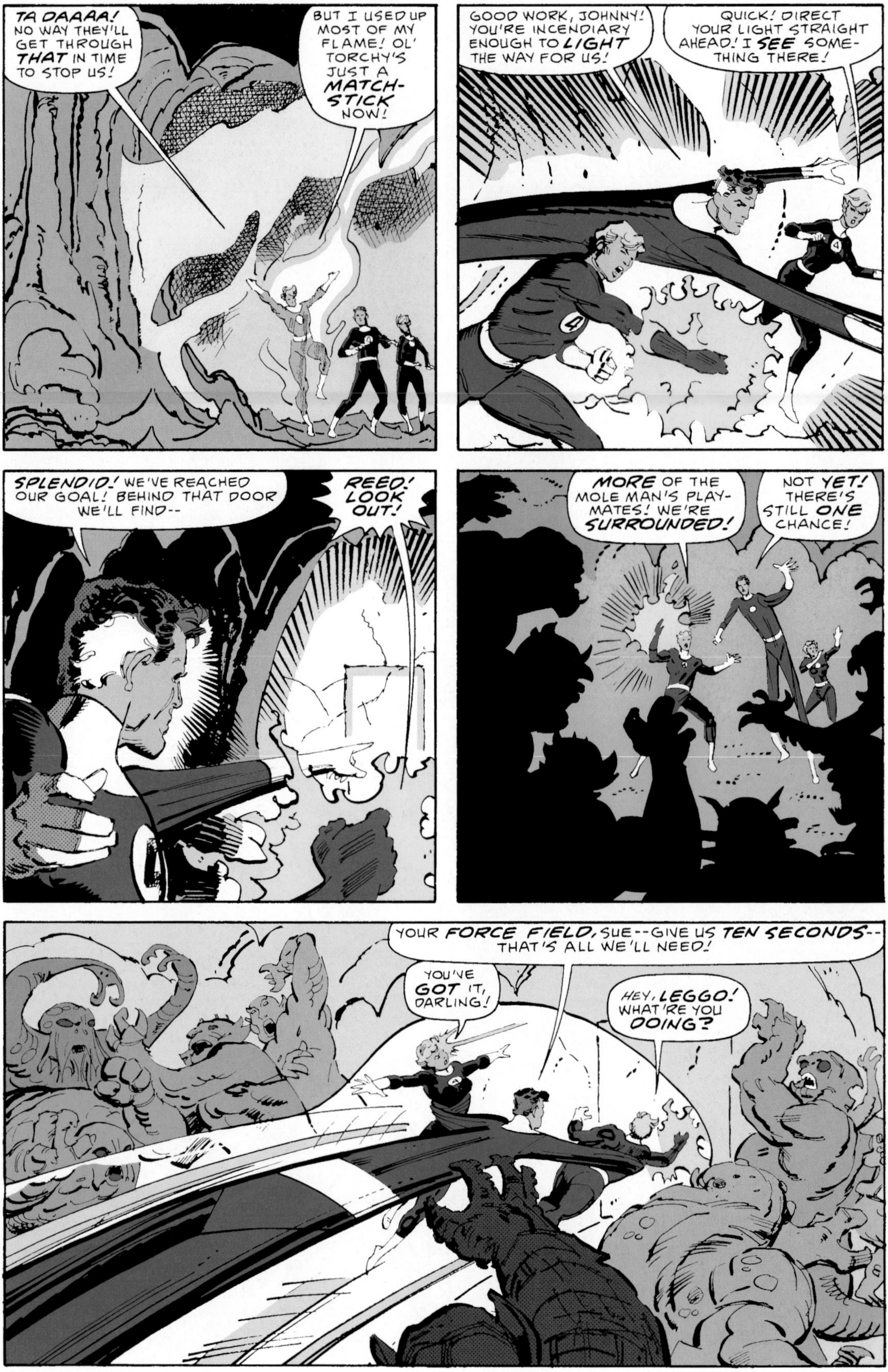
TA DAAAA! NO WAY THEY'LL GET THROUGH THAT IN TIME TO STOP US!
BUT I USED UP MOST OF MY FLAME! OL' TORCHY'S JUST A MATCH-STICK NOW!
GOOD WORK, JOHNNY! YOU'RE INCENDIARY ENOUGH TO LIGHT THE WAY FOR US!
QUICK! DIRECT YOUR LIGHT STRAIGHT AHEAD! I SEE SOME-THING THERE!
SPLENDID! WE'VE REACHED OUR GOAL! BEHIND THAT DOOR WE'LL FIND--
REED! LOOK OUT!
MORE OF THE MOLE MAN'S PLAY-MATES! WE'RE SURROUNDED!
NOT YET! THERE'S STILL ONE CHANCE!
YOUR FORCE FIELD, SUE--GIVE US TEN SECONDS--THAT'S ALL WE'LL NEED!
YOU'VE GOT IT, DARLING!
HEY, LEGGO! WHAT'RE YOU DOING?

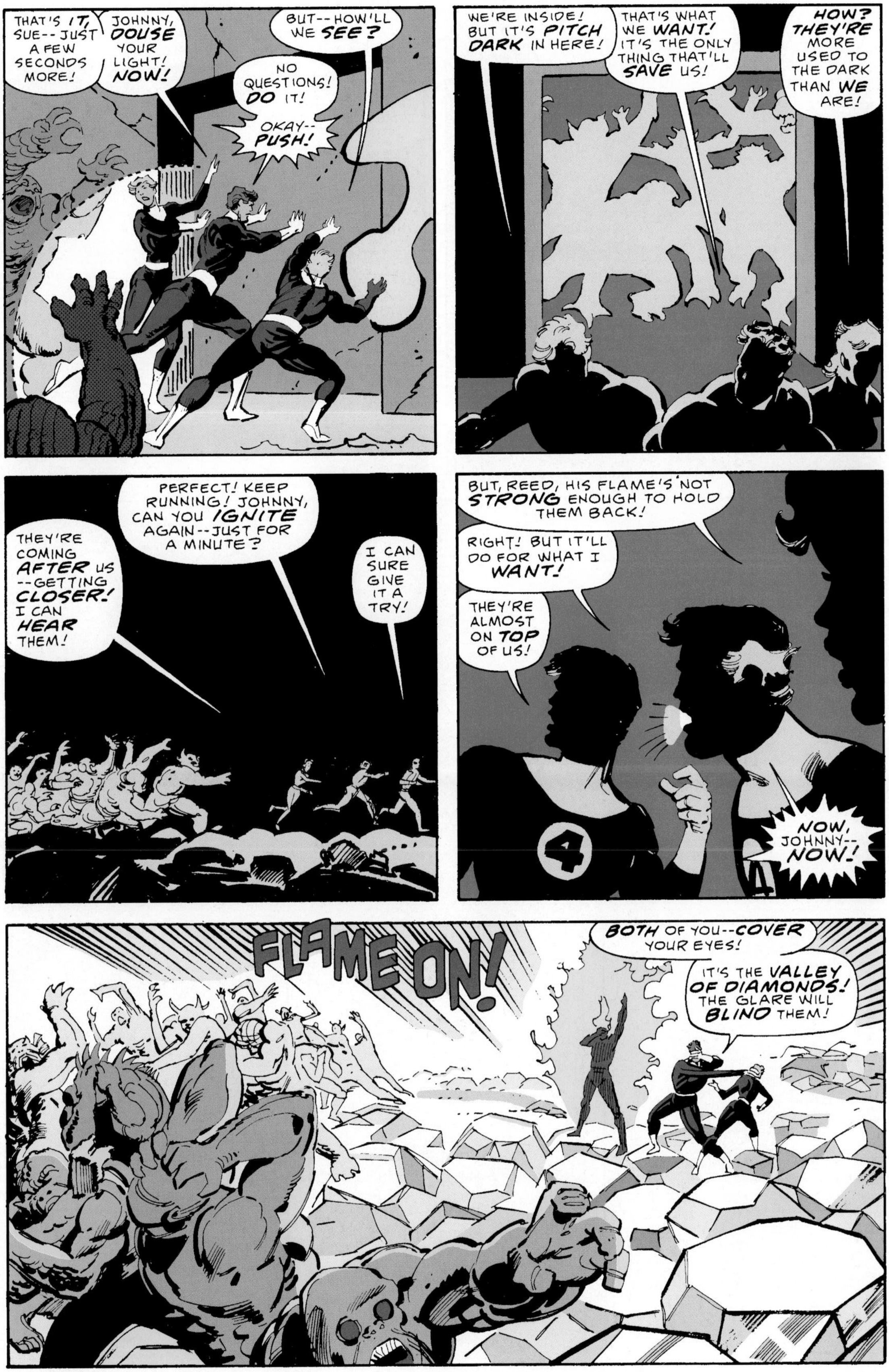
THAT'S IT, SUE--JUST A FEW SECONDS MORE!
JOHNNY, DOUSE YOUR LIGHT! NOW!
BUT--HOW'LL WE SEE?
NO QUESTIONS! DO IT!
OKAY--PUSH!
WE'RE INSIDE! BUT IT'S PITCH DARK IN HERE!
THAT'S WHAT WE WANT! IT'S THE ONLY THING THAT'LL SAVE US!
HOW? THEY'RE MORE USED TO THE DARK THAN WE ARE!
THEY'RE COMING AFTER US--GETTING CLOSER! I CAN HEAR THEM!
PERFECT! KEEP RUNNING! JOHNNY, CAN YOU IGNITE AGAIN--JUST FOR A MINUTE?
I CAN SURE GIVE IT A TRY!
BUT, REED, HIS FLAME'S NOT STRONG ENOUGH TO HOLD THEM BACK!
RIGHT! BUT IT'LL DO FOR WHAT I WANT!
THEY'RE ALMOST ON TOP OF US!
NOW, JOHNNY--NOW!
FLAME ON!
BOTH OF YOU--COVER YOUR EYES!
IT'S THE VALLEY OF DIAMONDS! THE GLARE WILL BLIND THEM!

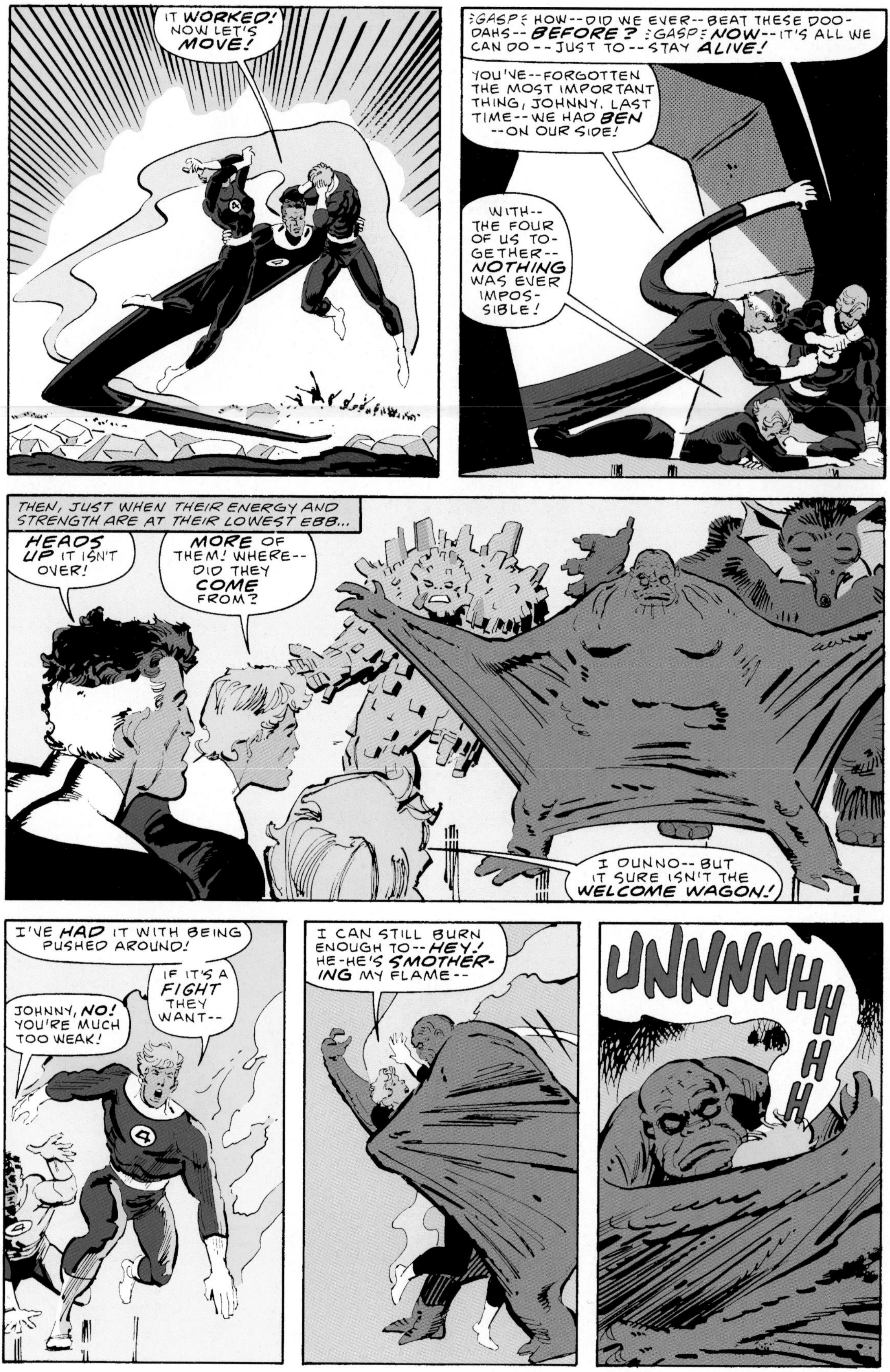

IT WORKED! NOW LET'S MOVE!
:GASP: HOW--DID WE EVER--BEAT THESE DOO-DAHS--BEFORE? :GASP: NOW--IT'S ALL WE CAN DO--JUST TO--STAY ALIVE!
YOU'VE--FORGOTTEN THE MOST IMPORTANT THING, JOHNNY. LAST TIME--WE HAD BEN --ON OUR SIDE!
WITH--THE FOUR OF US TO-GETHER--NOTHING WAS EVER IMPOS-SIBLE!
THEN, JUST WHEN THEIR ENERGY AND STRENGTH ARE AT THEIR LOWEST EBB...
HEADS UP IT ISN'T OVER!
MORE OF THEM! WHERE--DID THEY COME FROM?
I DUNNO--BUT IT SURE ISN'T THE WELCOME WAGON!
I'VE HAD IT WITH BEING PUSHED AROUND!
IF IT'S A FIGHT THEY WANT--
JOHNNY, NO! YOU'RE MUCH TOO WEAK!
I CAN STILL BURN ENOUGH TO--HEY! HE-HE'S SMOTHER-ING MY FLAME--
UNNNNHHHHH

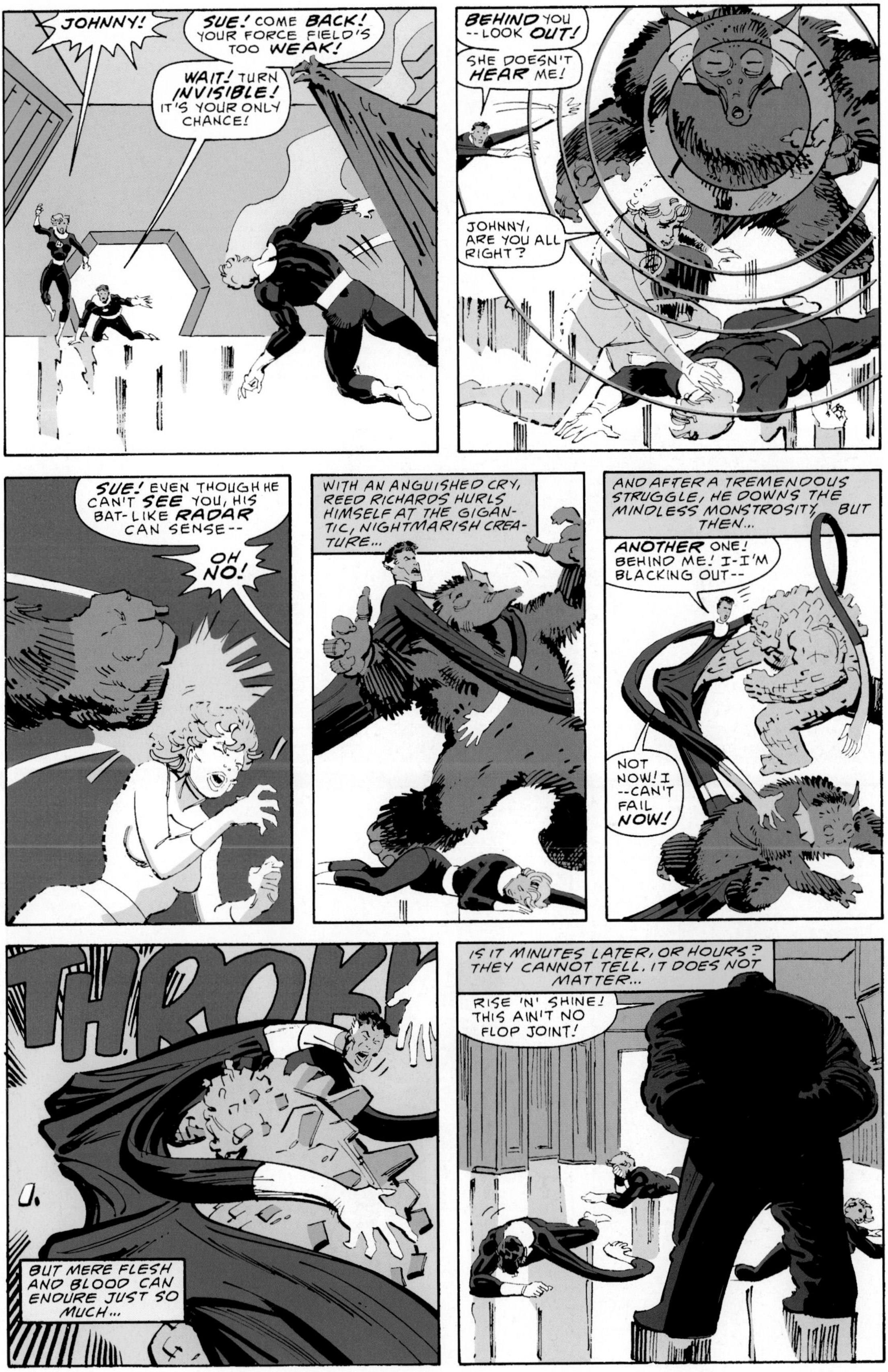

JOHNNY!
SUE! COME BACK! YOUR FORCE FIELD'S TOO WEAK!
WAIT! TURN INVISIBLE! IT'S YOUR ONLY CHANCE!
BEHIND YOU --LOOK OUT!
SHE DOESN'T HEAR ME!
JOHNNY, ARE YOU ALL RIGHT?
SUE! EVEN THOUGH HE CAN'T SEE YOU, HIS BAT-LIKE RADAR CAN SENSE--
OH NO!
WITH AN ANGUISHED CRY, REED RICHARDS HURLS HIMSELF AT THE GIGANTIC, NIGHTMARISH CREATURE...
AND AFTER A TREMENDOUS STRUGGLE, HE DOWNS THE MINDLESS MONSTROSITY, BUT THEN...
ANOTHER ONE! BEHIND ME! I-I'M BLACKING OUT--
NOT NOW! I --CAN'T FAIL NOW!
THROK!
BUT MERE FLESH AND BLOOD CAN ENDURE JUST SO MUCH...
IS IT MINUTES LATER, OR HOURS? THEY CANNOT TELL. IT DOES NOT MATTER...
RISE 'N' SHINE! THIS AIN'T NO FLOP JOINT!

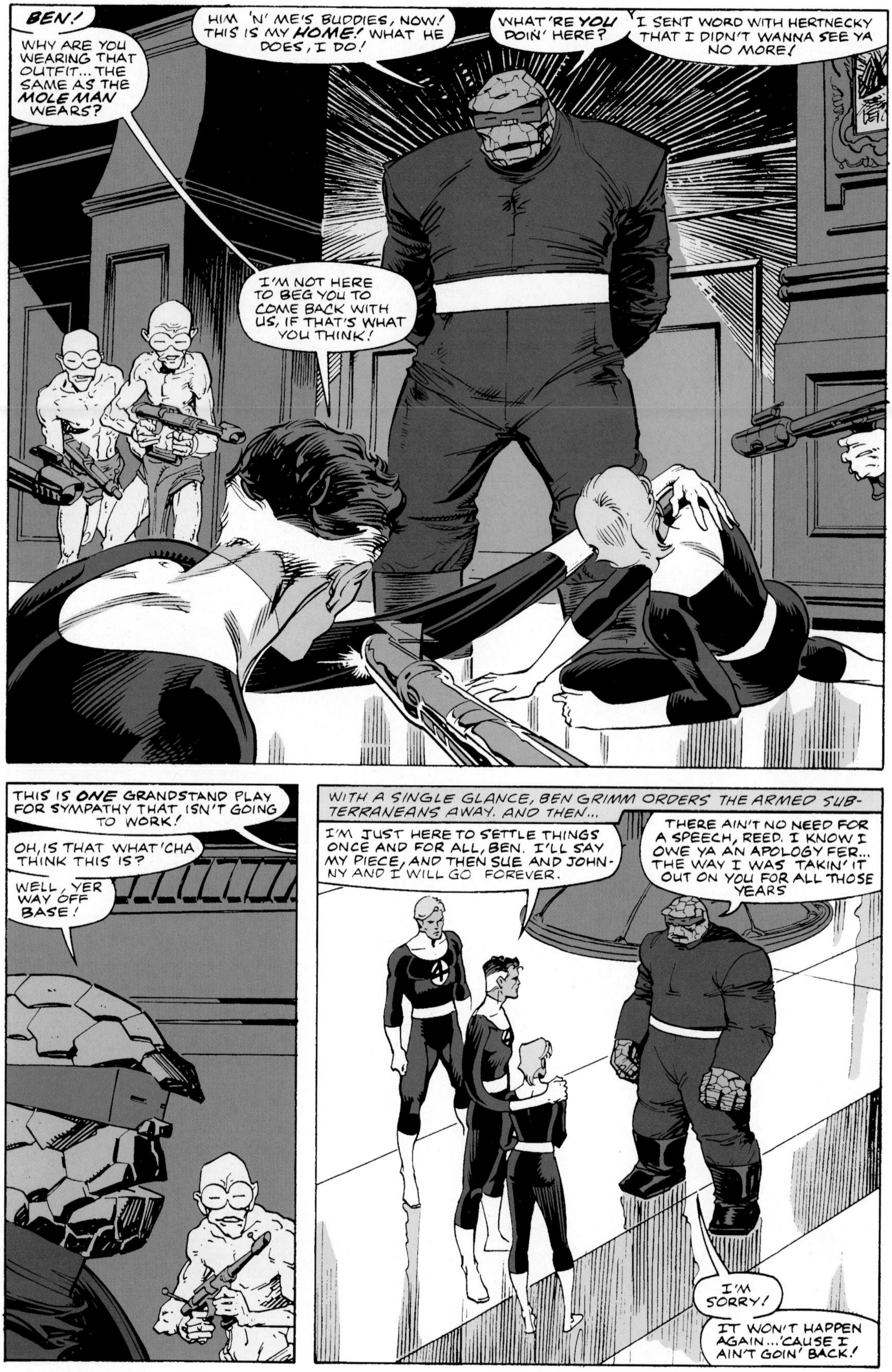

BEN! WHY ARE YOU WEARING THAT OUTFIT... THE SAME AS THE MOLE MAN WEARS?
HIM 'N' ME'S BUDDIES, NOW! THIS IS MY HOME! WHAT HE DOES, I DO!
WHAT'RE YOU DOIN' HERE?
I SENT WORD WITH HERTNECKY THAT I DIDN'T WANNA SEE YA NO MORE!
I'M NOT HERE TO BEG YOU TO COME BACK WITH US, IF THAT'S WHAT YOU THINK!
THIS IS ONE GRANDSTAND PLAY FOR SYMPATHY THAT ISN'T GOING TO WORK!
OH, IS THAT WHAT'CHA THINK THIS IS?
WELL, YER WAY OFF BASE!
WITH A SINGLE GLANCE, BEN GRIMM ORDERS THE ARMED SUBTERRANEANS AWAY. AND THEN...
I'M JUST HERE TO SETTLE THINGS ONCE AND FOR ALL, BEN. I'LL SAY MY PIECE, AND THEN SUE AND JOHNNY AND I WILL GO FOREVER.
THERE AIN'T NO NEED FOR A SPEECH, REED. I KNOW I OWE YA AN APOLOGY FER... THE WAY I WAS TAKIN' IT OUT ON YOU FOR ALL THOSE YEARS
I'M SORRY!
IT WON'T HAPPEN AGAIN...'CAUSE I AIN'T GOIN' BACK!

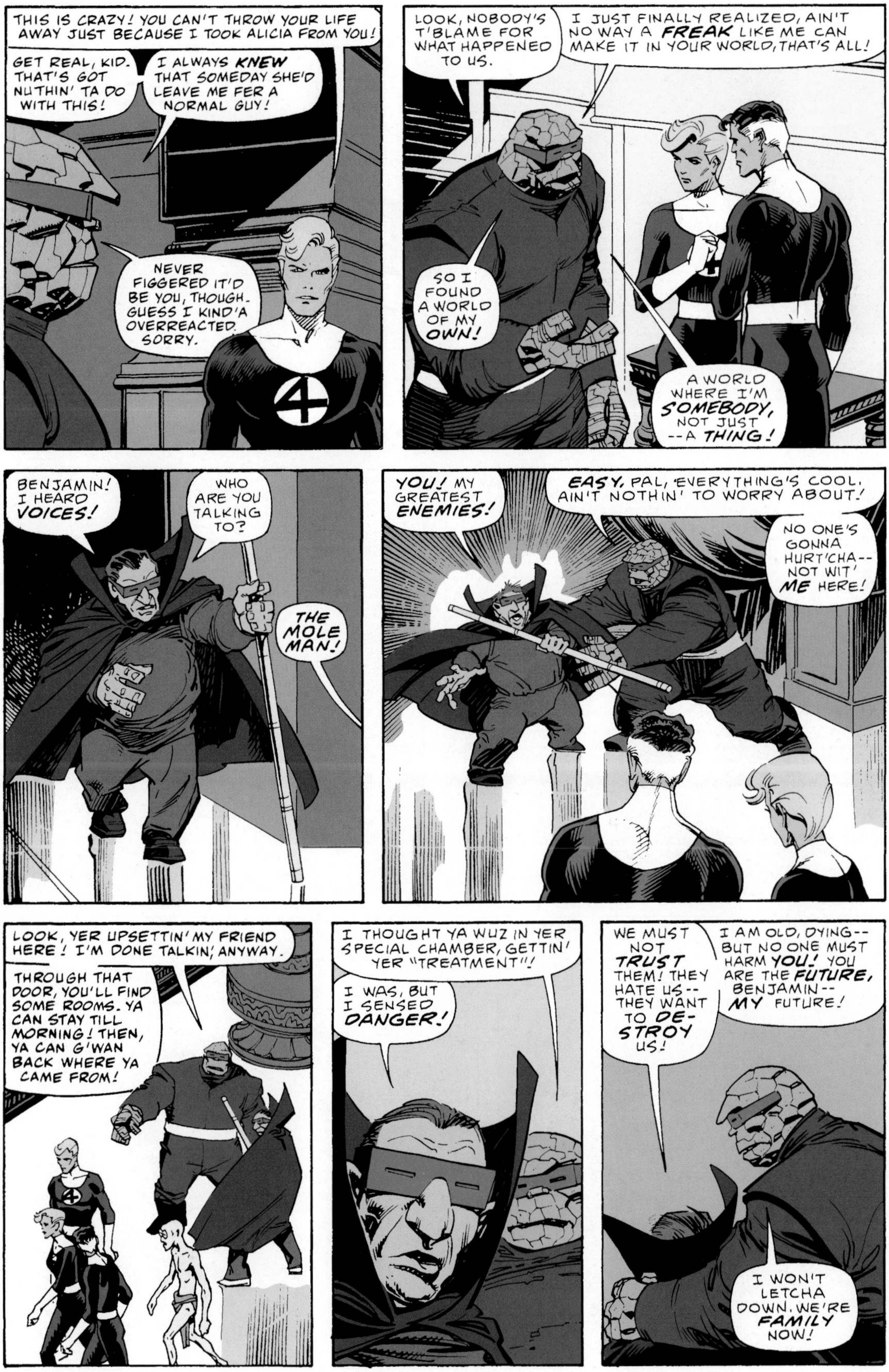

THIS IS CRAZY! YOU CAN'T THROW YOUR LIFE AWAY JUST BECAUSE I TOOK ALICIA FROM YOU!
GET REAL, KID. THAT'S GOT NUTHIN' TA DO WITH THIS!
I ALWAYS KNEW THAT SOMEDAY SHE'D LEAVE ME FER A NORMAL GUY!
NEVER FIGGERED IT'D BE YOU, THOUGH. GUESS I KIND'A OVERREACTED. SORRY.
LOOK, NOBODY'S T'BLAME FOR WHAT HAPPENED TO US.
I JUST FINALLY REALIZED, AIN'T NO WAY A FREAK LIKE ME CAN MAKE IT IN YOUR WORLD, THAT'S ALL!
SO I FOUND A WORLD OF MY OWN!
A WORLD WHERE I'M SOMEBODY, NOT JUST --A THING!
BENJAMIN! I HEARD VOICES!
WHO ARE YOU TALKING TO?
THE MOLE MAN!
YOU! MY GREATEST ENEMIES!
EASY, PAL, EVERYTHING'S COOL. AIN'T NOTHIN' TO WORRY ABOUT!
NO ONE'S GONNA HURT'CHA-- NOT WIT' ME HERE!
LOOK, YER UPSETTIN' MY FRIEND HERE! I'M DONE TALKIN', ANYWAY.
THROUGH THAT DOOR, YOU'LL FIND SOME ROOMS. YA CAN STAY TILL MORNING! THEN, YA CAN G'WAN BACK WHERE YA CAME FROM!
I THOUGHT YA WUZ IN YER SPECIAL CHAMBER, GETTIN' YER "TREATMENT"!
I WAS, BUT I SENSED DANGER!
WE MUST NOT TRUST THEM! THEY HATE US-- THEY WANT TO DE-STROY US!
I AM OLD, DYING-- BUT NO ONE MUST HARM YOU! YOU ARE THE FUTURE, BENJAMIN-- MY FUTURE!
I WON'T LETCHA DOWN. WE'RE FAMILY NOW!

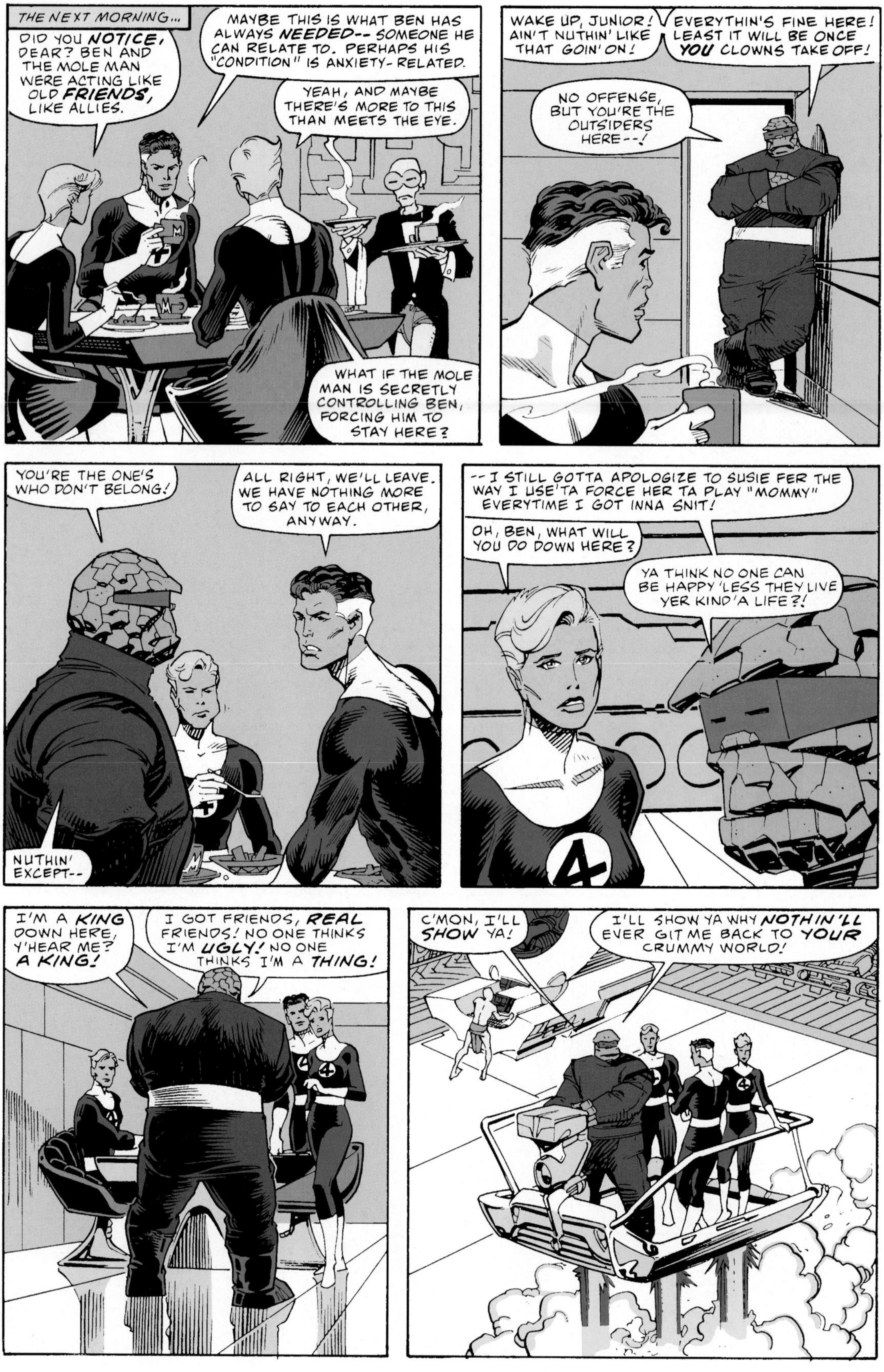
THE NEXT MORNING...
DID YOU NOTICE, DEAR? BEN AND THE MOLE MAN WERE ACTING LIKE OLD FRIENDS, LIKE ALLIES.
MAYBE THIS IS WHAT BEN HAS ALWAYS NEEDED-- SOMEONE HE CAN RELATE TO. PERHAPS HIS "CONDITION" IS ANXIETY-RELATED.
YEAH, AND MAYBE THERE'S MORE TO THIS THAN MEETS THE EYE.
WHAT IF THE MOLE MAN IS SECRETLY CONTROLLING BEN, FORCING HIM TO STAY HERE?
WAKE UP, JUNIOR! AIN'T NUTHIN' LIKE THAT GOIN' ON!
EVERYTHIN'S FINE HERE! LEAST IT WILL BE ONCE YOU CLOWNS TAKE OFF!
NO OFFENSE, BUT YOU'RE THE OUTSIDERS HERE--!
YOU'RE THE ONE'S WHO DON'T BELONG!
ALL RIGHT, WE'LL LEAVE. WE HAVE NOTHING MORE TO SAY TO EACH OTHER, ANYWAY.
NUTHIN' EXCEPT--
--I STILL GOTTA APOLOGIZE TO SUSIE FER THE WAY I USE'TA FORCE HER TA PLAY "MOMMY" EVERYTIME I GOT INNA SNIT!
OH, BEN, WHAT WILL YOU DO DOWN HERE?
YA THINK NO ONE CAN BE HAPPY 'LESS THEY LIVE YER KIND'A LIFE?!
I'M A KING DOWN HERE, Y'HEAR ME? A KING!
I GOT FRIENDS, REAL FRIENDS! NO ONE THINKS I'M UGLY! NO ONE THINKS I'M A THING!
C'MON, I'LL SHOW YA!
I'LL SHOW YA WHY NOTHIN'LL EVER GIT ME BACK TO YOUR CRUMMY WORLD!

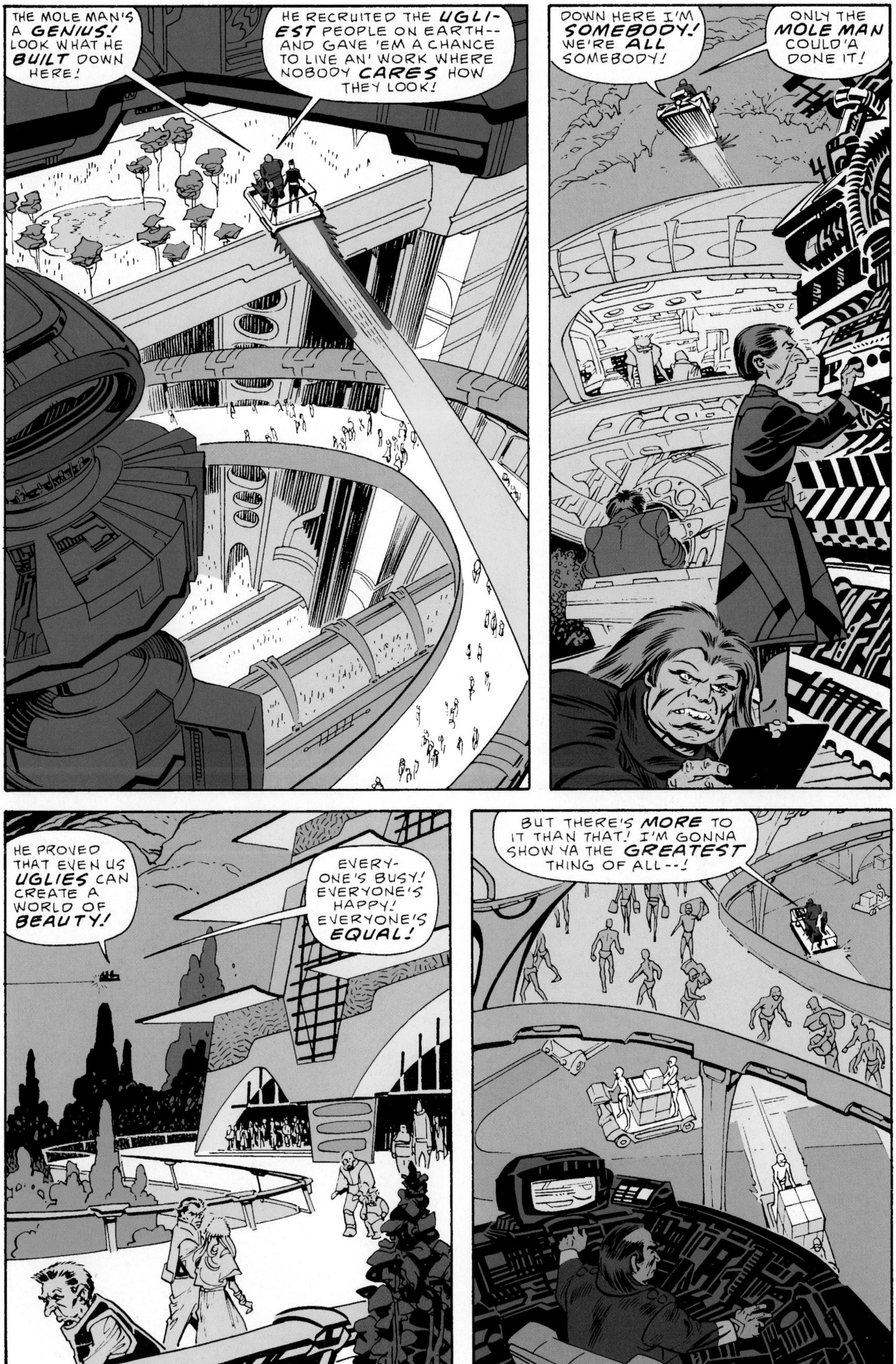
THE MOLE MAN'S A GENIUS! LOOK WHAT HE BUILT DOWN HERE!
HE RECRUITED THE UGLIEST PEOPLE ON EARTH-- AND GAVE 'EM A CHANCE TO LIVE AN' WORK WHERE NOBODY CARES HOW THEY LOOK!
DOWN HERE I'M SOMEBODY! WE'RE ALL SOMEBODY!
ONLY THE MOLE MAN COULD'A DONE IT!
HE PROVED THAT EVEN US UGLIES CAN CREATE A WORLD OF BEAUTY!
EVERYONE'S BUSY! EVERYONE'S HAPPY! EVERYONE'S EQUAL!
BUT THERE'S MORE TO IT THAN THAT! I'M GONNA SHOW YA THE GREATEST THING OF ALL--!

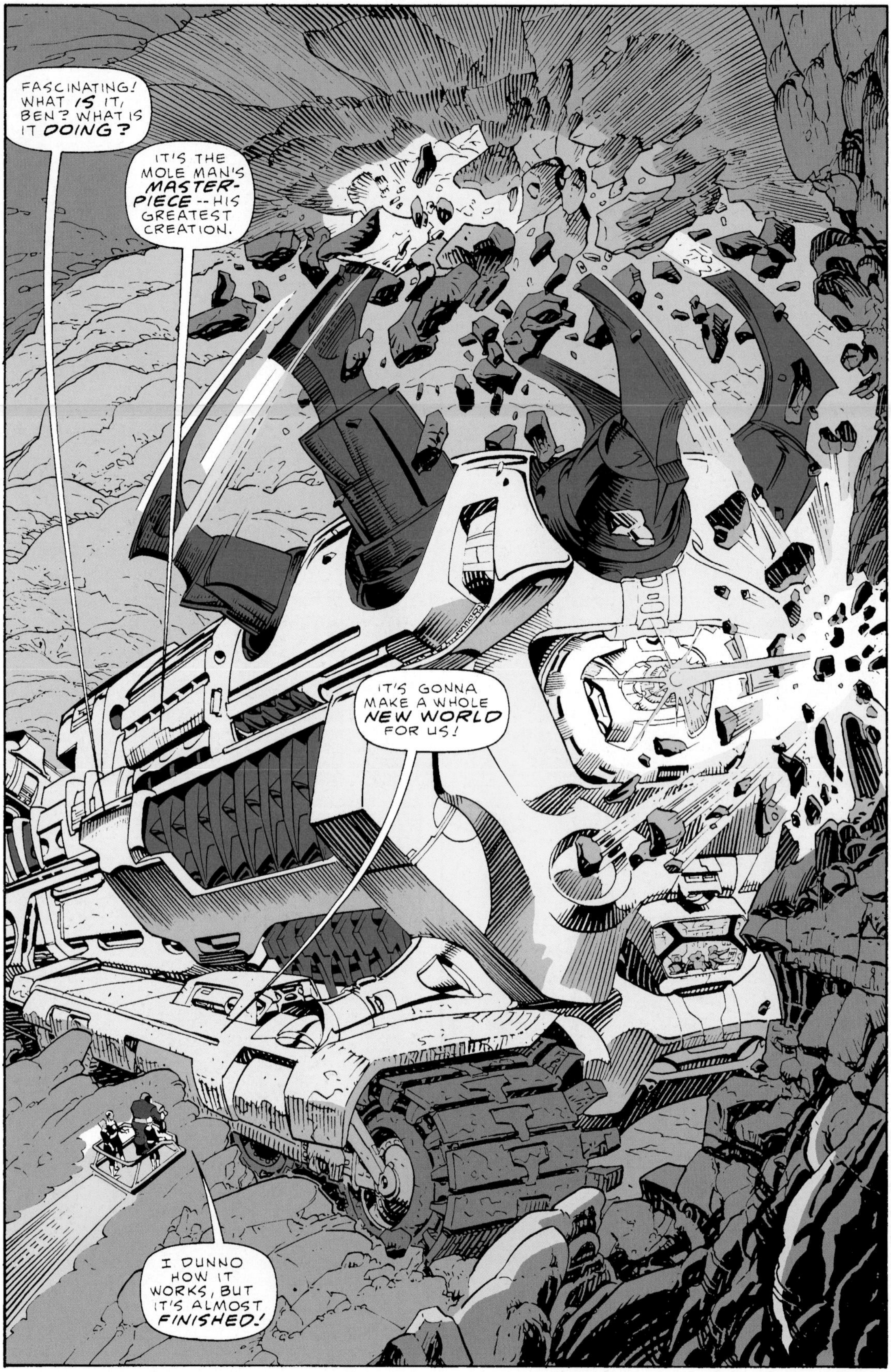
FASCINATING! WHAT IS IT, BEN? WHAT IS IT DOING?
IT'S THE MOLE MAN'S MASTER-PIECE--HIS GREATEST CREATION.
IT'S GONNA MAKE A WHOLE NEW WORLD FOR US!
I DUNNO HOW IT WORKS, BUT IT'S ALMOST FINISHED!

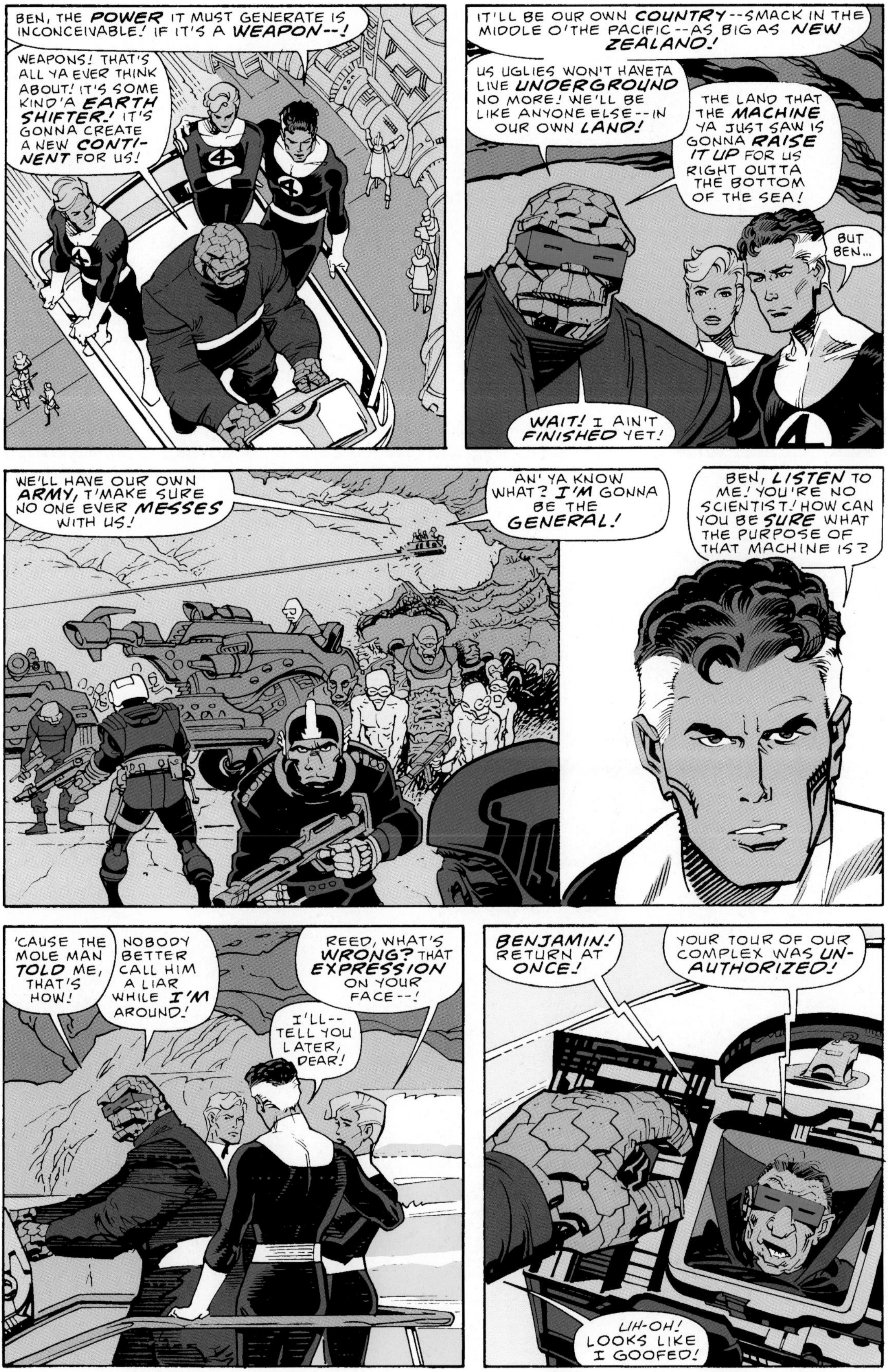
BEN, THE POWER IT MUST GENERATE IS INCONCEIVABLE! IF IT'S A WEAPON--!
WEAPONS! THAT'S ALL YA EVER THINK ABOUT! IT'S SOME KIND'A EARTH SHIFTER! IT'S GONNA CREATE A NEW CONTI-NENT FOR US!
IT'LL BE OUR OWN COUNTRY--SMACK IN THE MIDDLE O'THE PACIFIC--AS BIG AS NEW ZEALAND!
US UGLIES WON'T HAVETA LIVE UNDERGROUND NO MORE! WE'LL BE LIKE ANYONE ELSE--IN OUR OWN LAND!
THE LAND THAT THE MACHINE YA JUST SAW IS GONNA RAISE IT UP FOR US RIGHT OUTTA THE BOTTOM OF THE SEA!
BUT BEN...
WAIT! I AIN'T FINISHED YET!
WE'LL HAVE OUR OWN ARMY, T'MAKE SURE NO ONE EVER MESSES WITH US!
AN' YA KNOW WHAT? I'M GONNA BE THE GENERAL!
BEN, LISTEN TO ME! YOU'RE NO SCIENTIST! HOW CAN YOU BE SURE WHAT THE PURPOSE OF THAT MACHINE IS?
'CAUSE THE MOLE MAN TOLD ME, THAT'S HOW!
NOBODY BETTER CALL HIM A LIAR WHILE I'M AROUND!
REED, WHAT'S WRONG? THAT EXPRESSION ON YOUR FACE--!
I'LL--TELL YOU LATER, DEAR!
BENJAMIN! RETURN AT ONCE!
YOUR TOUR OF OUR COMPLEX WAS UN-AUTHORIZED!
UH-OH! LOOKS LIKE I GOOFED!

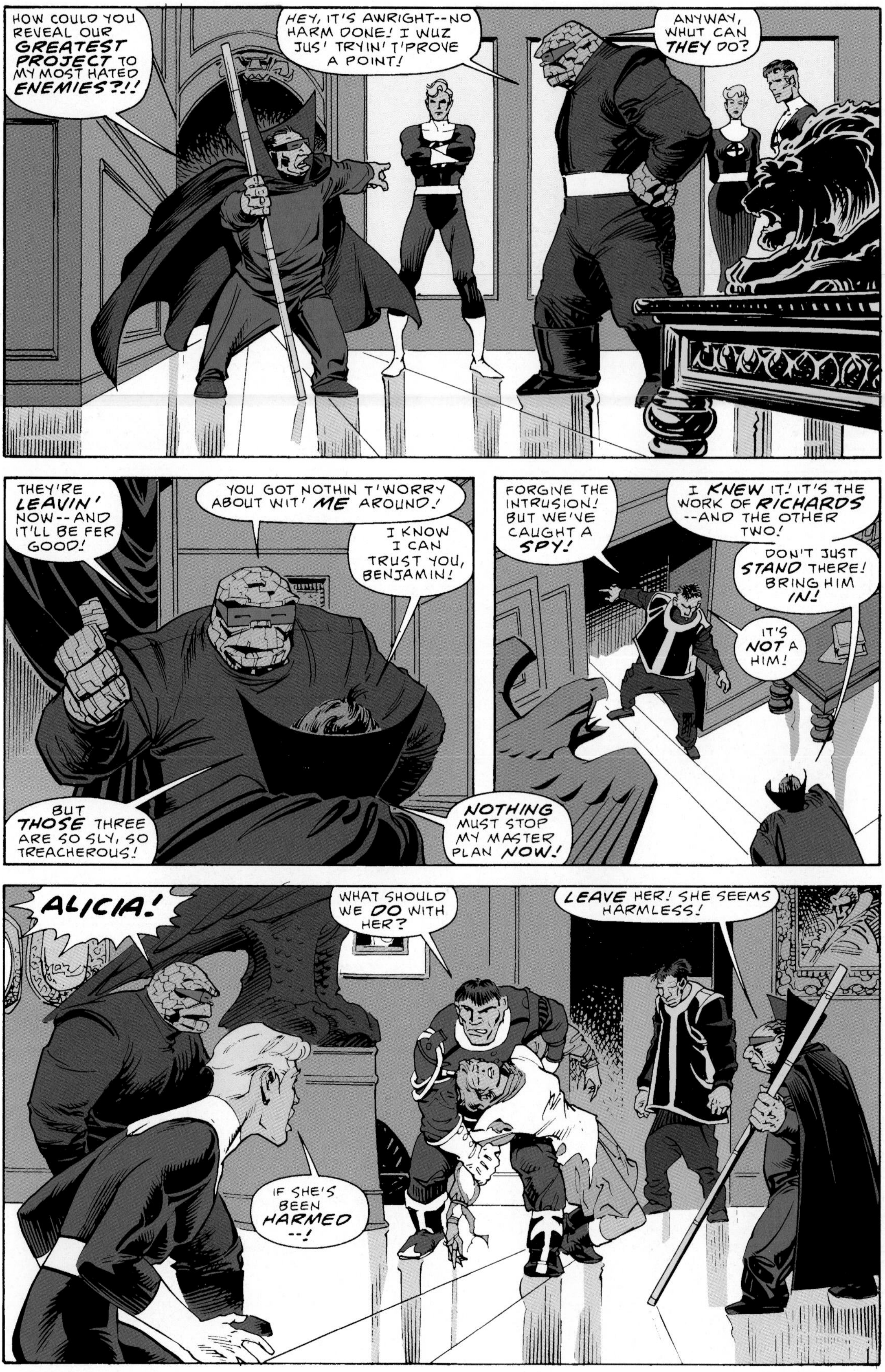
HOW COULD YOU REVEAL OUR GREATEST PROJECT TO MY MOST HATED ENEMIES?!!
HEY, IT'S AWRIGHT--NO HARM DONE! I WUZ JUS' TRYIN' T'PROVE A POINT!
ANYWAY, WHUT CAN THEY DO?
THEY'RE LEAVIN' NOW--AND IT'LL BE FER GOOD!
YOU GOT NOTHIN T'WORRY ABOUT WIT' ME AROUND!
I KNOW I CAN TRUST YOU, BENJAMIN!
BUT THOSE THREE ARE SO SLY, SO TREACHEROUS!
NOTHING MUST STOP MY MASTER PLAN NOW!
FORGIVE THE INTRUSION! BUT WE'VE CAUGHT A SPY!
I KNEW IT! IT'S THE WORK OF RICHARDS--AND THE OTHER TWO!
DON'T JUST STAND THERE! BRING HIM IN!
IT'S NOT A HIM!
ALICIA!
WHAT SHOULD WE DO WITH HER?
LEAVE HER! SHE SEEMS HARMLESS!
IF SHE'S BEEN HARMED--!

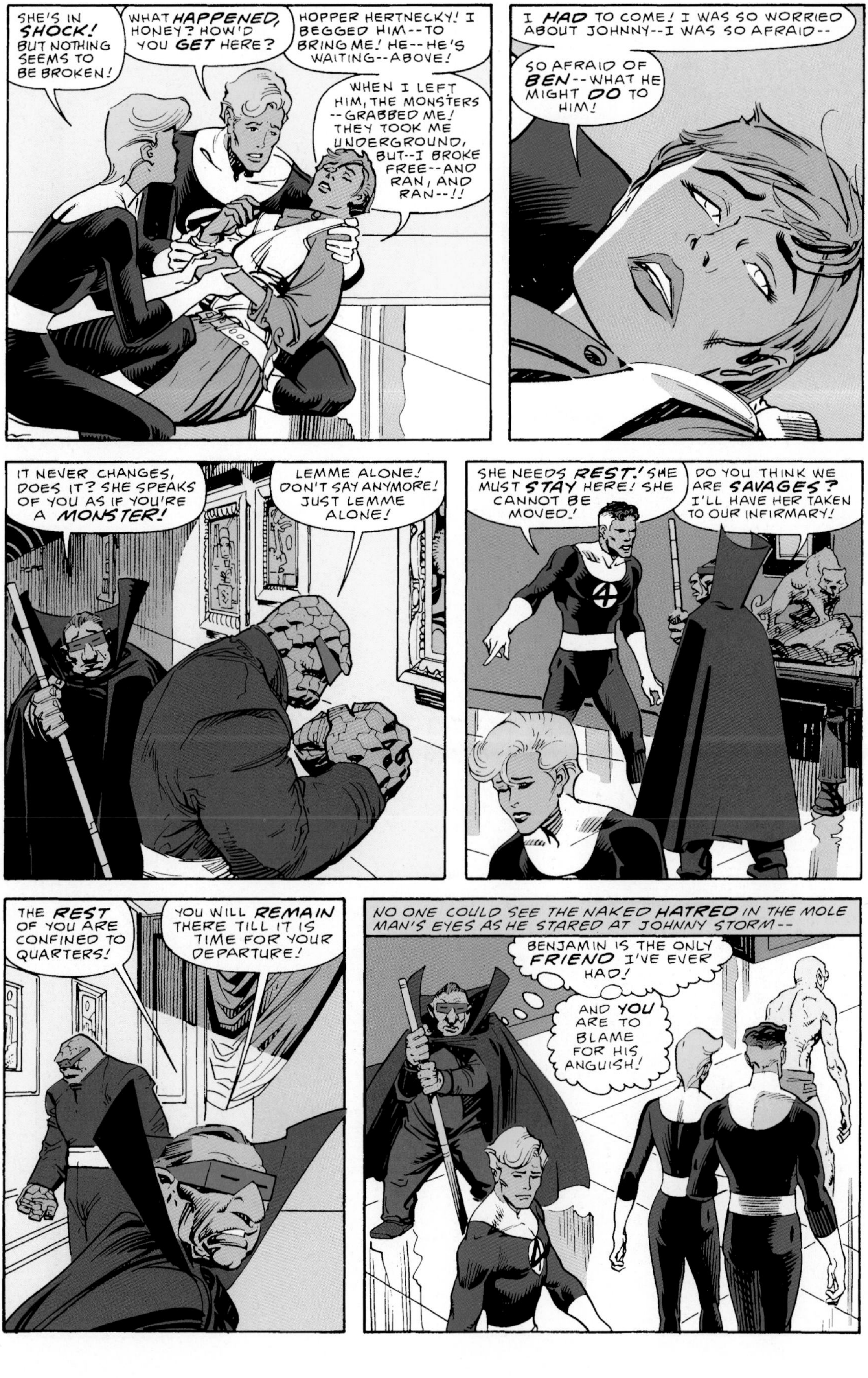
SHE'S IN SHOCK! BUT NOTHING SEEMS TO BE BROKEN!
WHAT HAPPENED, HONEY? HOW'D YOU GET HERE?
HOPPER HERTNECKY! I BEGGED HIM--TO BRING ME! HE--HE'S WAITING--ABOVE!
WHEN I LEFT HIM, THE MONSTERS--GRABBED ME! THEY TOOK ME UNDERGROUND, BUT--I BROKE FREE--AND RAN, AND RAN--!!
I HAD TO COME! I WAS SO WORRIED ABOUT JOHNNY--I WAS SO AFRAID--
SO AFRAID OF BEN--WHAT HE MIGHT DO TO HIM!
IT NEVER CHANGES, DOES IT? SHE SPEAKS OF YOU AS IF YOU'RE A MONSTER!
LEMME ALONE! DON'T SAY ANYMORE! JUST LEMME ALONE!
SHE NEEDS REST! SHE MUST STAY HERE! SHE CANNOT BE MOVED!
DO YOU THINK WE ARE SAVAGES? I'LL HAVE HER TAKEN TO OUR INFIRMARY!
THE REST OF YOU ARE CONFINED TO QUARTERS!
YOU WILL REMAIN THERE TILL IT IS TIME FOR YOUR DEPARTURE!
NO ONE COULD SEE THE NAKED HATRED IN THE MOLE MAN'S EYES AS HE STARED AT JOHNNY STORM--
BENJAMIN IS THE ONLY FRIEND I'VE EVER HAD!
AND YOU ARE TO BLAME FOR HIS ANGUISH!

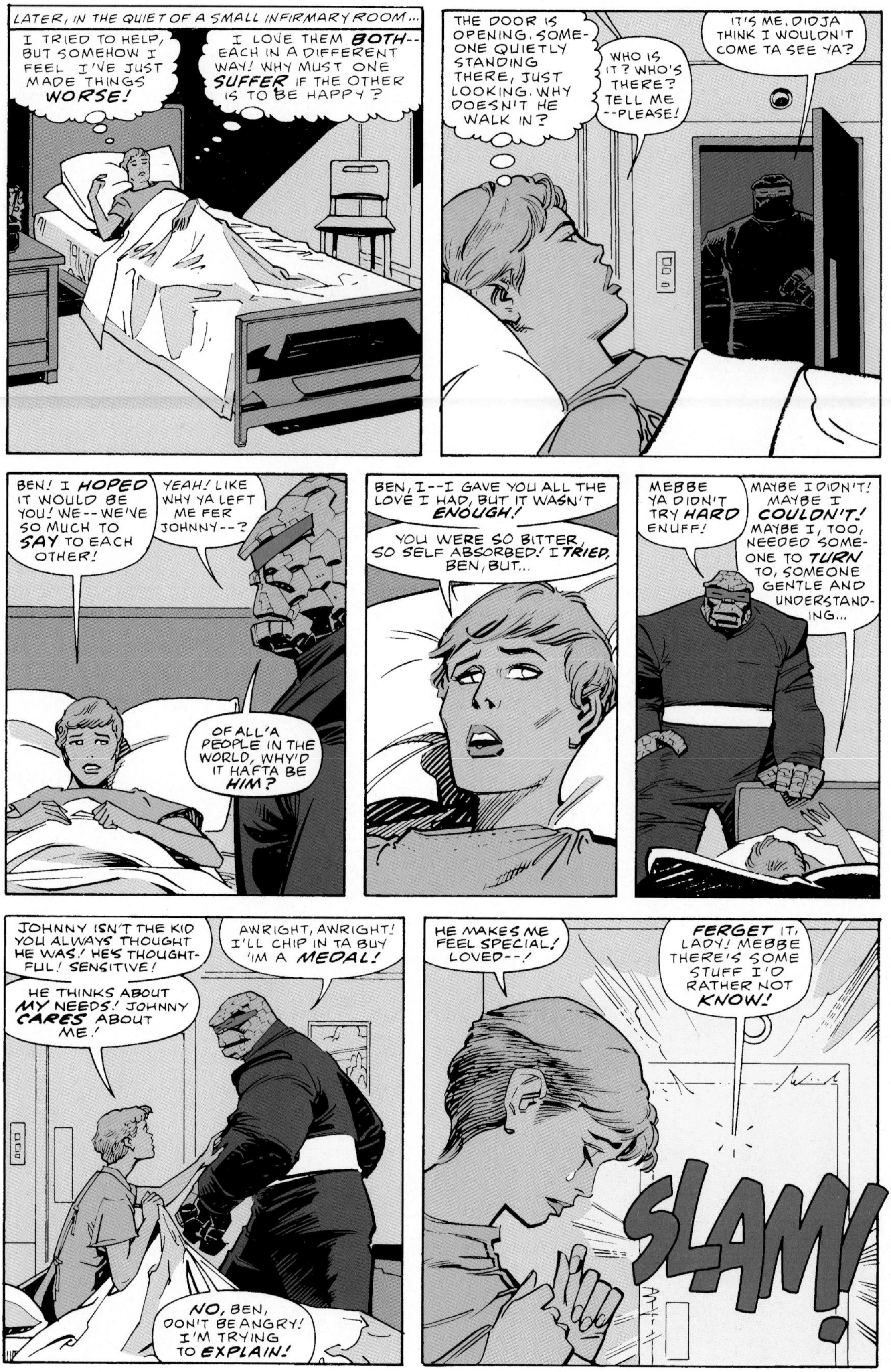
LATER, IN THE QUIET OF A SMALL INFIRMARY ROOM...
I TRIED TO HELP, BUT SOMEHOW I FEEL I'VE JUST MADE THINGS WORSE!
I LOVE THEM BOTH-- EACH IN A DIFFERENT WAY! WHY MUST ONE SUFFER IF THE OTHER IS TO BE HAPPY?
THE DOOR IS OPENING. SOMEONE QUIETLY STANDING THERE, JUST LOOKING. WHY DOESN'T HE WALK IN?
WHO IS IT? WHO'S THERE? TELL ME --PLEASE!
IT'S ME. DIDJA THINK I WOULDN'T COME TA SEE YA?
BEN! I HOPED IT WOULD BE YOU! WE--WE'VE SO MUCH TO SAY TO EACH OTHER!
YEAH! LIKE WHY YA LEFT ME FER JOHNNY--?
OF ALL'A PEOPLE IN THE WORLD, WHY'D IT HAFTA BE HIM?
BEN, I--I GAVE YOU ALL THE LOVE I HAD, BUT IT WASN'T ENOUGH!
YOU WERE SO BITTER, SO SELF ABSORBED! I TRIED, BEN, BUT...
MEBBE YA DIDN'T TRY HARD ENUFF!
MAYBE I DIDN'T! MAYBE I COULDN'T! MAYBE I, TOO, NEEDED SOMEONE TO TURN TO, SOMEONE GENTLE AND UNDERSTANDING...
JOHNNY ISN'T THE KID YOU ALWAYS THOUGHT HE WAS! HE'S THOUGHTFUL! SENSITIVE!
HE THINKS ABOUT MY NEEDS! JOHNNY CARES ABOUT ME!
AWRIGHT, AWRIGHT! I'LL CHIP IN TA BUY 'IM A MEDAL!
NO, BEN, DON'T BE ANGRY! I'M TRYING TO EXPLAIN!
HE MAKES ME FEEL SPECIAL! LOVED--!
FERGET IT, LADY! MEBBE THERE'S SOME STUFF I'D RATHER NOT KNOW!
SLAM!

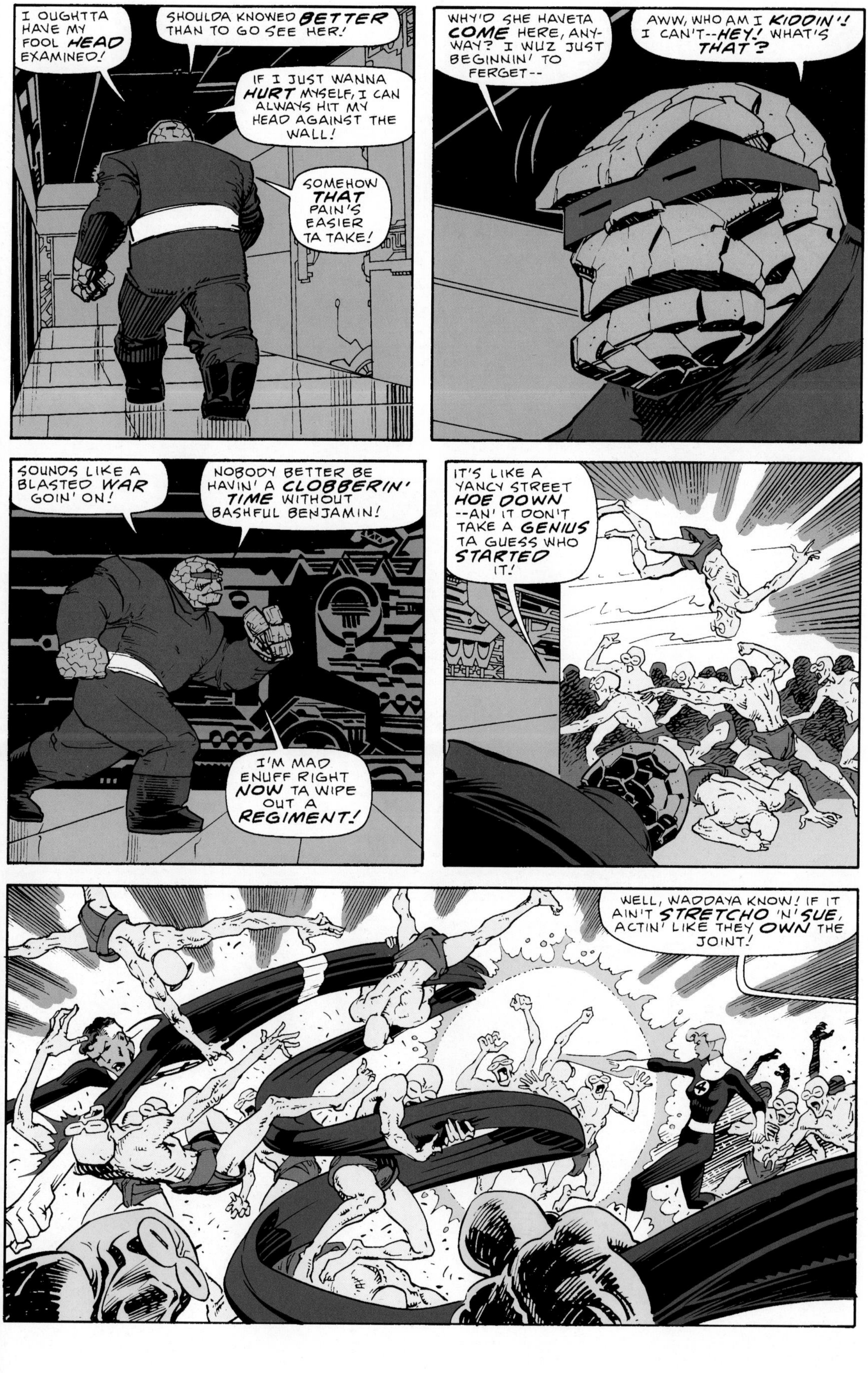
I OUGHTTA HAVE MY FOOL HEAD EXAMINED!
SHOULDA KNOWED BETTER THAN TO GO SEE HER!
IF I JUST WANNA HURT MYSELF, I CAN ALWAYS HIT MY HEAD AGAINST THE WALL!
SOMEHOW THAT PAIN'S EASIER TA TAKE!
WHY'D SHE HAVETA COME HERE, ANY-WAY? I WUZ JUST BEGINNIN' TO FERGET--
AWW, WHO AM I KIDDIN'! I CAN'T--HEY! WHAT'S THAT?
SOUNDS LIKE A BLASTED WAR GOIN' ON!
NOBODY BETTER BE HAVIN' A CLOBBERIN' TIME WITHOUT BASHFUL BENJAMIN!
I'M MAD ENUFF RIGHT NOW TA WIPE OUT A REGIMENT!
IT'S LIKE A YANCY STREET HOE DOWN --AN' IT DON'T TAKE A GENIUS TA GUESS WHO STARTED IT!
WELL, WADDAYA KNOW! IF IT AIN'T STRETCHO 'N' SUE, ACTIN' LIKE THEY OWN THE JOINT!

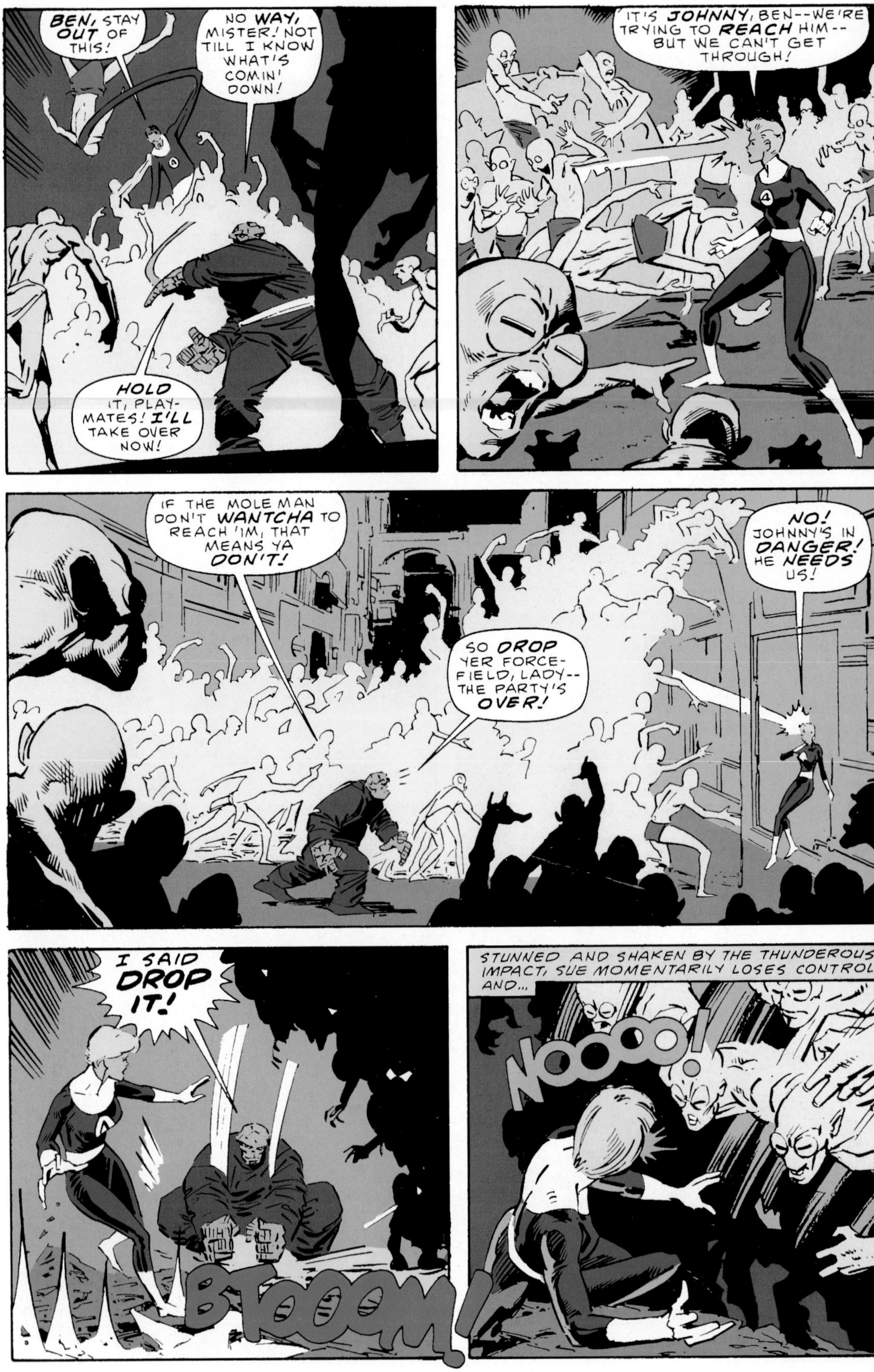

BEN, STAY OUT OF THIS!
NO WAY, MISTER! NOT TILL I KNOW WHAT'S COMIN' DOWN!
HOLD IT, PLAY-MATES! I'LL TAKE OVER NOW!
IT'S JOHNNY, BEN--WE'RE TRYING TO REACH HIM--BUT WE CAN'T GET THROUGH!
IF THE MOLE MAN DON'T WANTCHA TO REACH 'IM, THAT MEANS YA DON'T!
NO! JOHNNY'S IN DANGER! HE NEEDS US!
SO DROP YER FORCE-FIELD, LADY--THE PARTY'S OVER!
I SAID DROP IT!
BTOOOM!!
STUNNED AND SHAKEN BY THE THUNDEROUS IMPACT, SUE MOMENTARILY LOSES CONTROL, AND...
NOOOO!

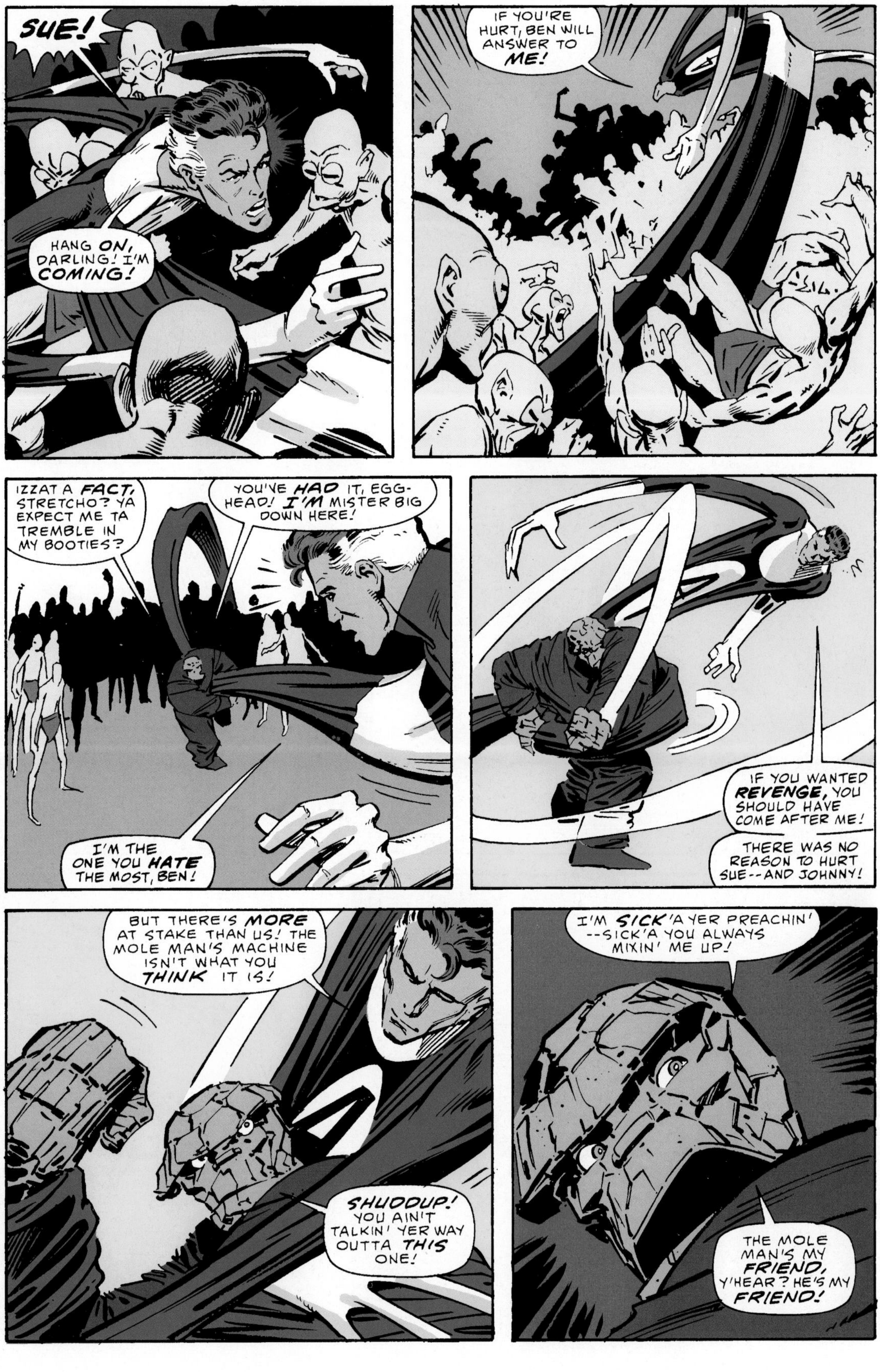
SUE!
HANG ON, DARLING! I'M COMING!
IF YOU'RE HURT, BEN WILL ANSWER TO ME!
IZZAT A FACT, STRETCHO? YA EXPECT ME TA TREMBLE IN MY BOOTIES?
YOU'VE HAD IT, EGG-HEAD! I'M MISTER BIG DOWN HERE!
I'M THE ONE YOU HATE THE MOST, BEN!
IF YOU WANTED REVENGE, YOU SHOULD HAVE COME AFTER ME!
THERE WAS NO REASON TO HURT SUE--AND JOHNNY!
BUT THERE'S MORE AT STAKE THAN US! THE MOLE MAN'S MACHINE ISN'T WHAT YOU THINK IT IS!
SHUDDUP! YOU AIN'T TALKIN' YER WAY OUTTA THIS ONE!
I'M SICK'A YER PREACHIN' --SICK'A YOU ALWAYS MIXIN' ME UP!
THE MOLE MAN'S MY FRIEND, Y'HEAR? HE'S MY FRIEND!

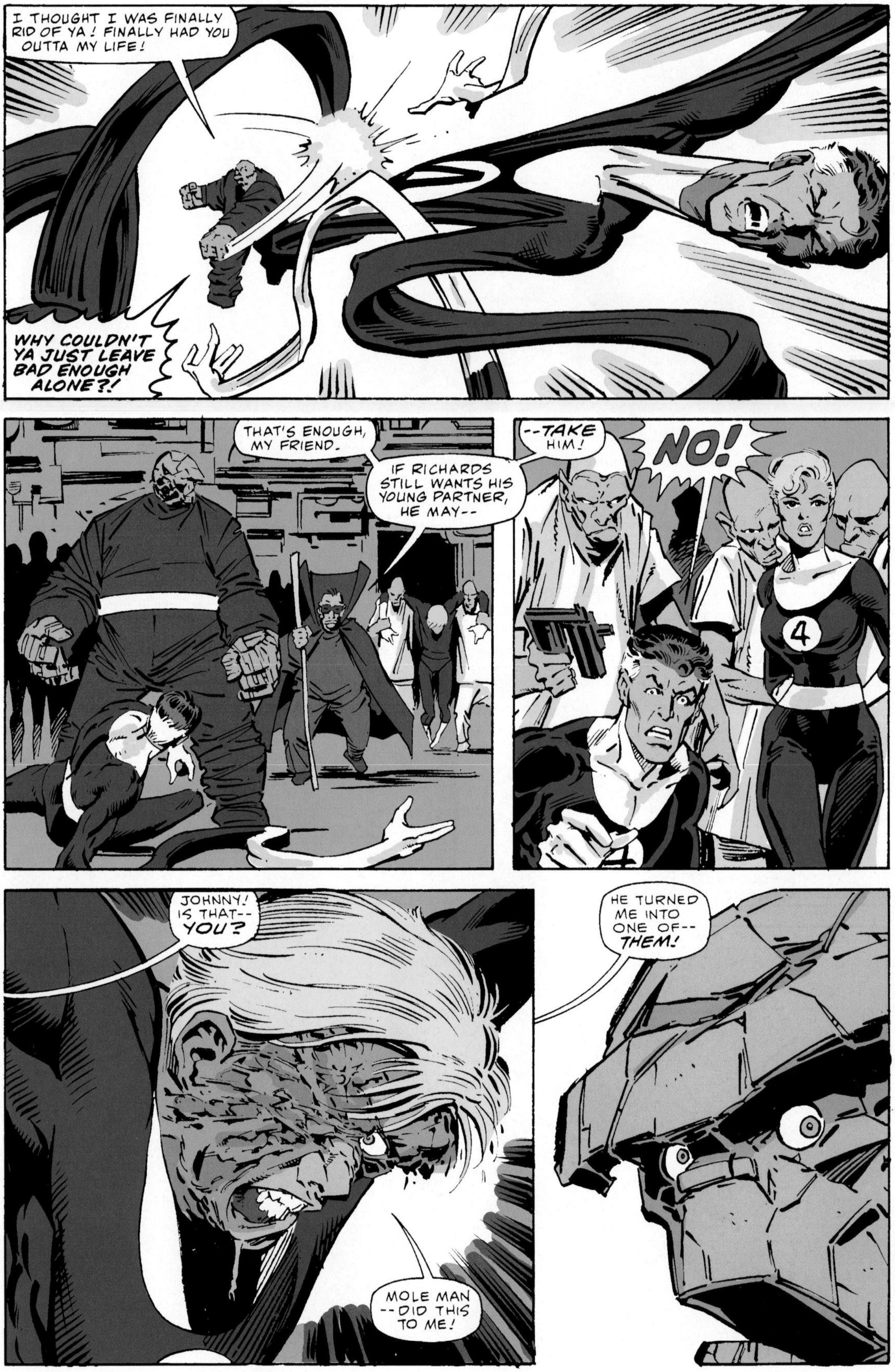

I THOUGHT I WAS FINALLY RID OF YA! FINALLY HAD YOU OUTTA MY LIFE!
WHY COULDN'T YA JUST LEAVE BAD ENOUGH ALONE?!
THAT'S ENOUGH, MY FRIEND.
IF RICHARDS STILL WANTS HIS YOUNG PARTNER, HE MAY--
--TAKE HIM!
NO!
JOHNNY! IS THAT-- YOU?
MOLE MAN --DID THIS TO ME!
HE TURNED ME INTO ONE OF-- THEM!

TOO STUNNED TO FIGHT ANYMORE, TOO SHAKEN BY THE SHEER HORROR OF WHAT THEY HAVE SEEN, SUE AND REED LOOK ON IN SHOCK AS BEN SOFTLY MUTTERS TO HIMSELF...

I TOLD 'EM--NOT TO COME.

WITHOUT LIFTING HIS HEAD, WITHOUT ANOTHER GLANCE, BEN ISSUES HIS FINAL ORDER, IN A VOICE AS LIFELESS AS LEAD...

IT'S OVER. TAKE THEM TO THE SURFACE--

THE BLIND GIRL, TOO.

MINUTES LATER, AS THE NUMBNESS SLOWLY WEARS OFF...

WHERE IS HOPPER? I NEED HIM TO LOOK AFTER ALICIA AND JOHNNY.

WHY, REED? WE'RE ALL TO-GETHER NOW. WE CAN LOOK AFTER THEM, WE WON'T LEAVE THEM ANYMORE.

HEY, DID I HEAR SOMEONE CALL MY NAME?

WE HAVE TO GO BACK, SUE! THERE'S NO OTHER WAY!

NO! IT'S MADNESS! THERE'S BEEN ENOUGH FIGHTING, ENOUGH HORROR!

REVENGE IS MEANING-LESS! LET IT REST!

I'M NOT THINKING OF REVENGE.

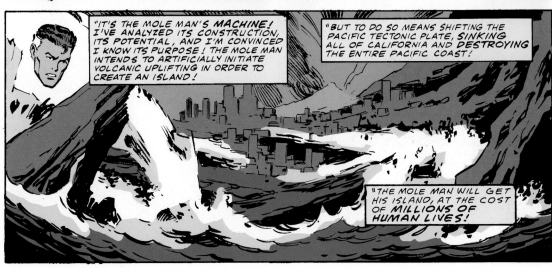

"IT'S THE MOLE MAN'S MACHINE! I'VE ANALYZED ITS CONSTRUCTION, ITS POTENTIAL, AND I'M CONVINCED I KNOW ITS PURPOSE! THE MOLE MAN INTENDS TO ARTIFICIALLY INITIATE VOLCANIC UPLIFTING IN ORDER TO CREATE AN ISLAND!

"BUT TO DO SO MEANS SHIFTING THE PACIFIC TECTONIC PLATE, SINKING ALL OF CALIFORNIA AND DESTROYING THE ENTIRE PACIFIC COAST!

"THE MOLE MAN WILL GET HIS ISLAND, AT THE COST OF MILLIONS OF HUMAN LIVES!

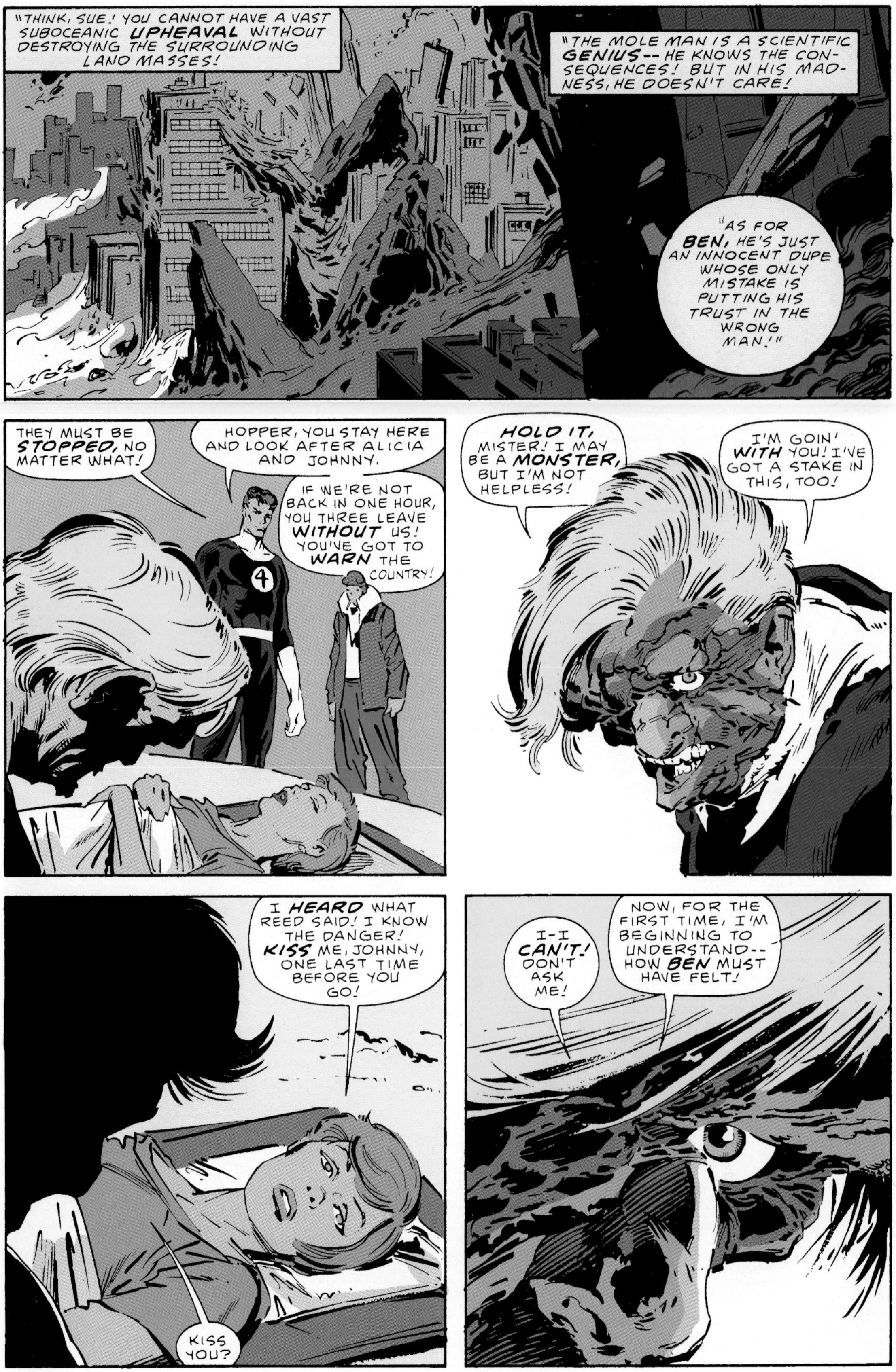
"THINK, SUE! YOU CANNOT HAVE A VAST SUBOCEANIC UPHEAVAL WITHOUT DESTROYING THE SURROUNDING LAND MASSES!
"THE MOLE MAN IS A SCIENTIFIC GENIUS -- HE KNOWS THE CONSEQUENCES! BUT IN HIS MADNESS, HE DOESN'T CARE!
"AS FOR BEN, HE'S JUST AN INNOCENT DUPE WHOSE ONLY MISTAKE IS PUTTING HIS TRUST IN THE WRONG MAN!"
THEY MUST BE STOPPED, NO MATTER WHAT!
HOPPER, YOU STAY HERE AND LOOK AFTER ALICIA AND JOHNNY.
IF WE'RE NOT BACK IN ONE HOUR, YOU THREE LEAVE WITHOUT US! YOU'VE GOT TO WARN THE COUNTRY!
HOLD IT, MISTER! I MAY BE A MONSTER, BUT I'M NOT HELPLESS!
I'M GOIN' WITH YOU! I'VE GOT A STAKE IN THIS, TOO!
I HEARD WHAT REED SAID! I KNOW THE DANGER! KISS ME, JOHNNY, ONE LAST TIME BEFORE YOU GO!
KISS YOU?
I-I CAN'T! DON'T ASK ME!
NOW, FOR THE FIRST TIME, I'M BEGINNING TO UNDERSTAND-- HOW BEN MUST HAVE FELT!

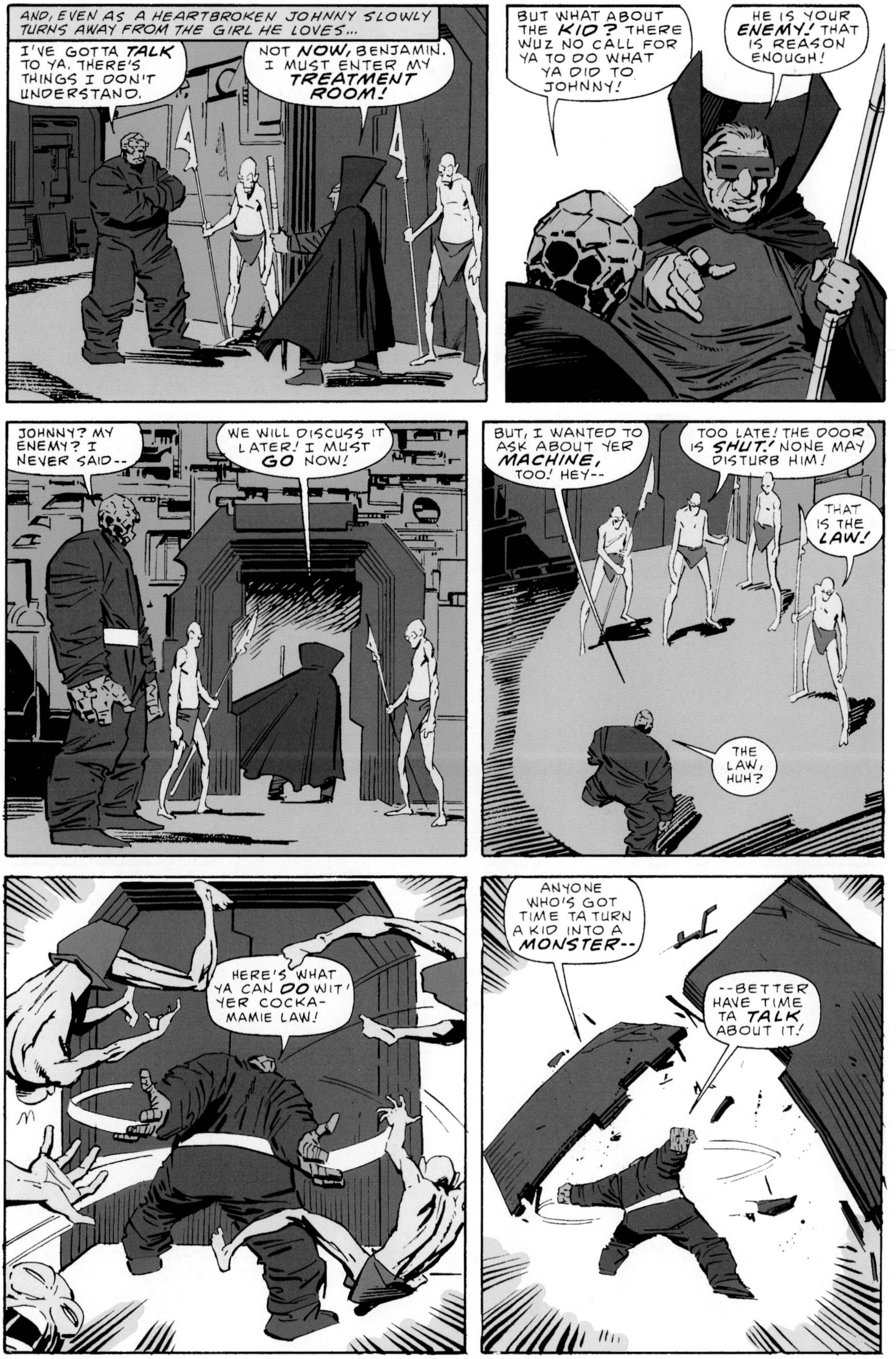
AND, EVEN AS A HEARTBROKEN JOHNNY SLOWLY TURNS AWAY FROM THE GIRL HE LOVES...
I'VE GOTTA TALK TO YA. THERE'S THINGS I DON'T UNDERSTAND.
NOT NOW, BENJAMIN. I MUST ENTER MY TREATMENT ROOM!
BUT WHAT ABOUT THE KID? THERE WUZ NO CALL FOR YA TO DO WHAT YA DID TO JOHNNY!
HE IS YOUR ENEMY! THAT IS REASON ENOUGH!
JOHNNY? MY ENEMY? I NEVER SAID--
WE WILL DISCUSS IT LATER! I MUST GO NOW!
BUT, I WANTED TO ASK ABOUT YER MACHINE, TOO! HEY--
TOO LATE! THE DOOR IS SHUT! NONE MAY DISTURB HIM!
THAT IS THE LAW!
THE LAW, HUH?
HERE'S WHAT YA CAN DO WIT' YER COCKA-MAMIE LAW!
ANYONE WHO'S GOT TIME TA TURN A KID INTO A MONSTER--
--BETTER HAVE TIME TA TALK ABOUT IT!

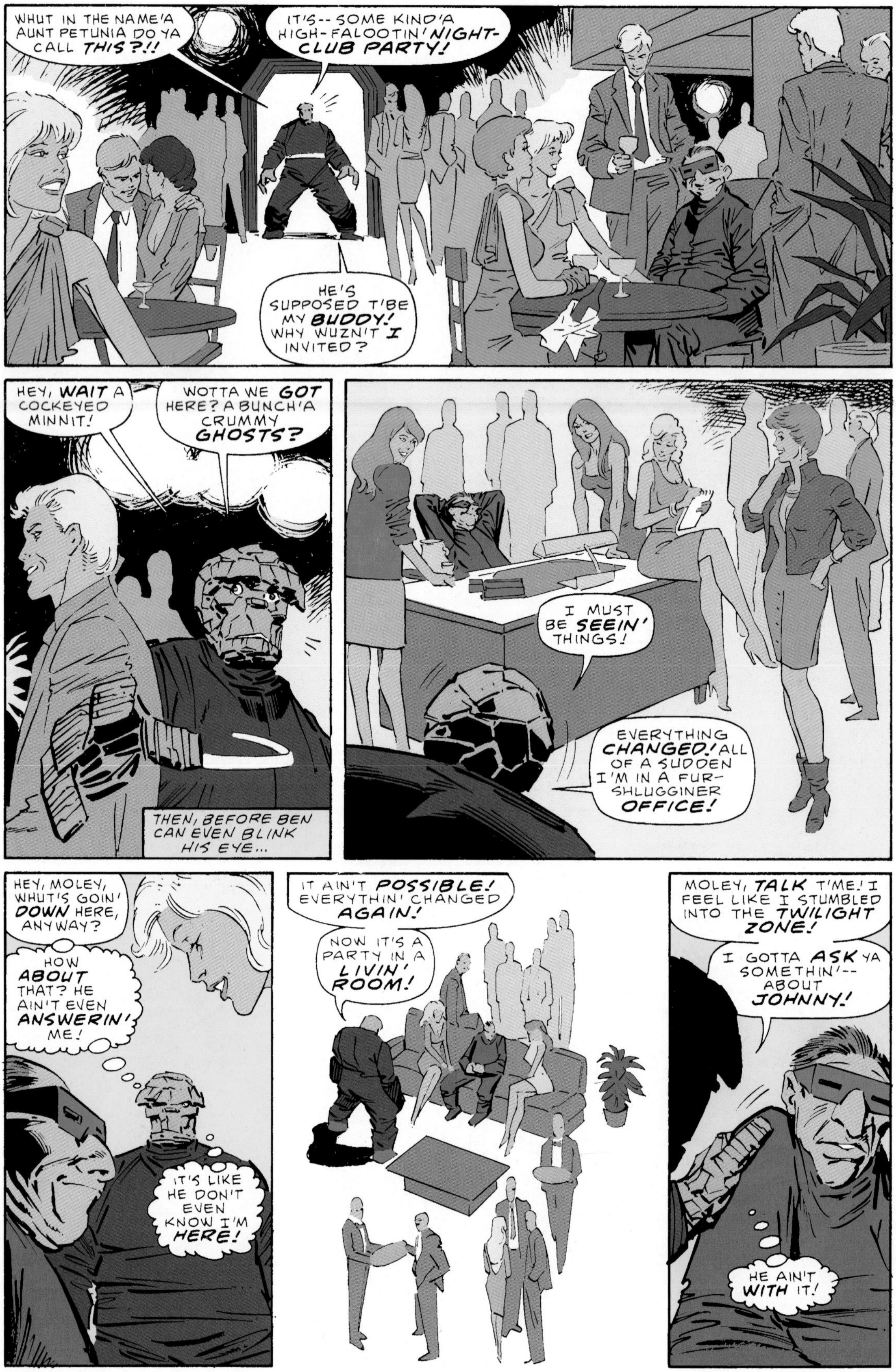

WHUT IN THE NAME'A AUNT PETUNIA DO YA CALL THIS?!!
IT'S-- SOME KIND'A HIGH-FALOOTIN' NIGHT-CLUB PARTY!
HE'S SUPPOSED T'BE MY BUDDY! WHY WUZN'T I INVITED?
HEY, WAIT A COCKEYED MINNIT!
WOTTA WE GOT HERE? A BUNCH'A CRUMMY GHOSTS?
THEN, BEFORE BEN CAN EVEN BLINK HIS EYE...
I MUST BE SEEIN' THINGS!
EVERYTHING CHANGED! ALL OF A SUDDEN I'M IN A FUR-SHLUGGINER OFFICE!
HEY, MOLEY, WHUT'S GOIN' DOWN HERE, ANYWAY?
HOW ABOUT THAT? HE AIN'T EVEN ANSWERIN' ME!
IT'S LIKE HE DON'T EVEN KNOW I'M HERE!
IT AIN'T POSSIBLE! EVERYTHIN' CHANGED AGAIN!
NOW IT'S A PARTY IN A LIVIN' ROOM!
MOLEY, TALK T'ME! I FEEL LIKE I STUMBLED INTO THE TWILIGHT ZONE!
I GOTTA ASK YA SOMETHIN'-- ABOUT JOHNNY!
HE AIN'T WITH IT!

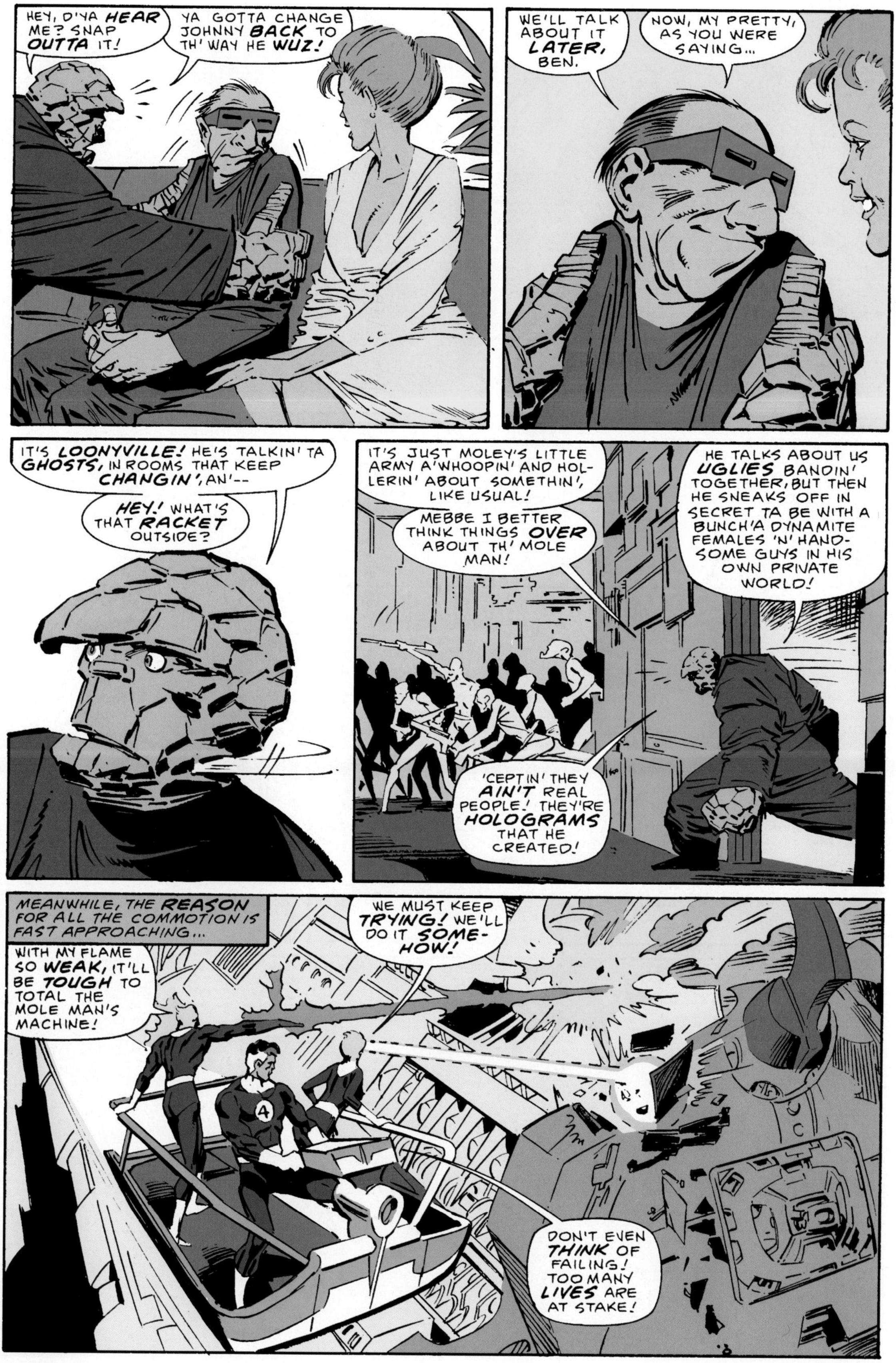
HEY, D'YA HEAR ME? SNAP OUTTA IT!
YA GOTTA CHANGE JOHNNY BACK TO TH' WAY HE WUZ!
WE'LL TALK ABOUT IT LATER, BEN.
NOW, MY PRETTY, AS YOU WERE SAYING...
IT'S LOONYVILLE! HE'S TALKIN' TA GHOSTS, IN ROOMS THAT KEEP CHANGIN', AN'--
HEY! WHAT'S THAT RACKET OUTSIDE?
IT'S JUST MOLEY'S LITTLE ARMY A'WHOOPIN' AND HOLLERIN' ABOUT SOMETHIN', LIKE USUAL!
MEBBE I BETTER THINK THINGS OVER ABOUT TH' MOLE MAN!
HE TALKS ABOUT US UGLIES BANDIN' TOGETHER, BUT THEN HE SNEAKS OFF IN SECRET TA BE WITH A BUNCH'A DYNAMITE FEMALES 'N' HANDSOME GUYS IN HIS OWN PRIVATE WORLD!
'CEPTIN' THEY AIN'T REAL PEOPLE! THEY'RE HOLOGRAMS THAT HE CREATED!
MEANWHILE, THE REASON FOR ALL THE COMMOTION IS FAST APPROACHING...
WITH MY FLAME SO WEAK, IT'LL BE TOUGH TO TOTAL THE MOLE MAN'S MACHINE!
WE MUST KEEP TRYING! WE'LL DO IT SOMEHOW!
DON'T EVEN THINK OF FAILING! TOO MANY LIVES ARE AT STAKE!

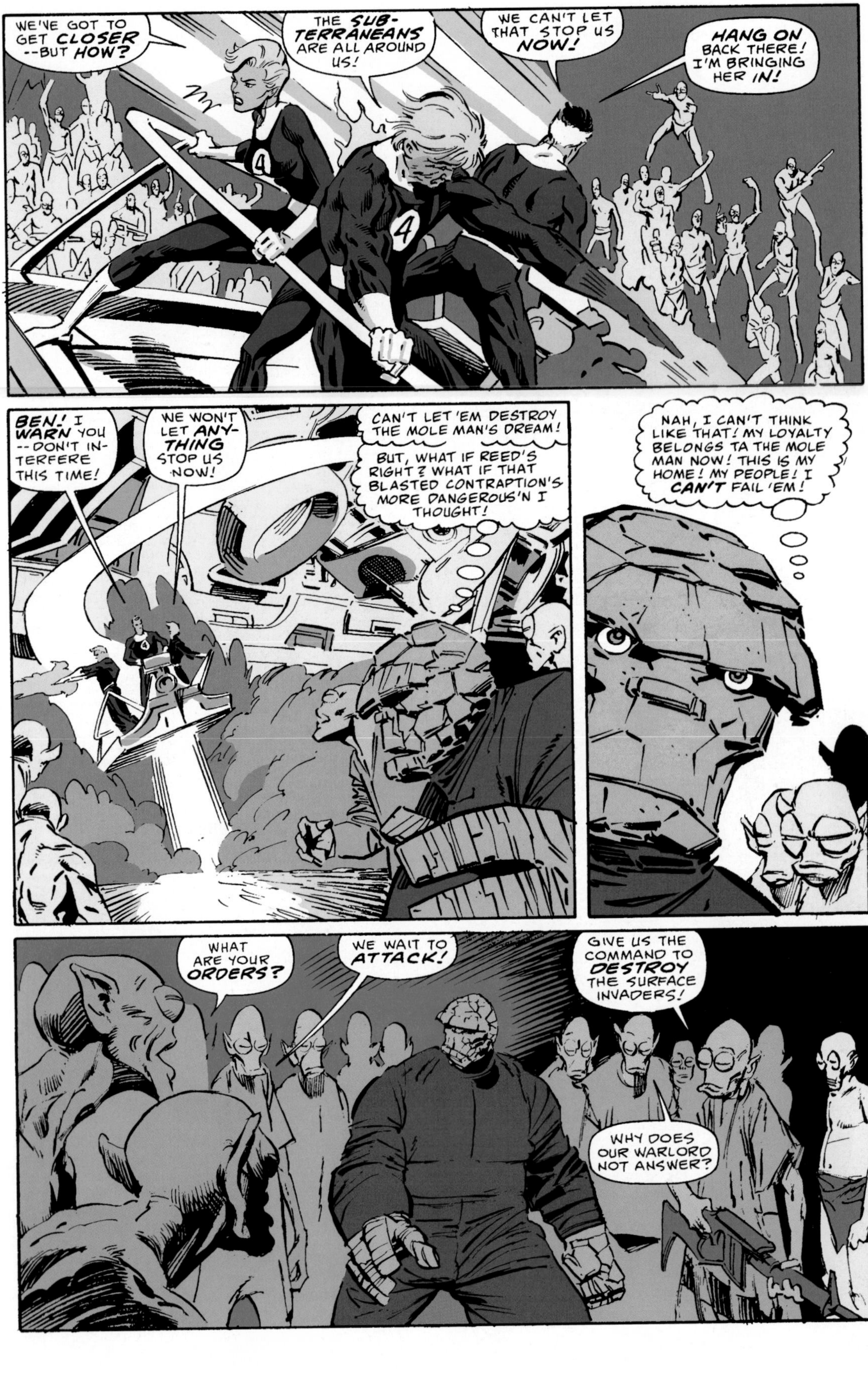

WE'VE GOT TO GET CLOSER --BUT HOW?
THE SUB-TERRANEANS ARE ALL AROUND US!
WE CAN'T LET THAT STOP US NOW!
HANG ON BACK THERE! I'M BRINGING HER IN!
BEN! I WARN YOU --DON'T INTERFERE THIS TIME!
WE WON'T LET ANYTHING STOP US NOW!
CAN'T LET 'EM DESTROY THE MOLE MAN'S DREAM!
BUT, WHAT IF REED'S RIGHT? WHAT IF THAT BLASTED CONTRAPTION'S MORE DANGEROUS'N I THOUGHT!
NAH, I CAN'T THINK LIKE THAT! MY LOYALTY BELONGS TA THE MOLE MAN NOW! THIS IS MY HOME! MY PEOPLE! I CAN'T FAIL 'EM!
WHAT ARE YOUR ORDERS?
WE WAIT TO ATTACK!
GIVE US THE COMMAND TO DESTROY THE SURFACE INVADERS!
WHY DOES OUR WARLORD NOT ANSWER?

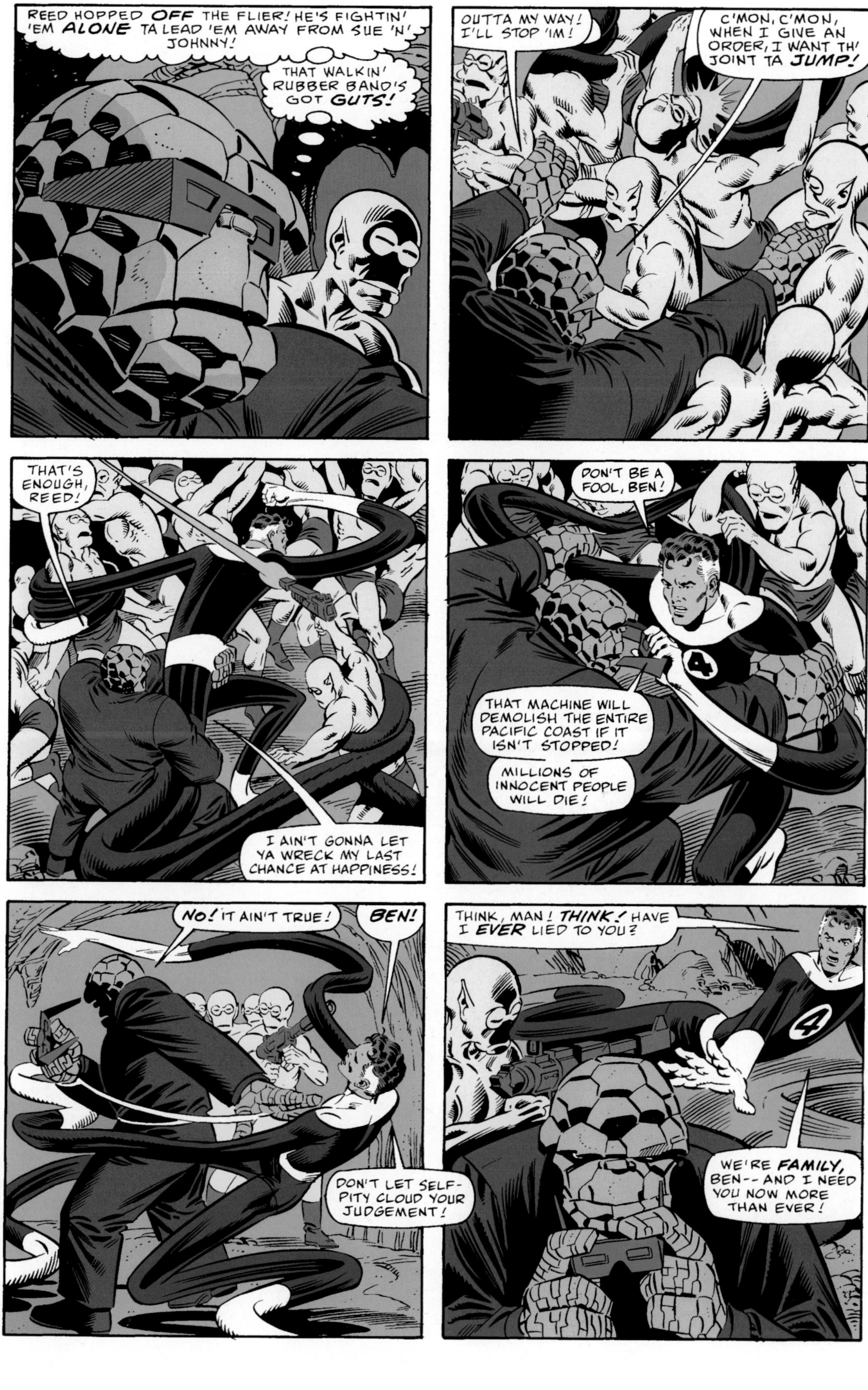
REED HOPPED OFF THE FLIER! HE'S FIGHTIN' 'EM ALONE TA LEAD 'EM AWAY FROM SUE 'N' JOHNNY!
THAT WALKIN' RUBBER BAND'S GOT GUTS!
OUTTA MY WAY! I'LL STOP 'IM!
C'MON, C'MON, WHEN I GIVE AN ORDER, I WANT TH' JOINT TA JUMP!
THAT'S ENOUGH, REED!
I AIN'T GONNA LET YA WRECK MY LAST CHANCE AT HAPPINESS!
DON'T BE A FOOL, BEN!
THAT MACHINE WILL DEMOLISH THE ENTIRE PACIFIC COAST IF IT ISN'T STOPPED!
MILLIONS OF INNOCENT PEOPLE WILL DIE!
NO! IT AIN'T TRUE!
BEN!
DON'T LET SELF-PITY CLOUD YOUR JUDGEMENT!
THINK, MAN! THINK! HAVE I EVER LIED TO YOU?
WE'RE FAMILY, BEN-- AND I NEED YOU NOW MORE THAN EVER!

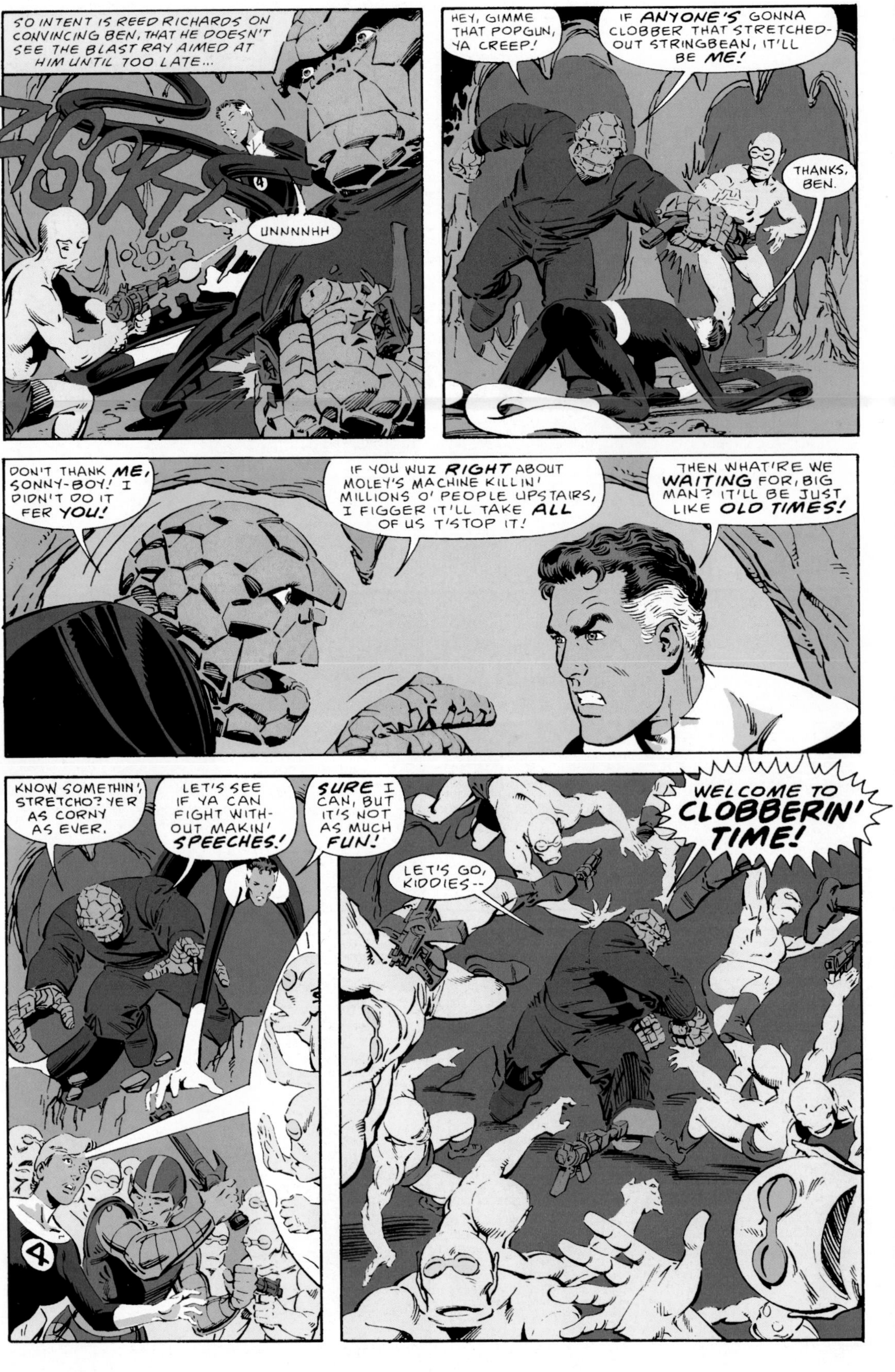
SO INTENT IS REED RICHARDS ON CONVINCING BEN, THAT HE DOESN'T SEE THE BLAST RAY AIMED AT HIM UNTIL TOO LATE...
ZSSKT!
UNNNNHH
HEY, GIMME THAT POPGUN, YA CREEP!
IF ANYONE'S GONNA CLOBBER THAT STRETCHED-OUT STRINGBEAN, IT'LL BE ME!
THANKS, BEN.
DON'T THANK ME, SONNY-BOY! I DIDN'T DO IT FER YOU!
IF YOU WUZ RIGHT ABOUT MOLEY'S MACHINE KILLIN' MILLIONS O' PEOPLE UPSTAIRS, I FIGGER IT'LL TAKE ALL OF US T'STOP IT!
THEN WHAT'RE WE WAITING FOR, BIG MAN? IT'LL BE JUST LIKE OLD TIMES!
KNOW SOMETHIN', STRETCHO? YER AS CORNY AS EVER.
LET'S SEE IF YA CAN FIGHT WITHOUT MAKIN' SPEECHES!
SURE I CAN, BUT IT'S NOT AS MUCH FUN!
LET'S GO, KIDDIES--
WELCOME TO CLOBBERIN' TIME!

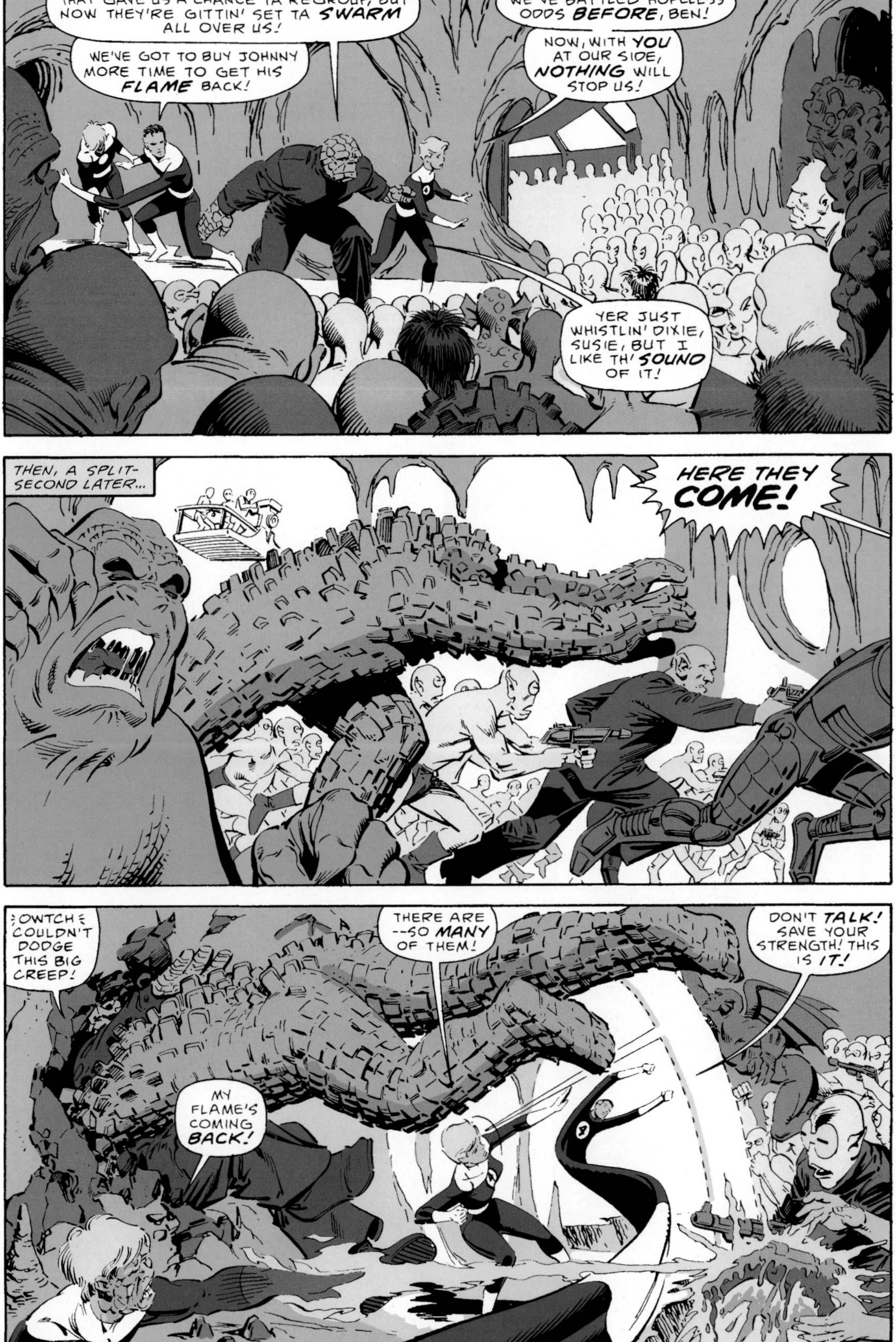
THAT GAVE US A CHANCE TA REGROUP, BUT NOW THEY'RE GITTIN' SET TA SWARM ALL OVER US!
WE'VE GOT TO BUY JOHNNY MORE TIME TO GET HIS FLAME BACK!
WE'VE BATTLED HOPELESS ODDS BEFORE, BEN!
NOW, WITH YOU AT OUR SIDE, NOTHING WILL STOP US!
YER JUST WHISTLIN' DIXIE, SUSIE, BUT I LIKE TH' SOUND OF IT!
THEN, A SPLIT-SECOND LATER...
HERE THEY COME!
OWTCH COULDN'T DODGE THIS BIG CREEP!
THERE ARE --SO MANY OF THEM!
DON'T TALK! SAVE YOUR STRENGTH! THIS IS IT!
MY FLAME'S COMING BACK!

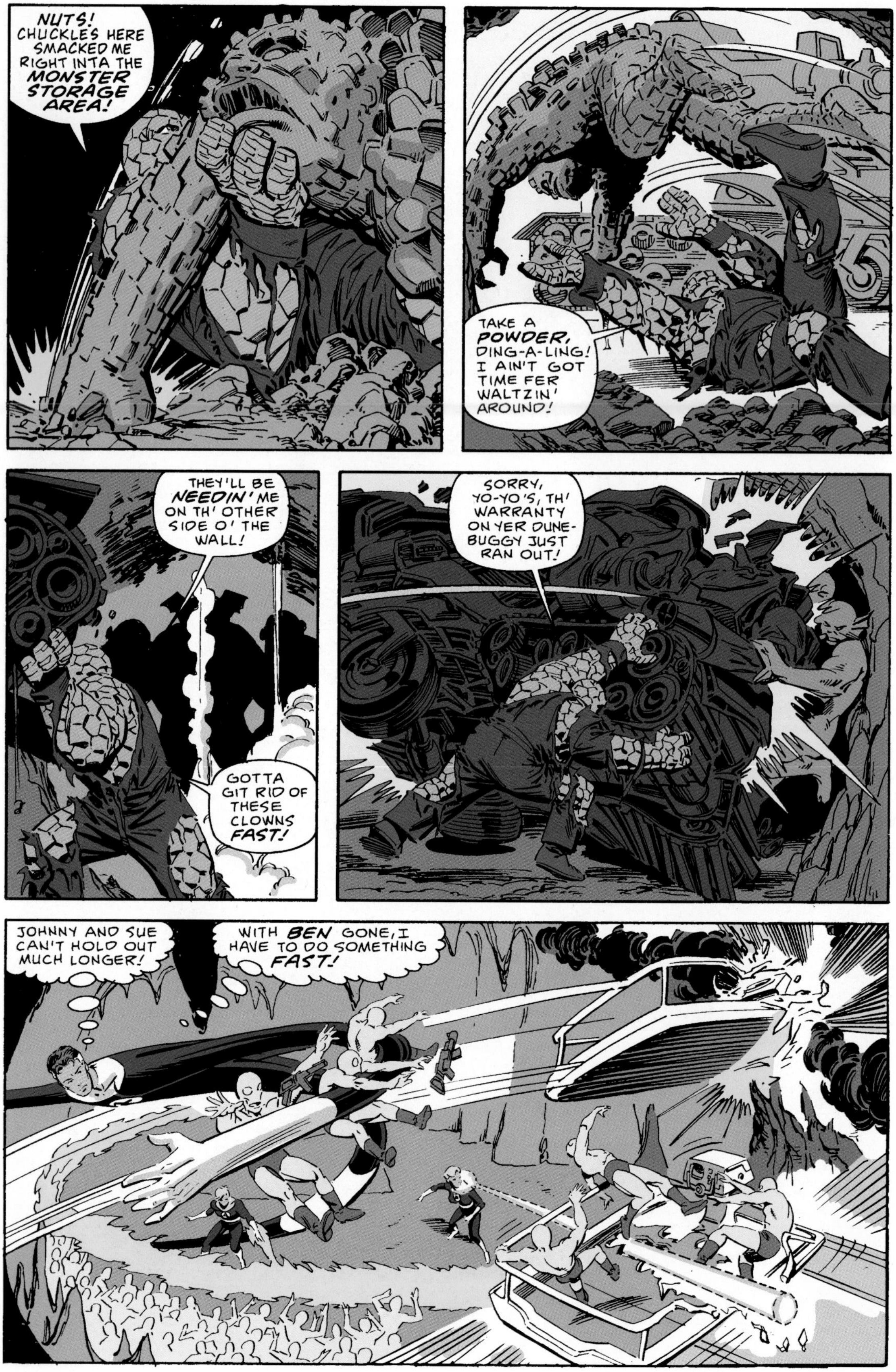
NUTS! CHUCKLE'S HERE SMACKED ME RIGHT INTA THE MONSTER STORAGE AREA!
TAKE A POWDER, DING-A-LING! I AIN'T GOT TIME FER WALTZIN' AROUND!
THEY'LL BE NEEDIN' ME ON TH' OTHER SIDE O' THE WALL!
GOTTA GIT RID OF THESE CLOWNS FAST!
SORRY, YO-YO'S, TH' WARRANTY ON YER DUNE-BUGGY JUST RAN OUT!
JOHNNY AND SUE CAN'T HOLD OUT MUCH LONGER!
WITH BEN GONE, I HAVE TO DO SOMETHING FAST!

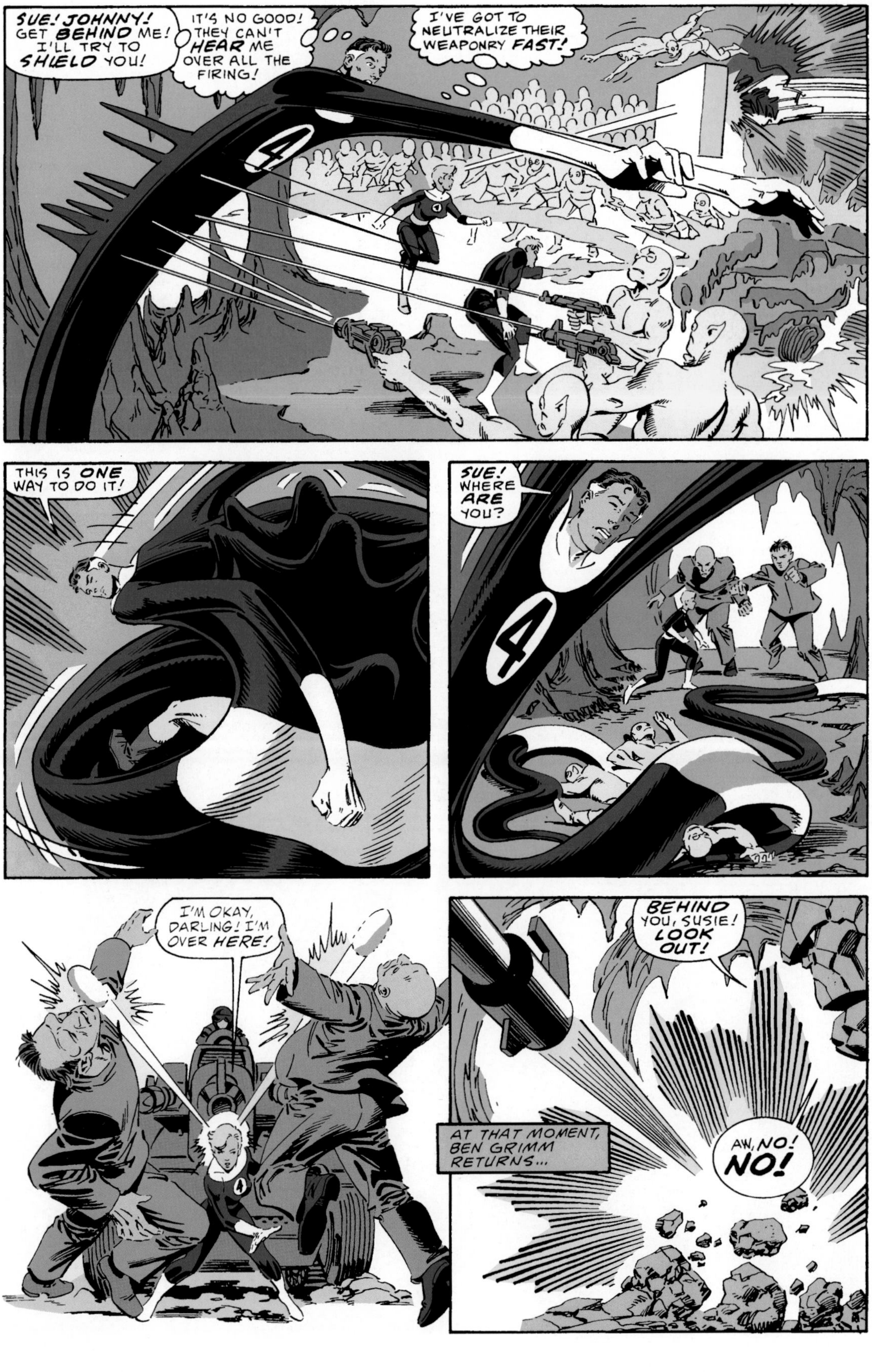
SUE! JOHNNY! GET BEHIND ME! I'LL TRY TO SHIELD YOU!
IT'S NO GOOD! THEY CAN'T HEAR ME OVER ALL THE FIRING!
I'VE GOT TO NEUTRALIZE THEIR WEAPONRY FAST!
THIS IS ONE WAY TO DO IT!
SUE! WHERE ARE YOU?
I'M OKAY, DARLING! I'M OVER HERE!
BEHIND YOU, SUSIE! LOOK OUT!
AT THAT MOMENT, BEN GRIMM RETURNS...
AW, NO! NO!

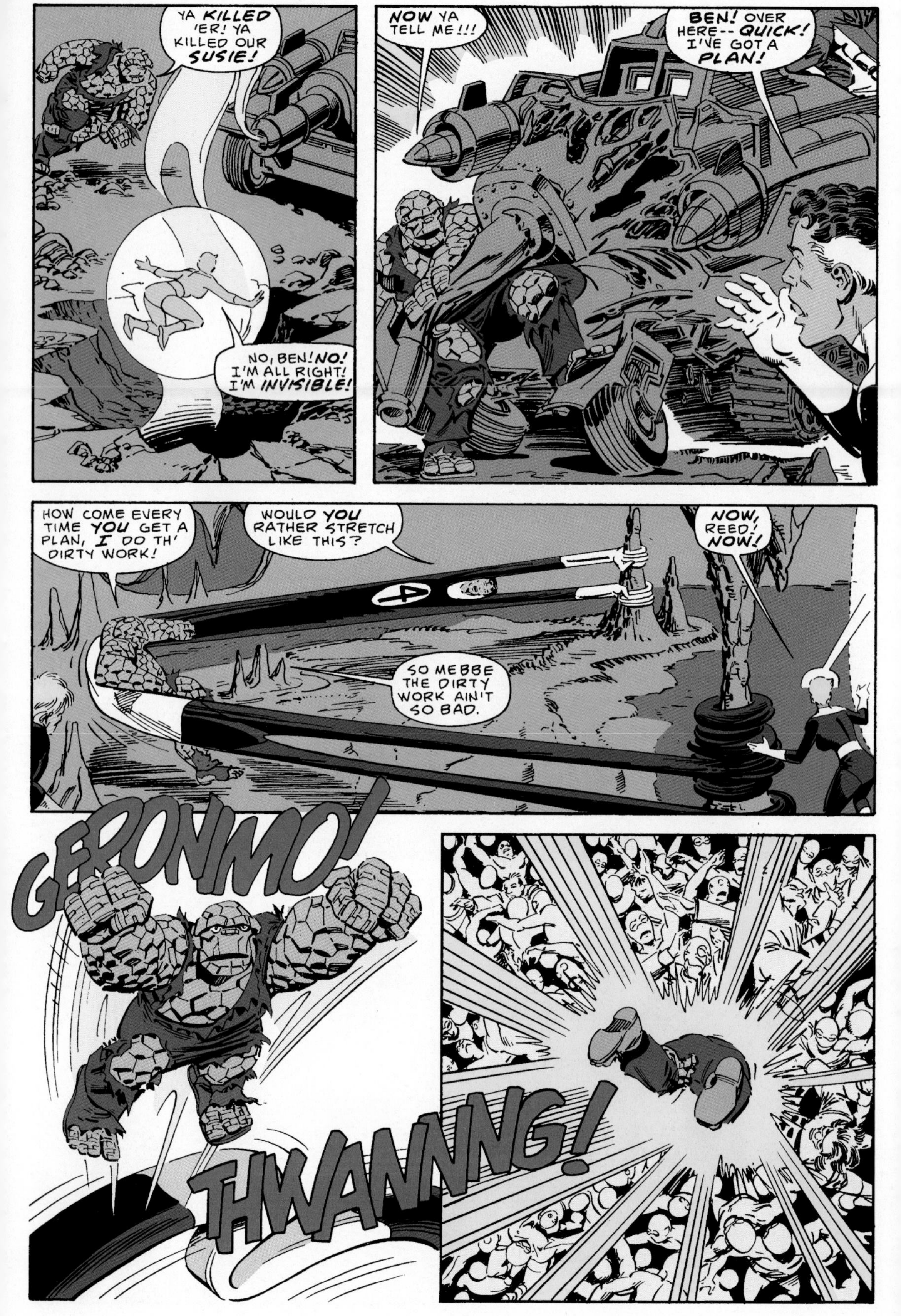
YA KILLED 'ER! YA KILLED OUR SUSIE!
NO, BEN! NO! I'M ALL RIGHT! I'M INVISIBLE!
NOW YA TELL ME!!!
BEN! OVER HERE-- QUICK! I'VE GOT A PLAN!
HOW COME EVERY TIME YOU GET A PLAN, I DO TH' DIRTY WORK!
WOULD YOU RATHER STRETCH LIKE THIS?
NOW, REED! NOW!
SO MEBBE THE DIRTY WORK AIN'T SO BAD.
GERONMO!
THWANNNG!

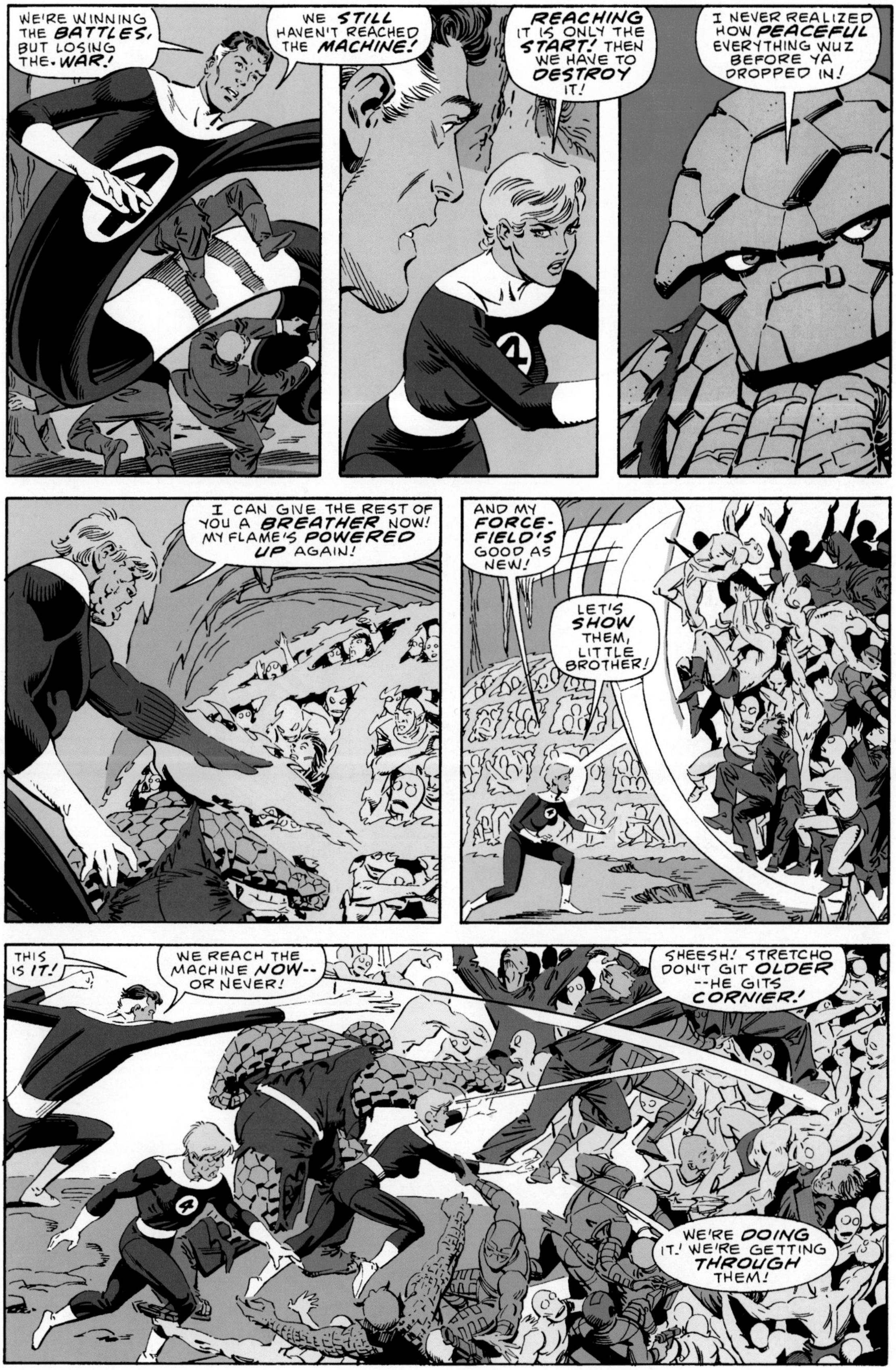
WE'RE WINNING THE BATTLES, BUT LOSING THE WAR!
WE STILL HAVEN'T REACHED THE MACHINE!
REACHING IT IS ONLY THE START! THEN WE HAVE TO DESTROY IT!
I NEVER REALIZED HOW PEACEFUL EVERYTHING WUZ BEFORE YA DROPPED IN!
I CAN GIVE THE REST OF YOU A BREATHER NOW! MY FLAME'S POWERED UP AGAIN!
AND MY FORCE-FIELD'S GOOD AS NEW!
LET'S SHOW THEM, LITTLE BROTHER!
THIS IS IT!
WE REACH THE MACHINE NOW-- OR NEVER!
SHEESH! STRETCHO DON'T GIT OLDER --HE GITS CORNIER!
WE'RE DOING IT! WE'RE GETTING THROUGH THEM!

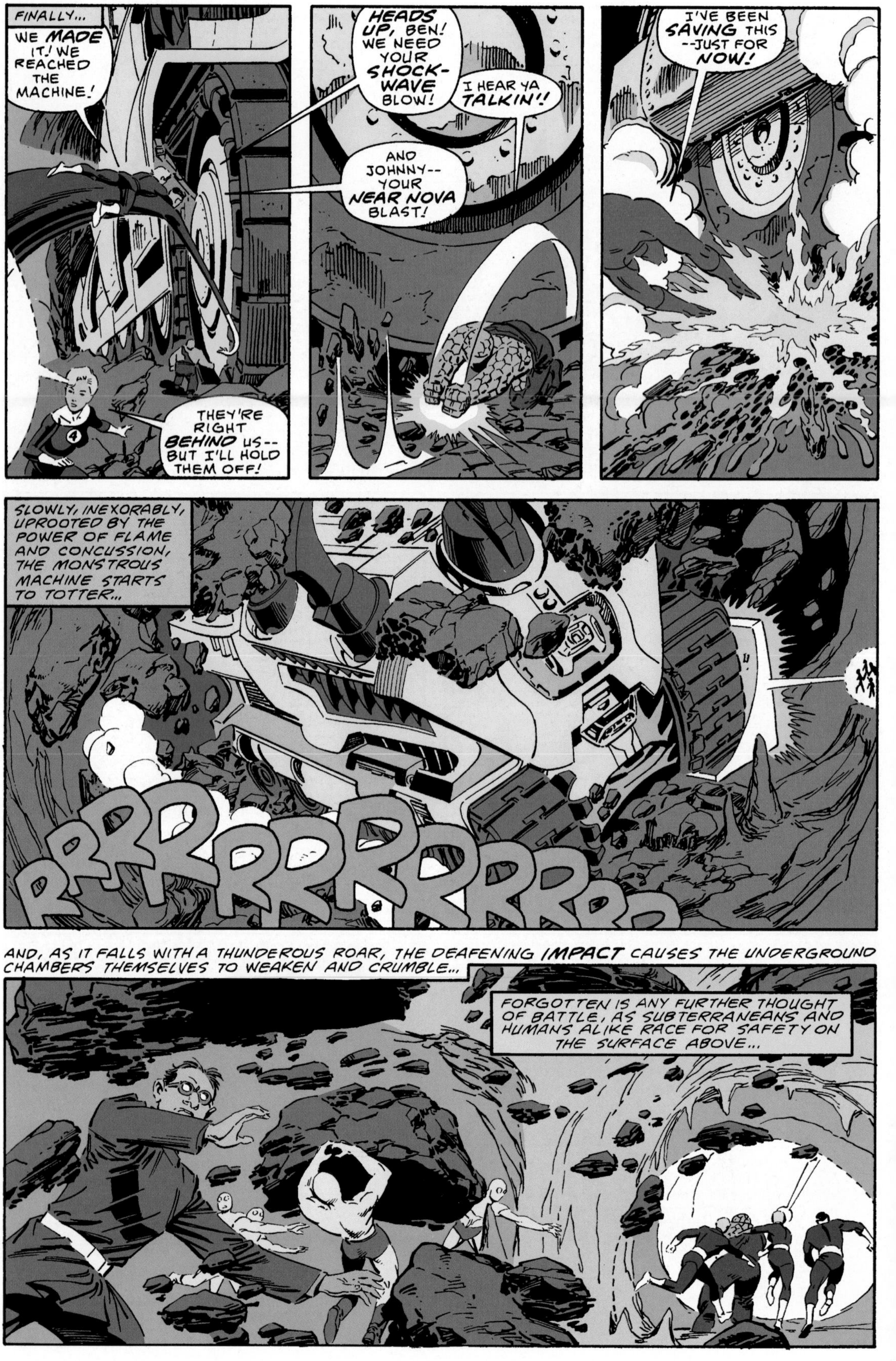
FINALLY...
WE MADE IT! WE REACHED THE MACHINE!
THEY'RE RIGHT BEHIND US--BUT I'LL HOLD THEM OFF!
HEADS UP, BEN! WE NEED YOUR SHOCK-WAVE BLOW!
I HEAR YA TALKIN'!
AND JOHNNY--YOUR NEAR NOVA BLAST!
I'VE BEEN SAVING THIS --JUST FOR NOW!
SLOWLY, INEXORABLY, UPROOTED BY THE POWER OF FLAME AND CONCUSSION, THE MONSTROUS MACHINE STARTS TO TOTTER...
RRRRRRRRRRRRRRRRR
AND, AS IT FALLS WITH A THUNDEROUS ROAR, THE DEAFENING IMPACT CAUSES THE UNDERGROUND CHAMBERS THEMSELVES TO WEAKEN AND CRUMBLE...
FORGOTTEN IS ANY FURTHER THOUGHT OF BATTLE, AS SUBTERRANEANS AND HUMANS ALIKE RACE FOR SAFETY ON THE SURFACE ABOVE...

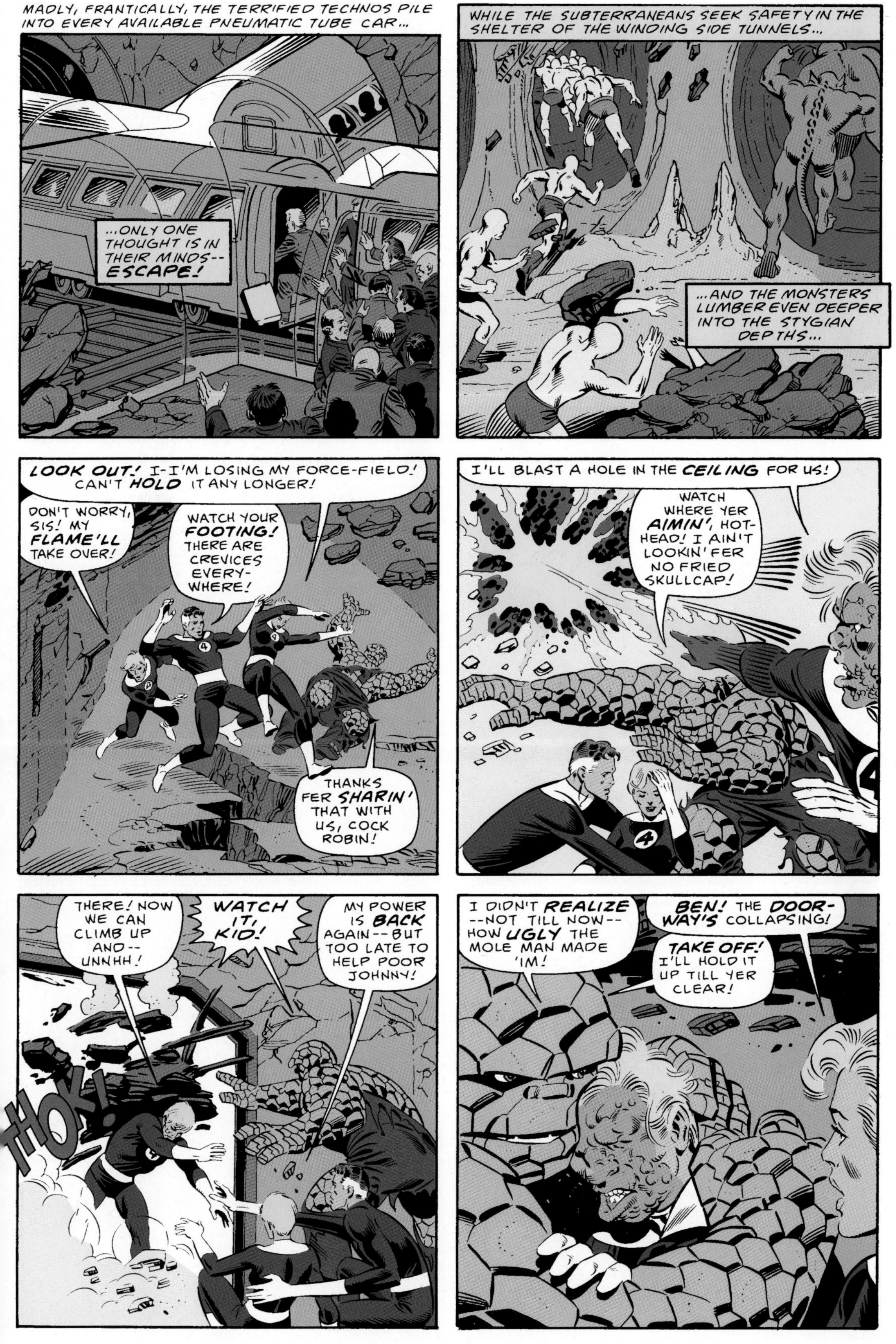
MADLY, FRANTICALLY, THE TERRIFIED TECHNOS PILE INTO EVERY AVAILABLE PNEUMATIC TUBE CAR...
...ONLY ONE THOUGHT IS IN THEIR MINDS-- ESCAPE!
WHILE THE SUBTERRANEANS SEEK SAFETY IN THE SHELTER OF THE WINDING SIDE TUNNELS...
...AND THE MONSTERS LUMBER EVEN DEEPER INTO THE STYGIAN DEPTHS...
LOOK OUT! I-I'M LOSING MY FORCE-FIELD! CAN'T HOLD IT ANY LONGER!
DON'T WORRY, SIS! MY FLAME'LL TAKE OVER!
WATCH YOUR FOOTING! THERE ARE CREVICES EVERY-WHERE!
THANKS FER SHARIN' THAT WITH US, COCK ROBIN!
I'LL BLAST A HOLE IN THE CEILING FOR US!
WATCH WHERE YER AIMIN', HOT-HEAD! I AIN'T LOOKIN' FER NO FRIED SKULLCAP!
THERE! NOW WE CAN CLIMB UP AND-- UNNHH!
WATCH IT, KID!
MY POWER IS BACK AGAIN--BUT TOO LATE TO HELP POOR JOHNNY!
THOK!
I DIDN'T REALIZE --NOT TILL NOW-- HOW UGLY THE MOLE MAN MADE 'IM!
BEN! THE DOOR-WAY'S COLLAPSING!
TAKE OFF! I'LL HOLD IT UP TILL YER CLEAR!

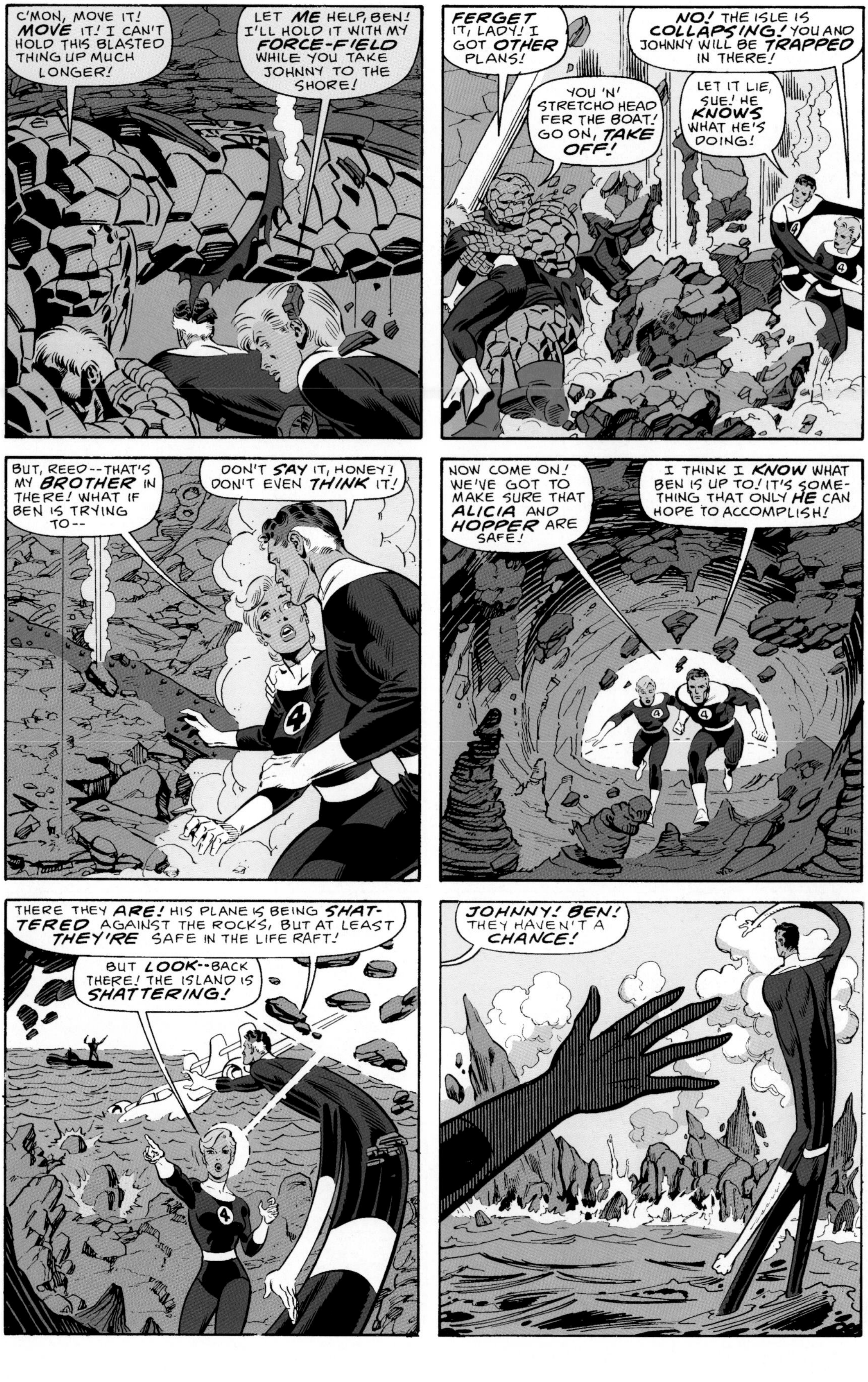
C'MON, MOVE IT! MOVE IT! I CAN'T HOLD THIS BLASTED THING UP MUCH LONGER!
LET ME HELP, BEN! I'LL HOLD IT WITH MY FORCE-FIELD WHILE YOU TAKE JOHNNY TO THE SHORE!
FERGET IT, LADY! I GOT OTHER PLANS!
NO! THE ISLE IS COLLAPSING! YOU AND JOHNNY WILL BE TRAPPED IN THERE!
YOU 'N' STRETCHO HEAD FER THE BOAT! GO ON, TAKE OFF!
LET IT LIE, SUE! HE KNOWS WHAT HE'S DOING!
BUT, REED--THAT'S MY BROTHER IN THERE! WHAT IF BEN IS TRYING TO--
DON'T SAY IT, HONEY! DON'T EVEN THINK IT!
NOW COME ON! WE'VE GOT TO MAKE SURE THAT ALICIA AND HOPPER ARE SAFE!
I THINK I KNOW WHAT BEN IS UP TO! IT'S SOMETHING THAT ONLY HE CAN HOPE TO ACCOMPLISH!
THERE THEY ARE! HIS PLANE IS BEING SHATTERED AGAINST THE ROCKS, BUT AT LEAST THEY'RE SAFE IN THE LIFE RAFT!
BUT LOOK--BACK THERE! THE ISLAND IS SHATTERING!
JOHNNY! BEN! THEY HAVEN'T A CHANCE!

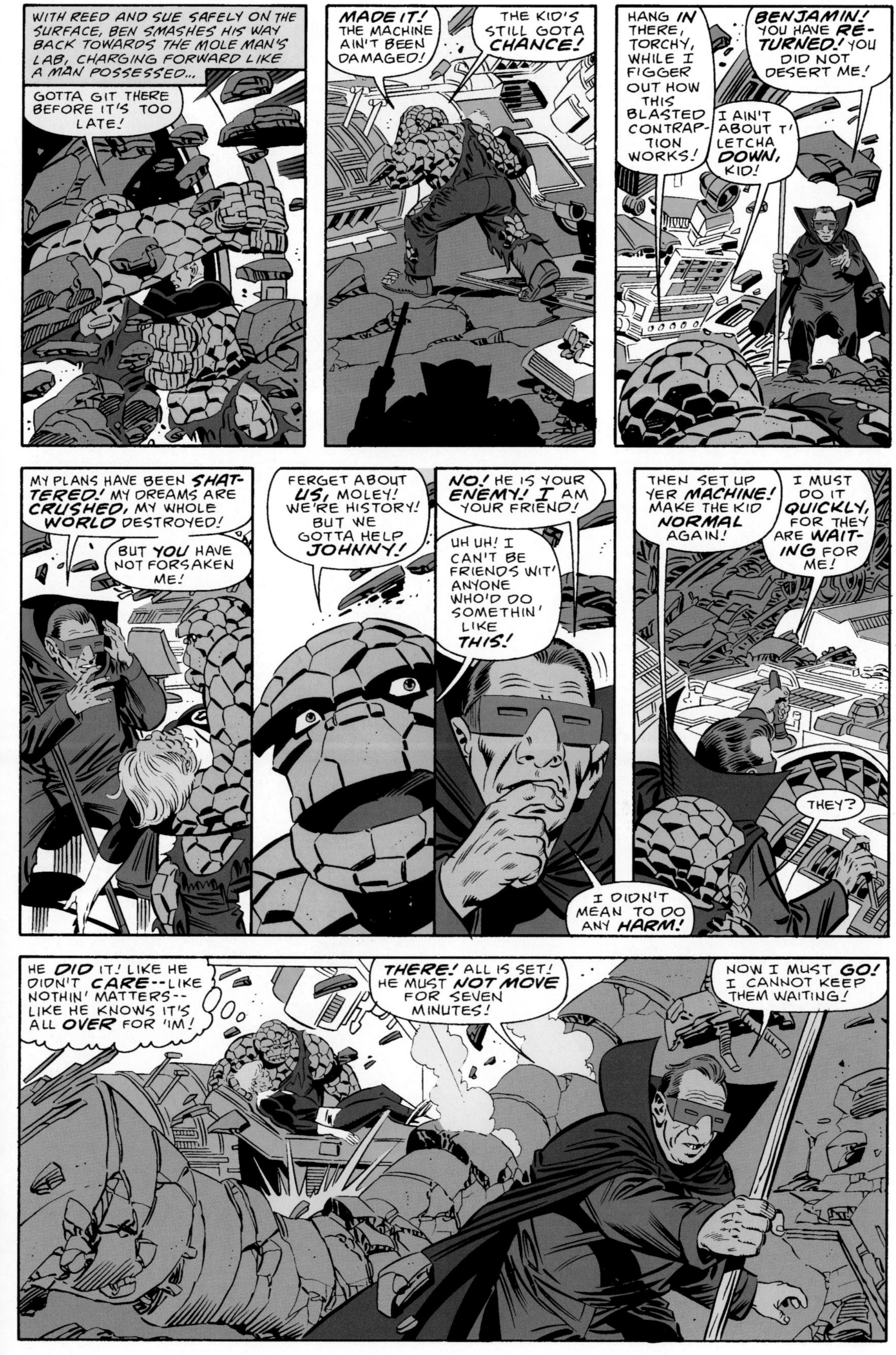

WITH REED AND SUE SAFELY ON THE SURFACE, BEN SMASHES HIS WAY BACK TOWARDS THE MOLE MAN'S LAB, CHARGING FORWARD LIKE A MAN POSSESSED...
GOTTA GIT THERE BEFORE IT'S TOO LATE!
MADE IT! THE MACHINE AIN'T BEEN DAMAGED!
THE KID'S STILL GOTA CHANCE!
HANG IN THERE, TORCHY, WHILE I FIGGER OUT HOW THIS BLASTED CONTRAPTION WORKS!
BENJAMIN! YOU HAVE RETURNED! YOU DID NOT DESERT ME!
I AIN'T ABOUT T' LETCHA DOWN, KID!
MY PLANS HAVE BEEN SHATTERED! MY DREAMS ARE CRUSHED, MY WHOLE WORLD DESTROYED!
BUT YOU HAVE NOT FORSAKEN ME!
FERGET ABOUT US, MOLEY! WE'RE HISTORY! BUT WE GOTTA HELP JOHNNY!
NO! HE IS YOUR ENEMY! I AM YOUR FRIEND!
UH UH! I CAN'T BE FRIENDS WIT' ANYONE WHO'D DO SOMETHIN' LIKE THIS!
I DIDN'T MEAN TO DO ANY HARM!
THEN SET UP YER MACHINE! MAKE THE KID NORMAL AGAIN!
I MUST DO IT QUICKLY, FOR THEY ARE WAITING FOR ME!
THEY?
HE DID IT! LIKE HE DIDN'T CARE--LIKE NOTHIN' MATTERS--LIKE HE KNOWS IT'S ALL OVER FOR 'IM!
THERE! ALL IS SET! HE MUST NOT MOVE FOR SEVEN MINUTES!
NOW I MUST GO! I CANNOT KEEP THEM WAITING!

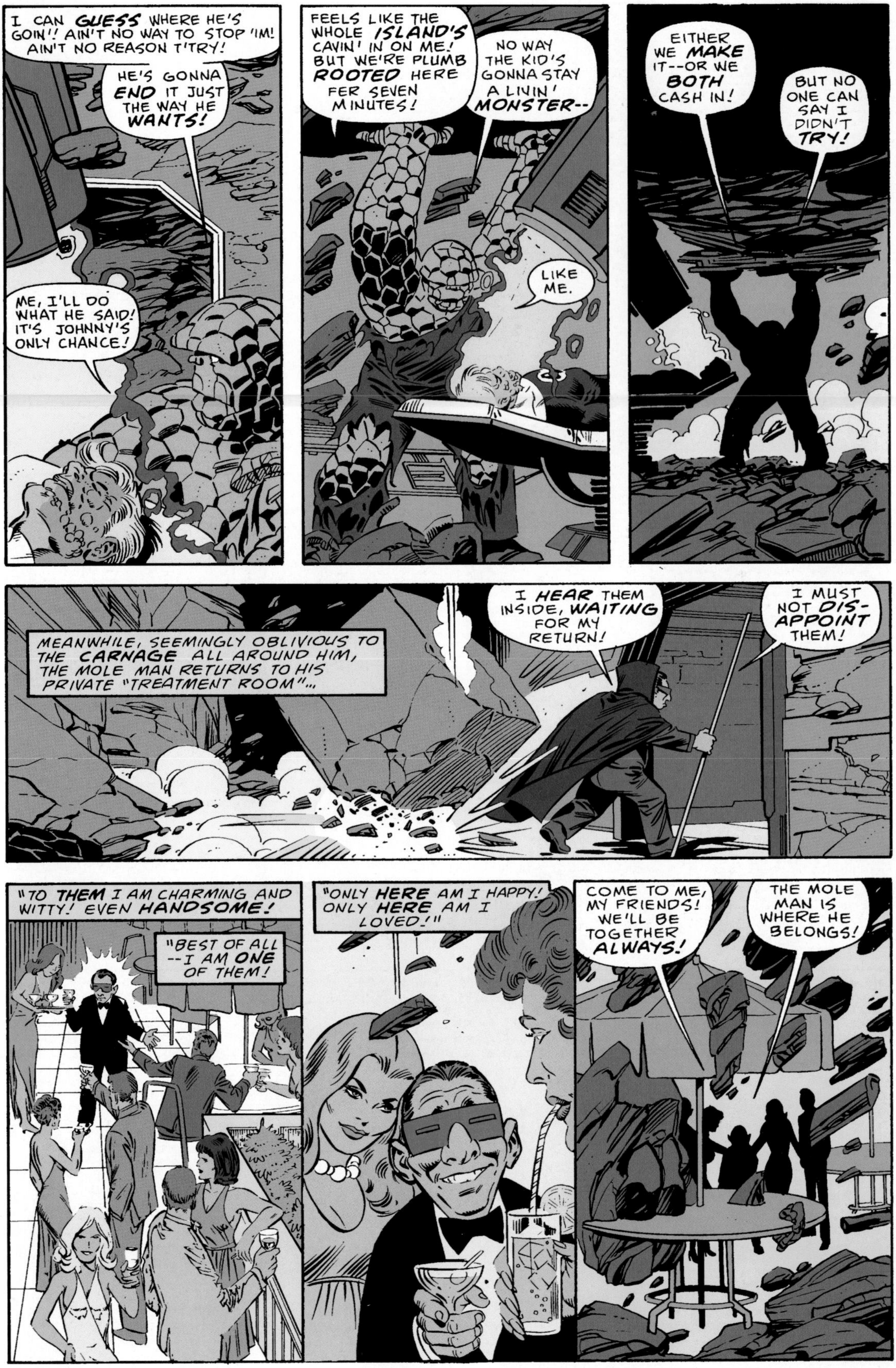
I CAN GUESS WHERE HE'S GOIN'! AIN'T NO WAY TO STOP 'IM! AIN'T NO REASON T'TRY!
HE'S GONNA END IT JUST THE WAY HE WANTS!
ME, I'LL DO WHAT HE SAID! IT'S JOHNNY'S ONLY CHANCE!
FEELS LIKE THE WHOLE ISLAND'S CAVIN' IN ON ME! BUT WE'RE PLUMB ROOTED HERE FER SEVEN MINUTES!
NO WAY THE KID'S GONNA STAY A LIVIN' MONSTER--
LIKE ME.
EITHER WE MAKE IT--OR WE BOTH CASH IN!
BUT NO ONE CAN SAY I DIDN'T TRY!
MEANWHILE, SEEMINGLY OBLIVIOUS TO THE CARNAGE ALL AROUND HIM, THE MOLE MAN RETURNS TO HIS PRIVATE "TREATMENT ROOM"...
I HEAR THEM INSIDE, WAITING FOR MY RETURN!
I MUST NOT DIS-APPOINT THEM!
"TO THEM I AM CHARMING AND WITTY! EVEN HANDSOME!
"BEST OF ALL --I AM ONE OF THEM!
"ONLY HERE AM I HAPPY! ONLY HERE AM I LOVED!"
COME TO ME, MY FRIENDS! WE'LL BE TOGETHER ALWAYS!
THE MOLE MAN IS WHERE HE BELONGS!

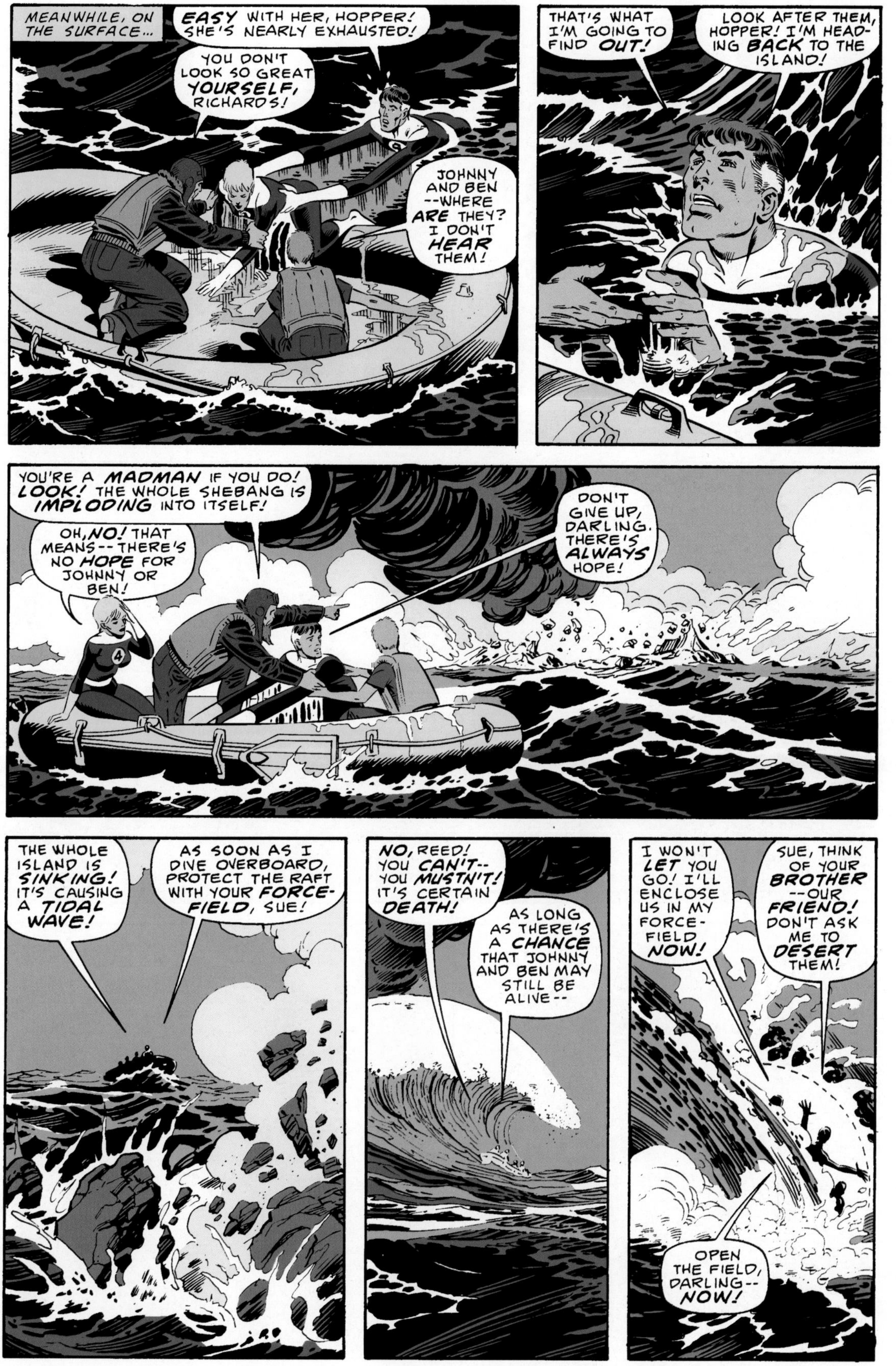

MEANWHILE, ON THE SURFACE...
EASY WITH HER, HOPPER! SHE'S NEARLY EXHAUSTED!
YOU DON'T LOOK SO GREAT YOURSELF, RICHARDS!
JOHNNY AND BEN --WHERE ARE THEY? I DON'T HEAR THEM!
THAT'S WHAT I'M GOING TO FIND OUT!
LOOK AFTER THEM, HOPPER! I'M HEADING BACK TO THE ISLAND!
YOU'RE A MADMAN IF YOU DO! LOOK! THE WHOLE SHEBANG IS IMPLODING INTO ITSELF!
OH, NO! THAT MEANS-- THERE'S NO HOPE FOR JOHNNY OR BEN!
DON'T GIVE UP, DARLING. THERE'S ALWAYS HOPE!
THE WHOLE ISLAND IS SINKING! IT'S CAUSING A TIDAL WAVE!
AS SOON AS I DIVE OVERBOARD, PROTECT THE RAFT WITH YOUR FORCE-FIELD, SUE!
NO, REED! YOU CAN'T-- YOU MUSTN'T! IT'S CERTAIN DEATH!
AS LONG AS THERE'S A CHANCE THAT JOHNNY AND BEN MAY STILL BE ALIVE--
I WON'T LET YOU GO! I'LL ENCLOSE US IN MY FORCE-FIELD NOW!
SUE, THINK OF YOUR BROTHER --OUR FRIEND! DON'T ASK ME TO DESERT THEM!
OPEN THE FIELD, DARLING-- NOW!

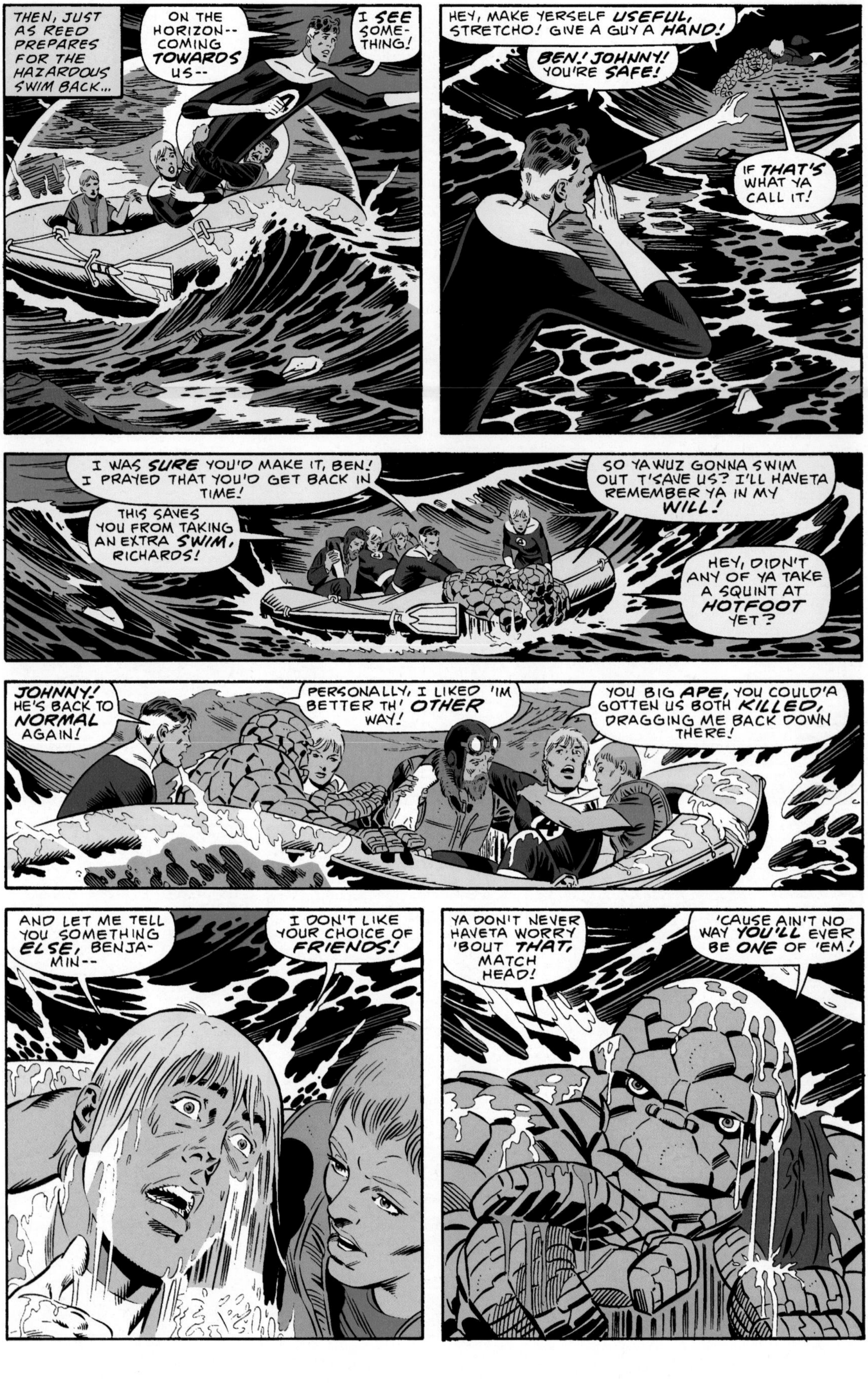
THEN, JUST AS REED PREPARES FOR THE HAZARDOUS SWIM BACK...
ON THE HORIZON-- COMING TOWARDS US--
I SEE SOME-THING!
HEY, MAKE YERSELF USEFUL, STRETCHO! GIVE A GUY A HAND!
BEN! JOHNNY! YOU'RE SAFE!
IF THAT'S WHAT YA CALL IT!
I WAS SURE YOU'D MAKE IT, BEN! I PRAYED THAT YOU'D GET BACK IN TIME!
THIS SAVES YOU FROM TAKING AN EXTRA SWIM, RICHARDS!
SO YA WUZ GONNA SWIM OUT T'SAVE US? I'LL HAVETA REMEMBER YA IN MY WILL!
HEY, DIDN'T ANY OF YA TAKE A SQUINT AT HOTFOOT YET?
JOHNNY! HE'S BACK TO NORMAL AGAIN!
PERSONALLY, I LIKED 'IM BETTER TH' OTHER WAY!
YOU BIG APE, YOU COULD'A GOTTEN US BOTH KILLED, DRAGGING ME BACK DOWN THERE!
AND LET ME TELL YOU SOMETHING ELSE, BENJA-MIN--
I DON'T LIKE YOUR CHOICE OF FRIENDS!
YA DON'T NEVER HAVETA WORRY 'BOUT THAT, MATCH HEAD!
'CAUSE AIN'T NO WAY YOU'LL EVER BE ONE OF 'EM!

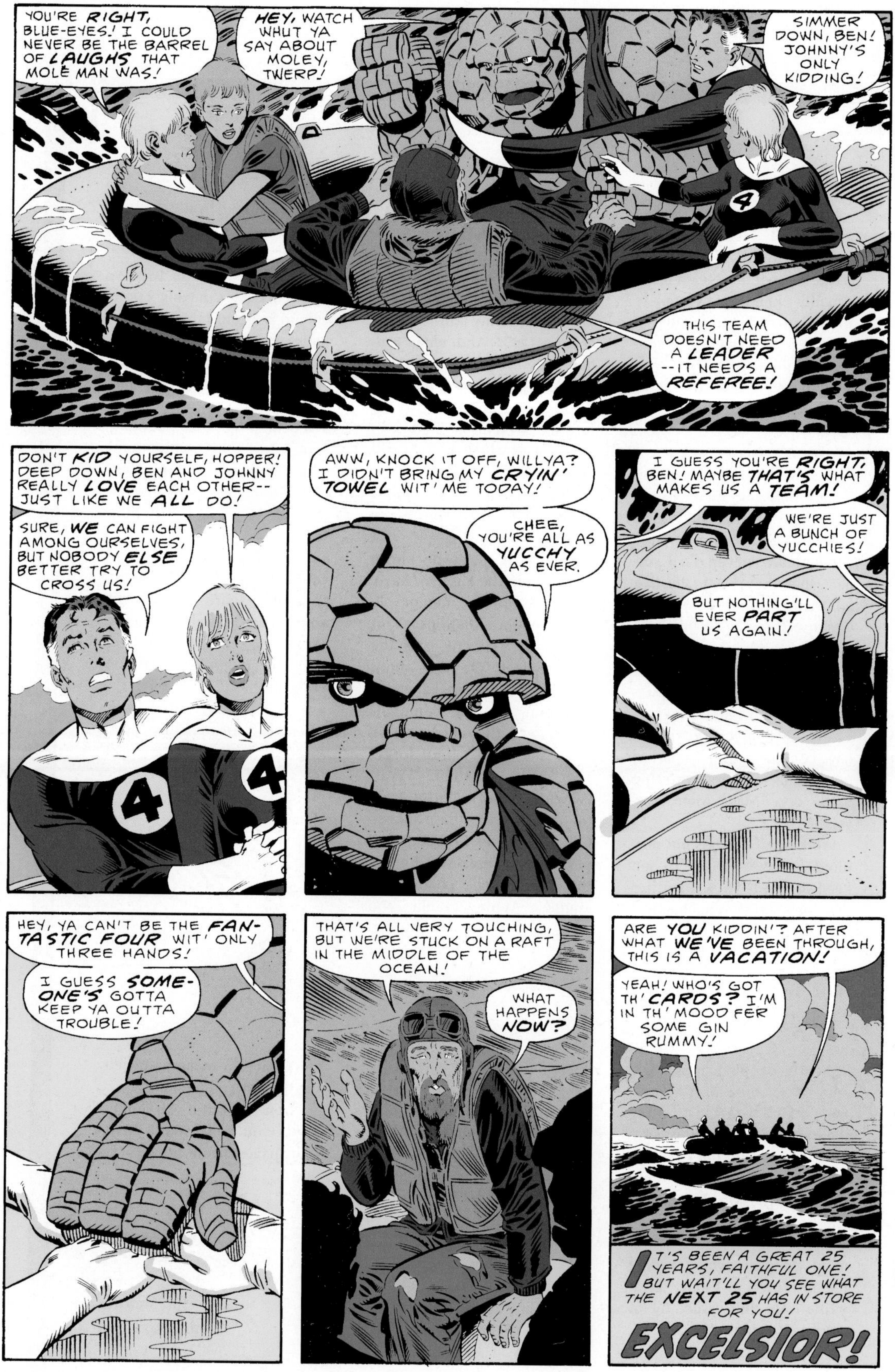
YOU'RE RIGHT, BLUE-EYES! I COULD NEVER BE THE BARREL OF LAUGHS THAT MOLE MAN WAS!
HEY, WATCH WHUT YA SAY ABOUT MOLEY, TWERP!
SIMMER DOWN, BEN! JOHNNY'S ONLY KIDDING!
THIS TEAM DOESN'T NEED A LEADER --IT NEEDS A REFEREE!
DON'T KID YOURSELF, HOPPER! DEEP DOWN, BEN AND JOHNNY REALLY LOVE EACH OTHER-- JUST LIKE WE ALL DO!
SURE, WE CAN FIGHT AMONG OURSELVES, BUT NOBODY ELSE BETTER TRY TO CROSS US!
AWW, KNOCK IT OFF, WILLYA? I DIDN'T BRING MY CRYIN' TOWEL WIT' ME TODAY!
CHEE, YOU'RE ALL AS YUCCHY AS EVER.
I GUESS YOU'RE RIGHT, BEN! MAYBE THAT'S WHAT MAKES US A TEAM!
WE'RE JUST A BUNCH OF YUCCHIES!
BUT NOTHING'LL EVER PART US AGAIN!
HEY, YA CAN'T BE THE FANTASTIC FOUR WIT' ONLY THREE HANDS!
I GUESS SOMEONE'S GOTTA KEEP YA OUTTA TROUBLE!
THAT'S ALL VERY TOUCHING, BUT WE'RE STUCK ON A RAFT IN THE MIDDLE OF THE OCEAN!
WHAT HAPPENS NOW?
ARE YOU KIDDIN'? AFTER WHAT WE'VE BEEN THROUGH, THIS IS A VACATION!
YEAH! WHO'S GOT TH' CARDS? I'M IN TH' MOOD FER SOME GIN RUMMY!
IT'S BEEN A GREAT 25 YEARS, FAITHFUL ONE! BUT WAIT'LL YOU SEE WHAT THE NEXT 25 HAS IN STORE FOR YOU!
EXCELSIOR!

I can't believe it!

Since Jolly Jack Kirby and I first bestowed the world's greatest super hero team upon a madly cheering, awesomely appreciative human race, I can't believe a quarter of a century has already sped by!

From where I sit, it doesn't seem like a day more than twenty-five years!

Y'know, never in my wildest flights of imagination did I dream that our quarrelsome and queasy little quartet would usher in a glorious new era for comicbooks. Never did I suspect that they'd actually live up to the title "The World's Greatest Comicbook" which I so frivolously added to the magazine's masthead in a burst of totally unwitting inspiration.

And now, the good ol' F.F. have become as much a part of Americana as that inspiring battle cry, "Make Mine Marvel!"

Who among us has not nurtured a secret desire to see Reed Richards stretch further than he's able? Who has not

been tempted to shout "It's Clobberin' Time!" when nobody was looking? Who wouldn't love to have a fire extinguisher near at hand the next time Johnny Storm shouts "Flame On"? And what red-blooded American youth hasn't wished that he had met the stunning Invisible Girl before ol' Stretcho latched onto her?—And when she was still visible, natch!

Hey, I could go on, but I might get exiled to Yancy Street for corniness!

Anyway, I guess no single comicbook title has ever introduced more memorable characters or situations. Want proof? Try Galactus and the Silver Surfer! Or how about Doc Doom and his Latverian kingdom? And the Inhumans —not exactly chicken fat, huh? And leave us not forget The Black Panther, Wyatt Wingfoot, The Frightful Four, the Mole Man, the Fantasti-Car, The Baxter Building, and our all-time biggest triumph, that celebrated, charismatic couple, Aunt Petunia and

Willie Lumpkin! Wow, I get all gushy and misty-eyed just thinking about 'em.

Now, here we are, twenty-five years later, having come full circle as our fabulous four-some once again battles the Mole Man, the first villain they ever tackled as a team! And I'm lucky enough to have been asked to script this landmark issue by that sentimental editor in chief, that peerless plotter and fellow scrivener, ol' High-Pockets Jim Shooter himself.

I loved writing it. I hope you'll love reading it. If you do, I humbly share and accept your plaudits and accolades. But if you don't, blame it on Jim! He could'a hired Irving Forbush!

And hey, better mark your calendar now before you forget. I'll be looking for you at our next big anniversary—the 50th!

Excelsior!

Stan

Nearly two and a half decades after reading *Fantastic Four #1* I was asked to write the plot for this, the Silver Anniversary issue of the *Fantastic Four*. Writing it, I felt the same sort of joyous thrill as I did while reading issue #1. I experienced that electric excitement yet *again* while reading the absolutely awesome script written for this issue, by of course, Stan himself.

That feeling of sheer joy made me glad to be a part of Marvel Comics all three times. It made me realize just how great a responsibility I have, as editor in chief, to safeguard and carry on the legends that mean so much to so many of us. I could ramble on about that, but if Ben Grimm were here, he'd probably tell me what he once told Reed Richards way back when: "You

don't have to make a speech, big shot! We understand!"

I hope so. But if you don't, I think you will soon—sixty-four pages from now to be exact.

Jim Shooter
Jim Shooter
Editor in Chief

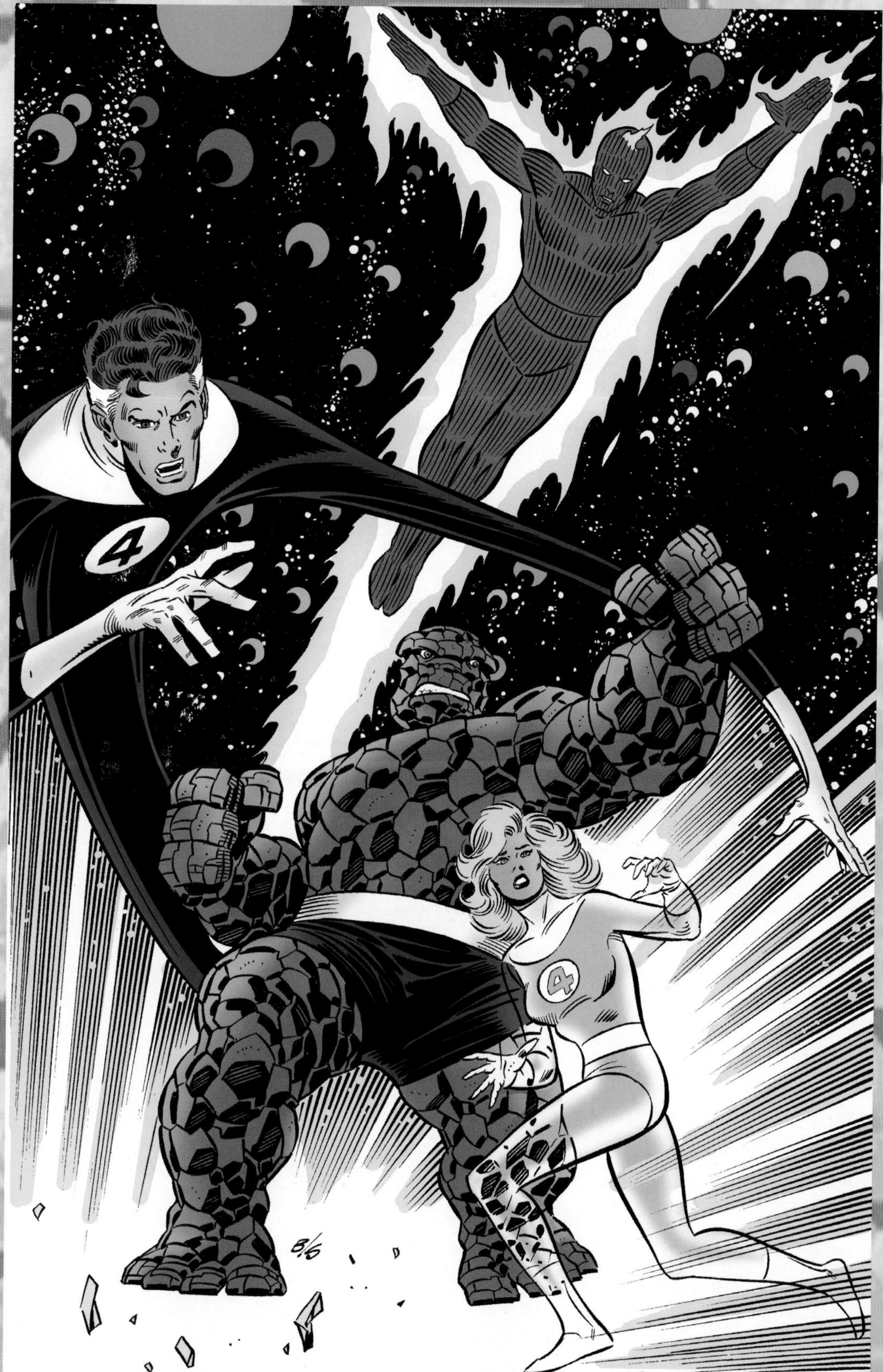

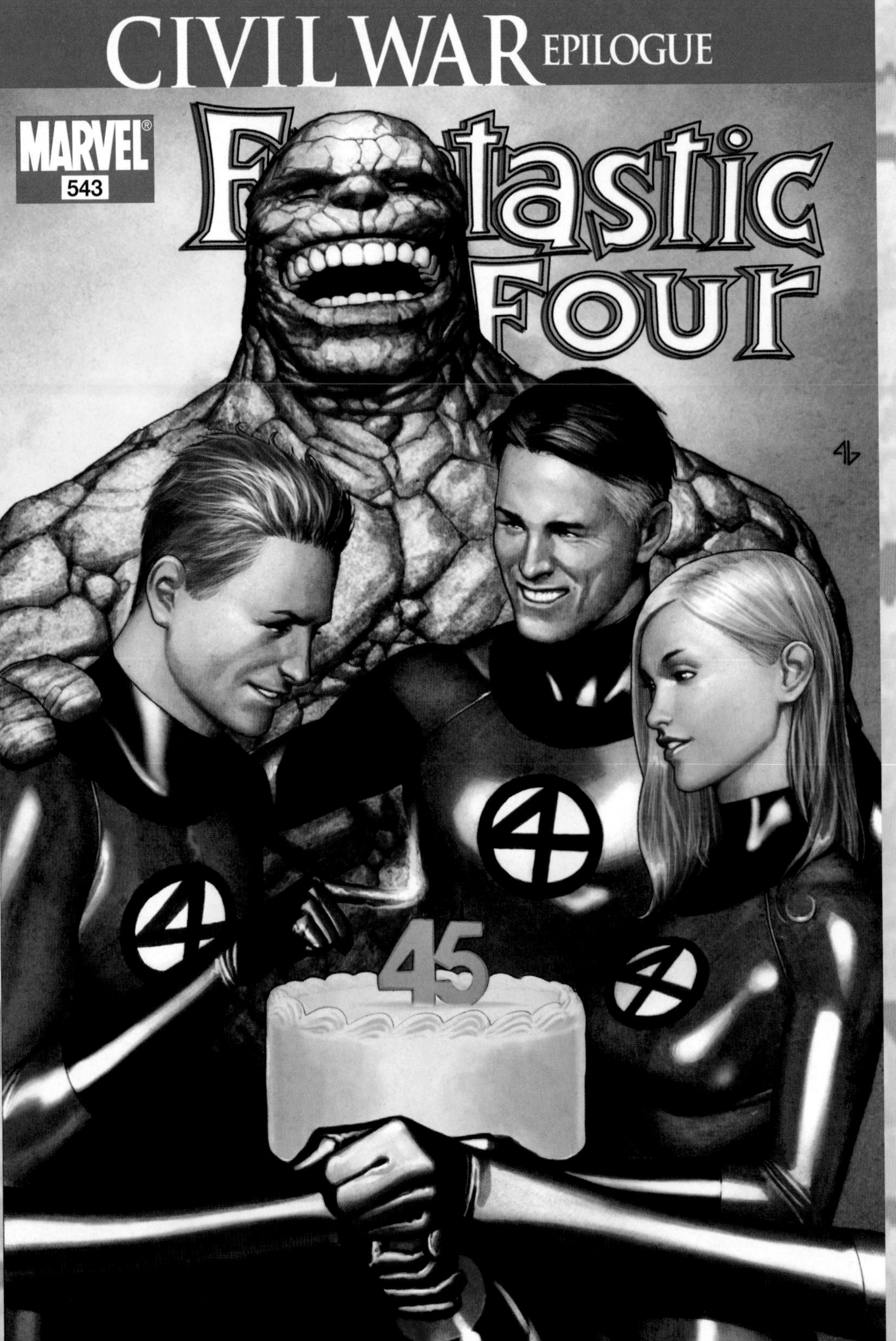

CIVIL WAR EPILOGUE
MARVEL
543
Fantastic Four
45

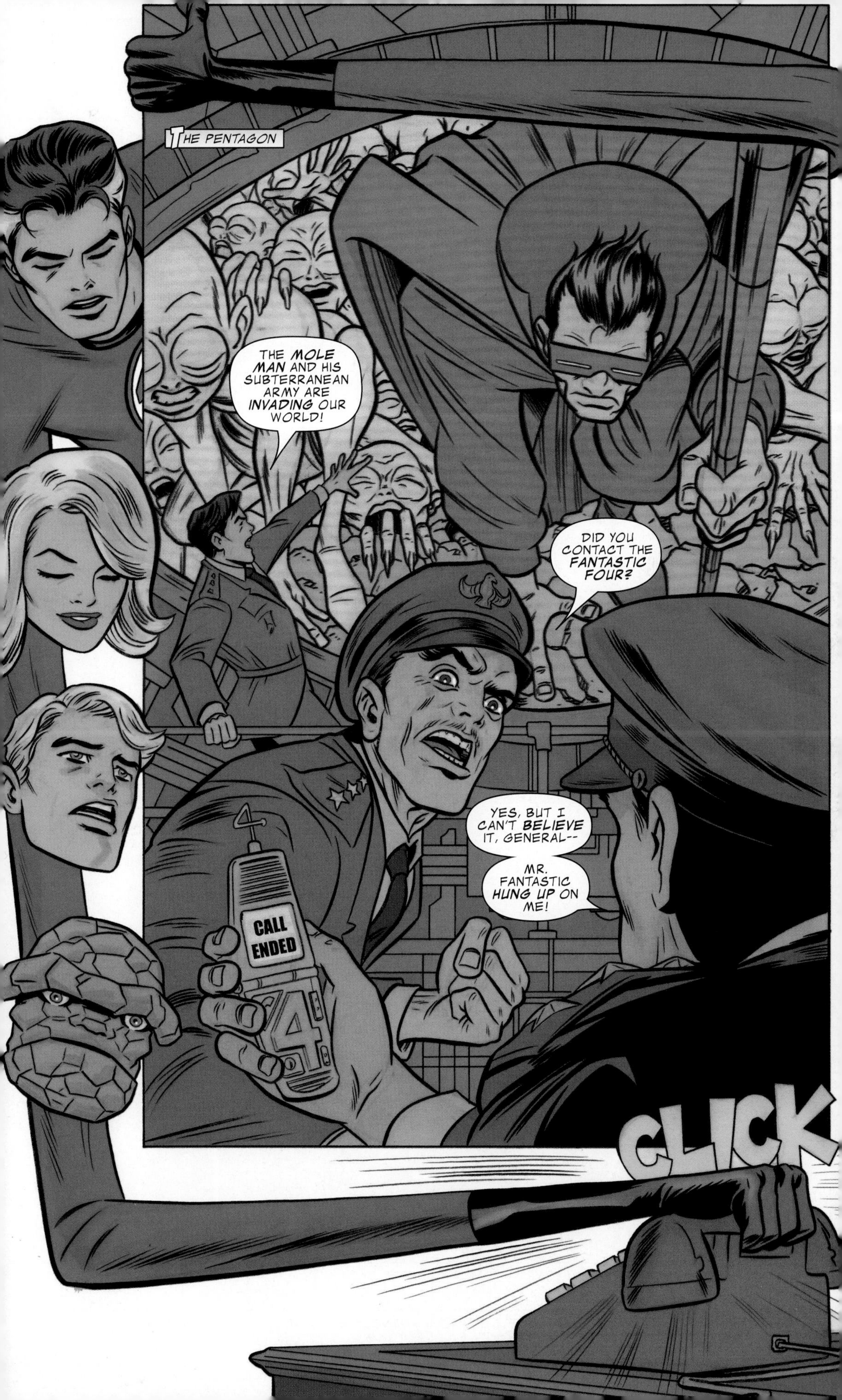
THE PENTAGON
THE MOLE MAN AND HIS SUBTERRANEAN ARMY ARE INVADING OUR WORLD!
DID YOU CONTACT THE FANTASTIC FOUR?
YES, BUT I CAN'T BELIEVE IT, GENERAL--
MR. FANTASTIC HUNG UP ON ME!
CALL ENDED
CLICK

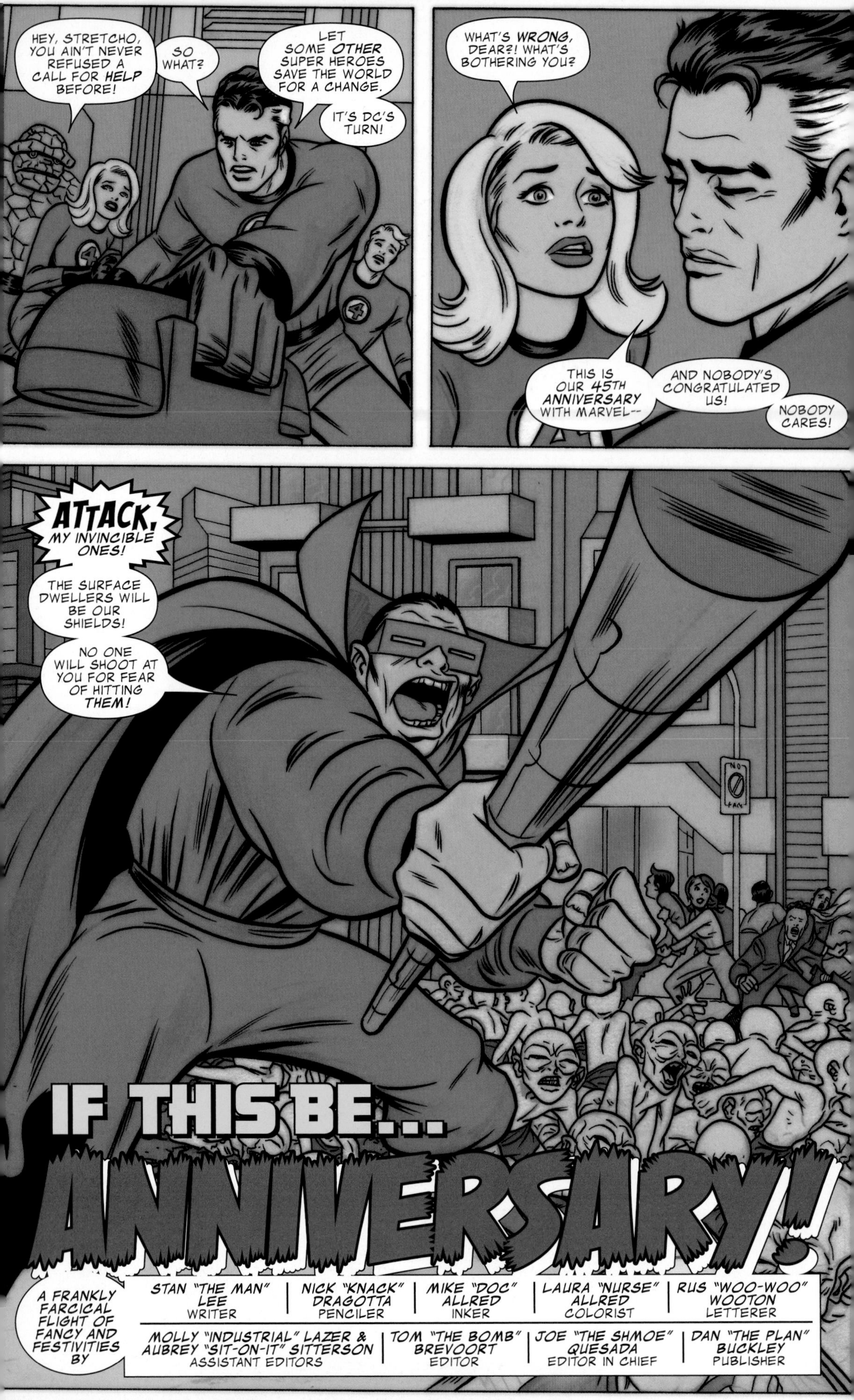

HEY, STRETCHO, YOU AIN'T NEVER REFUSED A CALL FOR HELP BEFORE!
SO WHAT?
LET SOME OTHER SUPER HEROES SAVE THE WORLD FOR A CHANGE.
IT'S DC'S TURN!
WHAT'S WRONG, DEAR?! WHAT'S BOTHERING YOU?
THIS IS OUR 45TH ANNIVERSARY WITH MARVEL--
AND NOBODY'S CONGRATULATED US!
NOBODY CARES!
ATTACK, MY INVINCIBLE ONES!
THE SURFACE DWELLERS WILL BE OUR SHIELDS!
NO ONE WILL SHOOT AT YOU FOR FEAR OF HITTING THEM!
NO FAN
IF THIS BE... ANNIVERSARY!
A FRANKLY FARCICAL FLIGHT OF FANCY AND FESTIVITIES BY
STAN "THE MAN" LEE WRITER
NICK "KNACK" DRAGOTTA PENCILER
MIKE "DOC" ALLRED INKER
LAURA "NURSE" ALLRED COLORIST
RUS "WOO-WOO" WOOTON LETTERER
MOLLY "INDUSTRIAL" LAZER & AUBREY "SIT-ON-IT" SITTERSON ASSISTANT EDITORS
TOM "THE BOMB" BREVOORT EDITOR
JOE "THE SHMOE" QUESADA EDITOR IN CHIEF
DAN "THE PLAN" BUCKLEY PUBLISHER

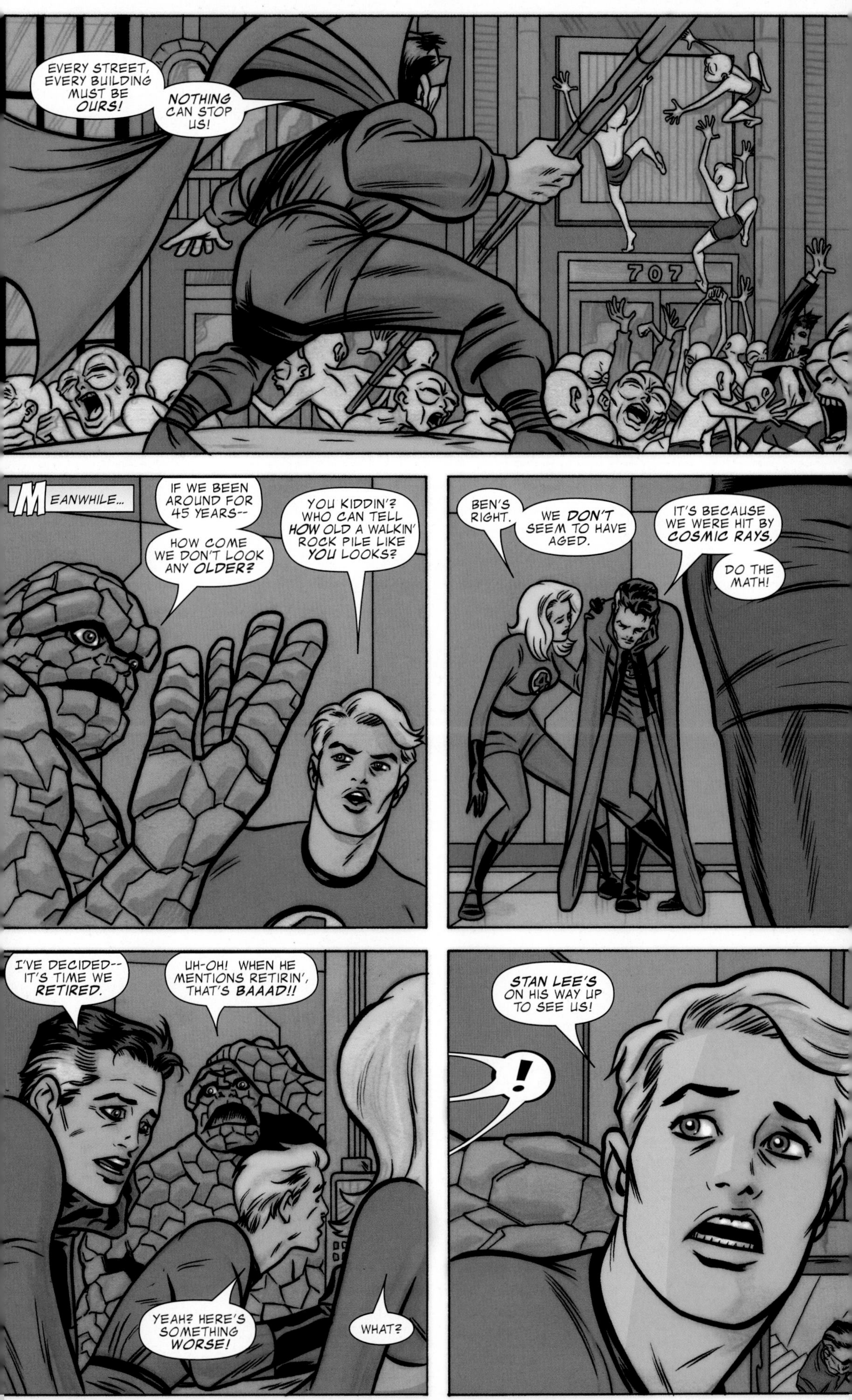

EVERY STREET, EVERY BUILDING MUST BE OURS!
NOTHING CAN STOP US!
707
MEANWHILE...
IF WE BEEN AROUND FOR 45 YEARS--
HOW COME WE DON'T LOOK ANY OLDER?
YOU KIDDIN'? WHO CAN TELL HOW OLD A WALKIN' ROCK PILE LIKE YOU LOOKS?
BEN'S RIGHT.
WE DON'T SEEM TO HAVE AGED.
IT'S BECAUSE WE WERE HIT BY COSMIC RAYS.
DO THE MATH!
I'VE DECIDED-- IT'S TIME WE RETIRED.
UH-OH! WHEN HE MENTIONS RETIRIN', THAT'S BAAAD!!
YEAH? HERE'S SOMETHING WORSE!
WHAT?
STAN LEE'S ON HIS WAY UP TO SEE US!
!

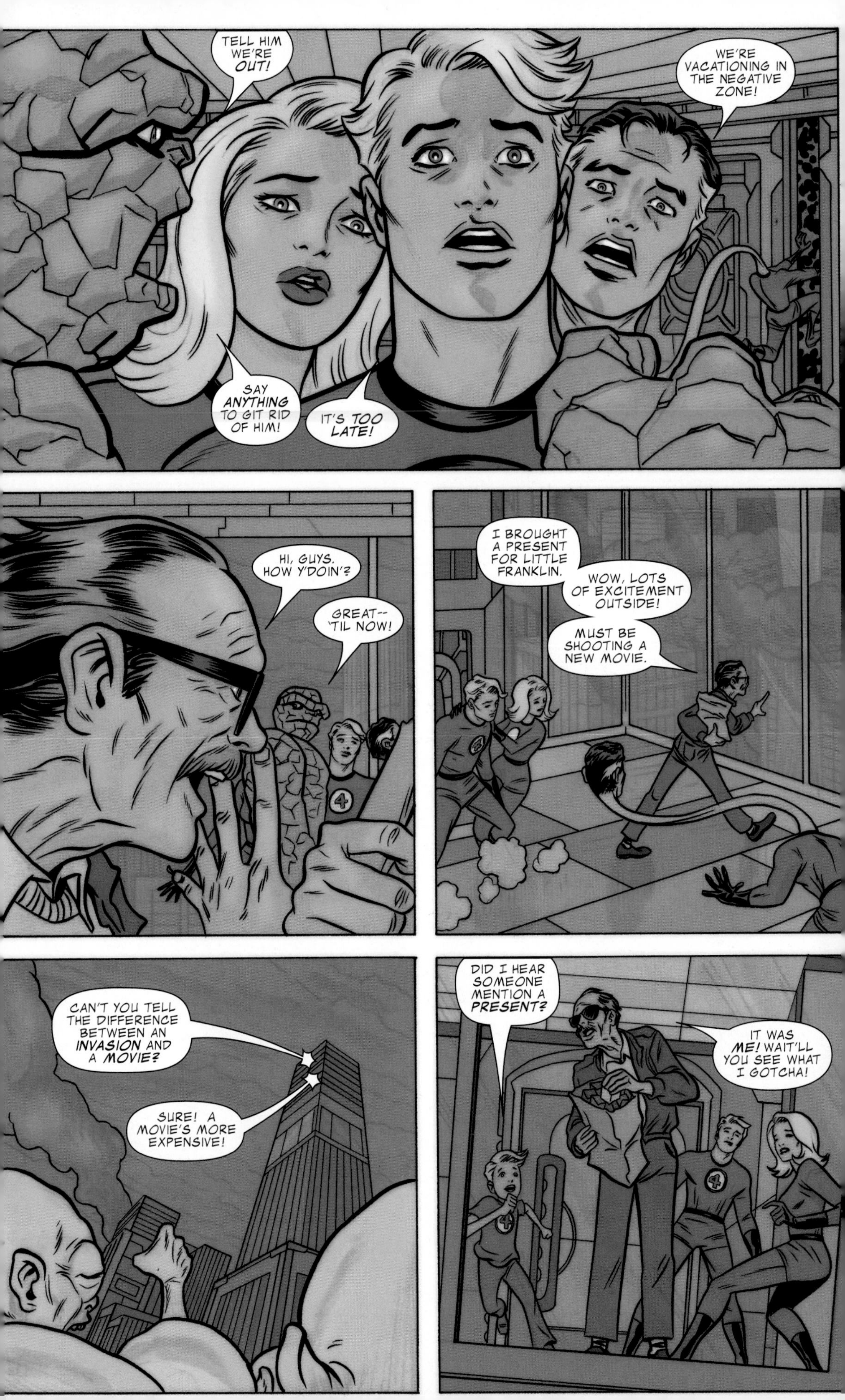

TELL HIM WE'RE *OUT!*
WE'RE VACATIONING IN THE NEGATIVE ZONE!
SAY *ANYTHING* TO GIT RID OF HIM!
IT'S *TOO LATE!*
HI, GUYS. HOW Y'DOIN'?
GREAT-- 'TIL NOW!
I BROUGHT A PRESENT FOR LITTLE FRANKLIN.
WOW, LOTS OF EXCITEMENT OUTSIDE!
MUST BE SHOOTING A NEW MOVIE.
CAN'T YOU TELL THE DIFFERENCE BETWEEN AN *INVASION* AND A *MOVIE?*
SURE! A MOVIE'S MORE EXPENSIVE!
DID I HEAR SOMEONE MENTION A *PRESENT?*
IT WAS *ME!* WAIT'LL YOU SEE WHAT I GOTCHA!

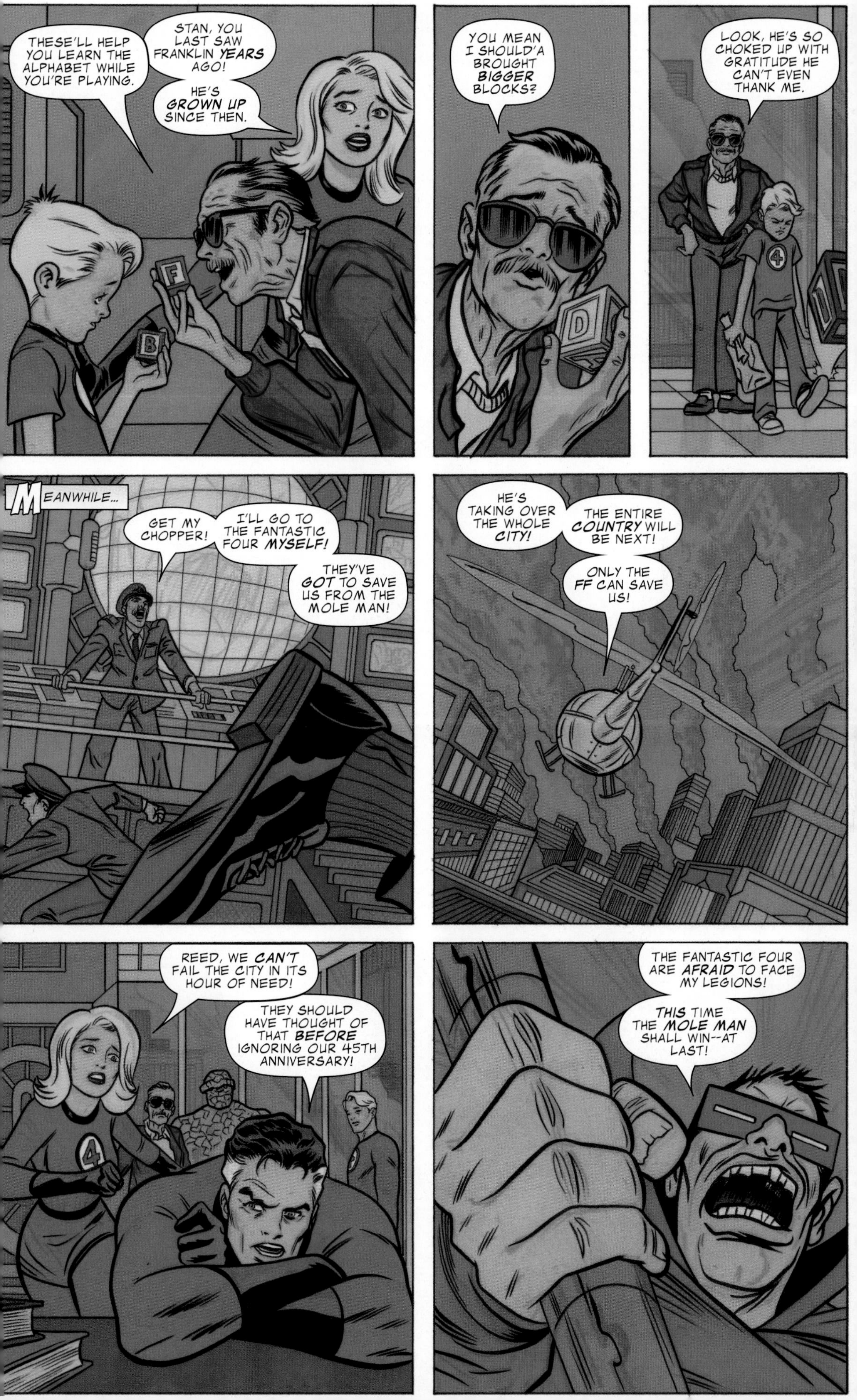
THESE'LL HELP YOU LEARN THE ALPHABET WHILE YOU'RE PLAYING.
STAN, YOU LAST SAW FRANKLIN YEARS AGO!
HE'S GROWN UP SINCE THEN.
YOU MEAN I SHOULD'A BROUGHT BIGGER BLOCKS?
LOOK, HE'S SO CHOKED UP WITH GRATITUDE HE CAN'T EVEN THANK ME.
MEANWHILE...
GET MY CHOPPER!
I'LL GO TO THE FANTASTIC FOUR MYSELF!
THEY'VE GOT TO SAVE US FROM THE MOLE MAN!
HE'S TAKING OVER THE WHOLE CITY!
THE ENTIRE COUNTRY WILL BE NEXT!
ONLY THE FF CAN SAVE US!
REED, WE CAN'T FAIL THE CITY IN ITS HOUR OF NEED!
THEY SHOULD HAVE THOUGHT OF THAT BEFORE IGNORING OUR 45TH ANNIVERSARY!
THE FANTASTIC FOUR ARE AFRAID TO FACE MY LEGIONS!
THIS TIME THE MOLE MAN SHALL WIN--AT LAST!

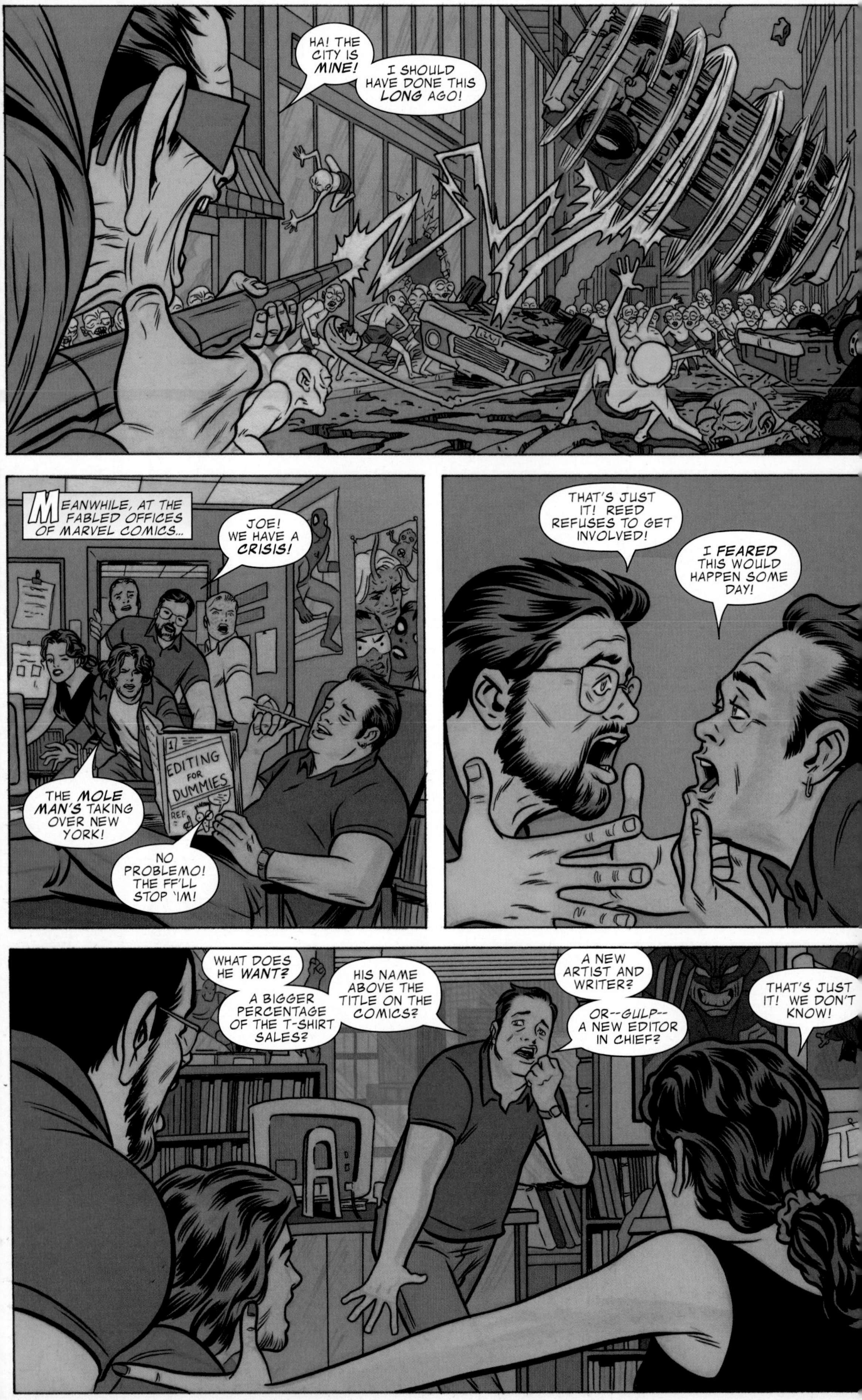
HA! THE CITY IS MINE!
I SHOULD HAVE DONE THIS LONG AGO!
MEANWHILE, AT THE FABLED OFFICES OF MARVEL COMICS...
JOE! WE HAVE A CRISIS!
THE MOLE MAN'S TAKING OVER NEW YORK!
EDITING FOR DUMMIES
NO PROBLEMO! THE FF'LL STOP 'IM!
THAT'S JUST IT! REED REFUSES TO GET INVOLVED!
I FEARED THIS WOULD HAPPEN SOME DAY!
WHAT DOES HE WANT?
A BIGGER PERCENTAGE OF THE T-SHIRT SALES?
HIS NAME ABOVE THE TITLE ON THE COMICS?
A NEW ARTIST AND WRITER?
OR--GULP--A NEW EDITOR IN CHIEF?
THAT'S JUST IT! WE DON'T KNOW!

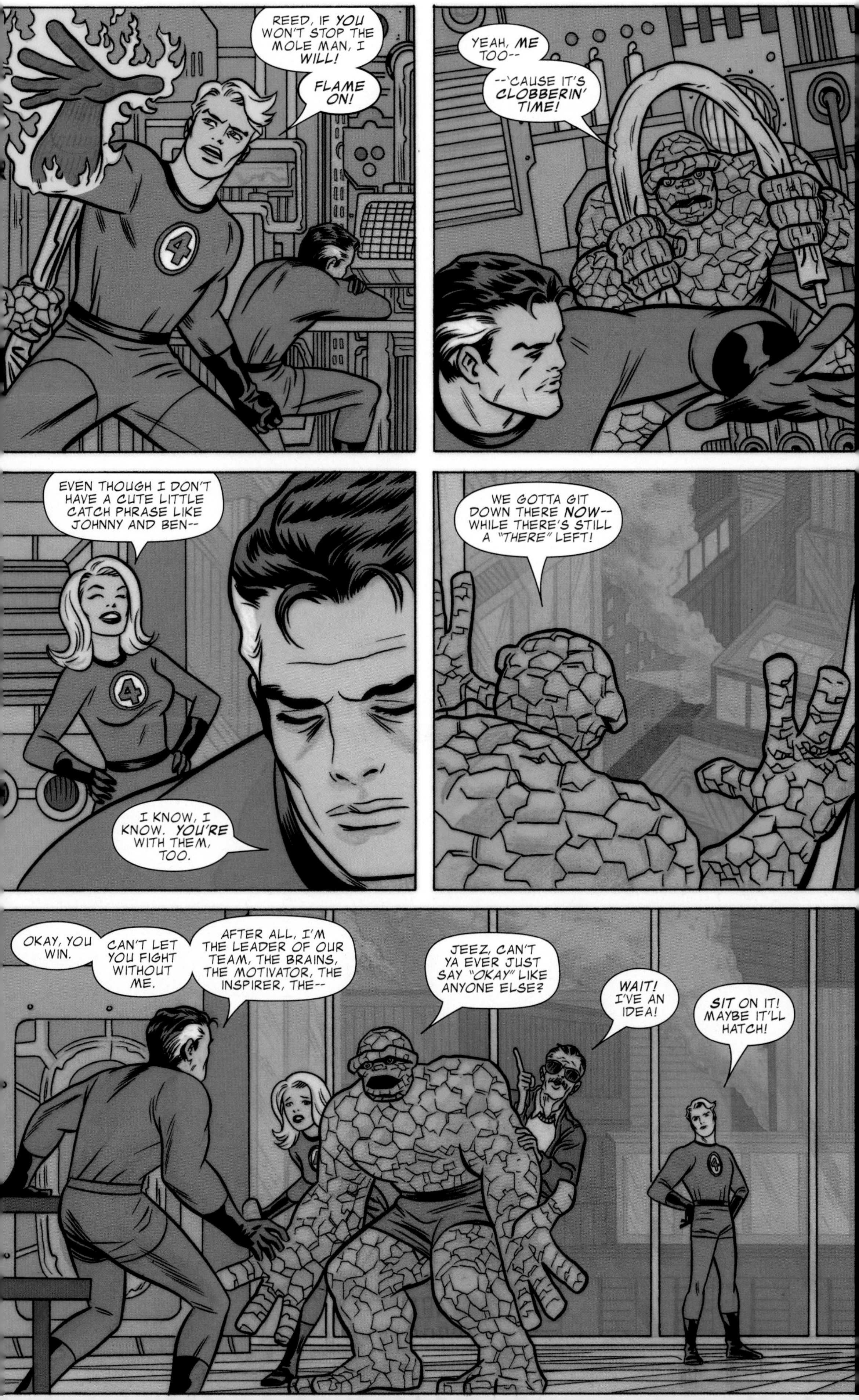
REED, IF YOU WON'T STOP THE MOLE MAN, I WILL!
FLAME ON!
YEAH, ME TOO--
--'CAUSE IT'S CLOBBERIN' TIME!
EVEN THOUGH I DON'T HAVE A CUTE LITTLE CATCH PHRASE LIKE JOHNNY AND BEN--
I KNOW, I KNOW. YOU'RE WITH THEM, TOO.
WE GOTTA GIT DOWN THERE NOW-- WHILE THERE'S STILL A "THERE" LEFT!
OKAY, YOU WIN.
CAN'T LET YOU FIGHT WITHOUT ME.
AFTER ALL, I'M THE LEADER OF OUR TEAM, THE BRAINS, THE MOTIVATOR, THE INSPIRER, THE--
JEEZ, CAN'T YA EVER JUST SAY "OKAY" LIKE ANYONE ELSE?
WAIT! I'VE AN IDEA!
SIT ON IT! MAYBE IT'LL HATCH!

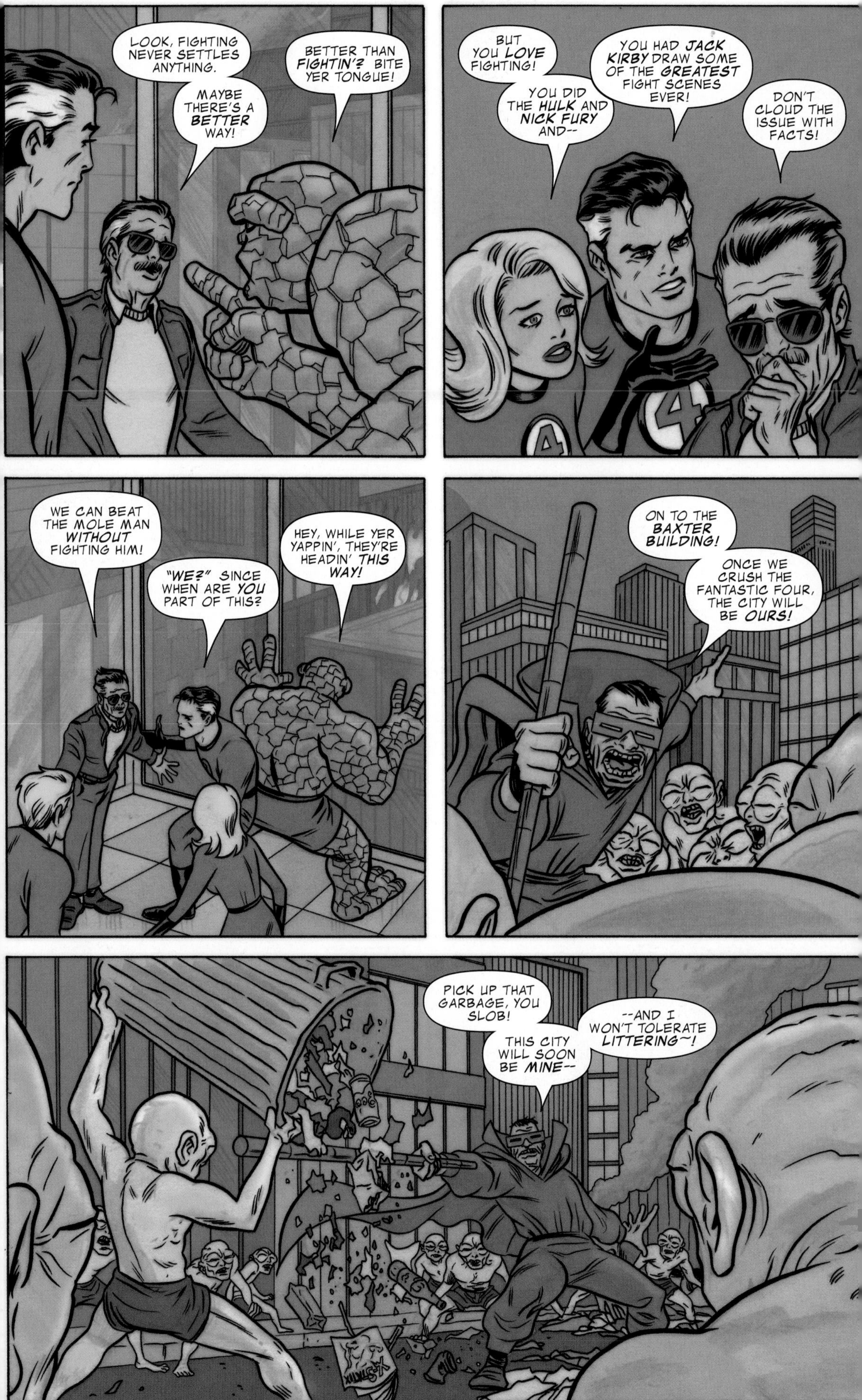
LOOK, FIGHTING NEVER SETTLES ANYTHING.
MAYBE THERE'S A BETTER WAY!
BETTER THAN FIGHTIN'? BITE YER TONGUE!
BUT YOU LOVE FIGHTING!
YOU DID THE HULK AND NICK FURY AND--
YOU HAD JACK KIRBY DRAW SOME OF THE GREATEST FIGHT SCENES EVER!
DON'T CLOUD THE ISSUE WITH FACTS!
WE CAN BEAT THE MOLE MAN WITHOUT FIGHTING HIM!
"WE?" SINCE WHEN ARE YOU PART OF THIS?
HEY, WHILE YER YAPPIN', THEY'RE HEADIN' THIS WAY!
ON TO THE BAXTER BUILDING!
ONCE WE CRUSH THE FANTASTIC FOUR, THE CITY WILL BE OURS!
PICK UP THAT GARBAGE, YOU SLOB!
THIS CITY WILL SOON BE MINE--
--AND I WON'T TOLERATE LITTERING~!

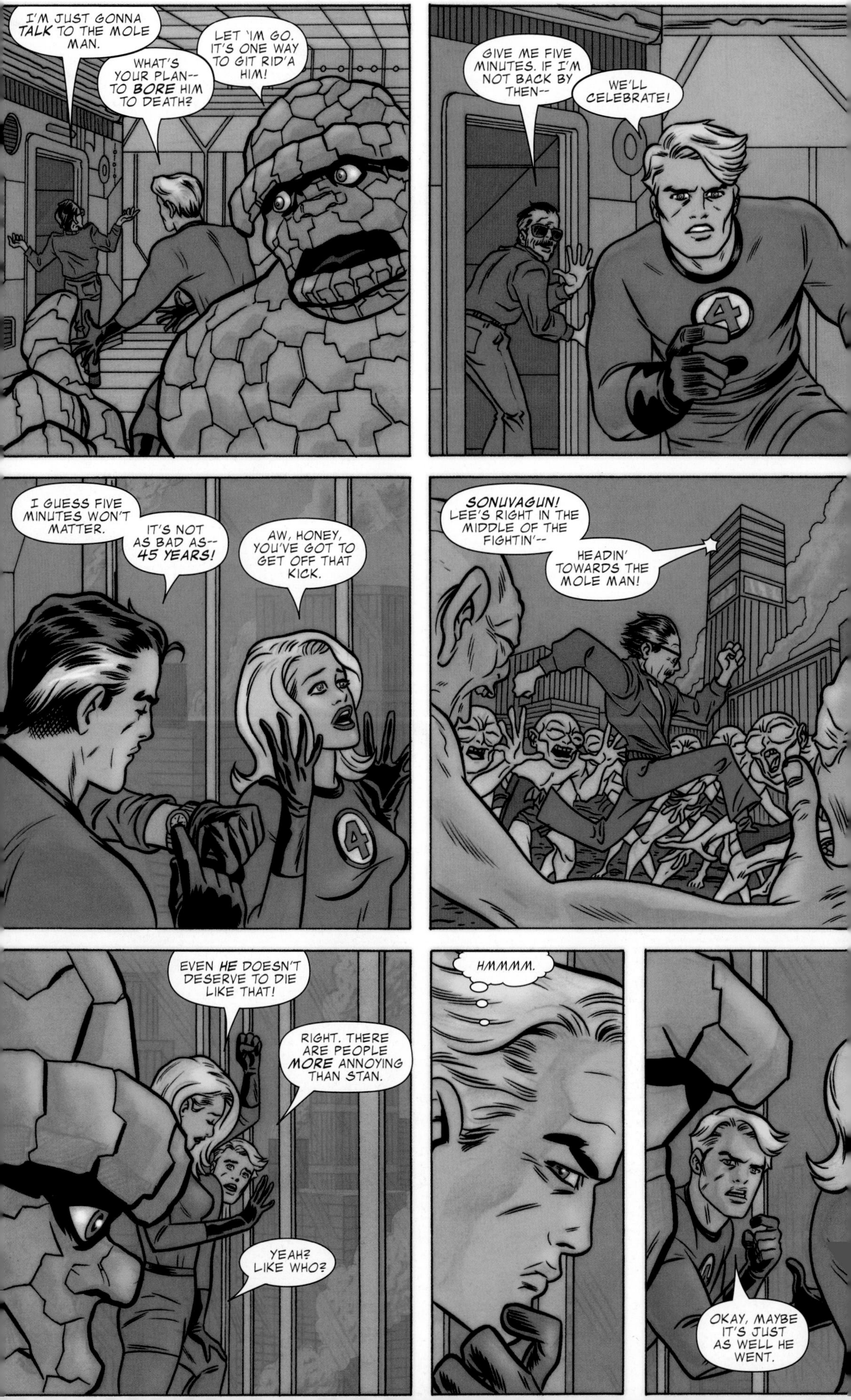
I'M JUST GONNA TALK TO THE MOLE MAN.
WHAT'S YOUR PLAN-- TO BORE HIM TO DEATH?
LET 'IM GO. IT'S ONE WAY TO GIT RID'A HIM!
GIVE ME FIVE MINUTES. IF I'M NOT BACK BY THEN--
WE'LL CELEBRATE!
I GUESS FIVE MINUTES WON'T MATTER.
IT'S NOT AS BAD AS-- 45 YEARS!
AW, HONEY, YOU'VE GOT TO GET OFF THAT KICK.
SONUVAGUN! LEE'S RIGHT IN THE MIDDLE OF THE FIGHTIN'--
HEADIN' TOWARDS THE MOLE MAN!
EVEN HE DOESN'T DESERVE TO DIE LIKE THAT!
RIGHT. THERE ARE PEOPLE MORE ANNOYING THAN STAN.
YEAH? LIKE WHO?
HMMMM.
OKAY, MAYBE IT'S JUST AS WELL HE WENT.

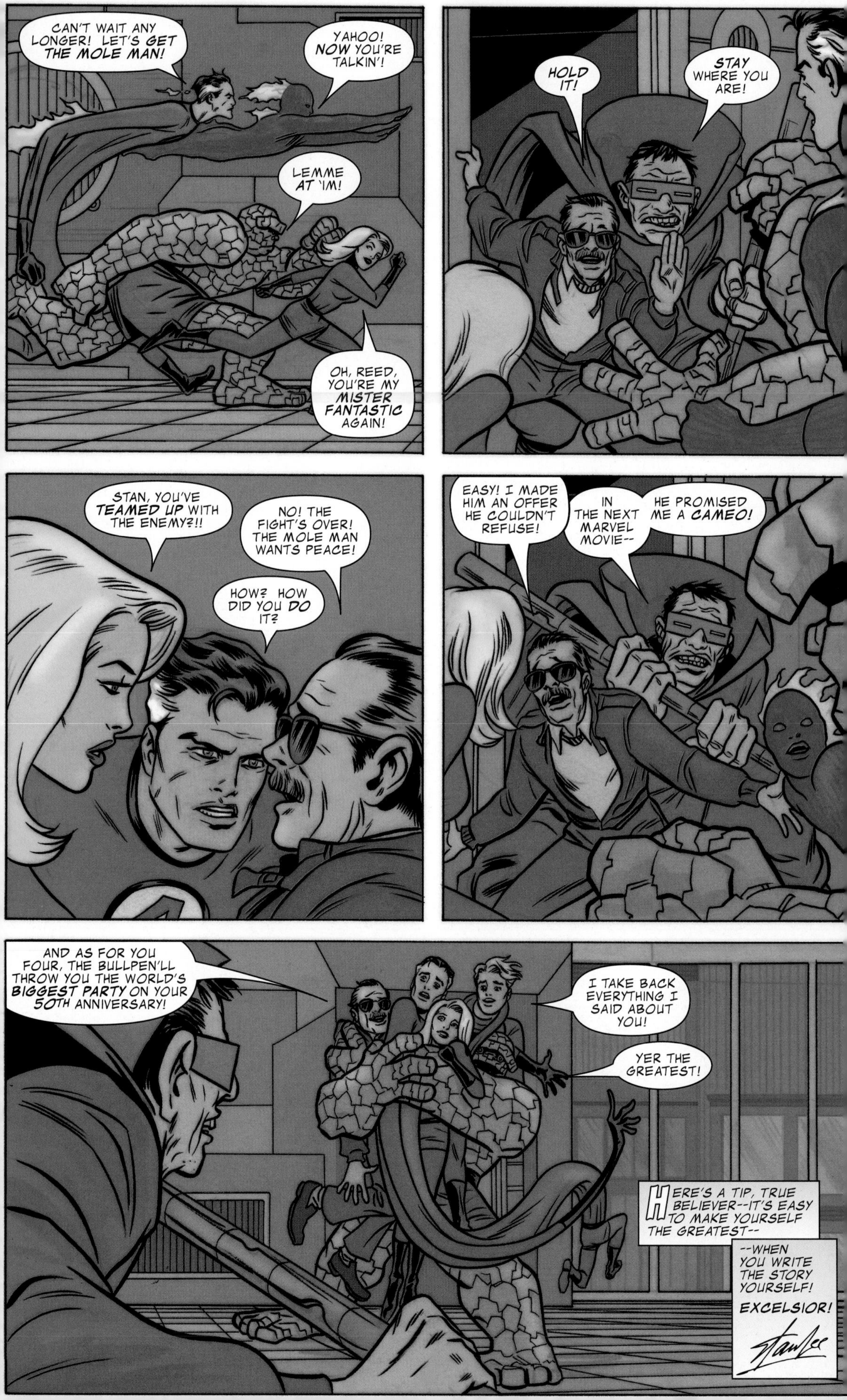

CAN'T WAIT ANY LONGER! LET'S GET THE MOLE MAN!
YAHOO! NOW YOU'RE TALKIN'!
LEMME AT 'IM!
OH, REED, YOU'RE MY MISTER FANTASTIC AGAIN!
HOLD IT!
STAY WHERE YOU ARE!
STAN, YOU'VE TEAMED UP WITH THE ENEMY?!!
NO! THE FIGHT'S OVER! THE MOLE MAN WANTS PEACE!
HOW? HOW DID YOU DO IT?
EASY! I MADE HIM AN OFFER HE COULDN'T REFUSE!
IN THE NEXT MARVEL MOVIE--
HE PROMISED ME A CAMEO!
AND AS FOR YOU FOUR, THE BULLPEN'LL THROW YOU THE WORLD'S BIGGEST PARTY ON YOUR 50TH ANNIVERSARY!
I TAKE BACK EVERYTHING I SAID ABOUT YOU!
YER THE GREATEST!
HERE'S A TIP, TRUE BELIEVER--IT'S EASY TO MAKE YOURSELF THE GREATEST--
--WHEN YOU WRITE THE STORY YOURSELF!
EXCELSIOR!
Stan Lee

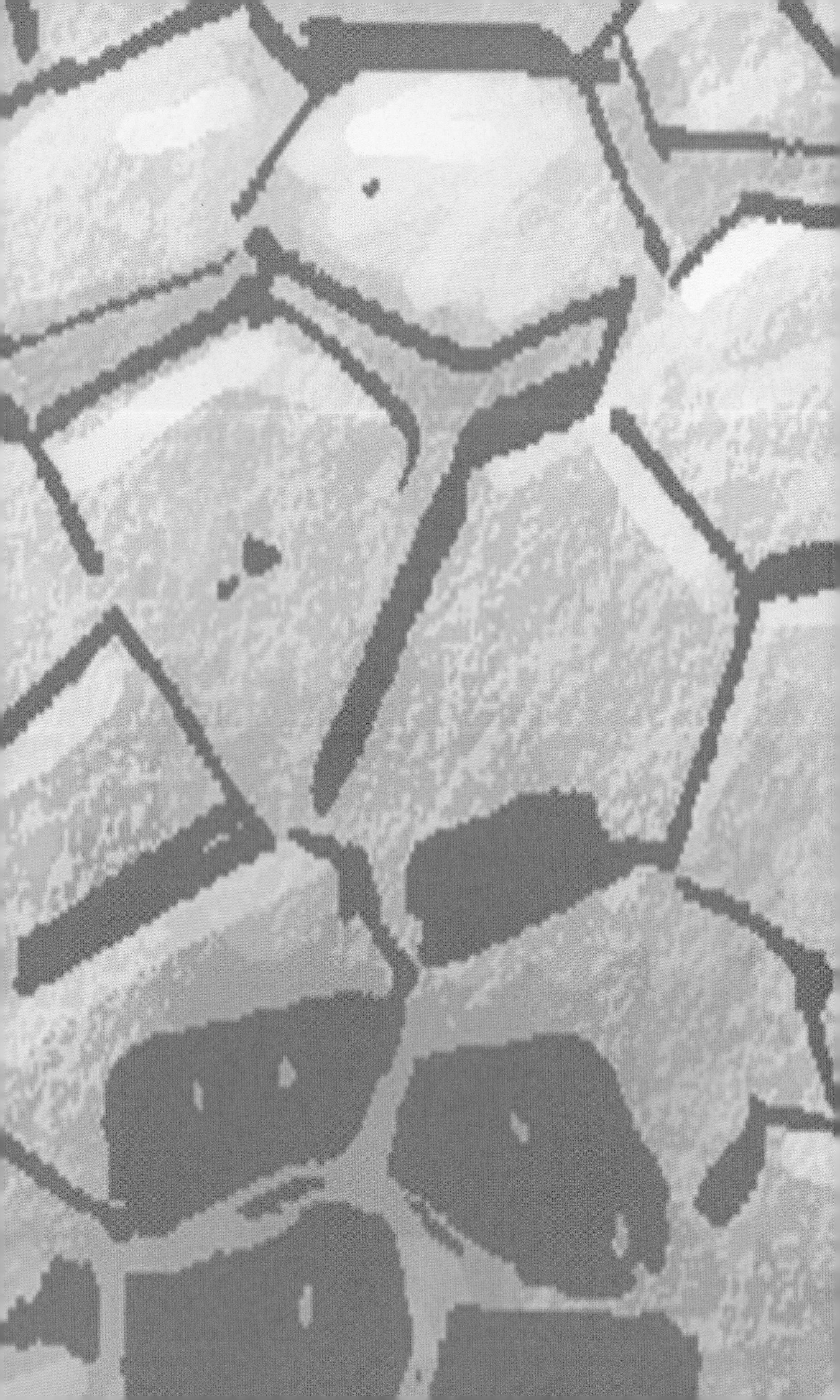

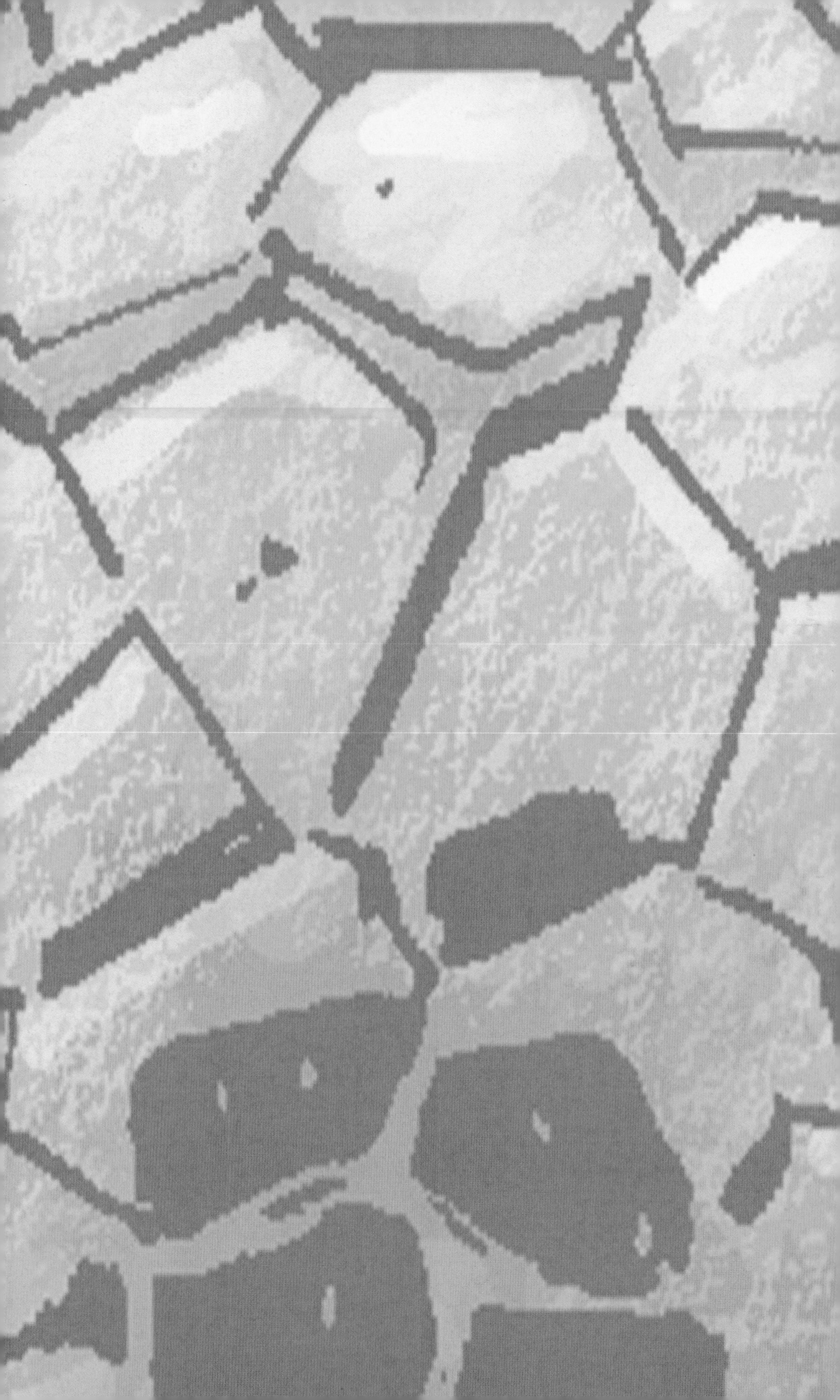